Hidden Champions in CEE and Turkey

Peter McKiernan • Danica Purg
Editors

Hidden Champions in CEE and Turkey

Carving Out a Global Niche

Springer

Editors
Peter McKiernan
Strathclyde Business School
University of Strathclyde
Glasgow
United Kingdom

Danica Purg
CEEMAN and IEDC-Bled School of Management
Bled
Slovenia

ISBN 978-3-642-40503-7 ISBN 978-3-642-40504-4 (eBook)
DOI 10.1007/978-3-642-40504-4
Springer Heidelberg New York Dordrecht London

Library of Congress Control Number: 2013954673

Printed on acid-free paper

Springer is part of Springer Science+Business Media (www.springer.com)

Foreword

Looking at the list of the most admired companies in the world as published annually by *Fortune* magazine, one must conclude that an excellent company must be large, indeed very large, and glamorous. Only well-known corporate giants appear in this list. And this is in accordance with the prevailing belief of the public, politicians, journalists, and business professors on role models of good management. If this view was right, a country and its politicians should focus on creating large corporations to compete internationally. But for most countries the reality is very different: 169 of the 206 sovereign states in the world have no firm in the Fortune Global 500 list for the year 2012. Only nine companies are from Central and Eastern Europe (CEE). Russia has seven, whereas Hungary and Poland have one global 500 company. And when we look at export performance, we detect another astonishing fact. In the last 10 years Germany was six times, and China was four times, number one in exports. In both countries more than two-thirds of the exports come from firms with less than 2,000 employees and not from large corporations.

What are the lessons here? The first lesson is that for most CEE countries it is, and will remain, a vain hope to create Fortune Global 500 companies. The second lesson is that outstanding export success can be achieved with many midsized companies. CEE countries seem well advised to build their economic future on Hidden Champions, i.e., midsized global market leaders. This strategy allows transformation and emerging countries to participate in the rapidly growing global economy, to create high-quality jobs and to flourish. The globalized world abounds in opportunities. How many separate markets are there in the world? Nobody knows the exact number. Let us assume that the number is 10,000. Fortune Global 500 firms only operate in 100 or 200 of these markets. The rest, 98 % of all markets, are smallish niche markets. Each of them offers the chance for a midsized firm to become a global market leader. And there is a fundamental difference from the world of the past. With the Internet, modern telecommunications, air traffic, and logistics, it is possible for small and midsized firm to do business on a global scale. Accidentally, the emergence of systems like the Internet and global logistics occurred parallel to the liberalization in CEE countries. This opened the stage for what we see in this book.

This book will surprise you, as it surprised me. I was flabbergasted when I first learned of the sheer number of Hidden Champions in the 17 CEE countries that were surveyed. I had not expected such a large number since I knew from my studies of Hidden Champions in other regions, especially the German-speaking countries, that it typically takes decades to become a global market leader. It is only a little over 20 years since the CEE countries became market economies and entrepreneurs could freely develop. And what impressed me even more were the high-level competencies of the CEE Hidden Champions. Many of these midsized world market leaders are truly high-tech and world class. The wide range of industries that these firms cover is also impressive.

I find the core traits of the CEE Hidden Champions remarkably similar to their counterparts from the rest of the world. This especially applies to their inner strengths, the passions, the deep knowledge, and the ambitions. When I read in this book of outstanding Hidden Champion founders and entrepreneurs, images of similar characters all over the world pop up in my head. An example is the proverbial "my work is my hobby" by Ivo Boscarol, the founder of Slovenian airplane maker Pipistrel. Or the statement that "in some cases it was impossible to differentiate between the identity of the leader and the company". Yes, the Hidden Champions are often characterized by an identity of person and purpose. It is also interesting to note that most CEE Hidden Champions are not located in big cities but in smaller communities to which they are closely attached. I found the same pattern in Germany. In their core values, the Hidden Champions and their leaders are remarkably similar across countries and cultures. I am happy that so many new Hidden Champions from CEE are joining the elite group of almost 3,000 companies on my global Hidden Champions list compiled over 25 years.

By providing an excellent analysis of the success factors of the CEE Hidden Champions, this book does not only set a record of tremendous achievements but in addition provides encouragement and recommendations for young people from CEE. The most striking differences I see between youth in saturated Western countries and in CEE lie in the ambitions and the energies of young people. Students, applicants, and high potentials that I got to know in CEE are almost always energetic, ambitious, and willing to work hard. In combination with a good education and language capabilities this is the ideal breeding ground for new Hidden Champions. This book encourages many of these young hopefuls to decisively go for Hidden Championship. Therefore, I am very optimistic that many more new Hidden Champions will emerge in CEE countries in the coming decades. This book reports on the beginning of a great movement and sets the stage for its continuation into the future.

Bonn, Germany
July 2013

Hermann Simon

Acknowledgment

On behalf of CEEMAN,[1] and the editors, we would like to acknowledge and thank all researchers that contributed to the success of this research and book. In particular we are grateful to Prof. Hermann Simon who generously offered his research methodology, adapted by Dr. Marek Dietl who was together with Dr. Melita Balas Rant involved in the initial stages of the project on HCs.

Our thanks go to the hidden champion companies and their presidents/owners who generously offered their time, opened their companies and minds, and let researchers explore and learn.

We are also grateful to language editors Gabrielle Walker and Eric Whittle from Murdoch University, Australia, Michael Minkov from International University College, Bulgaria and to the CEEMAN team, Olga Veligurska, Špela Horjak and Maja Medja Vidic who coordinated this complex activity so well.

A great thank you to everybody!

Bled, Slovenia — Danica Purg
Glasgow, United Kingdom — Peter McKiernan
July 2013

[1] CEEMAN, the International Association for Management Development in Dynamic Societies, was established in 1993 with the aim of accelerating the growth in quality of management development in Central and Eastern Europe. With more than 210 members from 52 countries in Europe, North America, Latin America, Africa, and Asia, it has become a global association with its focus on management and leadership knowledge in dynamically developing societies. Many researchers in this book have gained additional management knowledge at the CEEMAN International Management Teachers Academy, which has educated more than 470 management faculty from 135management schools and universities in 37 countries from all over the world.

Contents

The Context of Hidden Champions

Peter McKiernan and Danica Purg

1 The Mystery of Corporate Success

Books that search for the Holy Grail of "success" in the corporate world have been either light or heavy. Usually, the former derive from observation and anecdotal evidence and are written by consultants, reflective CEOs and journalists, and directed towards a target market of busy businessmen looking for the next quick fix. This is a volume industry where customers seem to have an insatiable appetite for the vast material offered in airport bookshops. These publications are purposeful and their beauty lies in their simplicity, which allows the material to be digested easily and applied quickly. Moreover, their large customer base means that the proposed techniques can take root over many sectors and so they can soon become the next contemporary fashion. The downside is that fashions come and go. Perhaps the finest example of the genre is Peters and Waterman's (1982) seminal study *In Search of Excellence*, a book that triggered a generation of these "success"-based publications in the modern era.

In contrast, the heavy material is usually supplied by academics. Professionally, they must pay due diligence to the methodology employed in researching a phenomenon like "success" such that confidence can be placed in their research findings. Sometimes, the scholarly language has been brutal to read with the applied message being lost in an impenetrable body of case evidence, as in Grinyer et alia's (1988) classic book on fast turnarounds, the *Sharpbenders*. But, as academics, initially American, harnessed the writing skills of investigative journalists, their messages became clearer and more poignant, as in Porter's (1980) seminal book on

P. McKiernan
University of Strathclyde, Glasgow, United Kingdom

D. Purg (✉)
IEDC – Bled School of Management, Bled, Slovenia

CEEMAN – The International Association for Management Development in Dynamic Societies, Bled, Slovenia
e-mail: danica.purg@iedc.si

P. McKiernan and D. Purg (eds.), *Hidden Champions in CEE and Turkey*,
DOI 10.1007/978-3-642-40504-4_1, © Springer-Verlag Berlin Heidelberg 2013

Competitive Strategy. Consequently, over the last 30 years, academics have amassed a significant body of knowledge that purports to explain "success" over the corporate whole and across many aspects of business operations. These messages have been distilled in accessible form and are now sold alongside the lighter offerings on the world's bookshelves.

2 The Problematics

Despite the utility of these books in the provision of general advice, two issues of concern remain. First, and expectedly, these offerings have suffered predictive imperfections. This is best witnessed in Peters and Waterman's (op cit) contribution, wherein many key corporate examples of excellence soon experienced financial trouble and in Gary Hamel's (2000) infamous glorification of Enron. Success may be a temporary phenomenon. Indeed, an analysis of the Forbes top-20 corporations in each decade over the last 100 years shows that few names appear in consecutive lists and none survive a longer historical observation. Business contexts change and what works in one context becomes less effective in another. In the evolution of the corporate species, failure to adapt strategic recipes to changing context suggests consequent underperformance and eventual failure. Hence, there may be contemporary examples of good business practice but no sustainable panacea for success.

Second, the majority of this literature has focused on larger, well-known companies whose corporate histories were relatively easy to etch out, as much of the information was publicly available. Many became prize cases in the MBA classroom, where the teaching mantra was how Hewlett-Packard, Honda, and Dell had made it big. But, as economists had long recognized, the engine of economic growth for many nations were the flourishing strata of small and medium-sized companies, whose invention, innovation and export-to-sales ratios drove country GDP. Unfortunately, these strata were not always detected on the radar screens of many business schools. The most famous collection are the craftsman-like Mittelstand of the German speaking nations, many of whom became the subject of Simon's (1996) pioneering thesis on Hidden Champions.

3 The Original Hidden Champions

Like many academics at the time, Simon had championed larger corporations. But, in the mid-1980s, he was inspired by the Harvard marketeer Theodore Levitt to inquire into the remarkable export-based success of SMEs in Germany and the role they played alongside their larger, well known multi-national counterparts like Bosch, VW, Siemens and BASF, in cultivating Germany's long-term export success. He labelled these small giants "Hidden Champions (HCs)" and observed how they avoided large company ailments like "inflexibility, bureaucracy, excessive division of labour, and remoteness from the customer" (Simon 1996).

4 Definition

In researching the phenomenon, Simon developed three qualifications for a HC:

(a) A HC should occupy the number one or two position in the world market and the number one position in the European market as measured by market share or, if the latter is unknown, a HC must be a leader relative to its strongest competitor (These measures are similar to those that underpinned the abscissa on the famous Boston Consulting Group matrix developed by Alan Zakon and Bruce Henderson in the 1970s);

(b) A HC must be small or medium-sized and, normally, its sales revenue would not exceed 1 billion US dollars (1996 terms);

(c) A HC must have a low visibility profile in the public domain.

Restrictive as these conditions may seem, Simon's research effort eventually uncovered nearly 500 such companies in Germany alone, leaving many undiscovered. In breaching the invisible wall, Simon offered an insight into their world.

5 Characteristics

The original HCs spanned many sectors but were mainly in mechanical engineering (37 %), miscellaneous industries—so obscure as to be statistically invisible, electronics (12 %), and metalworking (10 %). The remaining ones were in chemistry, paper, printing, food and textiles. As expected, the majority of their products (67 %) were in the mature phase of the life cycle. Average sales revenues were around 130 million dollars in 1996, with the smallest at 3.33 million dollars. Average annual growth rates were around 6.5 % and employment size was around 735 people. Remarkably, employment seemed impervious to the recession of 1989–1992, even growing in some cases. Indeed, the HCs proved to be major exporters, earning over 51 % of their sales revenue from direct exports and a good deal more from the indirect incorporation of their products in the final products of other businesses that are then exported. Their median age was nearly 50 years, but some had much longer heritages of over 200 years, having survived many generations of management.

Invariably, their product offerings were plain but had high global market shares. Examples of such HCs include Tetra (50 % market share in sales of aquariums), Baader (90 % in fish processing equipment), Hillebrand (60 % in wine shipments), Brita (85 % in water filters), Gerriets (100 % in stage lighting cloths), and Stihl (30 % in chain saws). Other HCs produce hops, gummi bear sweets, car sunroofs, book-binding textiles, model railways, skeletons, and more. The invisibility of these companies is guaranteed as many of their mundane products are subsumed either within the manufacturing processes or in other mainstream consumer products.

Hence, HCs deal in essential goods in niche markets, usually business-to-business, and are mainly family-run, single product entities. Global market exposure through exports gives them scale economies but their returns are based in superior service and quality rather than price discounting. The origins of their initial offerings stem from invention and innovation and much of this ongoing activity comes from staying close to their customers. Processes developed internally give their resource base the protection of non-imitability, which is reinforced by their eschewing of alliances and joint ventures. Old-fashioned values define cultures where employees work hard, imbue pride in their craft and remain perennially loyal. Their passionate and persistent leaders enjoy visionary skills and balance authoritarian strategic styles with cooperation at the operations level. They prefer controlled growth to explosive growth. Most important, they like to remain hidden:

> "But an equally important reason for the low profile of these world market leaders is that they relish their obscurity. They shy away from publicity, some through explicit policies of not dealing with the press-or, by the way, with academic researchers!" Simon (1996, p. 3)

This inconspicuous nature means that, unlike the strategies of their larger cousins, those of the HCs, remain largely invisible and so are tough to detect by rivals, yielding a significant competitive edge. But, perhaps the most important observation from Simon's original study is that the HCs, in Penrose's terminology, represent "a unique bundle of assets" that are managed in a common sense kind of way. They do their own thing in their own way and defy much of the body of knowledge generated from the study of large firms that forms much of the curricula of business schools. As Simon emphasizes, "a small company is not a little big company" and the mantra of big company success cannot be applied to the HCs. Ironically, his study reverses the dominant asymmetry of learning from big to small by suggesting that there are many lessons that can be taken from the HCs and delivered to larger, more complex corporations.

6 The Latter Hidden Champions

Simon's original book was published in 17 countries and so the story of HCs spread swiftly. Further research uncovered HCs in most economies, e.g. America, Brazil, Japan, South Africa and New Zealand, though Simon has estimated that 80 % still lie within the German-Scandinavian zone. More important, Simon found similarities in the cultures of theses global HCs and their approach to business strategy and corporate leadership…a sound, patriarchal, consistent, conservative, somewhat authoritarian style. This was at odds with much management teaching at the time, which advocated radical and continuous change, devolved and dynamic management, and dispersed leadership. The normal approach of the HCs contrasted with the prominent case examples in business schools that continued to emphasize large company prowess and among whose stars were IBM and General Motors. But, these stars lose their glitter with time and are replaced by the new stars of Microsoft and Nokia, who are then replaced by the new stars of eBay, then Google and Apple and so forth, as the fashion parade proceeds in front of credulous MBA students in a repetitive manner. For Simon, the more enduring lessons come from studying the relative monotony and mystery of the HCs.

In 2009, Simon's second book on *Hidden Champions for the 21st Century* brought much of the original information up to date and extended the coverage of HCs from Germany to include Austria and Switzerland. The consolidated HC list drew on data from over 2,000 HCs over a 20-year period, with 66 % in the German-speaking triangle. At 434 million US dollars, the average revenues of the HCs were almost three times higher than those of the companies in the 1996 sample, representing rapid growth over the period, but almost 25 % of HCs had revenues less than 70 million US dollars. Their average workforce grew from 735 to over 2,000 due to new job creation beyond the home territory. Again, most were in industrial goods (69 %), where engineering (36 %) and other, non-listed industrials (29 %) made up the majority, with only 20 % in consumer products. The median company age was 61 years with 32 % more than 100 years old.

Simon took a more qualitative approach to his analysis of these HCs, delving deeper into the culture and styles of these mysterious organizations. This allowed him to refine the lessons of his 1996 work. In particular, besides the themes developed in the original work, Simon added a deeper coverage of audit, strategy, financing and business context. He drew eight sharp lessons.

Hidden Champions...

1. Need will power, ambitious goals and decentralization to be world leaders
2. Need to maintain discipline and so inspire loyalty among employees
3. Need depth in value chains and must restrict outsourcing
4. Need to decentralize within their structure to encourage new HCs to emerge
5. Need to define markets precisely, focus on one thing and do it right
6. Need to suspend national boundaries to capitalize on globalization
7. Need to apply continuous innovation by creativity and quality, not by money
8. Need to privilege customer orientation over competitor orientation

A cursory examination indicates that these lessons differ from the modern management rhetoric of alliances, just-in-time outsourcing and transitory leadership styles. Such "wave"-based fads are displaced in HCs by a more consistent approach to affairs over the long run. Further and expectedly, these lessons mirror those of the earlier work while reflecting the dynamics of modern business in a globalizing world. The HCs have adapted as the world has altered around them, but have stuck to essential and proven ingredients. True, few of them accept that there is any formula for "success". Much is done in moderation, using common sense and tried and tested ways, while avoiding risky strategic moves. Many small things add up to a better whole and each has to be done with pride and to the best level possible. Guided by simplicity, HCs root out excess, become champions of "lean" and avoid distraction. Moreover, they do this with huge determination.

7 Hidden Champion in Central and Eastern Europe (CEE)

Clearly, HCs play a significant and essential role in driving growth in their national economies. After the chaos generated by the financial and economic crisis of 2008/2009, governments began to explore what was at the heart of their economies and what needed to be done to stimulate recovery and growth. The HCs gained a new, global audience as the notion that SMEs strength meant international strength was re-discovered.

Politicians and businessmen in the CEE were concerned for the continued dynamics of their region and its ability to escape the global recession in good shape due to perceived weaknesses in the SME sector and in entrepreneurship. The international business press was short of good examples of distinction amongst CEE firms and a leading global consultancy predicted that no key industrial firms would emerge from the CEE in the foreseeable future. Many reasons were offered. First, the strongest international firms in Poland, the Czech Republic, Slovakia, Hungary and Slovenia were an integral part of the supply chain for Western companies (mainly German). When those markets went into recession, supply was curtailed, causing suffering in many CEE companies. Second, despite some high-tech business location focus (as in Slovenia, the Czech Republic, Slovakia, Poland, Russia and Estonia), the absence of concentrated clusters of industry throughout the region raised the prospect of the CEE becoming a remnant in the global recovery battle. But was this a true assessment?

To answer this question, CEEMAN and IEDC-Bled School of Management embraced Simon's research on HCs in the CEE region and Turkey in the hope of discovering an engine of economic growth to spur the region onwards as the global economy stuttered. The journey was taken by 32 researchers and covered 18 countries from Russia to Albania, covering many contexts, political systems, cultures and infrastructures; 15 countries are included in the book. Moreover, some are full members of the European Union; during the creation of the book Croatia joined EU, some within the process of application and others without any membership aspirations. Despite this heterogeneity, all have in common their recent short experience of open economies which augers well for entrepreneurial SMEs like the hidden champions.

The main goals of the journey were to:

- Uncover examples of HCs
- Compare and contrast any examples with those of Simon's work
- Identify what support CEE HCs might need to get stronger

8 Structure of the Book

To emphasise the scholarship behind the research journey, the methodology follows this introduction. Every care was taken to design a project that could learn as it progressed by utilizing established, professional protocols. Of course, some HCs do not make it in the long run, but prior research suggests that their failure rate is much lower than the average of the country in which they are situated. Hence, failure is expected from the outset with lessons drawn from it and from the surviving companies. Their next chapters follow the key issues generated inductively from the research journey but are designed so that comparison with Simon's works is made easier. These chapters are: Leadership of Hidden Champions: From Vision to

Communityship; Three Bivalent Performance Factors of Hidden Champions: Ownership, Organization, Culture and Organizational Governance; Innovation Behaviour of Hidden Champions; In Search of Sustainable Business in Central and Eastern Europe; and Financial Aspects of Hidden Champions Business Model.

Following these interdisciplinary, cross-study chapters you will find individual country chapters containing an overview of each country's history, economic indicators and vignettes of the HC cases involved in this study.

References

Grinyer, P. H., Mayes, D. G., & McKiernan, P. (1988). *Sharpbenders, the secrets of unleashing corporate potential*. Oxford: Blackwell.

Hamel, G. (2000). *Leading the revolution*. Boston, MA: Harvard Business School Press.

Peters, T. J., & Waterman, R. H., Jr. (1982). *In search of excellence*. New York: Harper and Row.

Porter, M. E. (1980). *Competitive strategy*. New York: The Free Press.

Simon, H. (1996). *Hidden champions: Lessons from 500 of the world's business unknown companies*. Boston, MA: Harvard Business School Press.

Research Methodology

Melita Balas Rant

1 The Research Focus

This research project aimed to explore multilayer organisational behaviours of companies that successfully pursue leadership in a narrow market segment. In general, this is a subgroup of business organizations that follow a variation of differentiation strategy proposed by Porter (1980). Normally such strategy fits well in the contexts in which the target customer segment is relatively price-insensitive, the market is saturated, customers have very specific needs which are to a large-extent under-served, and the firm possesses unique resources and capabilities that are difficult to imitate, plus Intellectual Property (IP), exclusive technical expertise, talented personnel, a brand, or innovative processes (Porter 1980).

Hermann Simon (1996) undertook research on the internationalization patterns of small and mid-sized companies pursuing such differentiation strategies in a German context. He named this strategy "Focus & Depth & Internationalization" and labelled the companies "Hidden Champions (HCs)". The name was chosen because such companies were not well known to the general public since they mainly operated in the business-to-business market, producing inconspicuous, technologically complex products. Simon attributed their strong and sustainable market leadership to factors such as stability of ownership and governance structures, commitments and loyalties of local communities, intense and successful innovations resulting in high rates of patents, employee trust and closeness to customers, and strong, passionate, family-run leadership.

In 2008–2009, Simon re-examined his HCs to check how well they were doing a decade later and, more specifically, how resistant they were to the compression of market demands and financial volatility experienced with the financial markets melt-down in 2008. He discovered that the survival rate of HCs was significantly higher than the average in their sector. Besides, demand shrinkage had not affected

M. Balas Rant (✉)
Management and Organization Department, University of Ljubljana, Ljubljana, Slovenia
e-mail: melita.balas.rant@ef.uni-lj.si

P. McKiernan and D. Purg (eds.), *Hidden Champions in CEE and Turkey*,
DOI 10.1007/978-3-642-40504-4_2, © Springer-Verlag Berlin Heidelberg 2013

their market strength; on the contrary their market share grew on the account of bankrupt competition. If the organizational and leadership behaviour of HCs was more resistant to market instabilities, then this called for a deeper understanding of what accounts for this competitive superiority. Hence, *the primary purpose* of this study was to delve deeper into the phenomena of HCs to clarify and deepen the understanding of key factors contributing to competitive superiority indicated through consistency of revenue growth and growing market leadership strength. Special attention was given to the interpretations of core decision-makers (CEOs and/or founders) on factors that, in their minds, contributed the most to business growth and market leadership. Put differently, what core strategies do HC companies see, think and interpret as relevant and vital element to their business success? Coupling their interpretations with the original survey questionnaire developed by Simon (see below) allowed us to acquire an improved understanding of the drivers behind HC success.

In addition, *a secondary purpose* of this study was to touch upon patterns of the evolution of the HC phenomenon in an institutional context that was less stable and homogenous than that of Simon's original study. Contrary to HCs in the well-developed German context, CEE companies originated from the institutional environments characterized by only a short-history of market economy where the "rules of the game" were less clear (Boycko et al. 1995; Williamson 2000). Geographically, this research covered countries of the CEE region and beyond (Albania, Belarus, Bosnia and Herzegovina, Croatia, Czech Republic, Estonia, Hungary, Kazakhstan, Latvia, Macedonia, Poland, Romania, Russian Federation, Serbia, Slovak Republic, Slovenia, Turkey, and Ukraine).

2 Choices in the Research Design

The research endeavour aimed to "be rigorous while staying relevant" (Mirvis and Laweler 2011). To prevent the loss of relevancy and increased chance of coming up with novel understandings and relevant explanations of HC phenomena, the research design was deliberately conceptualized to allow for experimentations and adaptations to surprises (Campbell 1987, 1998). The design purpose was to produce a refined map of factors that contribute to the success (or, if missing, to the failure) of HCs (Azevedo 1997, 2005).[1] Presuming and hoping that such a map

[1] Azevedo (1997, 2005) compares theories with maps. Maps are selective representations of the world, and their content and form are selected by the map used in relation to the problems they are intended to solve. For example, if a map user wants to come from place A to place B in a city, a topological map of that city would be of smaller value that a quick sketch of how to come from point A to point B. So, because the usefulness of a map can only be assessed by how well it helps solve the problems of the user, its validity is interest-related as well. Hence, the interests of the user very much affect the methods used to construct maps. Since theories serve the same function as maps, being guides to action and decision making, this analogy of theories as maps is very useful. The validity depends on the interest of the user and the map. Reliability depends on how efficiently it meets these interests. Accordingly, our goals was to produce a more detailed, higher-resolution map of understanding the factors that drive the success and failures of HCs.

would, and could, be used not only by companies that wish to enact the HC successes but also by other stakeholders interested in the HC phenomena, the research deliberately invited and co-involved the interested stakeholders (academics, employees, managers, owners, investors, educators, governments) in the research process (Flyvbjerg 2006). In the approach to knowledge generation, the research design aimed to be positivistic whenever possible, but also interpretive at points when more meaningful and appropriate. In addition, it remained flexible in using both deductive reasoning derived from Simon's framework and employing inductive case-based reasoning when dealing with surprises from the field. The choice for such flexible and loosely structured research design was justified when dealing with ambiguous contextual properties (e.g., organizational, historical, political, and evidential). Ambiguity in contextual properties calls for an evolutionary approach to the research design (Buchanan and Bryman 2007).[2] Acknowledging Eisenhardt and Bourgeois' (1988) view that research methods should be regularly adjusted according to circumstances in a flexible manner as initial plans become inappropriate and as fresh lines of inquiry become apparent, researchers deliberately reflected on the signals from the field whether and where they could employ Simon's research methodology and where a more exploratory approach would create more value. Regardless of that deliberate incorporation of the reflection and exploration in the research design, Simon's past experience with the HC research to a significant degree constrained this research endeavour. In particular, Simon's conceptualizations of HC characteristics served as the research window through which researchers observed CEE companies. This window paid more attention to aspects of the HC phenomena as proposed by Simon in a mature market context and hence might have blinded the research to other, equally relevant aspects of the HC success that might have been overlooked.

Following the advice of Mintzberg (1979), Yin (1984), Miles and Huberman (1984), and Eisenhardt (1989), in each case multiple methods of data collection, qualitative and quantitative methods were employed. In addition to Simon's survey questionnaire (see below), interviews, observations and archival analysis from secondary sources were adopted. The interests of multiple stakeholder groups (management, investors and academic audiences) can be incongruent; e.g., academic colleagues expect new knowledge and theoretical insight; HC managers anticipate practical recommendations; field researchers wish to know that their contributions have been interpreted and used in an appropriate manner. Hence, this research adopted process theories (Dawson 2003; Pettigrew 1985) focusing more on local causality rather than the pursuance of the universal laws. To sum up, in order to come up with a relevant and useful map for HC stakeholders, flexibility and non-predetermination of the research design was applied, the merging of positivistic and interpretive epistemology; the incorporation of deductive and inductive reasoning; the co-involvement of multiple-stakeholders in the process,

[2] Predetermined and inflexible methods are less appropriate (perhaps inappropriate) where organizational context is changing (Buchanan and Bryman 2007, p. 488).

and a focus on local causalities rather than universal laws were all deliberate choices of our research design.

3 The Research Questions

Aligned with the flexible research design, the research questions were from two paths, confirmatory and exploratory. The confirmatory part of the research addressed questions such as: "Did the CEE region have Simon's HC type of companies and, if not, what could be the best approximation to Simon's HCs? How similar and different were these when compared to Simon's HCs?" The exploratory part of the research delved into: "How and why did these differences occur? What worked well in the specific cases and why? Was there a pattern? What important determinants of superior performance were missing and why?" In addition, the research incorporated extensive reflexivity. Hence, all researchers were continuously exposed to a series of value-related reflective questions (Flyvbjerg 2006) such as, "Where were you/we going? Was this development desirable? What, if anything, should you/we do about it to maximize research relevance and usefulness while preserving research reliability and validity?"

4 Frame of Reference

This research primarily addresses the phenomena of HCs through the eyes of the main company leader. He/she was the main decision-maker, the strategist. Most frequently in companies set up after the 1990s, this was the company founder who also stood in the shoes of CEO; in companies set up before the 1990s, this was usually the CEO and other members of the management board who, in most cases, also co-owned the major share of the companies. To reduce the subjectivity, the perspective of company strategists was supplemented with the archival data (mostly media articles and financial reports). In some countries, such as Kazakhstan, Belarus, Ukraine, and Albania among others, it was extremely difficult (or even impossible) to balance data from other sources (financial reports, media, web pages). Therefore, in a few case descriptions the interests and viewpoints of company strategists were favoured alone. However we do not consider this potentially in-balanced representation of HCs to be a problem as we were not "silent or naïve about whose interests are served and ignored in any study" (Van de Ven and Poole 2005, p. 868).

5 Entering the Field and Selecting the Cases

Overall 32 field-researchers from 18 countries[3] (Albania, Belarus, Bosnia and Herzegovina, Croatia, Czech Republic, Estonia, Hungary, Kazakhstan, Latvia, Macedonia, Poland, Romania, Russian Federation, Serbia, Slovak Republic,

[3] The list of field-researchers is included in the appendix to the book. All field researchers had training and knowledge of the organisation research methods. The majority of them came from faculties and universities that were members of CEEMAN association, a professional body for

Slovenia, Turkey and Ukraine) worked on the research project. They followed precise guidelines in each case. First, field researchers received Simon's book (2009) to inform themselves about the HC phenomena and then create a list of potential HCs in their respective countries by applying Simon's definition of HCs as the company search criteria. According to this definition, the company qualified as a HC if it was number one, two, or three in the global market, or number one in CEE region, as determined by market share.

In the process of the creation of the list of potential HCs, the field researchers carefully scanned various sources of information ranging from national and international statistical reports, economic studies; databases and networks of research and educational institutions; business rankings, articles in business magazines and other media; consultancy reports, information available through ministries, chambers of commerce, and other public bodies.

Despite this extensive search of multiple sources, Simon's search criteria proved insufficient and unsatisfactory due to four main research challenges:

- Research challenge 1: Companies, once identified, liked to stay hidden;
- Research challenge 2: Some countries did not have public reporting and so a systemic search for HCs was not possible;
- Research challenge 3: In some countries, Simon-like HCs did not exist;
- Research challenge 4: Even if researchers applied Simon's search criteria and identified the company whose leader confirmed that the company was first in the CEE in the specific market segment, the market segment might have been defined in a creative and narrow enough manner that even a small company could be positioned as first in the world or the continent.

To resolve the four research challenges in the best possible manner, the company search criteria were adjusted marginally and the following accommodation to the sample design enacted:

- Resolution of research challenge 1: Identified companies that wanted to stay hidden stay hidden; these were not included in the study. Roughly 45 % of identified companies (135 out of 300 identified companies) fell into this category.
- Resolution of research challenge 2: Any information that the researcher could get about the company was considered to be better than nothing. If the only informant was the company CEO and the researcher could not access the financial records and other information through other sources, trust was placed in their figures, for example, regarding growth of export and revenues.
- Resolution of research challenge 3: If Simon-like HCs could not be identified in a specific country,[4] field researchers looked for the best approximation of HC types in that local context. Therefore, if the company held market leadership in a narrow product category in a local geography extending over neighbouring

teaching and accreditation of business and management schools/departments in the CEE and beyond. EQUIS would be a similar global body based in Brussels in Western Europe.

[4] This was the case in seven countries: Bulgaria, Hungary, Bosnia and Herzegovina, Macedonia, Albania, Kazakhstan, and Belarus.

countries (Balkan, CIS region, Baltic region) and exhibited a consistent growth pattern over the last 3–5 years, the company was included in the sample. Though such companies were also incorporated in the research sample, they were categorized as "potential" hidden champions.
- Resolution of research challenge 4: If the company attributed itself as a market leader in a very narrow market segment by using creative market definition, the field researcher carefully scrutinized the market segment size and its specific regularities to assess the relevance of the self-stated market leadership. If this was considered to be weak and questionable, the field researchers were entitled to exclude the company from the sample.

6 Gathering the Data and Crafting Research Instruments

There were three stages to the data gathering section of the research design:

a) Adoption of the Resolutions

Field-researchers created their country list of HCs by applying the proposed resolutions outlines above.

b) Simon's Original Questionnaire; the Abridged Design

Field-researchers completed Simon's diagnostic questionnaire[5] on their target company. The concepts of HC phenomenon covered by this questionnaire were: general information about the company, nature of market leadership, growth indicators (revenues, export rates, employees), geographic markets in which the company held the strong market position, the nature of competition at these markets, nature and diversity of customers, factors driving the customers' purchasing behaviour, characteristics of the company products (life cycles stake, technological complexity, capital intensity), aspects in which the company product was superior to products of main competitor(s), general competence of the company (e.g., leadership, patents, financial strength, reputation, history), innovation practices, IP protection, performance indicators, financing instruments, and information about the general board. Each concept was assessed through multiple items and cross-examined through multiple questions. Both closed and open questions were used and closed questions applied a 1–7 Likert scale.

Initially, Poland was used as a test case for refining questionnaire for the CEE. This test proved invaluable as the original version proved to be too long and detailed for the context of the CEE. This forced the re-design of a shorter, more precise version. Hence, in other countries the new abridged version of Simon's questionnaire was applied. The latter covered exactly the same concepts as the original version, but used fewer indicators for each concept.[6] The abridged questionnaire was of the same reliability as the extended one, though shorter and

[5] The list of the HCs is included in the appendix to the book.

[6] Only the most reliable indicators of each concept were selected.

less time-consuming. Accordingly, it carried higher chances of completion by CEOs.

c) Company Interviews

In addition to the abridged questionnaires, the field researchers conducted in-depth exploratory interviews. In most cases, these were with the company founder and CEO. Questionnaires were used to study 165 companies; 95 of their leaders were interviewed for at least 90 min. In 30 cases, more than one interview was conducted on the company site where field researchers had requested a visit to the production area, R&D departments. This was done, among other reasons, to supplement the data from the interview with the researchers' own observations. In 10 cases, other members of the board and employees were interviewed. Field researchers started each interview by describing the research purpose, exploring the interviewee's background, and asking the interviewee to recount how they explain the nature of the company's market leadership and how they developed it. Most interviewees were eager to tell their stories and needed little prompting.

During the interviewing process, the field researchers probed into the nature of company leadership. Whenever possible, they inquired into aspects of company performance that were suggested by the interviewee as critical to company success. The field researchers tried to explore these aspects of company success deeply enough to comprehend how the relevant business issues interacted. In addition, they tried to capture the novel aspects of HC behaviour that were not initially addressed by the questionnaire (Dougherty 2005). The majority of interviews were audio-taped and later transcribed by the field researchers into extensive field notes. If interviews were not allowed, field researchers made short notes during the interviews and extensive notes after the interviewing process. Field researchers requested in-house memos, reports, and promotional material, and searched for stories about the organisation that appeared in trade journals or newspapers over the period 2000–2010, which was the temporal focus for the research. All these data were gathered with a retrospective method.

At the beginning of February 2011, all field researchers convened at a joint workshop to review and compare their data and early findings on the HC phenomenon. This meeting explored the joint sharing of unique data-gathering experiences (what approaches worked well and what approaches did not work), and the collective search resolution of specific data-gathering challenges (i.e., how to detect the company, how to probe their claims on stated nature of market leadership, how to gain additional material on companies, how to deal with information not to be disclosed in public). In this way, cross-learning was maximized and a uniform approach to data gathering was maintained across the CEE.

After the workshop, the field researchers produced their first drafts of the case studies. These write-ups aimed to unpack the main elements of the business success story for each of the companies in their countries. The first drafts were cross-examined by the research project leaders (Melita Rant of IEDC Bled and Marek Dietl of the Warsaw School of Economics) in order to pinpoint any discrepancies and insufficiencies in the interpretations, as well as to advise on additional data searches. At each opportunity, the project leaders advised all field researchers to remain committed to rigour in the data collection process with a deliberation to stay open-minded, ask the right questions, and to listen attentively to gain additional insights into the companies and their leaders.

After a further round of collecting the missing and supplementary data, field researchers re-wrote their cases to portray important "structures of meaning" as well as significant "repertoires of actions"[7] that contributed the most to the companies' success. While composing business success stories, the field researchers were asked to reflect on three important aspects: "Did the story articulate well the core themes of the HC phenomenon and the central dynamics among these themes? How could I best get an honest story honestly told?[8] How did the context-specific information, like regulatory and other institutional changes, affect the company path?" After completing the case writing stage, the field researchers circulated the final case studies write-ups to the interviewees, who re-examined and edited the writings with their own interpretations and reflections (Eisenhardt 1989). Though the case studies produced by the field researchers were infused by personal subjectivity (Dougherty 2005), the fabrication of a mass of subjective case studies allowed production of classification themes relevant to the HC phenomenon that tend to be fairly stable over these cases (Mohr 1998). The contributions to this book worked around these stable themes in the case studies.

To enable consistency of approach across the many country domains, the fieldwork was integrated by the project leaders, Melita Balas Rant and Marek Dietl. Their core role, besides project consistency, was to preserve the relevancy of the research. Accordingly, the coordinators frequently challenged themselves and other research colleagues with "so what" questions. Following the practice of Flyvbjerg (2006) to stay relevant in organizational science research, one needs to ensure the "fusion of horizons" on research findings by involving parties outside the research team in the research process. To achieve this fusion of horizons, an open conference on "Hidden Champions in CEE and Dynamically Changing Environments" was organized in Vienna, Austria on 17–18 November 2011 at the Austrian Federal Economic Chamber.[9] The conference served as the meeting platform where different parties interested in the HC phenomenon were invited to exchange their views and interpretations on findings and ideas proposed by the research team. At the conference, all researchers deliberately exposed their results to positive and

[7] Orlikowski and Yates (1994) showed how stylized conventions of communication genres make us see how organizational activates are bundled in standardized "repertoires of action".

[8] This important question is advised by Geertz (1988).

[9] The event brought together over 130 participants from 31 countries—HCs and other business leaders, business thinkers in the area of economic growth, international entrepreneurship and innovation, venture capital funds and other investors, management educators, and government officials. It enabled a rich exchange of viewpoints, insights and ideas, addressing developments down the championship road and beyond, more specifically: the economic, technological, and social importance of HCs; growth and financing issues; competitiveness, cooperation and cohesion; as well as leadership and sustainability aspects. More about the event can be found on http://www.ceeman.org/pages/en/hidden-champions.html.

Fig. 1 Flow of the HC research activities and challenges

negative reactions from the audiences interested in the HC phenomenon. In consequence, the conference created a set of novel interpretations, perspectives, insights and meanings about the HC phenomenon. Chapters in this book present the summary of a collectively improved understanding of the CEE HCs through this multilayer research process.

The summary of the temporal unfolding of the research activities with accompanying research challenges is presented in the Fig. 1.

References

Azevedo, J. (1997). *Mapping reality: An evolutionary realist methodology for the natural and social sciences*. Albany, NY: State University of New York Press.

Azevedo, J. (2005). Updating organizational epistemology. In J. A. Baum (Ed.), *Companion to organizations* (pp. 715–732). Malden: Blackwell.

Boycko, M., Shleifer, A., & Vishny, R. (1995). *Privatizing Russia*. Cambridge, MA: MIT Press.

Buchanan, D. A., & Bryman, A. (2007). Contextualizing methods choice in organizational research. *Organizational Research Methods, 10*(2), 483–501.

Campbell, D. T. (1987). Blind variation and selective retention in creative thought as an outer knowledge process. In G. Radnitzky & W. W. Bartley (Eds.), *Evolutionary epistemology, rationality and the sociology of knowledge* (pp. 91–114). Chicago: Open Court.

Campbell, D. T. (1998). The experimenting society. In W. N. Dunn (Ed.), *The experimenting society: Essays in honour of Donald T. Campbell* (Vol. 11, pp. 35–68). New Brunswick: Transaction.

Dawson, P. (2003). *Reshaping change: A processual approach*. London: Routledge.

Dougherty, D. (2005). Grounded theory research methods. In J. A. Baum (Ed.), *Companion to organizations* (pp. 849–866). Malden: Blackwell.

Eisenhardt, K. M. (1989). Building theories from case study research. *Academy of Management Review, 14*(4), 532–550.

Eisenhardt, K. M., & Bourgeois, L. J. (1988). Politics of strategic decision making in high-environments: Towards a mid-range theory. *Academy of Management Journal, 31*, 737–770.

Flyvbjerg, B. (2006). Making organization research matter: Power, values and phronesis. In S. R. Clegg, C. Hardy, T. B. Lawrence, & W. R. Nord (Eds.), *The Sage handbook of organization studies* (2nd ed., pp. 370–387). London: Sage.

Geertz, C. (1988). *Works and lives: The anthropologist as author*. Stanford: Stanford University Press.

Miles, M., & Huberman, A. M. (1984). *Qualitative data analysis*. Beverly Hills, CA: Sage.

Mintzberg, H. (1979). An emerging strategy of "direct" research. *Administrative Science Quarterly, 24*, 580–589.

Mirvis, P., & Laweler, E., III. (2011). Rigor and relevance in organization research: Experiences, reflections and a look ahead. In E. Lawler (Ed.), *Useful research: Advancing theory and practice* (pp. 113–135). San Francisco: Barrett-Koeahler.

Mohr, J. W. (1998). Measuring the meaning structures. *Annual Review of Sociology, 24*, 345–370.

Orlikowski, W. J., & Yates, J. (1994). Genre repertoire: Examining the structuring of communicative practices in organizations. *Administrative Science Quarterly, 39*, 541–574.

Pettigrew, A. M. (1985). *The awakening giant: Continuity and change in ICI*. Oxford, UK: Basil Blackwell.

Porter, M. E. (1980). *Competitive strategy: Techniques for analyzing industries and competitors*. New York: Free Press.

Simon, H. (1996). *Hidden champions: Lessons from 500 of the world's best unknown companies*. Boston, MA: Harvard Business School Press.

Simon, H. (2009). *Hidden champions of the 21st century: Success strategies of unknown* (World market leaders). London: Springer.

Van de Ven, A., & Poole, M. C. (2005). Field research methods. In J. A. Baum (Ed.), *Companion to organizations* (pp. 867–888). Malden: Blackwell.

Williamson, O. E. (2000). The new institutional economics: Taking stock, looking ahead. *Journal of Economic Literature, 38*(3), 595–613.

Yin, R. (1984). *Case study research*. Beverly Hills, CA: Sage.

Leadership of Hidden Champions: From Vision to Communityship

Ian Sutherland and Danica Purg

From Russia to Albania, Hidden Champion organizations (HCs) have many common features. Among these, as also argued in the original Hidden Champion work by Hermann Simon (1996, 2009), is the importance of leadership.

With few exceptions the narratives of these organizations attribute their beginnings and continuing success to visionary, passionate and expert leadership focused on building organizations of community. In this chapter these themes are followed in exploration of that ephemeral practice—leadership.

Drawing on national studies from Central and Eastern Europe (CEE), company descriptions, and interviews with CEOs, directors, and board members, this chapter explores the involved, social phenomena of leadership within HC's and identifies common leadership threads running through and across these organizations. We begin with the individuals running these companies—how they work from foundations of vision, passion and expert knowledge and provide continuity—before broadening the scope to consider the social nature of leadership as a cadre of people working together (Best 2011; Bolden 2011; Carroll et al. 2008; Crevani et al. 2010; Raelin 2011). Here we use Henry Mintzberg's (2009) concept of 'communityship' to discuss leadership not as something found in an individual, but rather as a social phenomena encompassing "...people's sense of belonging to and caring for something larger than themselves" (p. 140).

I. Sutherland (✉)
IEDC – Bled School of Management, Bled, Slovenia
e-mail: ian.sutherland@iedc.si

D. Purg
IEDC – Bled School of Management, Bled, Slovenia

CEEMAN – The International Association for Management Development in Dynamic Societies, Bled, Slovenia

P. McKiernan and D. Purg (eds.), *Hidden Champions in CEE and Turkey*,
DOI 10.1007/978-3-642-40504-4_3, © Springer-Verlag Berlin Heidelberg 2013

1 Leadership of Vision, Passion and Expertise

1.1 Vision

What does vision or, more specifically, visionary leadership mean? A "guiding vision" is posited by cornerstone leadership thinkers, such as Warren Bennis (2009, p. 33), to be the first ingredient of leadership, and it remains the subject of ongoing debate in leadership studies (Bennis and Nanus 1985; Lesourd 1992; Maccoby 2003; Meindl 1998; Nanus 1992; Sashkin 1988; Stam et al. 2010; Tellis 2006; Westley and Mintzberg 1989). At the heart of this debate is a focus on the future: leadership as a practice that brings people together to achieve future goals and aspirations.

In its original meaning, dating from the late thirteenth century A.D., the term "vision" was defined as something perceived or seen in the imagination, often related to the supernatural or spiritual, such as religious visions. While in the context of leadership the spiritual angle has been sidelined, there is still a focus on what is envisioned. In essence, the base of visionary leadership is the ability to think about, plan and consciously participate in creating the future through imaginative skill. This is a hallmark of leadership practice in HC companies.

ESET LLC, an important player in the constantly evolving malware protection field, was established in 1992 by Trnka and Pasko. ESET was founded on a vision of secure, protected access to information and communication technologies (ICTs). ESET, whose NOD32 anti-virus software is considered a global benchmark, is based on the visionary work of its co-founders, who in 1987 discovered one of the first computer viruses. When they diagnosed this early virus, they went a step further to imagine the future ramifications of its existence. Predicting the increasing centrality of the emerging globally interconnected, digitized world, they anticipated the need for a new kind of security and protection. Throughout the development of ESET, Trnka and Pasko have worked to provide responsible and reliable solutions to constantly emerging malware issues for both home users and corporate customers. Not only was the original work visionary, the ongoing competitive advantage of ESET relies upon the ability to envision new threats and innovate to overcome them. Their work is not just anticipation but proactive adaption—constant thinking, planning, and consciously participating in creating the future.

As visionary leaders, Trnka and Pasko are an exceptional example. They were able to analyze their 1987 discovery, when information sharing was still accomplished primarily through telephone, snail-mail and faxing, and imagine how this would affect the world in the coming decades. They foresaw an opportunity that would benefit others and worked towards creating that opportunity. Today the company continues to work at the cutting edge of anti-malware, still envisioning what the future developments and ramifications will be. A leading ICT trade magazine, *CRN*, has recognized the technological vision and innovation of the company, identifying CEO Miroslav Trnka as one of the most innovative managers in the field.

While Trnka and Pasko's visionary leadership lies in the realm of digital safety, DOK-ING Ltd's founder Vjekoslav Majetić's visionary leadership lies within the realm of physical safety, working to deal with the scourge of land mines. A medium-sized Croatian enterprise, established by Majetić in 1991, DOK-ING produces anti-mine, fire-fighting and underground mining vehicles. Between 1991 and 1995, Croatia was embroiled in a war of independence. During the first decade of DOK-ING's operation, Majetić led the company's development of technology to safeguard the lives of Croatians against an estimated 2,000,000 unexploded land mines scattered across the country. Through this vision and the commitment of DOK-ING's employees, they developed an unmanned, remote controlled anti-mine vehicle (AMV). This highly successful AMV has since spread around the globe, saving lives in many countries.

Majetić's leadership began as a concern for those around him and threats to human life. This developed into a vision to advance the cause of a mine-free landscape and he demonstrated the will and courage to pursue this. Through DOK-ING his vision has created an opportunity to improve life in Croatia and around the world. In turn he was able to establish, maintain and grow a strong and successful organization.

Through the actions of Trnka, Pasko (ESET LLC) and Majetić (DOK-ING Ltd.) is evidence of the practice of visionary leadership. Their activities, like so many of the other founder-leaders of HC companies, show how these organizations, through imaginative and visionary skills, are constantly planning for a future that will create a better global environment and a healthy bottom. Trnka and Pasko were able to imagine the digitized world and anticipate the necessity for security in it. Majetić's experiences of war and its aftermath prompted him to imagine a safer and healthier future. He saw the opportunity to create a sustainable company that would better his community and other communities around the world.

Yet, the visionary actions of these leaders are just the top of the leadership iceberg. In addition to enacting a vision, the founders of ESET, DOK-ING and their fellow entrepreneurial leaders, follow a passion.

1.2 Passion

Passion and leadership have long been linked and the exploration of the relationship between the two has been discussed by many (Bennis 2009; Hall 2009; Loye 1977; Marques 2007; Peters and Austin 1985) and is central to leadership discussions around charisma (Bass 1985; Conger and Kanungo 1987), authenticity (Eriksen 2009) and aesthetics (Ladkin 2008). The first written evidence of the word "passion" comes from the twelfth century, initially meaning suffering and/or endurance. This original meaning is relevant to some aspects of leadership, but we discuss passion in the modern sense referring to love, enthusiasm and predilection for a certain pursuit. This understanding of passion, which developed in the seventeenth century, seems inexorably linked to leadership. For example, Warren Bennis (2009) writes:

> The second basic ingredient of leadership is passion—the underlying passion for the promises of life, combined with a very particular passion for a vocation, a profession, a course of action. The leader loves what he or she does and loves doing it (p. 34).

There is something aesthetic about this description that invokes a sensory-emotional aura we sometimes feel emanating from leadership in action. This passion is infectious and inspiring; it spurs people into action. Yet this does not happen without struggle. Consider the following quote from entrepreneur Rok Uršič, founder and CEO of the Slovenian based company Instrumentation Technologies:

> Entrepreneurship is about creating artwork. Like artists, we entrepreneurs also struggle with moments of stuckness, restlessness and relentlessness before coming to moments of clarity, followed by action and ending with culmination, funneled towards a period of serenity and rest... If you walk around our company, you can sense the passion employees have for the supremacy of technology. They are burning for Libera [an Instrumentation Technologies product].

One can feel Uršič's passion from these words, describing the artistry of what Instrumentation Technologies does. The work is about emotion, struggle and accomplishment, about desire and achievement. As he describes the company, notably referring to it as "ours" rather than "mine", one experiences his development of a passionate workforce who "burn" for what they are doing. This is true of many of the leaders and organizations involved in this study. These leaders do not only have a vision, but also a predilection, enthusiasm and love—a calling, a vocation. In many cases this emanates from impassioned hobbies and professional pursuits.

The Slovenian company Akrapovič produces bespoke exhaust systems for motorcycles. It was established in the 1990s by Igor Akrapovič, a former professional motorcycle racer. During his racing days he spotted a niche market for high-quality exhaust systems for the bikes that he was using; his passion was interrupted too often by poor quality exhausts that hampered engine performance and caused mid-race breakdowns. He began to develop custom-made titanium systems to remedy the problems he experienced. By leveraging his experience and expertise, he was able to turn his passion into an internationally successful company.

The high-flying Pipistrel, a Slovene-based company, arose from a similar passion. Pipistrel was set up in 1982 when flying enthusiast Ivo Boscarol and friends began experimenting with lightweight, private planes for personal use. In 1987 his passion for the individual, personal experience of flight led Pipistrel to become the first private aircraft producer in Yugoslavia. With some ups and downs, Boscarol piloted Pipistrel to a top international market position. In a recent interview he said "I am fortunate that my work is my hobby. I enjoy my work enormously".

The Latvian company Blue Microphones has been connecting with customers for almost 20 years. BLUE Microphones was founded on the musical passion of Martins Saulesspurens. Behind the iron curtain, Martins discovered jazz and fell in love with it. At a time when the art form fell afoul of Soviet censors, his passion drove him to seek out jazz lovers around the world who were willing to exchange albums with him. In later years, this passion led him to study sound engineering and eventually become the director of sound recording at the Latvian Academy of Music. In 1988 Martins had the opportunity to travel to the United States, the birthplace of jazz, where he discovered a market for high-quality microphones. In Latvia Martins had access to a surplus of exceptional microphone and recording equipment that had been supplied to studios during the heyday of the Soviet Union. He began combining his passion with his knowledge to refurbish the equipment and sell it to the burgeoning markets outside Latvia. BLUE Microphones has by now become one of the most important and respected suppliers of top-notch microphones globally.

The passion, love, enthusiasm and drive of these individuals have fired their entrepreneurial spirit, leading them to see market opportunities for their unique products and services. With a strong vision, they have followed their passions to establish successful organizations that have become world leaders in their industries. The visionary passion with which they have pursued their work is palpable, inspiring and infectious. This was obvious to the researchers involved in this study. For example, Brkić and Berberović, who were looking into HCs in Bosnia and Herzegovina, noted:

> During the data gathering process, and especially during the interviews, we noticed something very interesting. Besides the ambitions that are common to successful companies, one cannot fail to spot the passion that the interviewees had for their businesses. The reason that these companies are champions is not limited to a pursuit of regular profit and a success drive.

For the leaders of these HC organizations, vision and passion came across as central and common descriptors of leadership activity. However, in virtually all cases, vision and passion were accompanied by a high degree of expert knowledge.

1.3 Expert Knowledge

In each of the aforementioned organizations the individual leader has not only acted in a passionate and visionary manner, but has done so by leveraging a high level of personal expert knowledge. Igor Akrapovič used his experience and expert knowledge of racing and exhaust system construction, whereas Trnka and Pasko availed themselves of their expertise in ICTs and programming. Extraordinary successes are often linked to expert knowledge. Take for example Malcolm Gladwell's (2008) popular work *Outliers: The Story of Success*. In his analysis of success stories from Bill Gates to The Beatles, he argues that there is a "10,000-hour rule": exceptional success comes from exceptional knowledge gained from 10,000 or more hours of study, training and practice. Regarding leadership, this phenomenon is discussed at length in Gosling et al. (2012) *Key Concepts in Leadership*.

Although we cannot claim that the leadership discussed here strictly met the 10,000-hour rule, it is clear that the majority of cases involved significant expert knowledge gleaned from study, training and practice. In Russia, for example, researchers found that most general directors of HCs graduated from some of the most prestigious Russian (Soviet) universities, specializing in engineering, mathematics and computer programming. In Serbia current or former professors and engineers founded many of the organizations. For example, DUOCHEM (a producer of high-quality rodenticides) was founded by Suren Husinec as a spin-off company, based on the results of his research and work as scientific advisor at the Institute of Chemistry, Technology and Metallurgy of the University of Belgrade. Similarly, in Hungary, the chemical company Cyclolab was founded by Professor Jozsef Szejtli. Szejtli, who was CEO and then honorary president until his death, was an internationally respected chemist, author or co-author of more than 250 scientific papers, wrote six books, and held more than 100 patents. Yet, it is not just knowledge from science and technology that has been leveraged to form HCs—recall the jazz aficionado Martins Saulesspurens and his founding of BLUE Microphones.

Another striking example of expertise from the creative and cultural industries comes from Albania. Venice Art Mask, a company producing Venetian carnival masks, was founded on the vision, passion, expert knowledge and artistic skills of Edmond Angoni. Formerly a practicing veterinarian, he employed his artistic creativity and knowledge to set up a successful company exporting high quality carnival masks. Angoni's story is one of struggle and courage. During the collapse of Yugoslavia in 1991 he was forced to leave his family for Italy to seek better employment. The self-taught visual artist took a job at an Italian factory producing carnival masks. Over 2 years he honed his craft and knowledge of the business and returned to his native Albania in 1998 to start his own mask-producing firm. Like the scientists and engineers that we discussed earlier, Saulesspurens and Angoni were able to leverage not just their passions and visions, but also their knowledge and skills, creating successful, internationally respected organizations in the creative and cultural industries.

Why is expert knowledge a key to success? In each case the expert knowledge gained by these individuals comes from a passion that they have for learning and doing something exceptionally well. In other words, their knowledge is an outgrowth of their predilection for a certain product, service, industry or purpose for doing business. In this sense, expert knowledge is part and parcel of passion. It is also very closely linked to vision. Without expert experience and knowledge, Akrapovič would never have discovered the niche market for high-quality exhaust systems, nor would Saulesspurens or Trnka and Pasko have been able to develop BLUE Microphones or ESET. Expert knowledge goes beyond the nuts and bolts of a specific technology, product or service. It encompasses a whole industry with all its strengths and weaknesses and the existing or potential needs of current or future markets.

The final piece in this puzzle is the presence of the visionary leaders in all these cases, imbuing their staff with their own passions and visions for a significant period of time. Echoing the findings of Simon (1996, 2009), these organizations were successful in part because of the sustained continuity of leadership. The leaders, upon whose vision, passion and knowledge the organizations were founded, remained (or still remain) a consistent, stabilizing force.

1.4 Leadership Continuity

Across the organizations that we have studied, the longevity of their leaders was a key component of success. In virtually all cases, the entrepreneurial founder (in the case of the start-ups), or the first CEO/director (in the case of formerly state-run enterprises) remained in a leadership role for many years, and many of them still hold the top position today. Very few organizations have experienced more than one change of top leadership, most have yet to go through a succession process. As reported by Dietl and Rant (2011), the aggregated average tenure of top leadership of the involved cases was 13.82 years, indicating significant leadership longevity.

These results are similar across most of the organizations studied. The Ukrainian Beer Company Group (UBC Group), founded in 1983, is still run by the original CEO Igor Gumennyy and the original two vice presidents. Privatization of the Ukrainian company KSEZO (producer of electric welding equipment) was overseen by Yaroslav Ivanovych Mykytyn who has been with the company since the Soviet period. Mykytyn remains CEO of the company today.

How does this longevity contribute to the success of these organizations? Thinking back to the quote from Rok Uršič (of Instrumentation Technology, Slovenia) one senses that it is first of all a continuity of vision and passion. Longitudinal leadership offers a bird's eye view of the organization, its past, present and potential future. As Uršič indicated, long-term leaders can contextualize and manage the experiences of "struggle" and "moments of stuckness, restlessness and relentlessness" with "moments of clarity... and action". Working from a deeply seated passion they supply a stabilizing motivation, becoming repositories of the memories of the organization's struggles (Linde 2009; Te and Frank 2008) and serving as emblems of hope, achievement and vision. As such, they carry the history and vision of the organization forwards. Because of that, they are able to communicate the living history of the organization to followers, customers and the general public. As Brkić and Berberović noted in their interviews with Bosnian HC leaders, the power of their ability to narrate the past, present and future of their organizations is palpable. This puts long-term leaders in the unique position to understand, oversee and adapt the wider processes and structures of their companies.

However, despite the benefits of leadership continuity, long-term leaders are not necessarily a desired element. Founder-leaders often have a great deal of difficulty letting go of the organizations that they start, even amidst overwhelming evidence that their presence is having detrimental effects. Such individuals are at risk of "founder's syndrome" (Block and Rosenberg 2002; Linsky 2006; Mcnamara 1998). Within this syndrome a leader can dominate the organization to the point of excluding the ideas of other members, stifling group inputs, leading to hyper-centralized decision making. In such cases decisions may frequently be made too quickly, without adequate influence from others. As this trend persists, the organization adopts a constantly reactive behaviour, rather than a proactive, strategic behaviour. This may eventually undermine the passionate vision of the founder and lead to a complete breakdown. Additionally, many organizations become inextricably linked to the identity of their founder-leaders. To employees, customers and the outside world, the founder may be seen *as* the company and the company *as* the founder. Without succession planning, such perceptions can cause the company to collapse if trust in the leadership is questioned, or if the founder retires or is unexpectedly incapacitated.

This issue is closely linked to the notion of "toxic leadership" (Goldman 2008; Kets de Vries 1989; Lipman-Blumen 2005; Pelletier 2010; Walton 2007). Leadership toxicity is often, though certainly not always, linked to long tenured leadership where a leader's behavior becomes erratic, self-obsessed, and self-serving. This kind of toxicity often filters throughout the organization, creating a toxic culture (e.g. Enron).

As many of the companies involved in this study are still relatively young, leadership toxicity arising from disproportionate tenures is not as yet an overriding concern. However, succession planning is, or will soon be, a significant concern for virtually all of these organizations. In this study we have seen examples of organizations that have successfully dealt with the succession issue. Despite the leaders' drive, passion and love for their organizations, their wisdom transpires also from their decisions to step down or step back from executive roles, often in favor of advisory roles. For example, in 2008 Transom Capital Group became the majority shareholder of BLUE Microphones as Martins stepped back to become chief engineer while his business partner stepped forward to become president. In other companies, such as Konti Hidroplast of Macedonia, the founding CEO has stepped aside to pass the leadership to a younger family member. Another two exemplary cases come from Slovenia. Studio Moderna, the leading multi-channel e-commerce and direct-to-consumer platform in CEE, was led by Sandi Češko from 1992 to 2007. In 2007 the Studio Moderna Group named Eivind Schackt CEO while Češko became Chairperson. In January 2009 Igor Akrapovič, referring back to the difficulties faced by the company in 2008, announced… "And today I am replacing myself. The new CEO of Akrapovič became Mr. Milos Deznak, ex-director of Johnson & Johnson for CEE" (excerpted from an interview with Melita Rant, 2011).

While these leaders had the vision, passion, knowledge and courage to take the lead in establishing or re-inventing their organizations, they also had the wisdom to know when their leadership had reached its end. They exhibited the courage to take a step back. It takes real courage and humility to realize that one's leadership has reached its limits. This ability is perhaps the greatest act of leadership. It indicates a deep sensitivity to the needs of community members—the social group that creates leadership. Often referred to as followers, it is the members of an organization, a community of people working together, that grant leaders their leadership. In what follows we use Mintzberg's concept of "communityship" to explore the social nature of leadership.

2 Leadership as Communityship

> I've never really thought about it as "leadership". I just want to be a part of a great group of people that work hard and are contented.
> —Xhevit Hysenaj, Founder and CEO of Xherdo Ltd, Albania

How does this statement relate to the concept of leadership? This man is the founding CEO of a successful company. Most people would doubtlessly see him as a leader. Yet, he himself has never considered his work leadership. This insight needs to be contextualized in the wider discussion in this chapter. So far the stories of successful organizations have been told in terms of the actions of single individuals, the de facto leaders. However, one of these individuals says plainly that he was not motivated by "leadership" but by being "part of a great group of people that work hard and are contented". In other words, he was never interested in being a leader, but wished to be part of an engaged and rewarding community.

There is a danger in looking for leadership in an individual. Such a viewpoint misses the subtle, dynamic, contextual and ultimately social nature of leadership. Leadership is not reducible to the actions or behaviors of a single person. It is a social activity negotiated between members of a group, and is often a highly ephemeral and illusive phenomenon (Alvesson and Sveningsson 2003). Leadership thinkers and researchers worldwide have come to focus on the wider social contexts that make leadership possible, recognizing that leadership is an emergent property of social systems, not single individuals (Best 2011; Carroll et al. 2008; Crevani et al. 2010; Pearce and Conger 2002; Raelin 2003, 2011; Spillane et al. 2004). To do otherwise is to undermine the social aspects and fail to see that what ultimately drives leadership is a community of people organizing to do things together. Until recently the idea of the social element was lacking in leadership research and the concept of "community" was largely absent from the annals of management and leadership studies. As Mintzberg (2009) has claimed:

> Beneath the current economic crisis lies another crisis of far greater proportions: the depreciation in companies of community—people's sense of belonging to and caring for something larger than themselves (p. 140)

The focus on, and popular belief in, the single leader, and indeed the focus of this chapter up to now, bespeaks Western hyper-individualism which, though having its benefits, is detrimental. Organizations, be they large or small, private or public, profit or not-for-profit, exist because people come together to accomplish things that they could not achieve alone. People work and are impassioned by being part of something bigger than their individual selves. Across the research on HCs the evidence points not so much to "depreciation in companies of community", but rather to an abundance of community. Moreover, the leadership of people like Xhevit Hysenaj (quoted above) evidences a focus on communityship. Mintzberg, who can be credited with adding the term to the management and leadership lexicons, describes communityship as being part of communities of practice. Leadership attends to the work (the practice), the members (the employees), and wider contexts, such as neighbourhoods, towns and countries.

Many of the organizations involved in this study exemplify these characteristics and many of the leaders are intently focused on being community organizers. But what is it in these organizations that creates this sense of community? How do people come to feel that they are contributing to something meaningful and more pervasive than themselves? The answers are actually quite obvious and direct: member respect, member investment and culture.

2.1 Member Respect

> "We consider each other [as] family. Employees of the company are one of the basic factors of success... In 15 years no worker has left the workplace. They have grown together with the business".
> —Edmond Angoni, Founder Venice Art Mask, Albania

"We consider each other [as] family". This statement speaks volumes of the kind of communityship exemplified by leaders such as Edmond Angoni. These leaders do not see employees as commodities or human resources. They are *human beings*, not nameless cogs in a wheel or assets to be exploited or disposed of when no longer useful. They are not even treated as followers or employees. They are respected members. At Hidria, a Slovenian company that operates in the automotive and climate control systems industry, one will hear Iztok Seljak, President of the Management Board, speak of concern for colleagues rather than employees, regardless of their status in the organizational hierarchy. In Mare Adriatic, an Albanian seafood company located in the small coastal community of Shelqet, Mark Babani and his wife Drande stress the flat, democratic structure of their business. They describe a familial concern and desire to help their employees. They value open communication and interactional teamwork. Furthermore their view of communityship does not stop at the doors of their business; they are committed to being responsible members of the wider Shelqet community.

In ACE Enterprise, a Slovak company producing information and measurement systems for utility companies, founder, owner and director Alexander Cimbalak focuses on eliminating physical and psychological borders between himself, the managers and the general employees. He seeks to be part of an organization that values and invests in all of its members. At ACE Enterprise the wider community of employee' is encouraged to participate in management decision making processes. Like Mare Adriatic, ACE is actively involved in the wider community, particularly in cooperation with universities. Their role involves encouraging, supporting and hiring young students from the Slovak Republic and abroad. In each of these organizations, and many others, there is a profound amount of respect, care and concern for all company members. These are not organizations with isolated leaders who undermine the employees' sense of community by envisioning their leadership as a one-man show, no matter how passionate, visionary, expert, or long-term it is. After all, for leadership to exist and for it to be passionate, visionary, expert and continuous, it has to be recognized as such by a community of individuals who create, support and maintain it. In these organizations, "family", "colleagues", and "open borders" are not just slogans. Their leaders must walk the talk of communityship by investing and re-investing in the development of the community and its members.

2.2 Member Investment

In the context of 'community' leadership, actions speak louder than words. In particular, community-oriented leaders are investing time, financial resources and effort in helping others develop. This investment pays great dividends for both the community and the employees. In the Serbian software development company EXECOM the managing partners focus on investing in youth development. This is also the case in Serbia's RT-RK Computer Based Systems, an ICT company, that invests heavily in the professional education of current and future employees. For example, RT-RK funds 35 scholarships at the University of Novi Sad.

These are not isolated examples, Mare Adriatic (Albania), ACE Enterprise (Slovakia) and Mikrosam AD (Republic of Macedonia), a composites manufacturing company, invest heavily in education and facilitates partnerships with local universities. Through the investment in education and other growth opportunities for employees and partnerships with the wider community, these companies put their words of respect, value and family membership into action. As Venice Art Mask's Angoni said "They have grown together, with their wider community". These kinds of community-oriented organizations exemplify engaging company cultures, a quality that ranks highly in the communityship activity of their CEOs.

2.3 Community Culture

Organizational culture (or corporate culture) has been, and still is, a significant focus for researchers and practitioners (Alvesson 1992; Ashkanasy 2011; Denison 1990; Frost 1991; Schein 1999). Organizational culture is intrinsically linked to organizational leadership and is a key aspect of leadership practice and the leadership literature (Argyris 2010; Schein 2010). Successful companies around the world make developing and maintaining an engaging culture a leadership priority.

At ACE Enterprises (Slovakia), Alexandar Cimbalak described his desire for employees to experience work as fun, as if it were a hobby. At EXECOM (Serbia), Petar Ulić described the need for all members to feel that they work in a challenging and motivating environment where everybody can achieve something. At Hidria (Slovenia), there is a focus on collegiality while at the Ukraine Beer Company, CEO Igo Gumennyy is concerned with having an organization that is creative and enthusiastic, and exudes a strong and unique cultural identity. By respecting employees and investing in them, the communityful leadership of many of these organizations creates cultures that are enjoyable, exciting, rewarding and impassioned. Rok Uršič of Instrumentation Technologies (Slovenia) states...

"We see ourselves as passionate designers of innovative solutions... If you walk around our company you can sense the employees' passion".

Throughout our discussion of leaders of passion and vision, a leader's qualities were described as an ability to instill motivation and create organizational development. These leaders have a collectivist vision:

> A company without a compelling culture is like a person without a personality—flesh and bones but no life force, no soul. Organizations function best when committed people work in cooperative relationships based on respect. (Mintzberg 2009, p. 142)

The leaders discussed so far exhibit a member-oriented leadership style representing communityship in action. Yet, this is only half the story. Some of these companies play a strong role in the wider communities of local neighbourhoods, towns, or countries. Thus, communityship extends beyond the physical and psychological boundaries of company offices and buildings. These are organizations that focus not only on creating an internal community, but on being integral parts of external communities.

2.4 Communities of Customers

For many of these companies, the family-oriented view of the organization expands outwards to include customers and the wider communities that the organizations are nested within. For example, the CEO of the Russian firm Luxoft describes the company's mission and vision as follows:

> Long-term partnerships are Luxoft's genuine philosophy and one of our core values. As your partner, we will bring passion for excellence, open and honest communication, and a proven track record of success.

We believe that this organizational culture of customer orientation, passion, excellence, and open and honest communication, is not just marketing lingo or a way to achieve good public relations. As these organizations do invest in community members, their actions speak louder than their words. Reminiscing on his company's history and current activities, Igor Akrapovič indicated that their designs for better motorcycle exhaust systems hinged on communication between the company and its clients. Similarly Rok Uršič spoke of communal relationships during Instrumentation Technologies' development: "On the way here we needed to go through many in-depth conversations with our clients, from whom we learnt the most". Here you can feel the coming together of multiple communities within the collective, rather than an individualistic, closed environment. The same can be said of many other organizations such as the Macedonian concrete admixture company Ading AD or the Slovenian luxury boat manufacturer and nautical consultancy firm Seaway Group that have long focused on reciprocal feedback from clients. In this instance, communityship is focused on customers and clients as more than sources of revenue. They are valued family members from whom the organizations learn important lessons and with whom they build history and cohesion.

There is one final aspect of the community-sensitive leadership of these HC organizations. It is perhaps the most important as it brings together the ideas of vision, passion, knowledge and continuity of leadership with the ideas and practices of holistic communityship. While the commitment, motivation and passion of these organizations can be seen as emanating from becoming a part of communities larger than themselves, there is an even larger context. For many of these leaders their work is part of something much more than even the totality of their organizations and customer bases. Their work is directed towards creating a better world for themselves, their employees and those external to the organization. This view to "communityful" leadership—working for the betterment of all—is the essence of holistic communityship.

2.5 Holistic Communityship

> I can feel successful only if I am acting responsibly towards people, the environment and society. This is the core of my business success.
> —Mr. Jakulin, CEO and co-founder of Atech Elektronika, Slovenia

Atech Elektronika (electronics design and manufacturing) CEO Mr. Jakulin highlights the holistic, socially responsible views that many of these leaders operate with and orient towards. They see their work as contributing to something outside themselves, their organizations and their local communities. They work for more general economic and social benefit. This is also seen in the cooperative partnerships and post-secondary education investments of companies such as RT-RK CBS (Serbia) and ACE Enterprises (Slovakia). It is a prominent feature of the visionary, compassionate anti-landmine work of Vjekoslav Majetić and DOKING.

Some of the clearest examples of this type of leadership come from Albania. Venice Art Mask's Edward Angoni returned to his native country from Italy to establish a new arts organization that provides meaningful work and socio-economic development to his small home city of Shkodra. In a nearby, isolated, mountainous region is the small town of Bajram Curri, home to Raiz Jahaj and the company AMLA, involved in chestnut harvesting and distribution. While AMLA has become a successful exporter of the unique, high-quality chestnuts from this region of Albania, improving his local community, culture, region and environment drives the work of Jahaj. He is motivated to combat local poverty, improve the working conditions of local harvesters, preserve a traditional agricultural pursuit and its culture, and contribute to the sustainable management of the region's forests. In his words: "It is our duty as businessmen to contribute somehow to the development of our local area".

Along the central coast of Albania, in the city of Durres, Xherdo Founder and CEO Xhevit Hysenaj understands that his work is about contributing in a similar manner. Active in the essential oils business since 1991, he runs Xherdo with social responsibility at the fore. Hysenaj is worried about the over-exploitation of Albania's natural resources, particularly the herbs and plants that supply his industry, and the use of inappropriate harvesting techniques that damage the environment. Xherdo is acutely aware of the well-being of the primary harvesters, many of whom are disadvantaged, elderly women. He is passionate and dedicated to his work. He understands that it is part of much wider social realities that have a long history and extend into the future: "I am in love with the field I have selected... I walked in the path of my ancestors... I am now working for my successors".

In the Baltic States a number of organizations are firmly grounded in holistic communityship and operate on social entrepreneurship models. One could describe these as beautiful organizations because of their concern for, and development of, the world in which we all live. Lotte Tisenkopfa-Iltnere, CEO of MADARA Cosmetics Ltd, producing high-quality, ecologically sound skin care products, has situated her business in the steadily growing green lifestyle movement. The Latvian social entrepreneurship company MAMMU started operations in 2010. It provides disadvantaged young mothers with opportunities to earn much-needed money to support themselves and their young families. The company creates a community of mothers, top fashion designers and photographers to produce eco-friendly sustainable products such as scarves. This initiative has inspired a growing global social media movement in social entrepreneurship.

Originating from Estonia in 2008, "Let's Do It" is a social network whose goal is to clean the planet and improve the quality of life for all. "Let's Do It" is an organization that defies many of the taken-for-granted assumptions of what an organization is, and certainly challenges the characteristics of a HC. It is a not-for-profit organization that has no physical footprint and is not led by a particular person or even a definable group of people. Its first activity was the bringing together of 50,000 people to clean up 10,000 tons of illegal garbage in 5 h. Today the organization is a socially networked community with more than 2,000,000 active members from Estonia, Latvia, Lithuania, Portugal, India, Slovenia, Serbia, Finland, Romania, Bulgaria, Moldova, Ukraine, Cambodia, Russia, Hungary and Brazil.

MADARA Cosmetics Ltd., MAMMU and "Let's Do It" can be classified in the category of potential HCs of CEE. As start-ups they exhibit great promise. As they develop into champions of the future, they exemplify emerging twenty-first century leadership trends. They are driven by socially, economically, culturally and environmentally sound ideas that are shared around the globe through networked communities.

In each of these examples, from the anti land-mine technology of DOKING to the socially responsible motivations of Albanian leaders, or the social entrepreneurship emanating from the Baltics, the work of HC organizations is influential. Socially, economically, culturally, environmentally, and temporally driven, this kind of orientation cultivates responsible, motivated, committed and impassioned followership. This manner of leadership is full of vision, passion, and expert knowledge and is focused on communities.

3 Concluding Remarks

Throughout the cases of these HCs, leadership was a central and important driver of organizational success. In this chapter leadership was considered from two interrelated viewpoints: (i) the individual founder-leaders and; (ii) the social nature of leadership involving communities of members and stakeholders. We began by highlighting the themes of vision, passion, expert knowledge and continuity.

Visionary leaders, such as Trnka and Pasko of ESET LLC., and Majetić of DOK-ING Ltd., lead through their ability to visualize and plan for the future through imaginative skill; of seeing a potential future and mobilizing an organization to meet or achieve that potential.

Across the leadership of the companies that have been studied, vision was always accompanied by passion—a love, an enthusiasm and a predilection for a certain pursuit. Uršič of Instrumentation Technologies, Akrapovič of Akrapovič, Boscarol of Pipistrel and Saulesspurens of BLUE Microphones embodied a passion for their business whether it was innovative particle accelerators, exhaust systems for motorcycles, personal planes or the world's best quality microphones. They led from a passion to be the best in their respective industries. In many cases these leaders turned earlier professional work or hobbies into world leading businesses. Their entrepreneurial spirit and courage is inspiring and contagious, spreading throughout their growing organizations.

However, vision and passion are not enough to grow a successful company. In virtually every case study, the leadership of these HCs was fed by expert knowledge. Whether it was expertise in the natural sciences, such as chemistry (DUOCHEM) or physics (Instrumentation Technologies), or in the fine arts (BLUE Microphones; Venice Art Mask), all leaders are experts. Closely linked with passion and vision, this expertise has allowed these leaders to work with what they love and see immense market opportunities that were hidden to others.

The final key point of the individual leadership focus is continuity. These organizations have been, or still are, led by their founder-leaders. This has provided stability and stamina and kept the fires of vision and passion alive. Each of these individuals serves not only an executive role, but as a repository of organizational knowledge and memory. However, herein lies the greatest danger of HC leadership. As these relatively young companies mature, they are in danger of falling afoul of the founder-syndrome, devolving into leadership and organizational toxicity. A key challenge for most of these companies will be succession planning. Central to this is maintaining a leadership of humility, a leadership in tune with organizational and contextual changes and limitations in relation to others, the wider organization and its future needs. A leadership of humility is one seeded with the courage to recognize the possibility that others may have more relevant knowledge and skills to take the lead in the future.

Widening the perspective to the social phenomena the leadership discussed throughout this chapter is focused upon, and sensitive to, what has been described as communityship. One of the essential elements of the success of these organizations has been a leadership not just of vision, passion, expertise and continuity, but a leadership that creates environments where people feel they belong to and care for something larger than themselves. They are, to further borrow from Mintzberg (2009), companies with compelling cultures of community. More than mere flesh and bones, they have a life force and soul and are imbued with personality and zeal.

As communityship, the leadership in these organizations develops member respect, the valuing of all members, and the investment in organizational development through the development of all involved. These are companies of great community culture, yet not just internally. What has been created in many of these organizations is a shared understanding that they are part of systems—whether local, regional, national or international—that are greater and more pervasive than the organizations themselves.

In the final estimation, there is much hope in the leadership of these companies. A leadership full of vision, passion, expertise and focused upon the betterment of all organizational members and wider stakeholders is, one hopes, not a hidden practice, but the championed practice of leadership for the twenty-first century.

References

Alvesson, M. (1992). *Corporate culture and organizational symbolism: An overview*. Berlin: W. de Gruyter.

Alvesson, M., & Sveningsson, S. (2003). The great disappearing act: Difficulties in doing "leadership". *The Leadership Quarterly, 14*, 359–381.

Argyris, C. (2010). *Organizational traps: Leadership, culture, organizational design*. Oxford: Oxford University Press.

Ashkanasy, N. M. (Ed.). (2011). *The handbook of organizational culture and climate*. Los Angeles: Sage.

Bass, B. M. (1985). *Leadership performance beyond expectations*. New York: Academic Press.

Bennis, W. (2009). *On becoming a leader: The leadership classic*. New York: Basic Books.

Bennis, W., & Nanus, B. (1985). *Leaders: The strategies for taking charge*. New York: Harper and Row.

Best, K. C. (2011). Holistic leadership: A model for leader-member engagement and development. *The Journal of Values Based Leadership, 4*(1), 54.

Block, S. R., & Rosenberg, S. (2002). Toward an understanding of founder's syndrome. *Nonprofit Management & Leadership, 12*(4), 353–368.

Bolden, R. (2011). Distributed leadership in organizations: A review of theory and research. *International Journal of Management Reviews, 13*(3), 251–269.

Carroll, B., Levy, L., & Richmond, D. (2008). Leadership in practice: Challenging the competency paradigm. *Leadership, 4*(4), 363–379.

Conger, J., & Kanungo, R. N. (1987). Toward a behavioral theory of charismatic leadership in organizational settings. *Academy of Management Review, 12*(4), 637–647.

Crevani, L., Lindgren, M., & Packendorff, J. (2010). Leadership, not leaders: On the study of leadership as practices and interactions. *Scandinavian Journal of Management, 26*(1), 77–86.

Dietl, M., & Rant, M. (2011, November 17). *Hidden champions in CEE and dynamically changing environments: Who are they, where do they come from, how different are they?* Summary of research results. Conference paper. Hidden Champions of CEE and Dynamically Changing Environments Conference, Vienna.

Denison, D. R. (1990). *Corporate culture and organizational effectiveness*. New York: Wiley.

Eriksen, M. (2009). Authentic leadership. *Journal of Management Education, 33*(6), 747–771.

Frost, P. J. (Ed.). (1991). *Reframing organizational culture*. Newbury Park, CA: Sage.
Gladwell, M. (2008). *Outliers: The story of success*. New York: Little, Brown and Company.
Goldman, A. (2008). Company on the couch: Unveiling toxic behavior in dysfunctional organizations. *Journal of Management Inquiry, 17*(3), 226–238.
Gosling, J., Jones, S., & Sutherland, I. (2012). *Key concepts in leadership*. London: Sage.
Hall, R. K. (2009). The personality, passion, and essence of a leader. *U.S. Army Medical Department Journal, October–December*, 47–53.
Kets de Vries, M. (1989). *Prisoners of leadership*. New York: Wiley.
Ladkin, D. (2008). Leading beautifully: How mastery, congruence and purpose create the aesthetic of embodied leadership practice. *The Leadership Quarterly, 19*, 31–41.
Lesourd, S. J. (1992). Attitude toward visionary leadership. *Journal of School Leadership, 2*(1), 34–44.
Linde, C. (2009). *Working the past: Narrative and institutional memory*. Oxford: Oxford University Press.
Linsky, B. M. (2006). Founder's syndrome: How to spot it and how to fix it. *American Venture Magazine, June*, 20–21.
Lipman-Blumen, J. (2005). Toxic leadership: When grand illusions masquerade as noble visions. *Leader to Leader, Spring*, 29–36.
Loye, D. (1977). *The leadership passion*. San Francisco: Jossey-Bass.
Maccoby, M. (2003). *The productive narcissist: The promise and peril of visionary leadership*. New York: Broadway Books.
Marques, J. F. (2007). Leadership: Emotinoal intelligence, passion and. . .what else? *Journal of Management Development, 26*(7), 644–651.
Mcnamara, C. (1998). Founder's syndrome: How founders and their organizations recover. *Communication, November–December*, 38–41.
Meindl, J. (1998). Invited reaction: Enabling visionary leadership. *Human Resource Development Quarterly, 9*(1), 21–24.
Mintzberg, H. (2009). Rebuilding companies as communities. *Harvard Business Review, 87*(8), 140–144.
Nanus, B. (1992). *Visionary leadership: Creating a compelling sense of direction for your organization*. San Francisco: Jossey-Bass.
Pearce, C. L., & Conger, J. A. (2002). *Shared leadership: Reframing the hows and whys of leadership*. Thousand Oaks, CA: Sage.
Pelletier, K. L. (2010). Leader toxicity: An empirical investigation of toxic behavior and rhetoric. *Leadership, 6*(4), 373–389.
Peters, T. J., & Austin, N. (1985). *A passion for excellence: The leadership difference*. New York: Random House.
Purg, D., & Rant, M. (Eds.). (2011). *HCs in CEE and dynamically changing environments. International management*. Bled, Slovenia: CEEMAN.
Raelin, J. (2011). From leadership-as-practice to leaderful practice. *Leadership, 7*(2), 195–211.
Raelin, J. A. (2003). *Creating leaderful organizations: How to bring out leadership in everyone*. San Francisco: Berrett-Koehler.
Sashkin, M. (1988). The visionary leader. In J. A. Conger & R. N. Kanungo (Eds.), *Charismatic leadership: The elusive factor in organizational effectiveness* (pp. 122–160). San Francisco: Jossey-Bass.
Schein, E. H. (1999). *The corporate culture survival guide: Sense and nonsense about culture change*. San Francisco: Jossey-Bass.
Schein, E. H. (2010). *Organizational culture and leadership* (4th ed.). San Francisco: Jossey-Bass.
Simon, H. (1996). *HCs: Lessons from 500 of the world's best unknown companies*. Boston: Harvard Business School Press.
Simon, H. (2009). *HCs of the 21st century: Success strategies of unknown world market leaders*. London: Springer.

Spillane, J. P., Halverson, R., & Diamond, J. B. (2004). Towards a theory of leadership practice: A distributed perspective. *Journal of Curriculum Studies, 36*(1), 3–34.
Stam, D., van Knippenberg, D., & Wisse, B. (2010). Focusing on followers: The role of regulatory focus and possible selves in visionary leadership. *Leadership Quarterly, 21*(3), 457–468.
Te, D., & Frank, A. J. (2008). Ontology-based evaluation of organizational memory. *Journal of the American Society for Information Science, 59*(9), 1454–1468.
Tellis, G. J. (2006). Disruptive technology or visionary leadership? *Journal of Product Innovation Management, 23*(1), 34–38.
Walton, M. (2007). Leadership toxicity: An inevitable affliction of organizations? *Organizations and People, 14*(1), 19–27.
Westley, F., & Mintzberg, H. (1989). Visionary leadership and strategic management. *Strategic Management Journal, 10*, 17–32.

Three Bivalent Performance Factors of Hidden Champions: Ownership, Organizational Culture and Organizational Governance

Arnold Walravens and Nenad Filipović

No specific reason can be identified to explain the success of Hidden Champions (HCs) (Flören 2002; Simon 2009; Venohr and Meyer 2007). Nevertheless there are a series of factors that can offer partial explanations. This chapter will focus on three of them: Ownership, corporate culture, and organizational governance. Each of these is a double-edged sword. Depending on how it is managed, it can lead an organization to prosperity or ruin. This thin line between success and failure involves strategic choices: to expand globally or remain local, to follow popular business models or develop new innovative initiatives so as to break into new markets. An appropriate choice often makes the difference between a successful and disastrous company leadership (See Breu 2001 or Fredberg et al. 2008). This research project deals exclusively with success stories. Yet, we also stress the fact that in certain circumstances success can turn into failure.

1 Ownership

In Herman Simon's studies on HCs (Simon 2009), the ownership issue does not attract much attention. A large majority of the firms in his sample are family-owned; therefore it seems logical to conclude that ownership structure is one of the important success factors of HCs (Table 1).

The companies in the CEE study are clearly smaller than those in Simon's studies. This is so because during the short transition to a market economy CEE, markets were small in most countries and companies did not have enough time to grow large. An interesting finding that emerged from the study is that nearly 75 % of the companies in the sample are fully or primarily family-owned. However, the observed forms of ownership are quite diverse and range from fully family-owned, to various types of mixed ownership, publicly quoted companies, and even several

A. Walravens (✉) • N. Filipović
IEDC – Bled School of Management, Bled, Slovenia
e-mail: arnold@walravens.org

P. McKiernan and D. Purg (eds.), *Hidden Champions in CEE and Turkey*,
DOI 10.1007/978-3-642-40504-4_4, © Springer-Verlag Berlin Heidelberg 2013

Table 1 Ownership and governance structure of Hidden Champions in this research

	Governance structure				
Ownership	CEO (founder/ owner)	CEO (founder/owner) + Board/Manag. team	CEO (not founder) + Board Manag. team	Board	Total (%)
Family owned companies	16	27	18		77.2
Cooperative ownership				1	1.2
Investment company/ private equity company			2		2.5
Joint-stock company			10		12.6
Limited liability company				2	2.5
Daughter company				3	3.8

cooperatives (such as Durante M.2 in Croatia or Grishko in Russia). Each of the companies in the CEE region has its own peculiarity in terms of ownership structure. For example Slovakia is an anomaly as none of the HCs in that country are family-owned. In contrast, four of the ten Turkish HCs are family-owned. This diversity suggests that ownership structure is not a key element of success.

This study finds that leadership structure is much more dynamic than was the case in Simon's original study. We believe that this can be attributed to the relatively early stage of development of CEE HCs, as well as the economic environments in which they operate. Some ownership changes are predictable as family or privately owned companies are sold to investment companies or multinationals, such as Blue Microphones in Latvia or Skype in Estonia. This process has been more pronounced in larger countries with more developed financial markets, such as Poland, but the overall readiness of the initial owners to cash out seems to be higher in CEE than in Simon's companies. Some other ownership structure transformations were more complex, such as that of the Tallink Group from Estonia, running duty free and travel shops, with a turnover of 813.9 million euros in 2010, employing more than 6,000 people. It started out as a joint venture; then the Estonian partners bought out the Finnish shareholders. At the time of this research, it was in mixed ownership (40 % large Estonian shareholders, 40 % foreign investment funds and banks, 20 % small shareholders).

Biochemie in the Czech Republic is an even more extreme example. It was set up more than 100 years ago as an Austrian company. It was nationalized, reprivatized, sold through a management buyout, and then sold to an investment fund. At the time of this research, it was getting ready for the IPO.

Finally, we observe relatively unorthodox changes, clearly influenced by the approach taken by the family owners, such as Radiation Meters (the real name is disguised) from Belarus. Initially family-owned, it was transformed into a cooperative.

1.1 The Origin or Location of the Entrepreneurial Initiatives

At this stage it may be interesting to look at another element related to company ownership: where the original owners of family companies originated from and what attracted them to business. This to a large degree determines a company's ownership philosophy, which in turn affects the ownership structure during the company's development and its culture and performance. It is interesting to note that despite the political, economic and cultural diversity of the countries in our sample, the majority of the companies that were studied came from outside the capital city or main economic centers. This peculiarity is in agreement with Simon's findings; as we shall see later, it strongly influences the relationship between the company and the local community. The only major exception is Russia, where practically all of the identified HCs are from Moscow and Saint-Petersburg. The size of Russia and the availability of information may suggest that the HCs in the other parts of Russia were not noticed by the researchers. However, there is a common opinion in Russia that, apart from companies related to natural resources, companies based outside of the biggest cities are oriented primarily to regional markets, rather than being international.

In several countries, most notably Albania and Estonia, quite a number of the HCs were started by individuals who returned to their homeland after spending some time working in a western country, bringing back with them not only entrepreneurial attitudes, but also technological know-how and market insights that were extremely important for the early success of their newborn enterprises. In some other cases, this expertise was obtained through individual or corporate contacts and partnerships in the West, which were later included in the ownership structure (as in the case of Blue Microphones). Another important factor worth noting is that the economies in transition, especially in the early days of market changes, created numerous opportunities for entrepreneurs, often leading to extremely fast profits. Most of these opportunities were short-lived as they stemmed from various market imperfections, such as distorted or deficient supply chains, monopolies, a lack of transparency, corruption and misuse of privatization processes. Still the company leaders in the CEE sample engaged in a more long-term pursuit of their ideas, which eventually led to regional or global dominance in their niche product or service area. As the owner of Kazakhstan's Tulpar-InTech put it, "they resisted the temptation of easier and 'faster' money". This is reflected in their approach to the ownership structure and the way that they manage their organizational culture and relationships with their local community.

The presentation of a strategy was often a barrier to obtaining external financing in the initial period. Banks and other investors were not familiar with these ventures and deemed them too risky. The owner of Venice Art Masks from Albania nicely summarized the situation: "In the beginning, when we needed investors, we couldn't find any. Now we could get a lot, but we don't want to." The limited access to financing in the early period of market changes influenced the present-day industry structure, with only a minority of the companies belonging to the industries that require relatively large up-front investments. In many cases HCs were created by finding a specific niche or a new business model in an otherwise mature industry that had a history in a particular CEE country. This allowed such companies to use readily available general knowledge about the industry and therefore decrease the perceived risk. They enhanced their ingenuity through creative business models as well as continuous improvements to organizational structure and the functions of the company.

1.2 The Overlap of Three Systems: Company, Family and Ownership

Orit Vaknin (2010) reviewed the schools of thought regarding family business performance. On one hand, family-owned business tends to be nepotistic. In Vaknin's view, nepotism is characterized by irrational decision-making processes and conflicts of interest between family members and other shareholders. On the other hand, Vaknin points out that family-owned companies have a high commitment to their business and are managed with a long-time horizon. Their employees are very loyal to the firm as they have a strong connection to the family. Due to the personal nature of the business, family management is characterized by very significant prudence and care, as the business is viewed as an essential element of the family's heritage, identity and pride. The results of this study suggest that, since CEE's HCs are so successful, they fit Vaknin's second description of family-owned businesses.

Overall, HCs appear to benefit from their ownership and governance structures. These can be described in terms of three systems—company, family and ownership. These systems overlap and can be a strength as well as a weakness. They contain a number of bivalent elements that continually interact within any structure (Flören 2002): the CEO, the company's strategy and culture, HRM, communication, ownership, and finances; and the balance between company and family interests. The spirit of ownership can be a binding element in a family and may also "dramatically influence the family business" (Donckels and Fröhlich 1991). In this respect one may think of family businesses as being less considerate of the interests of external partners and more reluctant to consider external financing by non-family stakeholders. This reluctance may hinder the expansion of the business. Other characteristics of family shareholders is that because of the overlap between the hierarchal family structure and the business structure, family members may allow their roles to overlap with their management responsibilities (Lansberg 1999). The aforementioned factors have been identified as a potential source of conflict in the family environment. This phenomenon is also known as the "cousin consortium", a stage of the family business at which a controlling owner passes down the enterprise to his or her children, who, in turn, hand the reins to the third generation.

Causes of conflict do not lie only in succession processes and management structures. A founder/owner crisis can run the business aground and negatively impact personal lives and family relationships. The functionality of the family ownership structure is tested as a business outlives the founder and the company is exposed to an increasingly large economic environment. Previous research analysis has led to a number of unequivocal conclusions. One premise is that family ownership creates value mostly during the first generation of owners (Villalonga and Amit 2006). This is challenged by the fact that companies such as Cargill, Lego, Michelin and Philips prospered through three or more generations. These cases have triggered a debate on whether family business is more resilient than non-family business in times of economic downturn and credit constraint. Although it is difficult to generalize, it appears that during economic downturns, family businesses are less likely to go bankrupt than large companies as the former are more risk-averse and in better financial health. The Tallink Group of Estonia confirms this theory despite its mixed shareholding. The group suffered less during the latest economic recession compared with other businesses in Estonia. Similarly, Latvia's Aerodium increased its market share during the 2009–2010 financial crisis, demonstrating that family business structures are able to withstand economic depression if their business structures are sound.

2 Organizational Culture

2.1 The Impact of Employees' Identification with Their Company's Mission and Values

Ownership does not operate in isolation and the differences between a good and bad company can often stem from their cultures. In an ideal situation that culture is accepted, embraced and enacted by all employees. This is not an issue specific to HCs as the correlation between culture and performance has been the subject of numerous academic studies, especially those related to the Resource Based View and related theories (Barney 1986; Fiol 1991; Gordon and DiTomaso 1992; Schein 1985). Small and middle-size enterprises (SME) have an advantage as they can more easily make their employees accept the company's goals and values. The culture of the smallest companies tends to resemble an extended family with patriarchal features and strong internal cohesion (Kets de Vries and Miller 1986). Companies such as Albania's Venice Art Mask offer positive examples of strong acceptance of the founder's goals and values by the employees. This creates a positive environment.

The other side of strong internal cohesion is that instead of formal hierarchical controls, a much more powerful mechanism of peer control is in use (Wilkins and Ouchi 1983). This in turn allows faster inclusion of newcomers with the right attitudes, faster learning cycles, better attainment of targets and faster departure of people who have been labeled "non-performers" or "social misfits".

HC leaders seem to be fully aware of the benefit that they get from having committed employees who strongly identify with the company and its mission. These leaders not only attempted to align staff with the company's goals, but also aimed to hire only people whose values and goals matched those of the company. This is what one of the owners of Aerodium said when asked how they found the best employees: "They are the ones with a spark in their eyes . . . their motivation and willingness to achieve something with us".

The influence of leaders on organizational culture was often observed not only in the way they defined the company's mission and created a reason for the employees to "be there", but also in the specific style of management and leadership that they were using. In most cases employees and business community referred to attributes of their style, using the words which in leadership literature are associated with the notion of "charismatic leadership". While one can easily admit the elusiveness of such a label, some concrete descriptions were offered. Probably the most vivid one was offered by ALSI from Kazakhstan, whose CEO (not a founder in the traditional sense, since the company came into being as a spin-off from a research institute) declined to be labeled as charismatic, yet his leadership style involved closeness to his people. He was humble, yet inspirational, creating a culture of high performance and a high level of mutual support.

A consequence of this leadership style is that the employees often identify much more strongly with the founder/owner/general manager than with the company. A good example is a company from Belarus, with the code name "Shutters", whose leader was described as a "strong, military type" (apparently a positive connotation in Belarus culture), creating an extremely strong culture of commitment and employee turnover rates well below Belarus averages.

In some cases, it was impossible to differentiate between the identity of the leader and the company itself. Leaders created powerful stories about the mission of the company (e.g. biodiversity in case of Xherbo) and used a charismatic leadership style to win the full commitment of the employees. They even made strong and potentially controversial statements, like "who we are is more important than what (financial) benefits we create"—a philosophy shared by several Slovenian owners/managers. However this leadership style also has a bivalent nature as it is often very difficult or impossible to transfer the charisma to the successor.

2.2 Company Culture, Leadership Style, and Succession Planning

Charisma has to be earned and it is understandable that the charisma of the founder cannot be inherited by the next generation. To assure a gradual and successful transfer of leadership, the positive commitment of both generations is necessary. In this research, succession planning has not been a major research topic. Nevertheless, this is clearly an issue across all companies in the sample. It is very conspicuous in the Polish HCs, where in the last 20–25 years there have been relatively few leadership changes. Table 2 shows that this is not only a Polish phenomenon. A relatively large group of companies are not prepared for a regulated transition.

Succession strategies for SMEs often explain why founders/owners maintain control for as long as possible and sometimes even stay longer than is healthy for the company. Sonnenfeld (1988) describes various types of retirement styles of founders or CEOs. "Monarchs" do not leave until they are forced out or pass away. "Generals" leave once forced out, but may often return to power to rescue the

Table 2 Number of companies prepared for regulated transition

Countries	Status of regulated transition: Prepared[a]	Status of regulated transition: Not prepared
Albania	–	4
Belarus	–	5
Bosnia and Herzegovina	2	4
Croatia	1	2
Czech Republic	1	7
Estonia	3	1
Hungary	2	2
Kazakhstan	–	2
Latvia	–	2
Macedonia	2	1
Poland	9[b]	9
Romania	–	3
Russia	1	4
Serbia	4	2
Slovakia	4	3
Slovenia	5	7
Turkey	6	4
Ukraine	2	3
Total	42	65

[a]Eighteen of the "prepared" companies are not family-owned and have a structure that is appropriate for leadership change

[b]There are no exact data available, only an indication that companies are "prepared"

company from an inadequate successor. "Ambassadors" leave willingly and become advisors to the firm whereas "governors" rule for a short term and then pursue other ventures. Lansberg (1988) finds that succession planning does not begin until the founder and his spouse enter the last stage in the life cycle, often in their 60s. As indicated previously, succession planning is a critical issue for family-owned firms of all sizes (Mandl 2004; Miller et al. 2001; Sten 2004). We believe that it is important to extend this research so as to examine the impact of succession style on company culture, specifically in the relatively late period when leadership is in transition. This would be especially relevant in CEE where economic liberalization began some 20 years ago. As a result the majority of family company founders, as well as the professional managers, have not reached retirement age.

2.3 The Culture of High Performance and High Support

Harrison (1995), a leading practitioner in the field of organizational development, outlines a number of cultural dimensions. In regard to performance and support, he has identified "rules and power" as strong influences on culture. Harrison has also come to the conclusion that the "performance and support" combination is by far the most effective in facilitating a productive and successful company culture, although all companies exhibit at least some aspects of all four dimensions. Practically all HCs have ambitious targets and organizational cultures that explicitly identify high-level performance as a core value. Furthermore the combination of a "high performance and high support" organizational culture was observed in the majority of HCs. Another company culture trait related to support is a very high level of cross-functional cooperation, observable in most HCs. The HCs were found to have strongly cross-functional corporate cultures as a powerful legacy of the previous economic system. Other companies, as in Belarus and Russia, report extreme silo-type cultures. The pronounced support dimension in the company cultures of CEE's HCs is an interesting finding as the countries in this region are characterized by fairly collectivist national cultures (Kolman et al. 2003). In some cases this is associated with a lack of trust and a negative reaction to the legacy of the communist ideology.

2.4 The Culture of Innovation and Loyalty

This study interviewed a number of leaders who professed a focus on employee satisfaction. A large number of companies emphasize organizational development and employees are encouraged to engage in these initiatives. However the leader is not the only factor in the building of a company's culture. An innovation culture requires a high level of loyalty from key employees who share their knowledge with their colleagues and bring new ideas to the table in order to improve existing products and processes.

There are two sides to this discussion. Companies with a high level of investment in R&D report high levels of teamwork and a clear ability to attract and retain star personnel by being able to offer them opportunities to engage in projects on the frontiers of their industries or professions. Still across our sample, even small companies that invest little in R&D, yield relatively successful initiatives!

Across our sample, there are large differences in the amount that companies spend on innovation. R&D budgets range from 2 % of revenue (Feal, Bosnia) to 20 % (DOK-ING, Croatia). While such a large difference can be partly explained by the nature of, and practices in, the respective industries, we also observe company culture differences with respect to innovation, mainly in allowing a drive for creative achievements without fear of retribution.

In some countries we found a positive innovation culture and unique educational structures for employees. In Poland we found companies where 50 % of employees have a university level education in Poland. In this case youth of high potential were identified at a very young age and offered a university education alongside their professional development at the company. However this practice is not confined to Poland. It was also observed at NT-MTD, Russia Elephant Orchestra, and an Internet innovator from the Czech Republic. The chairman of the Internet innovator company from the Czech Republic stated: "We intend to be the best in the world in what we do, and have fun while doing so".

This enjoyment of work has become a typical characteristic of numerous HCs, especially those relying on recruiting and retaining a younger workforce. However, as always, more in-depth interviews with employees and management reveal the other side of the coin. There was a thin line between "performance and fun" and "performance and support", and employees were often left to resolve personal performance issues without support from management while also coping with high expectations. A board member who wanted to remain anonymous stated, "You are expected to produce. We don't have patience for people who require high level of support from others". This type of attitude may produce high levels of stress that cannot be relieved by socializing if management does not provide adequate support In some cases, company-orchestrated events aimed at creating fun, gradually threatened individual performance and even company results. In some cases owners denied the reports of their employees and stated that they did not reflect reality. In several cases the owners were aware of the employee's frustration, yet they preferred to have management deal with it, as in the case of Akrapovič, rather than confront this issue themselves. Therefore it seems that fun was a nice-to-have element of culture, while support was the must-have factor in the creation of sustainable and profitable results.

2.5 The Identification of the Firm with the Environment

Besides the employees' identification with the firm, there is also a need for the firm to have a strong identity that employees, clients and other shareholders can relate to. As most HCs have their headquarters in rural locations, those organizations are shaped by their locations and the locations are shaped by the organizations (Simon 2009). This is demonstrated across this sample by both rural and urban companies. In essence, the inhabitants of the location are proud to have such an important firm in their environment and have a direct interest in the firm's wellbeing. Additionally, a clear relationship between locals and the company begins to develop. For example, Grishko, a Russian company, sells its ballet shoes at reduced prices to local customers, despite the fact that it is a clear global leader in the industry. This is a sincere commitment to the local ballet community, to which the founder belonged, and without which Grishko would not have reached its success. It is also a marketing tool that helps secure access to reputable customers, yet both the employees and the local community believe the latter is just a welcome consequence of the former.

Because of their financial needs, some companies created strong relationships with the local environment. For example the Albanian companies Amla and Xherdo had problems with financing as banks view their rural area (Tropoja) as highly risky. As a result Amla and Xherdo relied on their relationships with the community to finance and support the growth and development of the company. This phenomenon was found also in a number of other CEE countries, such as Romania and Bosnia and Herzegovina. According to Instrumentation Technologies in Slovenia, "the founder of the company creates something good for the local community".

A unique characteristic of HCs in CEE is a specific form of integration with their local environments and their support for them. Aside from anchoring the company in the community, these initiatives also help its drive for innovation. A number of companies, such as Mikrosam, a Macedonian producer of composite materials, or Yandex, a Russian leader in internet search engines in the former CIS, have started external educational institutions that create educational and employment opportunities for the poor local environments, but also secure a steady source of scarce talent. Some, like Gliga in Romania, opened kindergartens and even schools for the children of their employees, further fostering their loyalty and motivation but also providing much needed services to the local community. As we indicate later in this chapter, these efforts were sometimes combined with broader alliances created with other partners.

The challenge for many HCs is to foster an international and global orientation while maintaining the local culture and interests, so as to combine an innovative culture with the conservative elements of a local community. Internal cohesion in family-owned HCs is strong and the high level of integration in the local community creates common resistance to external intervention, be it financial or managerial. The preference for self-financing indirectly creates a culture of frugality. A good example is Slovenian company Hidria in the automotive business. Although it now operates predominantly in global markets, it has chosen to maintain small management, R&D and sales teams and is extremely reluctant to hire anyone outside Slovenia.

One of Simon's (2009) important conclusions is that although HC employees strongly identify with their companies we can expect a change in their labor orientation. We believe that his conclusion that people will be increasingly unwilling to work for money alone concurs with the findings of our CEE research as people now expect their work to provide more meaning, to bring enjoyment, and satisfy overarching goals and values.

2.6 Commitment and the Question of Employee Ownership

Perhaps it is too easy to bring up the question of employee ownership. Simon advocates a similar model for managers. Therefore one can legitimately ask how long employees will be motivated solely by wages. How long will they maintain a high level of identification, particularly if they are the innovative force of their firm, without becoming co-owners, sharing in the long-term value that they create? At the moment of the research, many HCs thrive in hostile environments, with limited employment opportunities, let alone opportunities for working with global winners. Once the market develops and more opportunities exist, what will happen to employee loyalty? As mentioned earlier, there are only a few examples of co-ownership or cooperative models across our the sample. In several cases this particular form of ownership structure was created for legal reasons, as in Rotomatika in Slovenia (out of which Hidria grew), where it became a key element in the privatization process of the once state-controlled company. Another example is Radiation Meters in Belarus, where it was mandated by law. However, wherever it existed it was seen as a major motivation factor for the employees.

3 Organization and Governance

3.1 The Right Organization as a Strategic Success Factor

The right organization is without a doubt a strategic success factor (Simon 2009). The question then of course is, what is the right organization structure? This can be answered only by taking into account the nature and stage of development of the business. Organization and governance is always a major topic of interest, be it in smaller HCs, mostly led by one or two persons, or in larger ones, that span large product or geographical markets and face market situations where a classical functional organization is not appropriate any more.

In more than half of the organizations in this research, the founder/owner is the sole hierarchal level and the division of labor begins only on a lower organizational or managerial level. It is fair to assume that this simplicity of organization and governance leads to lean processes, high speed and direct contact with the customers, and contributes to the success of HCs in the early stage of their development. However, as found by Simon (2009) and confirmed in this research, HCs favor and maintain simplicity despite their intensive growth. This is remarkable since the next stages of growth, which for the average company in our sample means a 10-fold increase in revenues over a period of 10 years (e.g. Belarus "Lid" grew from 3 to 50 million US$ and had 1,500 employees), diversification and globalization lead to complex organizational challenges and a need for new structures, divisionalization, regionalization, and so forth.

An interesting example of how a larger HC avoids complexity in its organization is ALSI of Kazakhstan. This is an information technology company with 500 employees. The CEO of ALSI explained that the company did not have a receptionist or secretaries and that he maintained an open door policy whereby the employees could always come directly to him. Although this is not a unique example, one can only wonder how sustainable this approach would be, if growth continued at the same or similar rate.

One of the challenges of growth is to stay close to customers and this is one of the key strengths of HCs. In practice, it is not only a question of organization, but also of behaviours or attitudes (Simon 2009). Governance becomes an issue also in times of growth and internationalization, when the organizational culture can lead to original innovative solutions. Some HCs are innovative network organizations and employ modern information technology to control their global structures with a very small amount of limited resources (Simon 2009).

3.2 Building and Using External Networks

Building and using external networks, rather than relying on their own internal resources, is often observed as a typical sign of entrepreneurial thinking. Our research confirms that this approach is very common across the HCs in our sample. It is also interesting to note that it takes on many different forms. Some of these networks are specifically related to access to industry know-how, such as a network of scientists organized in Slovenia. Instrumentation Technologies prepares workshops on the topic of beam control systems for particle accelerators, the company's main market niche. Another example from the same company is a consortium of high-tech organizations, which Instrumentation Technologies has helped set up to gain access to government funding for research and educational projects. This network will possibly lead to the company's diversification and is viewed as a potential necessity for future growth. In a similar manner, Tulpar-InTech from Kazakhstan planned to start an educational incubator, while a number of Russian high-tech HCs focused on creating value for their external R&D stakeholders, such as research institutes.

Some other companies, such as Albanian Venice Art Masks and Xherdo, developed associations of companies competing in their own niches, which allowed them to regulate the market and impose higher quality standards. As they are market leaders, they do not see this effort as help to their competitors, but as a smart move to secure their own dominance over low-cost competition.

Finally, another comment from ALSI's CEO points to the very essence of the observed behaviour of HCs when it comes to forging partnerships of different kinds. The company, according to his words, "was capable not only of finding water [in the 'business desert'], but also of populating the ground so as to preserve the water for new plants to evolve". They achieved that by developing "trust-based business networks" with multinational companies and with own customers.

This example evidences the paradox of "co-opetition"—simultaneous competition and cooperation among global multinationals and HCs—observed several times during the research. Even if the bivalent relationship was working at the time of the research, was it sustainable? Simon's (2009) answer is positive. Successful HCs carefully select niches that are, not too large to attract the attention of powerful multinationals, yet they are large global enough to allow for growth and dominance. This research elucidates another more specific feature of the HCs' business model. Given the very specific local economic situations in CEE, characterized by diverse peculiarities of the transition towards a free market economy, quite a few companies in our sample had to adapt global business practices to their own business environments. This proved to be an additional obstacle to global multinationals, decreasing their interest in competing with the HCs. Success in local markets was then used as a financial and knowledge basis for international expansion. Meanwhile, the HCs reorganized their business models and organizational structures as soon as the old ones had become dysfunctional, although some companies preempted this need. Understanding the tendency of many entrepreneurs and executives to "stick to the winning formula", this is an admirable achievement.

3.3 Changing Scale and Leadership

Another major issue related to the HC's fast growth that can easily be predicted is the capability of the founder/owner, or the family, to lead the company once the scale of the business and environment have changed. About 30 % of the family-owned companies in our sample, mainly the larger businesses, have hired CEOs from outside the family, while the remaining 70 % have remained family-run. A study of management practices in medium-sized manufacturing firms in the USA, UK, France and Germany showed that "primogeniture family firms"—those that passed management on to the eldest son—are significantly better managed than those managed by the founder or by outside professional managers (Bloom and Van Reenan 2005). In many cases the family members realize that they can remain owners of their companies only by separating management from ownership. It is a fact of life that managing skills are not always inherited and today's skills differ from those in the genes of the owner (A. Davis 2006). This is well illustrated in Turkey, where the share of family managers has been falling sharply and, by the time of this research, the majority of managers of family-owned companies were already professionals coming from outside the family. However, as in the case of Hidria, very few of these firms were truly international and preferred to remain local in their selection of a CEO.

Despite their relatively simple governance systems (see Table 1), many of the companies studied in this research were aware of the bivalent nature of this challenge. Poland is a clear case, displaying outstanding leadership continuity, with 58 % of leaders staying in place for more than 18 years whereas the average CEO tenure in USA in the last decade was 4 years. On the other hand, more than 50 % of the companies in the CEE state that they have a "regulated transition" plan and are relying on internal recruitment to replace their management teams. The success of this strategy remains to be seen. Will the successors be able to follow in the footsteps of the successful leaders?

Estonia's Tallink, provides a good example of a successful transfer of leadership from the experienced founders to a professional board of middle-managers. Similarly, Eesti Energia, also in Estonia, appointed a new CEO and formed a new professional management team whereas Studio Moderna of Slovenia hired a professional manager as CEO, although the owner remained active in the development of the company. Slovenia's Akrapovič, whose founder stepped back, announced, "In 2008, when we were facing major challenges, I promised to say 'thank you for your cooperation' to anyone I was not happy with. If that had been me, I would have replaced myself. And today I am replacing myself." He welcomed the new CEO although he remained very active in the technological field.

However, despite these success stories, at times leaders find it difficult to remove themselves completely from leadership positions. In several of the CEE companies, managers indicated that the owners occasionally trespassed back into active management roles, or that the family members tried to influence the owners or the managers to change the course of the company, going beyond the regular governance mechanisms. This phenomenon was found to be consistent with previous research findings and will continue to be an area of negotiation between the new management team and the former owners.

Conclusions

In this chapter we focused on three important factors that in our view contribute to the success of HCs: (1) ownership; (2) corporate culture; and (3) organization and corporate governance. We pointed out that these are also bivalent factors and can result in a high level of success as well as a high level of failure. The discussion of ownership concluded that the positive relationship between performance and family ownership is confirmed in this research on CEE HCs. However, we concede that other ownership structures can yield equal success.

We also replicate Simon's findings on the HCs' relationship with their local communities. We note that our research demonstrates that economies in transition create numerous opportunities for entrepreneurship. Concerning the impact of organizational culture, we note that the vast majority of HCs are small and middle-sized; as a result, they exhibit a high degree of identification with the values and goals of the company. This strong identification is often closely associated with the founder/owner/CEO. The style of leadership in many cases is defined as "charismatic". The bivalent element here is that this identification with the person and the charismatic leadership style can be a hindering factor in the transition of leadership or power to the next generation. Generally speaking, HCs have a strong, open innovative culture (Chesbrough 2003, 2011) and the identification and loyalty of their employees a positive factor. Although this was outside the scope of our research, the high level of identification and motivation brings up the question of how long these attitudes can be maintained without employees desiring more from the employers.

As Simon (2009) stated, the right organization is without doubt a strategic success factor. Following an in-depth analysis, we identified some examples of successful transfer of leadership that might serve as examples for others. Still, more than half of the HC leaders continued to maintain some element of control, even when intensive company growth was experienced. As our research deals only with successful and predominantly young companies, we could not identify any cases of mismanagement. It would be interesting to see how successful their organizational strategies will be in the future.

There are several issues related to the HCs' governance that are very specific to this research. Many HCs were started in very unfavorable business environments. As noted earlier, from a purely entrepreneurial point of view, this presented an opportunity rather than a threat. Yet, it typically led to HCs "thriving in the shade". These companies literally stayed underground and did not seek attention from anyone except their customers, suppliers, and potential talent. This low profile is part of some HCs' identity. For example, most Belarusian HCs requested anonymity during the research. In many cases the companies were intentionally kept less than transparent in terms of financial results, which was possible in view of the low reporting and corporate governance standards in their home countries. Of course, some of the companies in our sample, especially those going to capital markets, developed their governance systems well beyond the required standard. Nevertheless, the majority kept their governance mechanisms at an extremely basic level.

This fact, combined with insights from analyzing the HCs' strategies, leads to a major question that could ideally be answered in follow-up research in an appropriate time frame. In particular, given their little formal governance that cannot ensure that strategic risks are identified and taken care of, can the observed HCs remain sustainably successful once the business environment significantly changes? Some HCs already display remarkable flexibility in their business histories, but some of the predictable changes are likely to interfere with the very basic assumptions behind their business models. These include low labour costs, little competition in the talent market or a low equity base, not allowing for the internationalization that these companies desire. Of note, only a few of the owners/managers facing these challenges mentioned them explicitly. It may be that the others were still feeling more comfortable developing their plans in solitude rather than discussing them with the researchers. Or perhaps those interviewees preferred not to expose the weaknesses of their companies.

At the end of this overview, on the basis of the analysis of the research outcomes, it seems reasonable to conclude that family ownership with professional governance may combine the best of two worlds. Family control ensures a long-term investment horizon and a balanced stakeholder philosophy, while professional managers contributed state-of-the-art management practices (See also Bloom and Van Reenan 2005).

The point remains that HCs are a peculiar sample of businesses. Their corporate governance and management structures are unique. In this chapter we have focused on how leaders manage and function in a variety of paradoxical situations. Working in highly demanding circumstances and breaking into unique market niches, HC leaders all too often faced choices between short- and long-term, self and team, national and international, centralized and decentralized, as well as predictable and dynamic, to name just a few. These leaders are highly successful not by selecting the better of two opposing choices, or balancing between them, but by embracing both at the same time.

References

Barney, J. (1986). Organizational culture: Can it be a source of competitive advantage. *Academy of Management Review, 11*(3), 656–666.

Bloom, N., & Van Reenan, J. (2005). *Measuring and explaining management practices from firms and countries* (Working Paper, pp. 6–7; 31). Department of Economics, Stanford University and Centre of Economic Performance, London School of Economics.

Breu, K. (2001). The role and relevance of management cultures in the organizational transformation process. *International Studies of Management and Organization, 31*(2), 28–47.

Chesbrough, H. W. (2003). *The new imperative for creating and proposing from technology.* Harvard Business Press.

Chesbrough, H. W. (2011). *Open service innovation: Rethinking your business to grow and compete in a new era*. Wiley.
Davis, J. A. (2006). *Best practice in corporate governance: Building reputation and sustainable success*. Farnham: Gover.
Donckels, R., & Fröhlich, E. (1991). Are family businesses really different? *Family Business Review, 4*(2), 149–160.
Fiol, C. (1991). Managing culture as a competitive resource: An identity-based view of sustainable competitive advantage. *Journal of Management, 17*(1), 191–211.
Flören, R. H. (2002). *Crown princes in the clay. An empirical study on the tackling of succession challenges in Dutch family farms*. Assen: Van Gorcum.
Fredberg, T., Beer, M., Eisenstat, R., Foote, N., & Norrgren, F. (2008). *Embracing commitment and performance: CEOs and practices used to manage paradox* (Working Paper). Harvard Business School.
Gordon, G., & DiTomaso, N. (1992). Predicting corporate performance from organizational culture. *Journal of Management Studies, 29*(6), 783–798.
Harrison, R. (1995). *The collected papers of Roger Harrison*. Jossey-Bass.
Kets de Vries, M., & Miller, D. (1986). Personality, culture, and organization. *Academy of Management Review, 11*(2), 266–297.
Kolman, L., Noorderhaven, N. G., Hofstede, G., & Dienes, E. (2003). Cross-cultural differences in Central Europe. *Journal of Managerial Psychology, 18*(1), 76–88.
Lansberg, I. S. (1988). The succession conspiracy. *Family Business Review, 1*(2), 119–143.
Lansberg, I. S. (1999). *Succeeding generations: Realizing the dream of families in business*. Harvard University Press.
Mandl, I. (2004). *Business transfers and succession in Austria*. Paper presented at the ISBE Research and Policy Conference, Teesside University, November 2–4, 2004.
Miller, N. J., McLeod, H., & Ob, K. J. (2001). Managing family business in small communities. *Journal of Small Business Management, 39*(1), 73–87.
Schein, E. (1985). *Organizational culture and leadership*. Jossey-Bass.
Simon, H. (2009). *HCs of the 21st century: Success strategies of unknown world leaders*. London: Springer.
Sonnenfeld, J. (1988). *The hero's farewell*. New York: Oxford University Press.
Sten, J. (2004). *Succession and business transfers; Two different processes – two different outcomes*. Paper presented at the EFMD's 34th EISB Conference, Turku, Finland, September 8–10, 2004.
Vaknin, O. (2010). *The family business risk profile*. The Leonards N. Stern School of Business.
Venohr, R., & Meyer, K. E. (2007). *The German miracle keeps running: How Germany's HCs stay ahead in the global economy*. Berlin School of Economics.
Villalonga, B., & Amit, R. (2006). How do family ownership control and management affect firm value? *Journal of Financial Economics, 80*, 385–417.
Wilkins, A., & Ouchi, W. (1983). Efficient cultures: Exploring the relationship between culture and organizational performance. *Administrative Science Quarterly, 28*, 469–481.

Innovation Behaviour of Hidden Champions

Peter Baloh

Peter Drucker (1986) once wrote that a company has two basic functions: marketing and innovation. To win customers and stay ahead of the competition, to survive and compete, innovation is critical (Chesbrough 2003; Drucker 1986). The ability to innovate, and do so both effectively and efficiently, is required to achieve and maintain world market leadership. Outstanding and continuous innovative performance is *the* competency that firms have to master. The amount of money put into research and development (R&D) depends on the dynamics of the industry and the markets, yet it is not an indicator of success. In the early 2010s there are examples of key Western companies whose R&D expenditure is not related to profitability. For example Apple, doubtlessly a leader in the smartphone market, invests only 5.9 % of its profits in R&D, whereas the industry's average is 7.6 %. As Procter and Gamble, a world leader in personal care and household items, decreased its investment in R&D from 4.8 % to 3.4 %, its product success rate rose from 35 % to 75 %.

Similarly, the amount invested in R&D does not indicate previous successes. Consider the case of Google, an advanced internet search engine and a symbol of innovation. Recently, Google has lowered its output. While the concept and practice of "Google labs"—a page created by Google to demonstrate and test new products—are viewed as a revolutionary way to test cutting-edge ideas and prototypes before their release, Google's recent products have not fared well in the marketplace. Recent Google product releases, such as Wave and Buzz, that attempt to erode Facebook's dominance of the social web networks, have not done well. The prospects for the company's latest creation—Google+—are not good either. If *the* company seen as the symbol of innovation does not have success down to a fine art, there is still a lot to be learned in terms of mastering the innovation process and doing it smartly.

P. Baloh
IEDC – Bled School of Management, Bled, Slovenia
e-mail: peter.baloh@bisol.si

P. McKiernan and D. Purg (eds.), *Hidden Champions in CEE and Turkey*,
DOI 10.1007/978-3-642-40504-4_5, © Springer-Verlag Berlin Heidelberg 2013

It would be safe to predict that hidden champions (HCs) do master this process to some extent. They are top performers in their niches. But can these companies sustain that position as they grow? What are the best methods to maintain their innovativeness and, having limited resources, still play against the big companies? Do HCs really leverage their superior products as much as they could? The HCs studied in Central and Eastern Europe (CEE) are each navigating these questions in different ways. In this chapter we will try to highlight the most crucial challenges and issues surrounding their innovation processes. More important, we will uncover what strategies work for which HCs and why. These examples allow us to learn which pieces of the innovation puzzle are most important and suggest what skills are needed to master them.

1 What Kinds of Innovation Do Hidden Champions Perform?

The term "innovation" is broadly used, and can at times be seen as a buzz-word. Still, innovation is the best word to describe the creation of better or more effective products, services, processes, business models, and ideas. In essence innovation describes something new that draws upon old ideas, services, products, and processes. This new product is provided to customers who are willing to pay for it. The famous economist Joseph Schumpeter (1934) called innovation "romantic" due to the "creative destruction" that it causes: something new arises from something that is already there.

1.1 Service Innovation

The stories of innovation in CEE are diverse. The Hungarian company Kürt has successfully used innovative ideas to improve its services. In the 1990s, it became synonymous with IT security and data recovery in the local market. Since then it has expanded into the Western European market. Kürt's solutions recover data from seriously damaged storage devices when they are broken, soaked, burnt, erased or unreadable. Today Kürt has more than 20 years of experience developing solutions for information security and data recovery. Past experiences, and the work of its highly innovative experts, resulted in Kürt becoming a leading data recovery company globally.

Another example of service innovation is Slovakia's ACE enterprise, the market leader in integration of information systems of utility companies, providing solutions for intelligent metering and monitoring of utility networks. The ACE enterprise developed a unique technology for the quick modelling of central integration hubs and generating complete professional applications for metering and maintenance support for existing systems, mainly SAP. The company has created a unique connection point for over 300 types of solutions, enabling it to respond promptly to customers' needs. The ability to deliver service in hours, as opposed to weeks, is cherished by ACE's customers and provides great motivation to other companies aiming to streamline their services.

1.2 Innovation Through the Business Model

BISOL, a Slovenian photovoltaic module producer, demonstrates innovation through its business model. BISOL is one of the top five technological leaders in the world, exporting 90 % of its module-production to foreign markets. Instead of delivering only solar modules, it designs, engineers and produces other components of solar power plants for turn-key projects around Europe. BISOL positions itself distinctly as a builder of high quality and financially feasible plants. With more than 350 projects, BISOL has developed competency in logistics, roof covering, and energetic renewal of buildings. This has added numerous revenue streams to the initial one. These changes have allowed BISOL to begin building its own solar power plants with the ambition to become the biggest supplier of solar energy in Slovenia. The company designs and builds high-quality, efficient, and durable power plants to engage in the electricity selling business. BISOL provides a CEE example of innovation that changes the rules of the game in a particular technological and market niche.

1.3 Product Innovation

Feal, a metallurgic company from Bosnia and Herzegovina, expanded the notion of its product and offers a package that is customized closer to the customers' needs. While competitors focus predominantly on production, processing or design of aluminium products, Feal includes all three in its offer. Feal designs and produces aluminium systems. Its clients appreciate the highest quality product in the market, with a competitive price and a high quality of pre-sales and post sales services. Previously the aluminium industry did not have the concept of a one-stop shop. Moreover, the flexibility in the design and production (mass customization) is now a capability and core value of the company. Feal provides an example of a company that successfully expanded its core product with services to serve customers better and decrease the demand-to-delivery time.

The history of Prvi Partizan Užice (PPU), a Serbian ammunition manufacturer, goes back to 1928. PPU has always strived to address customers' needs better than its competition and has maintained very high product quality standards. Several sources list PPU as one of the few manufacturers of certain cartridges, such as the 7.92 × 33 mm Kurz cartridge used in the StG 44 rifle, and the 7.65 × 53 mm Argentine cartridge. At the beginning of 2009, the company introduced the 8 × 50 mm Lebel, becoming the first commercial manufacturer in decades to produce it. While PPU bases its long-term competitive advantages and services on its employees' expertise, it has expanded its business model from manufacturing of ammunition into sales of other products and services. In the early years, the company had its own school for training of riflemen; this seems to have served as a marketing tool. Moreover a long history of design and innovation in the manufacturing process and manufacturing lines has allowed the company to begin selling equipment and tools for ammunition production. Today PPU is one of the very few companies in the world to offer turn-key solutions for an ammunition manufacturing plant, from building and manufacturing process design to manufacturing equipment. Similarly, using its engineering competencies, the company has been able to expand its product range into medical equipment. PPU is thus an excellent example of innovation that builds upon core competencies and leverages them in the market in new and unique ways, other than those needed for cashing in on the core product.

Some HCs admit that they still do not have sustainable and ongoing innovation in their organizations. For example, the main product of Plastex, a company in Bosnia and Herzegovina, is klip-klap (a plastic frame). This innovation has not necessitated large investment or an intentional effort as it occurred by accident. The main driver of the innovation process at Plastex are the customers' needs in conjunction with internal technological competencies; the latter have dominated the process. Yet, Mr Terzic, CEO, complains, "There is no clear innovative idea selection process in our company".

1.4 The Importance of a Process of Innovation

Even if a company is generating new ideas, discoveries and solutions to client problems or new business models for revenue generation, a CEO might ask: How good are we at coordinating resources to leverage the value of this innovation? Are we exploiting each of the ideas to the maximum? Are we able to give these ideas the business consideration we should? Can we craft our ideas in the most efficient manner? Are the appropriate experts involved in evaluating these ideas? How shall we develop the ideas to their materialization? There are several forms of innovation and companies are continually redesigning and changing their products, services, internal technologies, processes, and business models. Sustained innovation rarely happens by chance and Drucker (1993) contends that there is no "flash of genius" that turns into innovation in isolation. Business practice and research (Desouza et al. 2009; Mariello 2007) emphasize the importance of a tangible, stage-based innovation process that is possible to manage, measure and develop. This should ideally be achieved through a framework of innovation to facilitate discussion and initiatives, and establish metrics and goals for each stage of the innovation process.

In essence, innovativeness requires a systematic, disciplined approach. While many organizations have embraced the concept to redesign and optimize processes around sales and production, they do not apply innovation processes to their company cultures. As a result there are few employees who know how to take their ideas from mere concepts to artefacts with business value. In essence employees spend great amounts of energy without actually creating anything of value (Desouza 2012). This does not mean that employees are not having great ideas. Yet, these may be hindered by not knowing how to have discussions about follow-up or new-product-creation or how to involve key people. Having employees overwhelmed by other tasks may be another organizational inefficiency with a detrimental effect on innovative activity. The ability of employees to practice entrepreneurship—behaving like an entrepreneur in a large company—is often hindered. At times, there is no clear procedure for developing ideas from the conception stage to their commercial application.

Consider the following comment by the vice-president of research of an information technology organization:

> A process of innovation is missing in this organization. . .One reason why I have been harping on setting up a process, or at least a template, is the need to measure our efforts. . .We spend money on [R&D] workshops, brainstorming retreats, experimentation, and a million other things; some of these work and some don't. . .I could not tell you where the strengths and weaknesses of our innovation capacities are. . .I can guess that we are very good at getting ideas from our employees, and not so good at the ways we commercialize the ideas. . .but these are my guesses. . .It is difficult to manage with guesswork.

This kind of comment is not uncommon. Most senior executives identify a need for better and more innovation in their organizations, yet few of them can define a business process that could help them meet that need. This may be because innovation remains informal, circumstantial and serendipitous. Few organizations take the time to articulate innovation processes or communicate this desire to their employees. Organizations that have a systematic procedure for leveraging ideas fare significantly better than organizations that do not, as waiting for inspiration to strike is not a sustainable method of securing a competitive advantage.

But how does a company go about developing an innovation culture? There are several innovative process models in the academic literature, yet these are limited in their ability to translate into real life business situations. These include levels of maturity of innovation processes, or simply a supply of desirable characteristics without further elaboration. Tajfun, a European leader in the production and supply of forestry equipment, defined a strategic roadmap for the company and the owner realized that a proactive approach to innovation was needed. Tajfun drew upon academic research that summed up the best practices of the most innovative companies (Desouza et al. 2009) and is designing a process consisting of several stages: generation and mobilization of ideas, advocacy and screening of ideas, experimentation, commercialization, and diffusion and implementation. The growth trajectory that the company anticipates cannot be achieved without new products, markets, and cost optimization.

Mr Sandi Češko, owner and the president of Studio Moderna, a CEE leader in electronic retailing and direct marketing, shared his view on innovation: "The realization of strategic plans and an innovation agenda depends on military discipline in the execution of internal tasks and processes". This demonstrates that HCs understand the need for a defined and implemented innovation process yet they experience difficulties in practice... By definition, HCs are small and young players that have competed (very) successfully in a particular niche segment. Each HC has a different growth trajectory but, in general, their CEOs have wanted their companies to grow. To be able to do that after the early successes, new products and markets are required and more employees have to be involved. This is not an easy task, as noted by Dr Rok Uršič, CEO of Instrumentation Technologies, a Slovenian nano-technology venture and a world leader in production, supply and advice in instrumentation:

> Having people organized and making them innovate in a collaborative fashion are two completely different things. At the beginning we were a few people who shared a passion. We would stay in the lab for weeks to find a solution to a problem. Everything was focused on a solution and, as we found it, we placed it shyly on the market and there was the success. Now, the group of people from whom I expect innovation is 10 times larger. To be able to do that, they need to be creative in finding new solutions. They need to be successful in using the existing knowledge and experience that has accumulated in the company. I want them to share that knowledge across groups. I want them to find the customers and really address their needs. All that is needed for a product to ultimately be a success. I want this to be somehow organized. I want to find the best horse to bet on every time it runs. It is very difficult to organize this kind of a collaborative movement that will flow in the same direction, and will replicate across the company, on and on.

There are obvious advantages in articulating and setting up an innovation process. First, taking a process view allows a company to open up the black box of idea development and pinpoint the discrete activities and stages involved. Management interventions can be developed to support and enhance these activities so as to boost up the collection of ideas from the business floor. A process view allows the company to develop the intrapreneurship quotient of the organization and measure each individual stage of the "process view". To achieve this, managers or departments can allocate 10 min of the weekly meeting to discuss new potential ideas and appoint a person to train managers in recognizing and developing innovation. Secondly, the process view enables organizations to precisely identify the roles played by various personnel at each stage of the innovation process, and to identify the role they should play in the future. Thirdly, the process view allows the company to use a baseline framework, albeit with some customization, and sort out ideas for incremental and radical innovation. These measurements enable organisations to more finely track the success and maturation of intrapreneurship and predict what results it will yield.

An ongoing issue with CEE HC companies is a lack of mature innovation capabilities. However we believe that when companies understand that organized ongoing innovation does not come quick or easy, they are more open to fine-tuning the process. Uroš Merc, CEO of BISOL, explains:

> After the initial frustration of not being able to do serial innovation in a jumpstart, I refocused. We did a lot of reading and talking, and the members of the board agreed that the company had gradually to learn how to do it. We believe it is the whole process of innovation that has to be developed jointly, organically. It is just like a kid when growing up from a helpless newborn baby to a walking and talking child, and then to an adult. Different aspects of a human being develop more or less simultaneously to maturity, and this is also how I believe it is with companies' innovation processes. If you can generate many ideas but if you don't follow up you will fail. If you over-analyse each idea and then come up with no product candidates, you will fail. If you can manufacture but have bad idea generation

> and selection, you will fail. Thus, we approached this maturation of innovation in our company by simultaneously focusing on each aspect of the innovation process to the same extent. When we have developed all of them to the same level, we will take another cut, again by addressing all aspects to the same extent. I am quite certain this will work.

2 Important Attributes of Successful Innovators

Several important attributes of successful innovators arose from the interviews with CEE HCs. We identified them as:

- Being close to customers
- Integrative practices
- Speed to market
- Commercialization of innovation
- Leaders' role
- Patents

Many HCs tackle the top three obstacles to innovation revealed by the 2010 Boston Consulting Group Survey on Innovation: risk-averse culture, lengthy development time and difficulty selecting the right ideas to commercialize (Andrew et al. 2010).

2.1 Being Close to Customers

Selecting ideas to commercialize is one of the main challenges in the innovation process (Desouza et al. 2008). Companies wish to select ideas for commercial success. As this depends on how well the customers receive the product, who else can evaluate the potential of an idea better than the customers themselves? However obvious this truth may seem, very few companies take their R&D outside of the company.

Across the HCs of CEE, there are abundant examples of closeness to the customer. Ansis Egle, CEO of Latvia's Aerodium, considers this the crucial success factor:

> We carefully address each market segment—either existing ones, or those that we create—and we make wind tunnels accordingly. We look at customers' specific requirements for flying conditions. For example, we produce tailor-made, wind tunnels for military parachutists. We also consider specific requirements for cost and extra safety measures such as those we receive from exhibition organizers or individual buyers. Right now we are carefully listening to the Shaolin monks in China to develop a wind tunnel tailored to their requirements. We are innovating in order to create demand for Aerodium products on the world market. In our business, this is possible only if you have better technology than your competitors. Technology-wise we are indeed very ambitious: if there is an opportunity, we do everything it takes to take advantage of it.

Another Latvian company, BLUE Microphones, considered the "Mercedes of microphones", owes its success to its proximity to their customers. Originally, the company restored expensive microphones of other producers. Its turnover grew from 40,000 euros in 1996 to 10 million in 2009 and 14 million in 2010 as the company rapidly upgraded and produced improved microphone models in response to the US market. As the price was not an issue, BLUE Microphones could sell their own first microphone for 5,000 euros. Although Mr. Martins, owner and CEO, thought this was a ridiculous price, he realized "by accident" that there were demanding customers who were willing to pay any price for very high added value and high prestige. This was the start of success and Mr. Martins implemented a strategy of designing microphones for specific uses.

> For instance, we offered microphones that are best for female voices, while other microphones were designed for a lower voice. Then there were microphones for drums, different kinds of guitars or any other particular instrument.

Overall, the way BLUE Microphones diversified its products was very innovative in this market, as most of the major producers were trying to offer "universal microphones". By understanding the main users of the product to the core, BLUE Microphone offers solutions to customers' task-related problems and charges a high premium for that service.

Being open and close to the customer is also considered crucial at Vipro, a Macedonian producer of ethnic food, whose global market share of Balkan foods is estimated at 50 %. Vipro collected feedback from emigrants from all over the world and identified and modified the flavours of particular dishes for different world markets so as to suit the tastes of local populations. Adding a high-quality, fresh, and organic philosophy to each product, Vipro is steadily creating a core brand that will guarantee the success of the products that it will add to their product line in the future. Similarly Slovenia's Seaway, a globally leading designer of sailboats for OEMs, ascribes its success to its proximity to the customer. Mr Japec Jakopin, co-owner of the company, explains:

> Our business is to really understand what the customers want, what their cultural roots are, what values drive them. Effective communication and trustworthiness are crucial for getting closer to the client. These things usually take years to develop... However, we need to understand the cultural base to be able to come up with the products that suit many cultures and hence be really global, since our customers cannot compete only locally.

New customers are attracted by the great number of design awards that Seaway has received at international expositions and fairs.

The Russian company Grishko is a monopolist leader in ballet shoes in Russia and has 30 % of world market share. Grishko has a sophisticated technology and premium quality philosophy. It works closely with ballet dancers to produce top-notch hand-made shoes for different levels and purposes of use. In the same manner Grishko has diversified and is developing footwear for theatre performance, circus actors, and gym sportsmen. It is also creating products for non-professional activities, fitness, and leisure. Grishko views closeness to the customer as one of the most important competitive advantages.

2.2 Integrative Practices

The point that we are making is that there are constraints to innovative practices. Closed innovation circles usually do not bring much success. R&D labs have numerous natural constraints that can limit the true potential of experimentation. R&D personnel are often detached from the day-to-day running of the business and may not be the best people to experiment on business solutions. In addition, R&D labs are often physically secluded from the operational centres of a business, so transporting ideas from the lab to where they are needed on the ground is a problem. Most important, no matter how brilliant your best people are, a company will be at a loss if you cannot find ways to tap into the 85–90 % of your organization's employees who do not work in the lab (Wilson and Desouza 2011). The loss will be even greater if you cannot tap into the potential outside the organization. Organizations in today's competitive marketplace are increasingly recognizing the need to innovate in partnership with their customers. Smart organizations are consciously tapping into their lead users, who possess knowledge to help an organization plan for the development of new products and the improvement of existing products (von Hippel 1986). As customers become increasingly connected with a firm, they become partners in product and service innovation. Opening up the innovation process to external stakeholders has been shown to be a successful path for companies, as some authors point out, for instance H. Chesbrough (2003), who coined the term "open innovation". In essence, in the view of CEE's HCs, being open and working with customers is crucial as it is the only way to stay ahead of the competition.

2.3 Speed to Market

An important way to increase the speed to market and improve the idea selection process is by increasing the pace of development and learning quickly. The stronger a company's growth performance, the more likely it will prefer experimentation as the first step to identify an opportunity. Just under a third of the companies with 1–10 % growth prefer experimentation to other methodologies, such as statistical analysis, to identify revenue and operational improvement opportunities. Almost half (46 %) of the companies with 11–20 % growth prefer experimentation as do well over half (56 %) of companies with more than 20 % growth (Wilson and Desouza 2011). It is crucial to deliver a product to the market as quickly as possible. Consider Procter & Gamble's launch of Febreze, which removes odours from fabric. Febreze was in premarket testing for 2 years before the official launch and the competition developed similar products in that time. SC Johnson, Clorox, and others introduced competing versions within a year. Similarly, Microsoft Surface, a gesture and touch-based device, was in public pre-testing for a number of years. Apple overtook Microsoft and in 2008 successfully commercialized many improvements that could be learned from Surface's flaws. As a result, the first iPhone was the first usable end-user mass market touch-based device. With the emergence of new generations of iPhones and iPads, MicrosoftSurface never took off.

How do CEE's HCs fare in this sense? As a number of interviewees indicate below, they understand that ideas improve products and should be immediately integrated and communicated. A member of the board of BISOL says:

> When talking about the speed of innovation, I always remember the scene from *Through the Looking Glass*, the sequel to *Alice in Wonderland*. The scene takes place on a large chessboard. Alice and the Red Queen are trying to get across the board; their feet are moving but they are not getting anywhere. When Alice expresses her frustration, the Red Queen Says 'If you want to get somewhere else you have to run at least twice as fast'. The lesson I can share is that it is not enough to be an innovator; you have to out-innovate the other companies that are innovating as well.

Mr Petar Ulić, co-owner of Serbian company EXECOM, a leader in custom software solutions in Western Europe, shared this view:

> We have one simple rule for new ideas. Try it out and see if it works; learn from failure and improve on what went wrong. If it works, implement it in the process. We do not have time to overanalyse. If you spend a month only talking about a potentially good idea, it is a few too many weeks that you have spent.

Slovenia's Akrapovič is a world leader in exhaust systems for racing bikes. It has always functioned in close collaboration with its customers. The company is now diversifying into the global market of high-performance cars. Because of Akrapovič's winning portfolio of racing bike exhausts, companies such as BMW, Mercedes, Porsche, and Ferrari, are happy to work with Akrapovič as soon as they can. The more options that there are on the market for "pimping your ride", the more appealing a particular car is to a typical buyer. As Akrapovič produced the only titanium after-market car exhaust system, and did that ahead of the competition, it acquired an important advantage. This highlights the importance of time in a product launch. Akrapovič is known for active engagement and constant experimentation with motorbike exhausts. Mr Akrapovič, began the business in a small workshop in the early 1990s and was one of the best racers in the then-Yugoslavia. Frustrated by the low quality of exhausts and motivated by the opportunity to make a difference, he was extremely open to learning and improving exhaust systems. He improved some products after each race basis. He views experimenting and putting products to a "live test" as an important element of his company, even after he gave up the CEO role in 2008.

Nevertheless a quick innovation mode can lead to the cannibalization of products. It is true that each innovation has an adoption curve (Rogers 1962) and there are innovators, early adopters, early majority, late majority and laggards. It is also true that if one cuts into the life-curve of a product too quickly, the mass profit and volume groups of customers might be missed. Yet the answer from successful companies is that it is not the curve one should be afraid of. Anything should be done to compress that curve to the lifespan that a product can afford. The CEO of Instrumentation Technologies says: "If we don't do it, someone else will."

Of course, each of these innovations is for the customer. CASON, a HC from Hungary, offers control systems for gas and oil transport systems and engages in novelty inflation in order to stay number one globally. They have built their success on the path blazed by their competitors. Whenever the latter imitate CASON's technology, they introduce more efficient solutions, thus acquiring a competitive advantage. CASON is not afraid to inflate their technologies in order to further increase the efficiency gap. For companies to be able to cash in, they have to be a significant step ahead of the previous model and the competition.

2.4 Commercialization of Innovation

An invention only becomes innovation when commercialized. The commercialization stage is of crucial importance and many organizations stumble as they approach this stage with little preparation. In the commercialization stage, an organization may look to its customers to verify that the innovation actually solves their problems. At this stage communication is essential. It is very important to clarify the benefits of the product to key customers through language and perspective.

A very strong aspect of commercialization was discussed in the sections on closeness to the customers and experimentation. But how do companies get potential customers outside their traditional markets that are interested in their new products? Hi-tech companies excel at this stage of marketing as customers are often involved in the experimentation or idea generation stage. When the quality and technological superiority are bases for a competitive advantage, this is a very straightforward approach. However, as companies are unable to involve every potential customer in the earlier stages of the innovation process (although they can rely on representatives of each market segment), other solutions have to be developed.

One issue that many HCs identified was the lack of trust in CEE companies. Western firms may be reluctant to do business with companies from CEE countries. Some companies use interesting counter-measures. One of these is to invite potential customers to the manufacturing plant and show off the hi-tech production facilities. The CEO of Microsam, a Macedonian producer of integrated solutions for manufacturing of products from composite materials and a world leader in its sector, notes:

> It is hard to persuade the customers that in Macedonia we are developing and producing such advanced high-tech products, but when we bring them and when they see our solutions and facilities everything goes much more easily.

Another way to demonstrate technological leadership and facilitate commercialization is through publications. The Hungarian company CycloLab is a world leader in pharmaceutical products that enhance drugs with quicker absorption possibilities. CycloLab's name became prominent through its employees' scientific publications. They have so far published approximately 500 scientific papers and conference presentations. In their business, it is very important that the CEO have a strong scientific reputation because only this can make him and the company legitimate. It is interesting to note that even the CFO holds a PhD degree in genetics.

However, it is not only the commercialization aspect that drives companies to employ highly educated people. Another reason is that this also leads to product validity. The founder and the leaders of IPG Photonics, a Russian manufacturer of high-tech devices and instruments that holds an 80 % market share in fibre lasers, have degrees in physics and mathematics, including doctoral degrees. CEO Dr Valentin Gapontsev notes:

> Finishing a PhD degree requires you to be a self-motivated, self-driven, systematic, hard-working, creative and passionate person, capable of making decisions. Besides the obvious expertise in particular narrow areas and besides the broader understanding of the field of the degree, these are some of the necessary qualities of people in the leading positions in fast-changing, innovative companies, such as IPG Photonics.

Finally, consider an example from Instrumentation Technologies. Driven by a quest for the best solution, the company searched for the best experts in the world, motivated to create cutting-edge technological knowledge and highly committed to the company's mission. Out of 60 employees, 40 hold PhDs. They see themselves as "*scientists in the world of business… not producing science, but serving science*."

2.5 Leaders Driving Innovation

The role of top management and the owner cannot be overemphasized in our HC sample. Innovation is continually driven by a passionate and dedicated person, or a team of people who believe in a particular area of technology, product or competency. Mr. Mark Pleško, owner and CEO of COSYLAB, a world leader in control systems running in large physics facilities, strongly believes in the potential of scientific excellence for creating a better world, and in no-compromise delivery of projects. By stressing the importance of these two areas, and acting as a role model, Pleško spreads this passion across his employees. Mr. Seradji, owner of Albanian company A.F.C. is a strong believer in environmental sustainability and sees wood as a "green existence" of mankind. This passion and drive allows the company to be a leading supplier of olivewood utensils to Western Europe.

One of the roles of a corporate leader is to create a culture that will hamper and boost innovation. Providing innovative mission and vision statements, enabling democratic communication, creating safe spaces where people can experiment and learn, enabling collaboration within and across department borders, allowing rule bending, and providing incentives, are organizational interventions that create a warm environment (Dombrowski et al. 2007). Slovakia's ACE Enterprises is a regional leader in integration and optimization of information systems and winner of multiple awards. Its owner and director, Mr. Alexander Cimbalák, says: "I am a believer in people's abilities and I create environments where others can participate in decision making". Leaders are role models and employees will not seek new solutions nor share ideas if they feel their managers criticize them and do not value their input. A risk-averse culture is one of the most common inhibitors of successful innovation as people do not like taking chances since they have been trained to think that failure is bad.

2.6 Patents

Securing intellectual property rights through patents is a reasonable way of hiding something from competitors for a certain period in a certain market. It allows the owner a legal right to be the only one to cash in on the product he invented and is a reward for finding a new solution for a particular problem. HCs often base their competitive advantages and market positioning on technological advancements in products or services. Therefore it would be reasonable to assume that they are active in patenting. Nevertheless, despite patents being popular academic measures of innovativeness, across the CEE HC sample it is not the best indicator of how successfully a company innovates. Even the Coca Cola formula is not patented but is a trade secret, guarded by the owners themselves.

Some HCs take advantage of patent registration while others do not. Macedonian Microsam has four patents and bases its competitive advantage in deep and secured technical knowledge. The 70 employees have access to more than 4,000 books in hard copy and more than 50,000 electronic ones. All engineers attend international trade fairs, conferences, seminars and training events and actively propose improved solutions to their existing and potential clients. Hungarian CycloLab has filed over 100 patent applications. Although the company has numerous patents, it only uses a few of them actively as long-lasting patents are expensive and do not pay back their costs.

However, many HCs do not believe in patents and intellectual property because they do not trust their protection ability. The CTO of BISOL explains:

> Even though we have a few very interesting and efficient superiorities and advancements in specific tasks in the manufacturing process (as compared to the whole industry standards), we wouldn't like to brag about them. First of all, we have a feeling that some of these patents would not be approved as they originate from existing science theories. Our fear is that once we file for a patent, our specific procedures and algorithms will become public; yet the patent will not be granted. We trust that we can better protect our knowledge by treating it as a trade secret internally, rather than by sharing it publicly as a patent that expires after a while.

Companies are put off by the slowness and complexity of the protection process. EXECOM's CEO notes:

> Patent protection is a costly, cumbersome and resource-consuming task. I would rather keep innovating and cashing in on the market's novelties as quickly as possible, than lose time dealing with lawyers and the IP office.

Instrumentation Technologies, a technologically highly advanced business, rarely uses patent protection. Though its Libera products are internationally protected by property rights, the company remains selective in terms of what to reveal through patenting, bearing in mind the time-consuming bureaucracy. Nonetheless as Mr Uršič, the company's CEO, meaningfully explains, Instrumentation Technologies is aware of the consequences of ignoring patent protection:

> One should internalize the competitive dynamics and constant battle for remaining upfront in the area of technological innovations... You must know that being the first is always a transitory category. Competitors are just behind the corner.

Conclusion

Innovation in today's market place is necessary for survival. To grow, and to sustain that growth, companies must become serial innovators. They need to look into how they are managing and executing their innovation processes. The understanding that innovation is not a few eureka moments but a multidimensional tangible process inside an organization allows companies to foster innovation as the norm. If the innovation process is outlined clearly, management interventions should be able to assess the state of each stage of the process and improve its maturity. CEE's HCs vary in the maturity of their innovation processes. A lack of financial resources and knowledge about how to proceed, and a lack of awareness of the necessity to innovate, can hinder the establishment of an innovation culture.

Innovating inside a company requires structure and flexibility to deliver products that will thrive in the market. It is crucial to open this process and engage in close relationship with customers. Obvious as it may seem, many companies are still not doing this today. Successful HCs engage with customers to a great extent, so as to be able to first understand the needs of their customers in detail. They do this through extremely competent and motivated individuals, who first assertively uncover the hidden or partly invisible needs of the customers. Secondly, they create world-class solutions that will satisfy those needs. One attribute of the HCs is their awareness that "nothing but the best works". Another one is the stance of the leaders that "today's best solution can and should be replaced tomorrow, not the day after tomorrow, by an even better solution".

The speed to market of the next superstar product is another critical success factor. Experimentation is the mother of learning and it helps select the right ideas to commercialize and speed up the time to market. There are a few HCs that are striving to democratize and engage as many employees as possible in the process. This is a way to become a serial innovator. Many of the HCs are not there yet and many are dependent on the owner or CEO as the main person that experiments and innovates. However if this is integrated into key business practices, innovation should take care of itself! We conclude this discussion with a quote from one of the success stories, that of Mr. Igor Akrapovič:

The ability to learn and deliver new ideas to the market much faster than our competitors was a key driver on our wining path to global market leadership. Moreover, if you have superior quality and competences, doing business is pretty simple!

References

Andrew, J., Manget, J., Michael, D., Taylor, A., & Zablit, H. (2010). *Innovation 2010: A return to prominence and the emergence of a new world order*. Boston: The Boston Consulting Group.

Chesbrough, H. W. (2003). *Open innovation: The new imperative for creating and profiting from technology*. Boston, MA: Harvard Business School Press.

Desouza, K. C. (2012). *Intrapreneurship: Managing ideas within your organization*. Toronto: University of Toronto Press.

Desouza, K. C., Awazu, Y., Jha, S., Dombrowski, C., Papagari, S., Baloh, P., et al. (2008). Customer-driven innovation. *Research-Technology Management, 51*(3), 35–44.

Desouza, K. C., Dombrowski, C., Awazu, Y., Baloh, P., Papagari, S., Jha, S., et al. (2009). Crafting organizational innovation processes. *Innovation: Management, Policy and Practice, 11*(1), 6–33.

Dombrowski, C., Kim, J. Y., Desouza, K. C., Braganza, A., Papagari, S., Baloh, P., et al. (2007). Elements of innovative cultures. *Knowledge and Process Management, 14*(3), 190–202.

Drucker, P. F. (1986). *Innovation and entrepreneurship: Practice and principles*. New York: Simon and Schuster.

Drucker, P. F. (1993). *Post-capitalist society*. Oxford: Butterworth Heinemann.

Mariello, A. (2007). The five stages of successful innovation. *Sloan Management Review, 48*(3), 8–9.

Rogers, E. M. (1962). *Diffusion of innovations*. New York: Free Press of Glencoe.

Schumpeter, J. A. (1934). *The theory of economic development: An inquiry into profits, capital, credit, interest, and the business cycle*. Cambridge, MA: Harvard University Press.

von Hippel, E. (1986). Lead users: A source of novel product concepts. *Management Science, 32* (7), 791–805.

Wilson, H. J., & Desouza, K. C. (2011). 8 ways to democratize experimentation. *Harvard Business Review Blog Network*. Available at http://blogs.hbr.org/research/2011/04/8-ways-to-democra tize-experime.html

International Marketing

Nenad Brkić and Denis Berberović

Within the discussion surrounding the Hidden Champions (HCs) from Central and Eastern Europe (CEE), this chapter will offer a brief international marketing perspective. Seeking to draw valuable conclusions from research that was conducted for more than 2 years in 17 CEE countries the authors will bring a blend of academic and business theory into a single workable frame of reference. The most prevalent and outstanding anomalies of this CEE HC cohort that have been studied in depth during this research will be emphasized and discussed in detail. This chapter will give a brief outline of major business environment dynamics in the last 25 years in CEE countries. It will demonstrate that this part of the world has become a popular source of business opportunity because of its emerging markets. The HCs support the argument that the business communities of the CEE countries' consist of emerging companies that are becoming a threat to existing successful organizations.

Following this contextual outline, the discussion will move to international marketing strategies, as many of the HCs have internationally orientated business strategies. In essence, we will examine what HC require for success and the core elements of their marketing strategies. Moreover, many of the HCs have a very specific target group of customers. Following this, the discussion will go further and analyze the specificities that draw customers towards these niche markets. Marketing analyses indicate that the four Ps (product, price, place and promotion) are of great importance. Therefore we will discuss marketing strategies surrounding product or service development, price choices, distribution markets and promotion options.

N. Brkić (✉) • D. Berberović
Department of Marketing, School of Economics and Business, University of Sarajevo, Sarajevo, Bosnia and Herzegovina
e-mail: nenad.brkic@efsa.unsa.ba

P. McKiernan and D. Purg (eds.), *Hidden Champions in CEE and Turkey*,
DOI 10.1007/978-3-642-40504-4_6, © Springer-Verlag Berlin Heidelberg 2013

1 Dynamic Environments

The last 25 years have been turbulent for the CEE countries. Most countries experienced significant political changes and upheavals involving social and economic adjustments, which continue to the present day.

Following the dissolution of the Eastern Bloc in 1991, all of its former members became independent states (Kenney 2006). This made communism redundant as a political and social ideology, although it had been followed for 50 years, or longer in the case of the Soviet Union. The one-party system was dismantled and many countries distanced themselves politically from Russia, introducing a Western-style democratic republican system. Nevertheless, Henderson and Robinson (1997) argue that the change in the political system was an easier undertaking than the economic changes required for this new system. In economic terms, each individual country was required to transform its national economy from centrally planned to market-oriented (Parker et al. 1997). The first step was privatization of state-run companies. These companies were generally not market-oriented. They were an instrument held by the communist governments of the Eastern Bloc countries. This lack of a market economy drive indicated a lack of Western business practices and knowledge in the business communities of CEE. By now, the privatization process has been completed more or less successfully and it appears that CEE has gained a critical dose of modern business knowledge.

Globally Information Technology (IT), and in particular the Internet, developed rapidly. These changes were embraced by the business sector (Ognjanov 2002). This means that companies in the ex-communist countries had to deal not only with the social upheaval and reorientation, but also with the lack of technological infrastructure in CEE. Because of insufficient financial resources, technological improvement was stagnant during the last years of communism. The CEE countries struggled with bad macroeconomic indicators, such as low incomes and inflation (Henderson and Robinson 1997). To keep up with the competition in domestic and international markets, CEE companies had to find a way to utilize their IT and at the same time modernize their production facilities.

2 Market Segments

The concept of marketing is based on the notion that companies regard their markets through the segmentation lens. Customers are grouped according to their demographical, psychological and behavioural characteristics. These groups are called market segments. By targeting individual groups, companies can offer better and more tailored products or services (Kotabe and Helsen 2010).

When it comes to geographical segmentation, this research has shown that HCs follow a variety of logics and strategies. While some HCs place their main focus on Western markets because of their higher purchasing power, others focus on emerging markets. One of the key characteristics of HCs in Simon's research is that these organizations seek to stay close to their customers. This study replicates his findings. Understanding customers, satisfying their needs, and customizing a product or service are of the same importance to the HCs of CEE as it is to those in Simon's sample. But each HC has different views on the best financing strategies, penetration of new markets, methods for launching new products, and a plethora of other business concerns. Nevertheless, they agree on one thing: the need to remain as close as possible to their clients. Each HC operates within different markets and with different goals customization appears on different levels. Product customization differs as a fully customized product requires a different marketing strategy compared to a partly customized product. The point that we are making is that it is necessary to understand the clients, know their preferences, and explore what needs to be done to satisfy them in the best possible way. Following this logic, Mr Cimbalak, founder and CEO of Slovakia's ACE Enterprise, argues that his company is successful because it analyses its customers in depth and the problems that they face. The company has managed to address these issues by becoming an essential part of the clients' daily routine. Mr Cimbalak firmly believes that his Slovakian HC has secured this important marketing achievement by becoming intertwined with its customers' behaviour.

The fact that the CEE's HCs are excellent marketers can also be seen in their devotion to creating loyal customers. Not only do they seek to satisfy their clients' needs, but they also appreciate the relevance of their customers' loyalty. HCs understand that client loyalty is highly cost-effective. An example of this type of company, fostering loyalty, is Grapefruit—a branding company from Romania that pays special attention to its loyal and passionate customers as a key strategy for business development.

Another marketing issue that is unique to HCs is the focus on marketing niches. As most HCs are small or medium-sized companies that do not have sufficient resources at their disposal, they tend to focus on one particular product market or niche. The development of a market niche requires customization as niche clients have specific needs, and therefore require greater attention than the average customer who is content to purchase from more mainstream companies. Although the interaction with these clients can be time and resource-consuming, these challenges stimulate the HCs to develop their product expertise which has been shown to have a positive impact on the bottom line. This is demonstrated by Estonia's Tallink Group, one of the world's top players in sea transport provision for passengers. The Tallink Group began small and focused on a narrow market place. This specialization has allowed the company to become globally renowned for its mini-cruise ferry operations and consequently the profits have shot through the roof.

Market niches do not always remain small; they often evolve into large market segments. This is a lesson that Latvia's, MÁDARA Cosmetics is now learning. That company offers eco-cosmetics. The need for such products is created by the increasing number of women who are environmentally aware and seek cosmetic products in line with their philosophy of acquiring aesthetic beauty in an environmentally friendly manner. At this point, MÁDARA Cosmetics has no significant competition; low competition is another specific trait of market niches. This is likely to change as potential competitors recognize the growing need of this group of customers.

Finally, many HCs have a strong focus on business-to-business marketing. This focus upon the B2B market may be the reason that many companies are less known outside of their industry. In particular Slovenian HCs are narrowly focused on the business-to-business market with specific and often highly customized solutions for their clients.

This research has shown that HCs use the whole range of different market entry modes. The rule of thumb is that companies rely on export when they start doing business in a specific market and in cases of high-risk environment. As time goes by and the business expands, HCs move to more hierarchical modes of market entry, i.e. they form joint ventures or establish own full subsidiaries abroad (Hollensen 2011).

3 Marketing Mix

The subsequent sections discuss the specific decisions that CEE's HCs have made concerning four important issues, known as the four Ps: product, price, place, and promotion. When deciding what market entry strategy should be followed, Johansson (2007) asserts that companies need to pay great attention to their marketing mix as each of these business elements becomes an essential message that the HCs send to the market about their company.

3.1 Product

The current findings are consistent with Simon's original research which indicated that HCs relied upon high-quality products to enter and conquer markets. For example, Bodren Ltd. in Croatia produces high-quality sweet and ice wine. Its distinct competitive advantage is the consistent development of the quality of their wines. Bodren achieves this by engaging the best wine connoisseurs in the region. Likewise, the high-quality of the products distributed by Ukrainian's Kakhovka Plant of Electric Welding Machines (KZESO) has allowed it to build an impressive 97 % market share in welding equipment. The longevity of a company has often been perceived as a guarantee of quality. A considerable number of HCs support this view, be they a food-processing company in Macedonia (Vipro) or an oil-processing firm in Estonia (Eesti Energia). Each HC believes that experience and maintaining tradition has helped it to create and offer a superb quality product, recognized by the market.

Product uniqueness requires product quality (Stark 2007) and many CEOs indicated that this product specialization was highly relevant to their company's success. Thus Venice Art Ltd., an Albanian company that manufactures carnival masks, has never produced two identical masks. The need for a carnival mask is specific; therefore the management believes exclusiveness is essential. This is achieved by manufacturing hand-made products with a unique design pattern, allowing the workers to express their creativeness.

And what about products, like oil, that are not in a niche market? Two Estonian companies, Enefit Energia and Viru Keemia Grupp, have found that there is more than one way to satisfy the need for oil. Envisaging a high demand for shale oil in the near future, these companies are focusing on improving and expanding their production. Crude oil is currently the most used kind, whose derivatives are used in vehicles and boilers. Yet, these Estonian companies are focusing their energies on shale oil, which they believe is a good substitute for crude oil. It appears that the prospects for shale oil are bright as its quality is equal to that of crude oil. At the current time, reserves for shale oil are 3.5 times larger than those of crude oil. Production is costly; however Enefit Energia and Viru Keemia Grupp aim to decrease production costs. They are exploring various ways in which shale oil can substitute the commonly used but potentially scarce crude oil.

However not all HCs rely solely on high quality or uniqueness to gain clients. Among others, Turkish companies regularly utilize the quality/price ratio strategy to attract more customers. We will discuss this strategy in more depth in the price section. In addition, successful products from CEE's HCs rely on some specificities. One successful practice involves paying attention to global social trends. For example, there has been a dramatic increase in the number of people attempting to become physically fit for personal, social or health reasons. People are also becoming increasingly aware that fitness and a healthy diet go hand in hand. As a result, this social trend has led to a range of bio products, all intended to help consumers stay fit and healthy. The Albanian essential oil producer Xherdo is successfully capitalizing on this trend by being one of the leading companies in West European countries, such as Germany and France. But it gets even better! This trend is creeping into each pore of our everyday lives. Consumers are rapidly becoming attached to the idea of eco and bio products and even the popularity of eco-cosmetics is rising.

The research on CEE's HC has highlighted the ability of these companies to offer products in highly competitive markets. What attracts customers to choose the HC's products over those of their competitors? We believe the answer lies, in part, in the constant improvement and development of the products. This is how the Bosnian-Herzegovinian producer of underwear, Alma Ras, has achieved a regional brand status in a record period. When asked what the secret to success is, Alma Ras CEO Rasim Memagić states: "You see, it's all about details. It's the small pieces that need to be put together in order to achieve success". Hungary's Energotest, a leading company dealing with modular, network-integrated technical testing stations in the car diagnostic industry, is another HC that is tirelessly devoted to the constant development of its electronic, mechanical and software solutions to retain its leading position.

However many of the HCs have limited financial resources to invest in extensive research and development (R&D). As a result, some companies have innovatively developed a new solution to offering scientifically backed products and they work alongside scientists and scientific institutes. For example, Russian scientist Viktor Bykov led a research project in 1990 resulting in the establishment of Nanotechnology MDT. The company launched an electronic and scanning probe microscope, which nowadays holds a fifth of the global market in zoned microscopes. Another example is the Slovenian Geneplanet Ltd. which offers services based on cutting-edge science. Based on a genetic analysis, Geneplanet provides advice on the prevention of potential curable diseases. The point we are making is that HCs are innovative with the scare resources that they have and must provide quality products.

To attract and keep customers, HCs often design all-encompassing products for their clients, particularly in the B2B market where extensive knowledge of products is needed. Serbia's RT-RK is a company that offers both software and hardware solutions for functional testing of multimedia devices, such as top boxes and TV sets. Feal is an aluminium company in Bosnia and Herzegovina whose history goes back to 1976. They both combine design and production in one place to satisfy their customers. Feal's product is highly customized and brings up a particularly interesting question: is standardization necessary when entering an international market? It is common practice for companies to customize to a certain point. However there is no best practice or clear answer to the question. Some HCs from CEE have even ignored the common recommendation for standardization when doing business internationally. As discussed previously, there are companies that rely on high product customization and many examples demonstrate that customers continue to be loyal despite the slightly higher prices of customized products.

It is usually argued that a product represents a solution to solving a particular problem or is a means to satisfying a particular need. This implies that one product can be used to satisfy one specific need. This study argues that some HCs find ways to extend a product's usage and operate in a number of markets. In other words, one product can be applied in different ways to satisfy a variety of different needs! Tulpar-Intech in Kazakhstan has patented a video-gram metric track-measuring system. It is a non-contact serial instrumentation system for railways. Tulpar-Intech is expanding the usage of this technology to the health sector, geological prospecting, agriculture, and construction.

The previous section discussed a variety of products produced by HCs in CEE. Many of them are savvy high-technology products. The need for constant technological innovation has been noted by Slovenia's Tajfun Planina Ltd., one of the world's leading producers of forestry equipment, specializing in logging winches and firewood processors. Mr Špan, a member of this family-owned business, notes:

"If you want to be competitive, you need to have your own effective R&D or you have to be cheaper than the Chinese. We will never be cheaper than the Chinese, so we need to be best in technological innovation".

The classic question of price or product differentiation arose several times in the research process. The majority of CEE's HCs prefer product differentiation, being aware that price competitiveness is difficult to achieve because of the strong international competition on price coming from Asia.

3.2 Price

In the previous section, we touched on the fact that price is a crucial in the creation of a successful product. The price must be economically profitable so that it covers expenses and it must be accepted by the target market. While cost cutting may be economically profitable, it is always a risky endeavour. Customers may be willing to accept a higher price as the reputation of many HCs rests on quality and the provision of unique products. This has been highlighted as being of great importance to clients (Cateora et al. 2011).

The Selena Group of Poland was mindful of the price/product dichotomy when it conquered the world with its polyurethane foam. The company offers an appealing price-value ratio which it found to be of crucial importance to its customers. The managers of Selena Group have realized that the right price-value ratio will not only attract customers to buy their product but also enable their sales force to offer additional products to the clients once they have had a satisfactory experience with Selena Group.

The research has shown that some HCs rely on the cost leadership strategy, well known to the business world. Lower your costs to keep your price down and you will stay above water. Kazakhstan's Tulpar-Intech manages to keep its R&D costs considerably under those of Western companies, which makes it capable of achieving a lower price on the market. Cost efficiency is pursued also by the Hungary's Energotest. The constant development of its products has helped the company offer a highly marketable product at a lower price.

To achieve lower prices, companies sometimes accept lower quality, as do customers. Turkey's Kanca Company, a producer of hand tools and forged parts, has realized this. It is strongly focused on achieving the right price-quality ratio. As a result, the company is a leader in Europe.

However some HCs have found another way to offer their products at a good price to their customers; they have simply increased their output and achieved economies of scale. Peter Hunt, the supervisory board manager of Wendre, an Estonian bedding manufacturer, believes that large production quantities are the key to achieving the right price-quality ratio.

All price issues are common dilemmas in the world of business. The HC research has discovered that companies are increasingly exploring less conventional ways of financing their business. Croatia's Durante M-KVADRAT is the only licensed credit reporting database in Europe and is successfully securing capital by charging the full price before even delivering the product. However, it is questionable whether holding this monopolistic position is the only reason that this model is working and if it would be sustained in the face of stronger competition.

3.3 Place

Due to its nature, distribution is highly dependable on company-specific international strategy. Of the four marketing mix elements, distribution is the one that the company is least able to control. While a company has full control of production, price and promotion, distribution is usually provided by other companies, argues Rakita (2005). However this study found that HCs seek to control the distribution system that they use, even if they cannot do that directly.

Therefore it comes as no surprise, that most of the HCs expressed their intention to gain a tight control of their distribution channels. The Ukrainian Beer Company Group (UBC Group) produces equipment for beer producers all over the world. This company also manufactures cooling equipment, as well as wood and cork, paper and paperboard, containers, and all other products necessary for beer producers. When asked about the competitive advantage of UBC, the corporate management named strict control over the distribution channel and customer orientation.

Nevertheless tight control over the distribution system is not always possible, particularly for newly founded companies. Latvia's Aboards Ltd. specializes in manufacturing kite boards and associated equipment. This company is a potential HC that has 5 % of the global market only 4 years after its establishment. According to founder Kriss Spulis, one of the reasons for this enormous success is the creation of a strong distribution network. Yet Aboards Ltd. does not have full control over its distribution network.

Most HCs are aware of the need to create distribution networks to leverage the connections of their company in their favour. This drives the integration of a distribution network within the value-chain framework. Mare Adriatika Ltd. is an Albanian fish-processing company that specializes in the processing of anchovies and sardines from the Adriatic Sea. After years of focusing on fish-processing, the company decided to expand its business and build its own distribution networks. This has been done with the aim to reduce distribution costs but, more important, to get full control of them so as to enhance performance.

3.4 Promotion

Research findings regarding promotion are mainly related to brand and reputation building. The values of these strategic assets are based not only on promotional activities, such as public relations (PR) or advertising, but also, and mainly, on business interactions with customers and suppliers. While this research did not focus in depth on promotional activities, the implications are striking. No matter how small or new the HCs are, each is well aware that brand building is crucial to its success. This finding is noteworthy because companies usually take a strategic approach to brand building only after years of doing business, when they believe that their existence is secured (Keller 2003). Most newly formed HCs have begun this practice early on in their company development. Similarly, Croatian, Latvian and Serbian B2B companies focus on building a strong brand and a positive reputation, and these are now paving the way to regional and global success.

Building a brand takes time. It takes even longer to maintain a well-known brand, and build and retain a good reputation (Argenti 2003). Data from this study indicates that HCs are able to secure a quality brand position without the usual trade-off between rapidity and quality. Creating an excellent image on the market in a short period has been achieved by transferring brand values from their partners to their own brands. This is very similar to what brands usually aim for when they hire famous people to advertize them (De Pelsmacker et al. 2010). An example is Louis Vuitton, which has an ongoing advertising campaign with a range of famous people to transfer their popularity to its own brands. The HCs are following this manner of doing business with world-class branded companies, and they communicate this to their client base. This is how they attract attention, popularity and even customer loyalty from the beginning. This is also how they communicate the reliability and quality of their products.

For example, Euro Plus Ltd. is a small Slovenian company, yet a global leader in the design and printing of labels with bar codes and radio-frequency identification. It has rapidly increased its market share in recent years. One of the major reasons for that is the fact that the company acts as a strategic partner to some of the extremely well-known companies around the globe. Euro Plus constantly communicates these names to the market.

Some HCs do not stop there, Lumen and Alma Ras, both from Bosnia and Herzegovina, are conscious that a good brand cannot remain valuable if there is not a quality product behind it. This is the reason that the transfer of know-how is an important part of the branding strategy of these companies. In other words, besides the transfer of brand values by their world-famous partners, they also accept their partners' know-how, and communicate this, too!

Conclusion

The intention of this chapter was to discuss, from a marketing perspective, the major findings concerning the HCs of CEE. The overriding question was how do these organizations compete internationally in terms of marketing? In general, CEE's HCs do business in a well-known manner, yet this is true only to a certain extent. It is striking that they also utilize uncommon methods to solve their international marketing dilemmas. One of the key findings of this research is that HCs in CEE not only explore new ways of doing business within emerging markets but also push the boundaries of marketing practices internationally and create their own marketing strategies. These companies do not only offer unique products; they market them in unique ways. Therefore, the conclusion will briefly reiterate these interesting findings.

As we pointed out, CEE has experienced large ideological and structural changes in the past two decades. This shift, combined with the IT revolution, made the transition challenging and had a strong impact on the business communities of the affected countries. This history has resulted in a completely new approach to doing business in CEE. It did not work for some companies but opened up opportunities to new businesses and markets for the HCs. The capitalistic approach to business, as opposed to the dismissed communist approach, had an important and immediate influence on CEE: Its companies began to operate on an international scale, targeting Western consumers with attractive disposable incomes. Therefore, CEE's HCs can be categorized as oriented toward Western or emerging markets.

Overall, CEE's HCs resemble those in Simon's original research in 1996. They focus largely on B2B markets and market niches. Yet, they do not stop there. These niches evolve to big market segments, leading to the HCs' strong growth. The magic of CEE's HCs is in the marketing mix, particularly in product development and production. Products are of high quality, unique and innovative. In combination with this innovativeness, HCs draw upon a tradition that helps them produce quality products and gain customer loyalty. The interviewees in the HC research emphasized that their success is not a result of big, world-changing innovation. Their achievements are the small, step-by-step improvements of products, offers and business processes. Scantiness creates creativity! This is one of the major findings of this research.

HCs usually begin by offering a product that demands high expertise. Yet, as time goes by, they aim to expand and develop their product and the markets in which they operate. This happens because these organizations become experts in their business fields. On the other hand, sometimes HCs have products that are technologically perfected to such an extent that a common person can hardly understand what they are supposed to do. In any case, HCs hold a great amount of expertise. The astonishing understanding of the products and their usage has led to another important finding: A product's usage effectiveness. Some HCs have created products in such a way that they can be used for several purposes. This seems like a clever way to increase the potential market.

High customization of the product leads to a more satisfied customer, which results in higher customer loyalty. In terms of finances, customization has a direct and positive impact on the corporate balance sheet. The price domain demonstrates minimal differences with respect to other companies. While cost cutting is usually a good thing, it should never endanger the overall quality of the product, or the brand name of the company. Customers are willing to pay more for a better quality. They are price-sensitive, yet they are more quality-sensitive. When asked about their competitive advantages, the HCs most commonly answered that it was their product. Yet a surprisingly high number of managers said that their success clearly depended on their tight control over the distribution system. This explains why many HCs seek to achieve forward integration of their value chain.

Finally, one of the impressing revelations of this research was the HCs' deep understanding of the strategic relevance of promotion. We found it surprising that most HCs are well acquainted with the brand and reputation concept and its relevance to business success. The majority of companies apply these practices from the first day of their foundation, which is quite unusual for start-ups. A number of these organizations even go a step further, as demonstrated by the Bosnian or Slovenian examples. They have found an interesting and financially less demanding way to brand their names by communicating their large clients' names to the market. In doing this, they offer a subtle guarantee to new customers that their products have passed the rigorous criteria of global companies. Each of these factors, in conjunction with the transfer of know-how from their big global partners, places the small-to-medium-sized HCs of CEE in an adequate position for the global battle in a dynamic business environment that will last well into the future.

References

Argenti, P. A. (2003). *Corporate communication* (3rd ed.). New York, NY: McGraw-Hill/Irwin.

Cateora, P. R., Gilly, M. C., & Graham, J. L. (2011). *International marketing* (15th ed.). New York, NY: McGraw-Hill/Irwin.

De Pelsmacker, P., Geuens, M., & Van den Bergh, J. (2010). *Marketing communications: A European perspective* (4th ed.). Harlow: Pearson Education.

Henderson, K., & Robinson, N. (1997). *Post-communist politics: An introduction*. Hemel Hempstead: Prentice Hall.

Hollensen, S. (2011). *Global marketing: A decision-oriented approach* (5th ed.). Harlow: Pearson Education.

Johansson, J. K. (2007). *Global marketing: Foreign entry, local marketing and global management* (5th ed.). New York, NY: McGraw-Hill/Irwin.

Keller, K. L. (2003). *Strategic brand management: Building, measuring, and managing brand equity* (2nd ed.). Upper Saddle River, NJ: Pearson Education.

Kenney, P. (2006). *Breme Slobode: Istočna Europa Nakon 1989 Godine*. Zagreb: Srednja Eeuropa.

Kotabe, M., & Helsen, K. (2010). *Global marketing management* (5th ed.). Hoboken, NJ: Wiley.

Ognjanov, G. (2002). Internet marketing in transition countries: A view from Serbia and Montenegro. In M. Čičić & N. Brkić (Eds.), *Transition in central and eastern Europe – challenges of the 21st century: Conference proceedings* (pp. 491–496). Sarajevo: Faculty of Economics.

Parker, S., Tritt, G., & Woo, W. T. (1997). Some lessons learned from the comparison of transitions in Asia and eastern Europe. In W. T. Woo, S. Parker, & J. D. Sachs (Eds.), *Economies in transition: Comparing Asia and Europe* (pp. 3–16). Cambridge, MT: The MIT Press.

Rakita, B. (2005). *Međunarodni marketing*. Beograd: Centar za izdavačku delatnost Ekonomskog fakulteta u Beogradu.

Stark, J. (2007). *Global product: Strategy, product lifecycle management and the billion customer question*. London: Springer.

In Search of Sustainable Business in Central and Eastern Europe

Nadya Zhexembayeva

Any modern literature, be it the scholarly work of Porter and Kramer (2006) or Prahalad (2004), the entertainment sections of Glamour magazine (Sole-Smith 2009), or even MTV television (Think MTV 2009), sends the message that the world is deeply concerned with social and ecological issues. Topics range from CO_2 emissions, water rights, and de-forestation, to child labour, peace, and social equity. The needs of society and the environment present a telling tale. However this concoction can be the perfect storm for the business manager, complex, disorienting, and maddeningly inscrutable and contentious. *Fortune Magazine* (2007) may have declared "Going Green" to be *the* business story of the twenty-first century but many managers struggle to understand even the most basic points of sustainable business practices (Berns et al. 2009). This chapter is not only concerned with the question of which issues merit consideration. It also asks if a business should focus on environmental concerns, *or* social concerns, or both? How is one to navigate the vast landscape of seemingly disconnected literature? Moreover, at the end of the day, why does it all matter to business? How does sustainability affect the bottom line? How can managers respond sustainably in order to support their business goals?

Finally—and this is the most important question—how have the HCs of Central and Eastern Europe (CEE) chosen to respond to these mounting issues thus far? The field of strategy is an apt place to begin this search for answers, a complex and beloved theme of management studies (Just ask any MBA student). The art and science of business strategy is implicit in identifying the best way for an organization to achieve its vision and objectives. Whatever its larger mission, a company must be able to develop its own unique path to value creation for customers, clients and other shareholders. To understand how the practicalities of sustainability impact business advantage, there can be no better guide than a successful business strategy.

N. Zhexembayeva
IEDC – Bled School of Management, Bled, Slovenia
e-mail: nadya.zhexembayeva@iedc.si

P. McKiernan and D. Purg (eds.), *Hidden Champions in CEE and Turkey*,
DOI 10.1007/978-3-642-40504-4_7, © Springer-Verlag Berlin Heidelberg 2013

1 Strategic Responses to Questions of Sustainability

Laszlo and Zhexembayeva (2011), in their book *Embedded Sustainability: The Next Big Competitive Advantage*, argue that sustainable models are possible without making economic trade-offs. Their two-decade study posits a set of eight strategic responses to ecological and social factors that affect businesses: risk mitigation, efficiency opportunity, product development and differentiation, brand protection, developing new market pathways, influencing industry standards and a driver towards radical innovation. All these can bring benefits if managers combine them sustainably and strategically. At first glance the categories seem fragmentary and at times contradictory. The first response frames sustainability in terms of a "trade-off" and "added cost" whereas the following seven responses argue that sustainability can create value for business. The final category, "sustainability as a driver of radical innovation", is a complex composite encompassing the previous responses. Dig a little deeper, however, and you will find that each of these responses are context-dependent. This chapter provides an overview of all eight responses, highlighting the specific choices made by the HCs of CEE. While many of the case studies examined have elected to follow a basic strategic response, others have ventured far into the innovative landscape of sustainable value creation. Taken together, the categories and case studies represent a rich canvas for thinking about how sustainability adds value to business.

1.1 Value Destruction: An Added Cost

In the wider business community, green and social responsibility initiatives have traditionally been considered an added cost, an inevitable trade-off with profits. This widespread belief is captured here (Reinhardt 2000):

> The idea that a business could ever "do well by doing good"... seems to violate economic logic... any business that tried to provide or preserve more environmental quality than is lawfully required would incur higher costs than its competitors, and its customers would abandon it in search of lower prices. (p. 5)

In short, the assumption is that socially or environmentally beneficial programmes are costly for business. One reason for the widespread trade-off assumption can be attributed to the dominance of awareness-raising efforts such as Rachel Carson's (1962) *Silent Spring*, and Ralph Nader's (1965) *Unsafe at Any Speed.* Each of these are powerful books built on the pioneering legacy of Aldo Leopold's (1949) *A Sand Country Alamanac, a treatise on* environmental ethics (Sharma and Aragon-Correa 2005).

> Early models discussing the integration of the natural environment into organizational decision-making and strategy were primarily derived from the deep ecology literature. Rather than addressing the issue of competitive advantage, they presented a conflict between the economy and ecology and thus between financial and environmental performance. (p. 1)

In just one of many available examples of this legacy, a 1994 *Harvard Business Review* article suggests that there is a necessary trade-off between profit and environmental improvement: "Ambitious environmental goals have real economics costs. As a society, we may rightly choose those goals despite their costs, but we must do so knowingly" (Walley and Whitehead 1994).

The overarching message is that sustainability means a hefty price tag. A large number of HCs, including Alma Ras, Lumen, and Plastex (Bosnia and Herzegovina), Bodren (Croatia), 2N, Adastra, Elephant Orchestra, Linet, Pixmac, Y Soft, and Zoom International (Czech Republic), Tallink Grupp (Estonia), CycloLab, Energotest, and Kürt (Hungary), ALSI and Tulpar-InTech (Kazakhstan), Aerodium and BLUE Microphones (Latvia), Mikrosam, Ading, Vipro, and Konti-Hidroplast (Macedonia) showed little to no evidence of interest in, or concern for, social and environmental management. Do these organizations consider sustainability a potential cost that can erode their strategic competitive advantage?

1.2 Value Creation #1: Risk Mitigation

Both sides of the argument are represented in the literature on the integration of sustainable programmes into business. An article in the *Journal of Economic Perspectives* argues that tougher environmental regulation must by its very nature reduce profits (Palmer et al. 1995). Managing sustainably-related business risks is often not primarily about value creation as much as it is about the bottom line. There are two levels of risk to be managed: the negative sustainability impact and the negative business consequence that may follow it. Both risks must be managed effectively to reduce potential economic loss. An environmental disaster, such as an oil spill, can be used as an example. This risk ought to be minimized by setting strong operational and risk management procedures. Nevertheless, if a spill does occur, the oil company is responsible not only for the clean-up, but also for limiting any environmental damage in the future. The oil company would also be required to compensate injured parties, manage reputational harm, and avoid potential customer and employee rejection, all of which are business risks distinct from the risk of damage to the environment.

The presumption is that sustainability is about managing potentially costly liabilities and that sustainability and businesses do not mix. However there are HCs that incorporate risk management in their business structures, such as CASON of Hungary, which operates in the risk management industry. As a provider of metering solutions for the oil and gas industry, the company helps its customers identify leakages, thus decreasing direct costs, and—most important—minimizing reputational damage that often stems from poorly-managed leakages.

Environmental strategist Andrew Hoffman (2000) lists four areas in which mitigating environmental risks can help a firm avoid significant business costs. These are (1) the reduced costs of environmental response by being proactive in preparing for disasters, such as accidents, spills and releases; (2) reduced remediation costs by proactively managing remediation projects and finishing ahead of schedule; (3) reduced product liability costs by addressing potential adverse impacts at the design stage; and (4) reduced insurance premiums by limiting environmental risk exposure for employees, contractors and customers. Sustainability scholar Marc Epstein (2008) believes sustainability-driven innovation strategies can be a critical component of mitigating risk. In essence, sustainability-related business risks are becoming broader and more varied than previously imagined, and have now expanded to include social issues such as child labour practices and minimization of political risks.[1]

1.3 Value Creation #2: An Efficiency Opportunity

"Of the possible ways to reconcile their need to deliver shareholder value with intensifying demands for improved environmental performance," says Harvard strategist Forest Reinhardt (2000), "perhaps the most straightforward is to provide environmentally preferable products and then capture the extra costs from consumers" (p. 17).

Rather than viewing sustainability as an added cost, improving efficiency is primarily about cutting the quantity and intensity of energy, waste, and materials being expended in the process of business, per unit of production. Reducing pollution at the initial stage is less costly than end-of-pipe treatment and remediation of effluents. Describing the economic value of pollution prevention, environmental strategist Alfred Marcus notes, "by increasing throughput, lowering rework rates and scrap, and using less material and energy per unit of production, a company can save money, enhance efficiency and become more competitive" (Marcus 2005, p. 1). Business strategists Michael Porter and Class van der Linde make a compelling argument that "the costs of addressing environmental regulations can be minimized, if not eliminated, through innovation that delivers other competitive benefits" (Porter and van der Linde 1995, p. 125). In these cases environmental impacts, such as air emissions and material waste, are indications of economic costs that can be eliminated in a win-win manner for business and society. Over a period of 10 years or more, companies like 3M, Chevron and DuPont have each reported saving billions of dollars from environmental cost-cutting initiatives (Reinhardt 2000). Walmart estimates that its sustainable packaging initiative launched in October 2005 will globally save 3.4 billion dollars by 2013 through eliminating 5 % of packaging materials in its supply chains. Many companies are finding that sustainability pressures assist in finding new savings in the areas of energy consumption, waste flows, and materials intensity. Short-term or long-term gains are driving firms in every sector to find exciting new cost-cutting opportunities. The moral is that sustainability is an eco-efficiency engine.

[1] Such as legal claims against directors and staff members which result from knowingly breaching environmental and social laws.

Some of CEE's HCs use eco-efficiency as a driver for new product development. Estonia's Eesti Energia has leveraged the rising prices of traditional crude oil into its competitive advantage by providing a sustainably alternative option and ensuring that Estonia enjoys one of the lowest electricity prices in Europe. By continuously searching for, and developing, more efficient and sustainable technologies for production, the company enjoys a strong financial performance. Other cases are also combining functionality with sustainable practice. Bochemie of the Czech Republic uses the demand for increased efficiency as a driver of its business success. A chemistry company, Bochemie helps its steel-producing clients decrease dangerous waste and increase productivity. In Slovakia, Media Control was the first company that "integrated the integration" into one product around four main axes: low energy consumption, fun, ecology and security. As a producer of control systems for "an intelligent home", Media Control channels the recent pressures for increased energy efficiency into a high value-added product.

1.4 Value Creation #3: It Is a Factor of Product Development and Differentiation

This leads us to use environmental and social attributes to differentiate products and services from the competition. With this response, the definition of "quality" or "performance" is simply expanded to include a sustainable dimension that encompasses green and social components, adding an additional weapon to a company's competitive arsenal. Strategy scholars Bob De Wit and Ron Meyer illustrate the point (De Wit and Meyer 2008):

> An ice cream manufacturer can introduce a new flavor and more chunky texture, a motorcycle producer can design a special "low rider" model for women, a pay TV company can develop special channels for dog owners and science fiction addicts, and a utility company can offer environmentally friendly electricity. (p. 238)

Therefore, even electricity can become green. This is a product attribute that helps differentiate a utility company from its competitors selling electricity from traditional "dirty" fuel sources, such as coal. Customers are increasingly willing to pay proportionately more for an environmental attribute. However a company must be able to provide credible information about that attribute (Reinhardt 2000). Once these conditions are satisfied, companies can expect to profit from adding new environmental attributes even if doing so incurs additional costs. The lesson is that sustainability is a product differentiator. Generally, the HCs from CEE do not consider this approach of product differentiation. However there are a small number of companies that are pushing the boundaries. Albania's Xherdo specializes in medicinal herbs and essences, and invests in official organic certification. This enables the company to gain a green competitive advantage against non-certified producers, thus distinguishing itself from the rest of the market. Additionally, MADARA Cosmetics in Latvia is using environmental trends as a channel for product differentiation. Established in 2006 as a high-quality ecological skin-care brand, and targeting the upper end of the market, by 2012 the company had entered more than 30 markets and was able to establish itself by focusing solely on eco-products in the highly competitive cosmetics market.

1.5 Value Creation #4: A Pathway to New Markets

Sustainability pressures create new market opportunities when businesses and consumers demand solutions. At the other end of the spectrum are opportunities for profitable provision of social and ecological *solutions*, such as life insurance and banking services to previously uninsurable and unbankable customers (Aviva, Erste Bank Group), a corporate mission to "bring health through food to as many people as possible" (Danone), and the growing number of clean energy and clean water options, such as those provided by P&G, Siemens, 3M, ITT or Filterboxx Water & Environmental. Additionally the needs of the world's poorest people present an opportunity for business to provide solutions to those living on less than 4 dollars a day. The World Resources Institute (2007) estimates the size of this consumer market at 5 trillion US dollars. By comparison, Canada's annual economic output is worth about 1.5 trillion US dollars. To use an example, Unilever's Indian subsidiary, Hindustan Lever Limited (HLL), developed Project Shakti as a way to reach India's poor rural population profitably with products such as shampoos, soaps, and iodized salt. By drawing upon the thousands of rural women's self-help groups established by the Indian government to facilitate local development, the company built a powerful new distribution and marketing system. The women sell products and promote the brands. They provide demonstration services in sanitization and hand washing that help reduce the incidence of diarrheal diseases and iodine deficiency. The project creates significant health benefits in neglected communities and further contributes to the local economy. Furthermore, HLL's parent company Unilever provides Project Shakti with access to a huge and growing market in what the company's director of new ventures calls a great win-win. The conclusion is that growing ecological and social needs are allowing companies to improve their products and even enter new markets globally. By addressing social or environmental needs in a profitable way, companies may create new solutions to the world's demands. This is a valuable lesson for the few companies that have demonstrated a desire to incorporate environmental or social solutions into their business models. A number of companies have attempted to follow this path. AMLA of Albania addresses unemployment and lack of community infrastructure or aid services by developing chestnut processing as an economically viable solution for a local community. The company was able to gain a cost advantage while simultaneously creating a real benefit for the local society. The owners elaborate:

> Poor families are especially dependent on chestnuts. It is our duty as businessmen to contribute somehow to the development of our area. Ermali and I do not see the company just as a source of profit. I was born and raised in Tropoja. This city has always been one of the poorest and forgotten areas of Albania. Imagine that those people have spent most of

their lives tending the chestnut forests, and now those forests are their main source of income.

Currently ALMA is developing programmes to provide investment support for chestnut gatherers who wish to become chestnut-processing professionals. While benefiting the company, this will also result in greater economic security for the gatherers and their community.

Croatia's company DOK-ING has connected high-tech and humanitarian needs by producing remote-controlled de-mining machines. The company focused on the needs of the region, which was infested with a high number of unexploded bombs from the Balkan conflicts. This unique specialization allowed the company to build a solid foundation for future product diversification. Similarly, Slovenia's Bisol has been driven by the growing prices of energy and the shift towards decentralization of electricity production. It is becoming the leading global producer of high-quality photovoltaic modules. With the highest electricity extraction ratio and the lowest outwear of photovoltaic modules in the world, Bisol is creating an entirely new market of high-output solar panels.

1.6 Value Creation #5: A Way to Protect and Enhance the Brand

Companies in a variety of sectors are finding that their brand name and corporate image are increasingly reliant on perceived environmental and social performance. Having a positive corporate image helps a company draw talent, secure loyal customers, become a supplier of choice and attract investors (Laszlo 2008). A company's image can help in negotiations with industrial or environmental regulatory bodies. A century ago a company's stock and tangible assets, such as production facilities, property and equipment, were its corporate value. Today, economists argue that corporate value (or "market capitalisation" for publicly traded companies) is increasingly tied to intangible assets, such as reputation, goodwill, employee know-how and stakeholder trust. At present intangible assets account for over 70 % of a company's value (Laszlo 2008). With rising expectations for green and socially responsible business, intangible value is increasingly driven by perceived sustainability performance. The financial consequence for BP from the Gulf oil disaster is a case in point. Within 2 months of the incident the financial cost to BP was assessed at more than 2 billion dollars. As a result, BP's stock price fell over 50 %, effectively wiping out approximately 90 billion dollars of its market value.

Additionally some companies may undertake corporate social responsibility (CSR) strategies, even if they do not follow through with action. However in a world of radical transparency, companies cannot *enduringly* make claims that are untrue and unverifiable, as social media, such as Facebook and Twitter, make companies increasingly accountable to the public. According to the UK Advertising Standards Authority (ASA), Renault and British Airways recently faced charges of misleading sustainability claims. Such charges—repeated in blogs and spread across social networks—can quickly undermine a company's overall image. This is a cautionary tale: Companies can gain or lose significant market value due to stakeholder *perceptions* of environmental, health-related and social impacts.

1.7 Value Creation #6: Influencing Industry Standards

Companies may try to shape government regulations or private industry standards to their advantage. This strategic use of government regulation or self-policing industry practices may raise the bar for competitors[2] (Nehrt 1998). When DuPont and a handful of other corporations lobbied the US government for strong national legislation regarding significant reductions of greenhouse gas emissions, including a cap-and-trade scheme,[3] it was counting on its expertise in low-carbon technologies to yield competitive benefits. DuPont's bet was that competitors would incur disproportionately higher costs as carbon emissions became regulated in the marketplace.

The Forest Stewardship Council (FSC) and the American Forest & Paper Association's Sustainable Forest Initiative (SFI), both founded in the early-mid 1990s, are two voluntary global certification systems for the forestry industry. They address issues such as illegal logging, deforestation, loss of wildlife habitat and climate change. Meanwhile lumber and paper companies unable to meet quality standards lose their membership and the right to carry the certification logo. In the years following the establishment of SFI, "a few companies decided not to commit to the SFI, and subsequently resigned their membership... and 15 company memberships were terminated after the companies failed to commit to the SFI" (Reinhardt 2000, p. 56). Such voluntary industry standards help raise industry-wide practices and differentiate, through certification schemes, those companies capable of meeting the emerging expectations of consumers, investors and other stakeholders. Additionally, Registration, Evaluation, Authorization and Restriction of Chemicals (REACH) legislation requires companies to register the chemical substances in their products sold in Europe. The registration process itself, and having to declare "substances of very high concern" (SVHC), is costly for competitors from outside the Euro zone, for example those in emerging markets· The lesson from this is that environmental regulations can create effective barriers to entry, especially if they help keep out low-cost imports.

[2] Nehrt (1998) demonstrated that companies that outstrip their competitors in advanced environmental practices and investments in technologies may obtain benefits if environmental legislation affecting the firm and the competitive scenario met certain conditions.

[3] The US Climate Action Partnership was founded in January, 2007, see: http://www.us-cap.org/

1.8 Value Creation #7: Drivers of Radical Innovation

Strategists have long seen the potential for environmental and social performance to drive deep innovation: "By thinking creatively about the fundamental nature of their business, executives in certain firms have been able to find ways to reconfigure the whole system by which they create value and deliver it to customers" (Reinhardt 2000, p. 106). A number of global cases provide some interesting examples of this trend. Consider the case of Tennant, a Minneapolis-based producer of walk-behind floor scrubbers for use in commercial buildings, sports stadiums and other large indoor and outdoor surfaces. While its competitors were busy working to reduce the harshness of their cleaning chemicals, Tennant simply eliminated the use of chemicals altogether. The company's flagship product, the ec-H2O, electrically converts tap water to perform like a powerful detergent. Tennant recycles water and, among its corporate goals, aims to use 70 % less water than in previous cleaning methods. Additionally, it aims not to release detergent into water systems. Having received several top awards, including the European Business Award for innovation, this small company now has visibility and reputation far exceeding its size.

The innovations taking place at the moment are unlimited. Nissan is preparing to move beyond fossil fuel engines, investing 6 billion US dollars into electric cars at a time when most of the industry is focused on improving fuel efficiency. Californian company Calera is developing a cement manufacturing process that captures and stores CO_2, while the rest of the industry is aiming to reduce CO_2 emissions.[4] Amazon's Kindle and Sony are questioning whether you need a paper book to read. This demonstrates that looking at your business through the lens of sustainability can be a source of tremendous creativity, helping to re-think the nature of your business venture fundamentally.

Serbian HC Prvi Partizan, a leading producer of ammunition, is truly taking the idea of radical innovation to the next level. Positioned among the top-five companies in its sector in the US and Canadian markets, Prvi Parizan is entering a new domain by developing "ecological" ammunition. Slovenia's Hidria, is a paragon of sustainability. The company has decided to work in two rather distinct areas: sustainable housing and sustainable mobility. Within the mobility domain, Hidria took a risk and focused on innovation for hybrid and electric vehicles. As a result, is now the number-one company in the world in the niche of range extenders, a critical component in the area of electric vehicle technology. Another Slovenian example, Seaway, demonstrates how social and environmental management drives new product development, enhances the brand and stimulates radical innovation. In 2008, Seaway designed a new hybrid carbon yacht, Greenline, as a reaction to environmental concerns such as CO_2-emission and the need for renewable energy. The yacht was offered to the company's partner, Original Equipment Manufacturer,

[4] Traditional cement makers are some of the largest carbon-emitting industries, contributing about 5 % of global emissions.

yet it was rejected. As a result, Seaway decided to market this product on its own. The product became a groundbreaking innovation for the entire industry and in 2009–2010 Greenline was the best-selling yacht by quantity worldwide!

The seventh value-creating response, radical innovation, is a complex composite. It draws on the nature of change in business models, product design, processes and technologies. Radical innovation enables the value-creating responses to interact, as innovation can be used across the business to lower costs, differentiate products and enter entirely new markets. Radical innovation is at the heart of the link between sustainability and profit, a core of the sustainable value concept.

To understand how companies develop the *capacity* for sustainability-driven radical innovation, one must dig deeper into the process underlying strategy. We turn now to an indirect, multi-layered theory, the "resource-based view" of competitive advantage, which helps to shed light on how shareholder value is created from superior environmental and social performance (Marcus 2005).

1.9 The Deep Link Between Sustainability and Profit

Early strategy research was exploratory. It lacked rigour and did not systematically address the link between sustainability and financial performance (Sharma and Aragon-Correa 2005). Rather than searching for comprehensive answers, research narrowly focused on topics such as the costs of pollution (Sharma and Aragon-Correa 2005). For anyone examining the texts of that period, it would be hard to disagree that "some of this literature is trivial and amounts to little more than the provision of green window dressing to disguise the activities of companies while the environmental impact of day-to-day operations remains unchanged" or that some writing was based on "simple moralistic exhortation or guilt-inducing rhetoric" (Sharma and Aragon-Correa 2005). Even management articles, such as Michael Porter's (1991) one-pager in *Scientific American* where he argued that tougher environmental regulation would lead firms to improve efficiency and competitiveness, were anecdotal and conceptual rather than systematic and empirical. From about 1995 onward, the environmental strategy literature began to attempt to uncover the mechanisms by which environmental and social strategy contributes to financial performance. New theoretical propositions and frameworks were introduced to assist managers understand *under what conditions* it "pays to be green".

In many instances, sustainability in itself does not increase profitability. This is hardly surprising. In contrast, environmental and social strategies force companies to acquire constituent *capabilities* that allow them to develop new *competencies*, leading to competitive and sustainability advantages. A subtle distinction but its logic, up to now well hidden in scholarly journals, is very convincing indeed. *Constituent capabilities* are "building-block" skills, both individual and organizational. These include pollution prevention, full cost analysis, design for environment (DfE), social auditing, community outreach, and stakeholder collaboration. These capabilities tie together over time to create new competencies, such as process innovation, continuous improvement, cross-functional management, and the ability to develop a widely shared strategy vision. In just one of many such examples, an analysis of the Canadian oil industry found that proactive environmental management leads to three organizational competencies—continuous high-order learning, continuous innovation, and stakeholder integration—which have positive effects on corporate financial performance. Other studies in the chemical, pulp and paper, and food industries reached similar conclusions (Sharma and Aragon-Correa 2005). In other words, successful management of environmental and social performance leads to new organizational competencies that apply broadly to every aspect of business management.

Are you confused by the distinction between capability and competence? Strategists Prahalad and Hamel (1990) first clarified the distinction in a manner that is crucial to understanding how sustainability creates competitive advantage. According to those authors, capabilities are the building blocks that aggregate into competencies. Companies can have many capabilities, 30 or more, but will have relatively few competencies, less than five or six. You can think of capabilities as separate skills sets that are only potentially of value to a firm, while competencies configure these capabilities into unique advantages. Competitive advantage arises from merging together complementary capabilities in a way that profitably serves customers, more so than competitors. Competencies involve a complex harmonization of capabilities and are hard to imitate. The more complex the integration of capabilities, the harder it is to imitate the competencies and the easier it will be for a company to maintain its competitive advantage.

This last point is of particular interest as environmental and social capabilities are relatively complex and imply bold disruptive change. The question of how to eliminate toxic chemicals, produce zero waste, or profitably serve consumers whose daily income is 4 dollars, is outside the usual purview of business. Many companies require what Andrew Winston, author of *Green to Gold*, calls "heresy": an enormous change in performance to meet customer demand. This includes radically minimizing resource use and waste, lowering carbon emissions, and attempting to engage with social equity issues (Winston 2009). Every company has its own heresy capable of driving disruptive, rather than incremental, innovation. Sustainability capabilities have scientific, technological, organizational and social dimensions. Developing and tying them together in a unique set of competencies can help establish a valuable competitive position that is hard for competitors to imitate.

2 The Strategist's View in a Nutshell

Of the eight responses, only one speaks about social and environmental performance in terms of value destruction. The idea that sustainability is an added cost is prevalent in mainstream business thinking. If present, it is a minor footnote in a strategist's work. In contrast, a strategist is more interested in knowing under what conditions sustainability becomes a source of value creation. He wishes to understand what type of value creation is viable for the company. With the value-creating responses, the strategy literature covers many basic questions and begins to guide the way forward for companies confronted with ecological and social pressures. These responses are potential sources of business value and opportunities for risk mitigation, improved efficiency, product revenue differentiation and new market entry, better regulatory rules, enhanced intangible value, and radical innovation.

There is no question that recent strategy studies have helped managers to understand how ecological and social pressures enter the calculus of business. Nevertheless, in our experience business practitioners continue to hold and practice beliefs about sustainability that prevent them from fully benefiting from its inherent value-creating opportunities. These views are widespread in every sector of the economy, which in our experience increasingly separates the winners from the losers. The former pursue sustainability strictly when it contributes to a competitive advantage. In contrast, the latter undertake CSR-type strategies that end up adding costs and fail to seize the ample opportunities for value creation.

In summary, the strategy field as a whole offers a number of ways to address sustainability-driven changes in the competitive environment. We believe that these responses are useful, yet not sufficient for practitioners seeking new methods to address sustainability for competitive advantage in a diverse number of markets. These competencies are merely suggestions to encourage businesses to begin considering sustainability actions. However, they do not provide much guidance on strategy implementation. For the most part, business practitioners, particularly in CEE, continue to believe that they must choose between shareholder and stakeholder value, much in the way that automakers a few decades ago were forced to choose between low price and high quality. What the field of strategy makes clear is that sustainability can become a *both-and* proposition fuelled by innovation to create less costly *and* more desirable products that profitably offer environmental and social benefits. Unfortunately, there continues to exist a widespread belief that such win-win initiatives are rare and violate the economists truism that there is no free lunch. They even seem to imply that there are lunches "one gets paid to eat" (Reinhardt 2000, p. 80). Certainly the lack of diversity in the HCs is one testament to this omnipresent belief. However ingenuity and innovation present a basis, and create sustainable value, for both business and society. These timid beginnings indicate that a much greater opportunity for embedding sustainability into business strategy and operation is biding its time.

References

Berns, M., Townend, A., Khayat, Z., Balagopal, B., Reeves, M., Hopkins, M., et al. (2009). *The business of sustainability*. MIT Sloan Management Review Special Report. Retrieved January 10, 2010, from http://www.mitsmr-ezine.com/busofsustainability/2009

Carson, R. (1962). *Silent spring*. Houghton Miffin.

De Wit, B., & Meyer, R. (2008). *Strategy synthesis: Resolving strategy paradoxes to create competitive advantage: Text and readings*. London: Thomson Learning.

Epstein, M. (2008). *Making sustainability work*. Greenleaf.
Fortune. (2007). Green is good. *Fortune, 155*(6), 42–74.
Hoffman, A. (2000). *Competitive environmental strategy*. Island Press.
Laszlo, C. (2008). *Sustainable value: How the world's leading companies are doing well by doing good*. Stanford, CA: Stanford University Press.
Laszlo, C., & Zhexembayeva, N. (2011). *Embedded sustainability: The next big competitive advantage*. Stanford, CA: Stanford University Press.
Leopold, A. (1949). *A sand country alamanac*. Oxford: Oxford University Press.
Marcus, A. (2005). Research in strategic environmental management. In S. Sharma & J. A. Aragon-Correa (Eds.), *Corporate environmental strategy and competitive advantage*. Edward Elgar.
Nader, R. (1965). *Unsafe at any speed*. Knightsbridge.
Nehrt, C. (1998). Maintainability of first mover advantages when environmental regulations differ between countries. *Academy of Management Review, 23*, 77–97.
Palmer, K., Oates, W., & Portney, P. (1995). Tightening environmental standards: The benefit-cost or the no-cost paradigm? *Journal of Economic Perspectives, 121*(4), 119–132.
Porter, M. (1991). America's green strategy. *Scientific American, 264*, 168.
Porter, M. E., & Kramer, M. R. (2006). Business and society: The link between competitive advantage and corporate social responsibility. *Harvard Business Review, 84*(12), 78–92.
Porter, M., & van der Linde, C. (1995). Green and competitive: Ending the stalemate. *Harvard Business Review, 73*(5), 120–134.
Prahalad, C. K. (2004). *The fortune at the bottom of the pyramid: Eradicating poverty through profit*. Upper Saddle River, NJ: Wharton School Publishing.
Prahalad, C. K., & Hamel, G. (1990). The core competence of the corporation. *Harvard Business Review, May–June*, 79–91.
Reinhardt, F. (2000). *Down to earth: Applying business principles to environmental management*. Harvard Business Press.
Sharma, S., & Aragon-Correa, J. A. (2005). Corporate environmental strategy and competitive advantage: A review from the past to the future. In S. Sharma, & J. A. Aragon-Correa (Eds.), *Corporate environmental strategy and competitive advantage*. Edward Elgar.
Sole-Smith, V. (2009). 70 new reasons to live green. *Glamour Magazine*. Retrieved July 27, 2009, from http://us.glamour.com/magazine/2009/03/70-new-reasons-to-live-green
Think MTV. (2009). *About*. Retrieved March 8, 2010, from http://think.mtv.com/Info/About.aspx
Walley, N., & Whitehead, B. (1994). It's not easy being green. *Harvard Business Review, 72*, 46–51.
Winston, A. (2009). *Green recovery: Get lean, get smart, and emerge from the downturn on top*. Harvard Business Press.
World Resources Institute. (2007). *The next 4 billion: Market size and business strategy at the base of the pyramid*. WRI/IFC.

Financial Aspects of HCs Business Models

Pavel Lebedev

An effective financial strategy is vital for the sustainable growth and development of any organization. It ensures that investment decisions align with the overall business strategy and allows the right mix of sources of funds to finance investments. Attracting finance is not an easy task for any company as it spills the risk-and-return discussion outside the boardroom to the premises of investors who are seeking an economically attractive investment on a long-term scale. At the same time, investors seek a transparent and understandable business. The quality of these factors, among others, affects important metrics such as the cost of capital and a level of dependency in managing a company.

This chapter begins with a summary of Simon's (1996, 2009) research surrounding the financing choices of hidden champions (HC) in developed markets. Following this outline, I examine a financial strategy dilemma of HCs and highlight the challenges of raising capital that both studies have revealed. Finally I illustrate how HCs in Central and Eastern Europe (CEE) finance their organizations. I identify the similarities and differences between the original research project and the current research.

In Central and Eastern Europe, each company works under an umbrella of national and international legislations. The level of compliance differs from country to country, economy to economy and within individual companies. I aim to outline how various HCs approach these challenges. The current trends in corporate communications indicate a shift towards integrated reporting that along with IFRS includes strategy, governance and risk disclosures and involves the external communications of the company. These are currently considered "best practices" internationally yet receive little attention in CEE. I propose that the IFRS reporting process is important for companies to grasp. They—and particularly small-to-medium-sized enterprises

P. Lebedev (✉)
Department of Finance and Banking, The Russian Presidential Academy of National Economy and Public Administration, Moscow, Russia
e-mail: p.lebedev@inbox.ru

P. McKiernan and D. Purg (eds.), *Hidden Champions in CEE and Turkey*,
DOI 10.1007/978-3-642-40504-4_8, © Springer-Verlag Berlin Heidelberg 2013

Table 1 Pros and cons of various capital sources for Simon's hidden champions

Category	For	Against
Self-financing	High equity ratio Positive profit Strong cash-flow Independence from capital markets	Growth rates are sometimes higher than the required generation of internal sources. Cost of capital might be optimized with an injection of reasonable amount of inexpensive debt.
External equity financing—private equity	Funds in-flow	The owner's longer view does not match the closer view of the private equity investor and his exit strategy.
External equity financing—going public	Funds in-flow	Much higher transparency level required. Hard to achieve adequate market valuation (mainly for niche-players).
Debt financing	High equity ratio Positive profit Strong cash-flow Excellent credit ratings Low capital costs	Need for disclosure Need to comply to creditor's requirements

Source: Adapted from Simon (2009)

(SME) across the globe, such as the HCs—should begin a discussion with the investment community.

1 Original Hidden Champions' Financing Issues

In the developed markets, 78 % of HC respondents described self-financing as the most important source of financing and claim that this will remain the predominant source in the future. Traditional bank loans are in second place, and Simon suggests funding via bank loans will decrease considerably in future. Private equity financing and financing on capital markets (going public, bonds) will similarly decrease. The percentage of respondents whose companies raise private equity funds and resort to financing from capital markets is relatively low (Simon 2009). Table 1 summarizes the main pros and cons of different forms of financing for Simon's HCs.

In summary, Simon points out that increasing equity rates over the last decade have resulted in excellent credit ratings and correspondingly low capital costs. In essence, financing is not a serious constraint for the further development of HCs and it appears not to limit their leeway for strategic investment. Therefore if a typical HC (operating in the conditions researched by Simon) decides to raise capital, it may reasonably count on both debt and equity markets. For CEE's HCs this is not always the case and operational and financial ratios are not as reliable as in established markets.

Table 2 Differences between financial and strategic investors

Category	Main typical characteristics	Portrait of the ideal company for the investor
Financial investors	• Financial value maximization • Mainly financial interest • Does not strive to execute control • Does not strive to change existing management team • Plans to have loan repaid within 3–6 years • Requires regular transparent information disclosures to monitor the activity of a company	• Effective and efficient business-processes • High growth rate of business • Explicit growth strategy • High level of proficiency and commitment on behalf of management team • Internal risks are well-managed
Strategic investors	• Value maximization plus extra benefits (synergies, integration, diversification) • Strives to control the company • Takes an active part in strategic and operational management • Investment horizon depends on investment strategy	• Current situation forces the company to seek a strong partner due to any type of constraints (lack of finance, competition, government regulations) • The company faces a takeover risk • Insufficient quality of management team • Operational failures and inefficiencies

Before we examine the differences between the two studies in what influences the financial choices that HCs make, let us focus on a financial strategy dilemma. In my opinion, it is common to all HCs and reflects many challenges of raising capital for this cohort globally.

2 A Financial Strategy Dilemma of HCs

The financial strategy dilemma of HCs is the choices that they must make when considering how to finance their business, specifically when neither debt nor external equity financing (including private equity and public equity) are suitable sources of funding. In terms of this option, capital providers may be classified as "financial investors" and "strategic investors". They are differentiated from each other by metrics, such as investment horizon, attitude towards the type and level of control that they will have over the company, their involvement in the company's strategic processes, and the manner in which they evaluate company success, among others. Table 2 shows the main characteristics of, and differences between, financial and strategic investors.

At first glance, financial investors should be preferred. Yet the CEE research demonstrates that HCs find it difficult to secure mutually beneficial external investments and partnerships. The ideal situation would be a well-run, sustainable company that attracts funding without losing financial control. However financial investors require transparency and expect businesses to outline financial, strategic, and business-model issues explicitly. In CEE the need to comply with the requirements and demands of equity providers may destroy the competitive advantage that HCs hold, thus decreasing their investment attractiveness. It may directly work against them when it comes to securing financing and disclosure of business strategy. We claim that HCs have a higher proportion of intangible key success factors. Therefore, the risk to a potential investor is higher than average. As a result, businesses may consider a mitigating strategy of disclosure to secure financing, which may act to commoditize and devalue key success factors.

In contrast, opting for the strategic investor option allows disclosure of information to be limited. Nevertheless, there is an unresolved question: are HC leaders ready to transfer the control of their beloved companies to new partners? They directly link their success to the company's high dependency on the owner's leadership and personality. If this dependency on the leader were reduced, an important success factor would be lost.

Another key success factor of HCs that may be at odds with the external financing process is that HCs trade in niche markets. Considering the narrowness of such markets, it can be difficult to attract external financing. In short, a fruitful partnership may be hard to achieve when a partner has little understanding of an inconspicuous market or product. For example, the markets of Russia's Grishko Ltd., a ballet a dance shoes producer, and those of Romania's Gliga Violins, a violin producer, are narrow and specific, making it difficult to secure funding from investment fund managers. This is because the factors that create the uniqueness of HCs and primarily contribute to their success, conflict with the fundamental criteria that investors traditionally use in evaluating a business. These evaluations are based strongly on classic risk assessment, a need for better understanding, transparency and control.

A key differentiator between Simon's research and the current research is that if a HC in an established market wishes to generate capital through investors it is able to count on debt and equity markets alike. In contrast, CEE's HCs have difficulty securing investment from external investors. In my opinion, the operating environments are key differentiators between these two cohorts of HCs. The HCs in the original research operate in developed Western markets. Compared to the CEE countries, these markets have effectively functioning economic and legislative institutions, which support commercial activities and ensure that business standards are followed. In contrast, CEE's HCs operate in environments characterized by a lack of established business culture, a high level of corruption and existence of black markets. These factors are accompanied by constantly changing business rules. To illustrate with a few examples, this research identified very few HCs in Kazakhstan. This can be attributed to the country's short history of a market economy and, in particular, to the young age of its companies, absence of business traditions, undeveloped markets, weak competition, corruption, and non-professional management. Similarly, one of the key challenges to the Latvian business environment and economic development seems to be the relatively high level of gray economy in the country. Among the factors explaining the large amount of tax evasion in Latvia is the "optimization" of expenses by avoiding taxes and thus increasing the companies' competitive advantage, the weak legal enforcement, the societal tradition of avoiding taxes and the low ethical standards.

In Ukraine the current fiscal, regulatory and legal framework is not conducive to the development of small and medium-sized companies as it favours the large financial and industrial groups. In numerous ratings by international research and financial institutions, Ukraine is constantly ranked low in competitiveness, simplicity of doing business, and sensitivity to corruption. The overarching differences between these economies and those in Simon's research include the inconsistency of public policy in the former as well as the reduced competitiveness of CEE companies by regulations and legal provisions, the low level of competition-boosting legislation, the low adaptation capacity of public policy to economic changes, bureaucracy, corruption, inaccessibility of stock markets, and poor methods of doing business.

Because of these specifics of the CEE environment, and the HCs' financial strategy dilemma, it is almost impossible for HCs to obtain debt or equity financing. Compared to larger companies operating in the same environment, HCs are rarely involved in debt financing, initial public offerings (IPO) and mergers and acquisitions (M&A) deals. Additionally we observe that venture financing and partnering with business angels—private companies that provide finance for business expansion—are not typical for CEE's HCs although these innovative companies might benefit from such activities. In spite of that, most of CEE's HCs continue to expand rapidly and flourish. Below, I explore how they develop and execute their financial strategies.

3 How Hidden Champions from Central Eastern Europe Finance Their Organizations

3.1 Historical Perspective of Central Eastern Europe HCs

The recent history of the CEE countries begins in the early 1990s and differs greatly from the economic environment described in the original research. It is only recently, in the 1990s, that the former socialist bloc began its transition to a Western model of market economy. The point is that the majority of HCs in the current research became incorporated only during the last three decades, although some companies trace their history prior to the launch of the reforms. A closer look at the CEE sample reveals different patterns of investment and financing, depending on the period of a company's creation.

Firstly, we can distinguish between the HCs that originated before the transition to a market economy and those that were created after the launch of the reforms. What makes these two groups very different is the way that they have obtained their initial investments and their amount. HCs established in the socialist period were created by the state and usually received large investments from it. On the contrary, companies that emerged after the reforms were created in most cases by capitalists without capital.

The companies that originated in the first decade of the transition period and those that emerged recently, in the 2000s, demonstrate very important differences in the way that they obtained their initial capital and fueled their business in the first years of operation. In the case of the first cohort, it was typical for new ventures to exploit social capital and networks from the socialist times. These networks maintained power and were eager to support each other in their new roles, thus gaining access to resources. Trading activities were a powerful source of initial capital as any company could engage in them. In contrast, the companies that emerged in the 2000s enjoyed a more mature economic and legislative environment. This type of financial environment is much more conducive to success, and organizations are able to rely on institutions and innovations, not only on personal relationships, to succeed. In these circumstances, strategic focus is important. For example, selling clothes or even crude oil would not be helpful for backing up an IT venture. Besides, the golden times of the Internet and IT have changed the structure of the assets required to run an innovative business. It is not solely financial assets that matter; human capital and knowledge have become extremely valuable in the current economic climate. Although difficult to attract, once found they can be financed from working capital rather than long-term investments. The descriptions of CEE's HCs in this book illustrate this.

Considering these examples, I suggest the following categorizations of HCs in CEE by the period of their creation:

1. HCs that were incorporated in the socialist times before the transition process started (up until 1990);
2. HCs that were incorporated in the 1990s;
3. HCs that were incorporated from the year 2000 onwards.

Most of the companies arising from the socialist era inherited the physical capital of their predecessors. In this case capital was most commonly in the form of undervalued tangible assets. These companies were generally privatized during the first privatization campaigns in the respective countries. This type of privatization usually meant that assets were either distributed free of charge or at a cheap nominal price, and were acquired by the groups (managers, representatives of the industry regulating authorities) that were close to the company. Technology also came with that physical capital; however as the economies became more open and integrated, the technology got obsolete because of the radical change in the competitive environment and the customers' requirements. Generally, undervalued assets, with the potential to increase in valuation as markets developed, contributed to the capital gains of the new owners. They could be used as collateral or as a basis for company development and sustainability. These HCs are mainly companies from traditional industries, involved in production, trade, extraction of raw materials, and engineering. Through their position and connections with partners, these HCs were able to provide huge sales and achieve large operating volumes.

As we see in the Russian and Turkish cases described in this book, CEE HCs with more than 30 years of history are now conglomerates which were either national holdings before the 1990s or had the state as the principal stake-holder.

HCs established in the 1990s relied on social capital or technical knowledge. As funds were hardly available in the early 1990s, previous know-how and social capital were essential for entrepreneurial start-ups in most of the countries in transition. Investing in social capital, often free of charge, the owners of these companies have built their success on leveraging networks and connections, which generally originated during the recent socialist years. Indeed, during that period social capital skills, emotional intelligence and other similar assets were fostered and developed as personal relationships with suppliers, customers, and the authorities among others, became a huge, albeit undervalued, advantage once the CEE countries began their transition to a market economy. In essence, if a start-up successfully monetized its social capital and various networks, this created a strong value stream.

Businesses from this period also leveraged technical knowledge and know-how. These assets were exploited commercially, mainly by scientists who had strong entrepreneurial skills and were employed by state scientific and research organizations. The cases of Hungarian pharmaceutical CycloLab, and JCG Nanotechnology NT-MDT of Russia, described in this book, illustrate this.

From the late 1990s to the early 2000s, HCs relied highly on knowledge and innovation, which they transformed into business models. These assets did not require high amounts of physical and financial capital, allowing companies to be created from scratch, without significant financial investments. Along the same line, the holders of knowledge assets, such as scientists, researchers and IT specialists, often became CEOs or major shareholders. The message here is that the value of the knowledge that these people possess allows their business models to function with low working capital ratios. As many of the assets are intangible and costs are fixed, specialists can maximize the assets that they have, whether they appear on the balance sheet or not. A Russian Internet search engine created by Yandex and ELEKS Software of Ukraine, both described in this book, are just two examples of this type of HC.

3.2 Initial Financing of CEE HCs Summarized

Figure 1 summarizes how HCs differ in the way that they initially financed their business depending on the period of their establishment. The "period" dimension was already explained. The "type of assets" dimension goes from tangibles to knowledge assets. The main source of funding is indicated in the appropriate sectors of the matrix.

The shift from privatization of undervalued assets to monetizing know-how can be clearly observed as the main direction of the HCs' initial funding strategies. However, further growth and development require additional funds. In the next section we take a closer look at how CEE's HCs address the challenge of financing further growth and development.

Main type of assets	Assets of certain type initially financed by		
Tangible assets	Privatization of assets at a symbolic price (mainly before early 1990s, rarely mid 1990s–2000s)	Amount of these assets is insignificant for the HCs originated in this decade	Amount of these assets is insignificant for the HCs originated in this decade
Social capital and technology	Amount of these assets is insignificant for the HCs originated in this decade	Capturing technology, monetizing and commercializing social capital and technology (mainly mid 1990s – 2000s, rarely early 1990s)	
Knowledge and innovation			Self-finance, no big initial investments required; Trade finance from a big customer
	... - 1990	1990 -2000	2000 - ...
	Period of company origination		

Fig. 1 How hidden champions from CEE initially obtained funds

3.3 Financing Growth and Development: Different Routes

As I mentioned earlier in this chapter, CEE's HCs are differentiated by a much higher lack of transparency compared to the original group. This includes the interviewees' unwillingness to discuss financial issues. In a number of cases (for instance in Belarus), no information on financing was disclosed at all and in many other cases it was just stated that finance was not a problem for the company. The interviewee from CASON, in Hungary, stated that if the company managed to solve its capital constraints, growth opportunities would be nearly infinite and CASON could become a well-known champion. Other interviewees complained about difficulties in obtaining external financing, without going deeper into specific details.

Still, there is evidence that CEE's HCs use all popular forms of financing. This includes equity financing (both private and public), M&A deals, debt financing, trade financing, and self-financing from retained profit and owner's funds. It should be noted, that HCs rarely resort to M&A, IPOs or debt financing. More popular forms are trade and self-financing and companies simply limit their growth when funds are scarce. Nevertheless there are distinct patterns in the financial decisions that HCs make. To reiterate, the economic differences between the CEE countries and those in the original research were controlled for so as to make some CEE companies eligible for inclusion in this research.

The economic environments in each CEE country are diverse. They are rapidly changing and adapting to economic and legislative changes. This is important to keep in mind when generalizations are made across the CEE cohort. There are globally important companies holding a high share of export revenues alongside small companies of regional importance. For example, Albania and Croatia have a considerate number of small businesses in our sample. Slovakia and Slovenia are represented predominantly by SMEs, whereas Turkey and Russia have powerful conglomerates. Each of these companies is categorized as a HC in this research, even though each country's business background and demographics are different. For instance, the majority of the Serbian population is employed in SMEs; in contrast, in Russia these companies accounts for only 20 % of employment. This also applies to legislation. There are countries that adopted EU legislation in the last decade and another set of countries that have not. Some—for instance Russia and Belarus—do not even expect to adopt any EU regulations.

Earlier in this chapter, I suggested classifying HCs by the decade of their origination, so as to clarify how they obtained the capital to fund the initial phase of their operations. However, the correlation between the initial investments and financial markets is low because of the future orientation of the latter. Thus the period of origination loses its relevance as an explanation of how companies finance their growth.

I propose the approach adopted during the research so as to distinguish between "strong HCs", "regional HCs", and "start-ups with an emerging competitive advantage". This could be useful for explaining patterns in the financial strategies of HCs.

1. "Strong HCs" satisfy Simon's original HC criteria. Accordingly, their financial options are better than those of the HCs in the next two categories.
2. "Regional HCs" are middle-sized businesses that are successful at a regional level. These enterprises currently lack formal governance procedures.
3. "Start-ups with an emerging competitive advantage" are small entrepreneurial companies organized around a leader-entrepreneur.

Figure 2 presents an overview of the typical financial strategies of CEE's HCs by category.

3.4 Closer Look: Self-Financing

Self-financing is the most common form of financing for all types of HCs. It consists of retained profit and the owner's contributions. Retained profit is a powerful stream of financing growth. In terms of return on assets and return on equity, HCs perform much better than the average company in their sector. Theory of financial management and corporate finance determine sustainable growth rate as such a rate that does not affect capital structure negatively (Higgins 2011; Hillier et al. 2010). A sustainable growth rate usually correlates with return on equity (ROE), provided that no profit distributions were made. As we see from the research, most of the HCs have high profits and reinvest them to achieve company growth.

In the case of ESET, a Slovakian developer of internet security solutions, the nature of the product enables the company to innovate and maintain a strong position without huge financial investments. ESET has a considerable number of product designs. This is because each additional product sold has a very little

Type of HC	Self-financing	Trade financing and partnerships	Debt-financing (Loans)	Debt-financing (Bonds)	External equity-financing
Strong HCs	Yes	Yes	Yes	Rare	Exceptionally rare
Regional HCs	Yes	Yes	Rare	Exceptionally rare	Exceptionally rare
Start-ups with emerging competitive advantage	Yes	Yes	Exceptionally rare	No	No

Fig. 2 How HCs in Central and Eastern Europe finance their growth

incremental cost, allowing the contribution margin to be nearly equal to the selling price!

Bosnia and Herzegovina and Hungary provide more interesting business models, described in the respective chapters.

3.5 A Closer Look: Trade-Financing and Partnerships for HCs

Trade-financing is the most popular form of external financing of growth and development of all types of CEE HCs. Trade financing is organized by means of short-term financing, obtained from customers in a form of prepayment or regular payments. A stable relationship with clients makes it easier to negotiate payment terms to obtain short-term financing. Plastex of Bosnia and Herzegovina (BiH) vividly demonstrates how such a strategy works.

It is beneficial for a company to be recognized globally and in its industry as this facilitates the decision-making processes of potential investors. A good reputation can be a vehicle for securing the necessary financing as demonstrated by BiH's HCs. It is typical of CEE HCs to obtain a large share of their revenues from three to five key clients. It can be reasonably assumed that being dependent on a few strong customers does not put a company in a good position to negotiate suitable terms of payment. However, as outlined above, there is a high level of interdependency between companies and their customers. Additionally, HCs' products and services have a high value added, meaning that the cost of inputs is relatively low compared to the price of outputs. The implication is that the interdependency between a supplier, a HC, and a customer often allows the relationship between clients and providers to be counterbalanced. In sum, these factors provide an opportunity for organizations to manipulate financial decisions in the short-term and mid-term and influence the financial and operating cycle to their advantage. Examples of smart management of the operating cycle are provided by a number of participants of this study, such as Durante M-KVARDRAT of Croatia, and Grishko Ltd. of Russia.

The demand for HC products, such as Grishko's ballet shoes, creates an opportunity for companies to take advantage of the financial benefits should they need customers to pay in advance. The downside of this model is that it is not sustainable in the long term and production and sales must continue to maintain a profitable business and a good reputation. The strategy of Durante M-KVADRAT is even more straightforward. The company operates in the construction sector and from the very beginning of its operations its policy has been to sell only prepaid merchandize.

Developing beneficial partnerships with local companies is a beneficial strategy for coping with financial constraints to growth. Latvia's Aerodium, a vertical wind tunnels producer, has developed its own strategy to enter global markets. Aerodium has realized that the best strategy for penetrating new markets is forming partnerships with local companies.

3.6 A Closer Look: HCs and Debt-Financing

As outlined previously, traditional avenues of financing, such as debt-financing, are available only to strong HCs as they comply with the standards that are set by debt providers. To secure debt-financing a company must have a well-managed development and financial infrastructure, including access to financial markets and institutions. Poland represents an example of an economy where financial markets and institutions have been developing at a greater pace and to a larger extent than in other small countries in CEE. In Poland access to financial resources began to develop early in the 1990s. At that time a wide variety of credit facilities became available. A highly liquid stock exchange and the local presence of major private equity investors played a key role in the development of the economy. Currently, approximately 75 % of Polish HCs reinvest profits into the company; 67 % reported using debt-financing and respondents pointed out that they have increased their use of this source in recent years.

Regional HCs rarely qualify for debt-financing. In contrast, new start-ups are practically never eligible for debt-financing. However, neither strong, nor regional HCs experience growth when using debt-financing. Ukrainian and Albanian cases illustrate both situations. KZESO is a Ukrainian company that manufactures modern electric welding equipment, with a history dating back to 1929. Prior to the recession, KZESO had invested its own assets and bank loans into the construction of a new plant for the manufacturing of rail machines, previously imported into Ukraine. However, in general, the Ukrainian HCs do not resort to scaled credit financing, and do not attract investments from external loan markets. This makes them similar to the HCs described in Simon's book.

Concluding Remarks

As we have seen in this chapter, CEE's HCs have many commonalities with Simon's original HCs as regards financing, and a number of key differences. All HCs are faced with a financial strategy dilemma as complying with the traditional requirements of investors is a potential threat to their competitive advantages. Additionally, most capital providers see investment in innovative companies as highly risky. Fortunately, this risk suites certain types of venture capitalists. Yet, they wish to control their investments until their exit, which may be an issue for HCs.

However, the companies in Simon's research have greater possibilities to attract external financing as they operate in developed economies with well-functioning institutions and strong business traditions and practices. For those in CEE it is more difficult to obtain finance. HCs that emerged in the 1990s have successfully privatized the assets that formed their initial capital base. In contrast, the next generations of HCs capitalized on social and intellectual capital. Along their way to success, they have managed to finance their growth largely on their own.

The CEE countries continue to be in a stage of rapid development and are still becoming fully integrated into the global economy. This environment is characterized by continuous turbulence, external shocks and a high level of uncertainty. In these economies, raising capital is a challenging task for any company, and increasingly challenging for SMEs, like most of the HCs. Therefore, it is crucial for companies seeking the right financial sources to learn the language of globalized financial markets, which is the language of transparency and understandability. For many HCs this will mean rethinking and reengineering their approach to management and implementation. In particular, their business models will at least require some of the "best practice" reporting appreciated by investors and often considered as unnecessary by SME's owners and managers. In this respect, three areas of focus could be recommended: formalization of strategic processes and execution, risk-management, and implementation of sound corporate reporting practices.

Today's best practices in corporate reporting include outlining the financial aspects of a company's performance in the language of the globally accepted standards (IFRS) in the wider context of the company's strategic processes, operating model, relationships with different groups of stakeholders and risk-management issues. This suggests a good command and regular use of sound management techniques.

The strategic processes of the HCs are often seen by external parties as something happening in a black box. Being prepared to tell the story of their own success in a way that is accepted and understood by investors could create a strong strategic advantage. Integrating strategic plans with risk-management issues and risk mitigation plans could contribute to assuring potential investors that the odds for success are high. Given the fact that the business model of a typical HC contains some very specific features, explaining how possible risks will be managed is of great importance in a fund-raising process.

Finally, preparation of financial statements in accordance with a widely accepted framework (e.g. IFRS) suggests that the presented information is reliable and explicitly indicates that the company that presents such statements fulfills the requirements of transparency expected from sound corporate governance.

References

Higgins, R. (2011). *Analysis for financial management*. McGraw Hill.

Hillier, D., Ross, S., Westerfield, R., Jaffe, J., & Jordan, B. (2010). *Corporate finance* (1st European ed.). McGraw Hill.

Simon, H. (1996). *Hidden champions – lessons from 500 of the world's best unknown companies*. McGraw Hill.

Simon, H. (2009). *Hidden champions of the 21st century – success strategies of unknown world market leaders*. Springer.

Hidden Champions of Albania

Vasilika Kume and Anisa Kume

Overview

Official name:	Republic of Albania
Type of government:	Parliamentary Democratic Republic
Population in 2011:	3.2 million habitants
Land area:	27,400 km^2

History

1913	Treaty of London of May 1913, mentions Albania as an independent state.
1941	Albania is occupied by Nazi Germany and Italy during World War II.
1944	At the end of the war, Albania becomes a Socialist Republic.
1990	The demise of communism. The country sets out on the road to a market economy.
1992	After the sweeping electoral victory of the Democratic Party, Sali Berisha becomes the first democratically elected president of Albania.
1997	The fall of pyramidal schemes causes a political and economic crisis.
2006	A Stabilization and Association Agreement (SAA) is signed with the EU in June.
2006	Albania joins other countries in the region and signs the Central European Free Trade Agreement (CEFTA).
2009	Albania becomes a NATO member country and applies for EU membership.

V. Kume (✉)
Department of management, Faculty of Economy, Tirana University, Tirana, Albania
e-mail: vasilika.kume@unitir.edu.al

A. Kume
Department of Budget Management, Ministry of Finance, Tirana, Albania

P. McKiernan and D. Purg (eds.), *Hidden Champions in CEE and Turkey*,
DOI 10.1007/978-3-642-40504-4_9, © Springer-Verlag Berlin Heidelberg 2013

1 Introduction: Context and History

Some 20 years after the demise of communism, Albania is finally on a solid road to economic development and economic integration. Situated in the south-western region of the Balkan Peninsula, Albania is predominantly mountainous but flat along its coastline with the Adriatic Sea. Geographically the country is at an advantage; it provides a bridge to Italy via the Adriatic Sea while being land-linked to Serbia, Montenegro, Macedonia and Greece.

When Dustin Hoffman, playing the part of Hollywood producer Stanley Moss, was asked in David Mamet's satirical movie "Wag the Dog" to create a media diversion for U.S. international problems, his first choice was to fabricate a fictional war in a country nobody knew anything about—Albania. When the film came out in 1997, the plot choice was effective, as indeed 40 years of dictatorial isolation under Enver Hoxha had made the southwest Balkan nation the most mysterious piece of land on the earth.

That veil of secrecy has been lifted since 1991 when a transition from restrictive communism to free market capitalism was set in motion. Slowly but surely Albania is beginning to project itself as a land of possibilities, opening its doors to foreign investments.

In November 1912, after 500 years under Turkish occupation, Albania was declared an independent country. Extraordinarily undeveloped, the Albania that emerged after World War I was home to less than a million people divided into two distinct classes: those who owned land and claimed semi feudal privileges, and those who did not. Through all the turmoil of the interwar years, Albania remained Europe's most economically backward nation without any serious industry. Oil represented the country's main extractable resource.

In the twentieth century, the main exports were petroleum, animal skins, cheese, livestock, and eggs. The prime imports included grain and other foodstuffs, metal products, and machinery.

The communist government that came into power after the Second World War took major steps to introduce a centrally planned economy. It nationalized all industries, transformed foreign trade into a government monopoly, brought almost all domestic trade under state control, and banned land sales and transfers. During this period, all kinds of industries and services were developed, mainly to preserve self-sufficiency. Bio-products, minerals and hand-made products were the core of Albanian international competitiveness and thus the country's main exports.

In the early 1990s, Albania ended communist rule and its centrally planned economy, and established a multiparty democracy set upon a market-driven economy. Over the last 2 decades Albania has experienced many of the problems of a transitioning economy trying to take off from a sticky ground, consisting of a poor population, predominantly engaged in small-scale agricultural activities and outdated production methods. Intensive macroeconomic restructuring with the IMF and The World Bank has tried to make Albania a more open economy.

For the time being, the take-off has been successful in relative terms. The Albanian economy is now growing at an annual rate of over 3 %. However, despite

Exhibit 1 Core economic indicators for Albania

	1999	2000	2001	2002	2003	2004	2005	2006	2007	2008	2009	2010	2011
GDP per capita (current US$)	1,118	1,200	1,329	1,440	1,819	2,389	2,666	2,893	3,377	4,076	3,796	3,701	4,030
GDP per capita growth (annual %)	10.33	7.33	6.81	2.49	5.12	5.28	4.93	4.51	5.46	7.30	2.93	3.13	2.63
Long-term unemployment (% of total unemployment)	n/a	n/a	n/a	n/a	n/a	n/a	n/a	n/a	n/a	n/a	n/a	n/a	n/a
Foreign direct investment, net inflows (% of GDP)	1.20	3.88	5.07	3.03	3.15	4.57	3.13	3.56	6.09	9.57	11.08	9.19	10.57
GDP (current $US m)	3,434	3,687	4,091	4,449	5,652	7,464	8,376	9,133	10,705	12,969	12,119	11,858	12,960
Exports of goods and services (current $US m)	594	705	839	909	1,165	1,608	1,866	2,291	3,080	3,827	3,443	3,845	4,380
Exports of goods and services (% of GDP)	17.29	19.14	20.52	20.42	20.62	21.54	22.27	25.09	28.78	29.51	28.41	32.43	33.80
Merchandise exports (current $US m)	351.12	257.93	307.19	339.55	447.95	605.40	658.00	798.00	1,077.58	1,354.83	1,090.60	1,544.61	1,956.38
Merchandise exports to high-income economies (% of total merchandise exports)	96.59	96.04	93.28	94.76	94.73	91.21	93.67	93.99	87.28	86.99	87.51	81.89	n/a
Merchandise exports to developing economies in Europe and Central Asia (% of total merchandise exports)	3.32	3.87	6.49	4.77	4.48	8.58	5.40	4.65	6.99	9.85	6.30	10.67	n/a
Ores and metals exports (% of merchandise exports)	3.92	3.71	2.91	3.43	4.10	5.52	24.14	37.86	13.56	32.63	9.56	12.83	11.90
Agricultural raw materials exports (% of merchandise exports)	4.47	5.91	5.52	6.51	5.13	4.46	13.89	13.08	3.38	7.65	2.98	2.39	2.57
Food exports (% of merchandise exports)	5.53	6.62	5.75	3.46	5.62	5.67	9.34	7.70	5.23	4.31	5.62	4.47	4.11
Fuel exports (% of merchandise exports)	1.98	1.85	1.45	2.01	0.94	2.63	8.66	13.69	7.45	21.81	11.60	17.97	21.19
	84.09	81.66	84.18	84.43	84.19	81.51	43.47	27.00	70.23	33.41	70.15	62.05	60.08

(continued)

Exhibit 1 (continued)

	1999	2000	2001	2002	2003	2004	2005	2006	2007	2008	2009	2010	2011
Manufactures exports (% of merchandise exports)													
High-technology exports (% of manufactured exports)	1.74	0.70	0.72	0.70	0.96	0.99	4.22	6.17	1.31	3.47	0.76	0.89	n/a

Source: World Bank (2013), http://data.worldbank.org/country

the wide range of institutional reforms, Albanian exports remain small, narrow, and undiversified. The main part of the exports consists of minerals, agricultural products, products based on bio raw materials, and bacon. The Albanian economy still suffers from a trade deficit, albeit a declining one. The country's main trading partners are Italy, Greece, Turkey, China, and Russia. More information about the Albanian economy is available in Exhibit 1.

The growth of the economy is induced mainly by Albanians working abroad and bringing money and experience back home. Many of the identified Albanian HC founders in fact started their careers abroad, and once they acquired sufficient finances, knowledge, and skills, they set up businesses at home. Albania's economic growth is also fuelled by some indigenous companies emerging from the agricultural field. Though none of them resembles the kind of companies to which a HC label might be attached, all of them are highly competitive internationally. Their competitive strengths have been developed internally solely by their founders. A quick summary of these companies can be found in Exhibit 2. All HCs from Albania can be categorized as regional leaders, and hence potential global HCs.

2 Four Case Studies

2.1 Venice Art Masks

Overview

Address:	Rr. VasilShanto, No.783, Shkoder, Albania.
Mob:	+355 672047291
Email:	edmondangoni@gmail.com

Company Information

Industry:	Carnival masks
Year of establishment:	1998
Sales revenue in 2010:	€1.55 million
Sales revenue in 2000:	€86,835
Average number of employees in 2010:	70
Brain(s) behind the company:	CEO and founder Edmond Angoni

2.1.1 Nature of Market Leadership

Venice Art Masks prepares carnival masks, according to the Venetian tradition. Its core market is Venice, from which it receives large orders for carnival celebrations. The company's masks are also sold at other traditional carnivals worldwide.

Exhibit 2 Hidden champions from Albania

Name	Short market leadership	Revenues 2010	Revenues 2000	Employees 2010
Venice Art	Venice Art Masks prepares carnival masks, according to venetian tradition. Venice Art Masks is the largest provider of traditional artistic masks. These venetial masks are characterized by high quality and above all are intended for a select clientele. Seventy per cent of production goes to venetia and 30 % is split between Las Vegas and Australia	1.3	0.9	70
Amla	AMLA is the unique formal company dealing with chestnuts in Albania. Company "AMLA" produces and exports 600 tons of chestnut per year, while the demand from international markets is up to 2,000 tons chestnuts per year. The company's products are exported to Italy, France and Switzerland, and there are requests by England and other countries of Western Europe	0.9	0.2	30
Xherdo	Essential oils (80 % of domestic market) and medicinal plants processing (20 % of domestic market). Germany, France, Italy, United States, and Greece are the main buyers. BIO products	3.1	0.3	120
Mare Adriatica	Refining, conservation and import–export of salted anchovy fillets. The largest producer of salted anchovies (BIO products) in Eastern Europe. Powerful competitors are Morocco and Southern Italy	1.8	0.3	150

Source: Authors of the chapter

2.1.2 Nature of Competitive Advantage

An advantage lies in the attractive price/value ratio: customers get a high-quality mask at a price lower than that of high-end competitors. The quality has been achieved through years of experience in producing masks, which has many production secrets. As a result, it is difficult for new entrants to be competitive in the market. A wide variety of products are hand-made, with low-cost labour. As it is very difficult for new entrants to create such a rich catalogue of high-quality handmade models, the company has erected an effective barrier.

2.1.3 Core Lessons Learned on the Path to Business Success

1. Try to create entry barriers for imitators, leveraging your years of experience and superior knowledge of the business relative to that of the newcomers.
2. Apply a wide range of innovative solutions to meet client expectations, particularly when it comes to design features—an extremely important factor of competitive advantage in the mask-making business.
3. Employees are the main assets. Invest in them, with an emphasis on training, trust, and respect.

2.1.4 Venice Art Masks: A Hidden Champion

Every year Shkodra (a city in the north of Albania) supplies the Venice carnival with 30,000 masks. Venice Art Masks is the largest provider of traditional artistic masks that accord with Venetian tradition. These are otherwise called Venetian masks, and are characterized by high quality, being intended for a select clientele.

The masks are not only popular at the Venice carnival celebrations, but are also exported to France, Greece, Japan, Canada and the USA. However, the company's main market is still Venice. Seventy per cent of the production goes to Venice and 25 % is split between Las Vegas and Australia. Though owning five shops in Venice, the company sells its products mainly through Venetian mask wholesalers, who cover not only the whole domestic market but also distribute worldwide.

The brain behind the company is Edmond Angoni, who emigrated to Italy in 1991. He was 34 years old and wandered between Pescara, Genoa and Padua working as a mason, dishwasher, and cook in restaurants for 10,000 liras per hour. In 1996 he had an opportunity to work in a factory in Venice producing carnival masks. At that point he had the idea to undertake the masks adventure. A self-taught artist in painting, he designed masks according to the orders of all the models and characters of "Comedia del Arte". He gathered people who gradually became professionals and created a laboratory, named after Arlecchino, 'the hero of carnivals'. "I did not have anything to loose when I entered this adventure. Investment was minimal and the only machinery, if we can call it that, was the casting mould," says Angoni.

Initially the company produced only the basis of masks (papier mâché), delivered to wholesalers in Venice. "We prepared only four or five models. The Italians were sceptical, but I was involved only in the first phase, producing the papier mâché and adding some simple decorations. The fine quality convinced the sceptics and the company started producing whole masks. The business grew. Today we prepare carnival masks according to the Venetian tradition. Everything is produced according to the typology of the Venetian mask. I am the largest provider of traditional artistic masks. The company counts 70 employers and produces 30,000 models. I am an important factor in the market of Venetian masks. There I have five specialized shops," says Angoni.

Since 1998, a lot of improvements have been achieved in mask production. As a result of experience and improved equipment, production time of a mask has been cut. Since a mask's uniqueness stems from handwork, we cannot talk about research and development as usual. Still the mask patterns keep changing. Each model differs from its predecessors. The way a mask looks also depends on customer requirements.

Over the years, Venice Arts has built a reputation for quality products and efficient response to client needs. It has adopted the mission statement: "Quality is our standard". The factory uses the labour-intensive mask production method (the papier mâché technique, with glue-moistened sheets of paper providing the mask's structure and its relief). The models range from simple, covering just the eyes, to the most extravagant full-face masks that are true works of art, incorporating various types of decoration, including painted scenes. "Everyone who knows something about masks, will notice that ours are pretty refined, containing all the details that the market requires".

In general, the masks market has been growing over the last 2 decades, but now the growth has stopped and the market has consolidated. Lately, Angoni has tried to "open the door" to carnivals in Shkodra, in order to revive this tradition in Albania. However, this carnival initiative has not evolved yet to full fruition. "It is too early to have a carnival market in Albania", Angoni says.

The competition in Venice is very strong. The market is filled with plastic masks made in China, sold in mixed shops. Slowly but steadily, Venice is losing the tradition of craft masks, therefore a Trust for the Production and Marketing of Carnival Masks in Venice has been established and Angoni is one of its most zealous associates.

The company's advantages lie in the experience gained from many years of production, as well as in trade secrets that every serious mask-maker has. As a result, it is difficult for new entrants to be competitive in the high-end of the mask market. Hand-made products are considered "luxury" goods—masks are sold at prices ranging from 20 to 150 euros. Besides, the company offers a rich catalogue of models, which is also very difficult for a new entrant in the market to create. Last but not least, the workshop has some famous customers from Hollywood. The company has provided masks for Stanley Kubrick's film *Eyes Wide Shut*. And many customers have told Mr. Angoni personally that Venice is the only place where they have seen what he makes with his hands. Hence, 2 decades of experience, trade secrets, hand-made production, and diversity of products, position the company above the emerging competition. Still, the main challenge the company faces is imitation of its masks by individual artisans who sell the hand-made copies at half price.

Angoni sees leadership as unique for each company. He says: "We just have to keep up the practical magic. I just want to be part of a group of people that work hard to make my ideas reality. At the same time they must be creative. If you are not, then you get neither art nor commerce." His uniqueness lies in the way he has brought his personal beliefs and philosophy into his management. Angoni's experiences of overcoming various difficulties, first as a refugee and later as an entrepreneur, formed the basis of some of the tenets of his personal philosophy—that people are the core of any success. "We consider each other family. The company's employees are one of the basic factors of success. It is their professionalism that makes my product unique. In 15 years no worker has left the workplace. They have grown together with the business."

Asked about expanding in the market, Mr. Angoni says: "We are advised to grow our market share and introduce the masks at low prices. But we would like to serve exclusively our customers. For that purpose, we have to be differentiated with focused products for a special segment of the market." And financing the business is not a problem anymore. "In the beginning, when we needed investors, we couldn't find any. Now we could get a lot, but we don't want to," he says.

The Venice Art factory teaches us that success has multi-faceted drivers, or as Mr. Angoni puts it: "Treating people with kindness and learning from them humbly are the most valuable human qualities, as well as being loyal to products and markets. Less is better if it does not undermine the standards".

2.2 AMLA

Overview

Address:	L. Dardania, (B. Curri), Tropojë, Albania
Tel:	0032/488875587
Mob:	+355 (0) 672892691
Email:	contact@amlashpk.com
Web:	http://www.amlashpk.com

Company Information

Industry:	Chestnuts processing and exporting
Year of establishment:	2006
Sales revenue in 2010:	€940,000
Sales revenue in 2006:	€220,000
Average number of employees in 2010:	30
Brain(s) behind the company:	CEO and founder Ramiz Jahaj

2.2.1 Nature of Market Leadership

European leader in the production and supply of chestnuts. The market is now expanding. The company is also building up a European market leadership position in half-processed chestnuts. The main competitors in the midterm are likely to be Greece and Turkey.

2.2.2 Nature of Competitive Advantage

The nature of the company's competitive advantage rests on the scarcity of chestnut forests relative to demand, on the quality of the product (chestnuts from Albania are considered of the highest quality), lower labour costs, and efficient organizational solutions for gathering and processing chestnuts.

2.2.3 Core Lessons Learned on the Path to Business Success

1. If you are in a labour intensive industry, such as harvesting chestnuts, make sure you create conditions for a good life for our fellow citizens, especially in disadvantaged areas. This will help create a climate of peace, security, and commitment.
2. In a country like Albania, which is under-developed in terms of services and product quality, there are many business opportunities but you need to have a

clear vision and the courage to pursue ambitious goals. Above all, you must offer something unique to all stakeholders, including your chestnut suppliers.

2.2.4 AMLA: Hidden Champion

AMLA is a unique 30-employee company dealing in chestnuts. Small businessmen bring the chestnuts into the factory directly from families. After a first manual selection, chestnuts are put into fresh water. They go through a calibration machine and then into a spin-drying and cleaning machine. They are finally dried with ventilators and put into bags. Chestnuts are sent to Italy in refrigerated trucks, and from there distributed to other global markets.

The Company was conceived in 1997, when Ramizi Jahaj decided to deal with trade, but it was only in 2006, after he connected with his son-in-law Ermali, that the chestnut business started. Both saw the opportunity in chestnuts, not only because of the vast chestnut forest in Tropoja, but also due to a large unemployed workforce there. In particular, in the early 2000s chestnut forests where transferred from state ownership to communal property. However, the communes let traditional owners take care of the forest and harvest them; communes are supposed to take care of the forest and control illegal cutting.

In Albania, chestnut trees are seen as having God-given qualities. In the view of most peasants, God planted the trees, around which different stories, myths and symbols have been created. Chestnuts from Tropoja are characterized by the highest secrecy and highest quality.

Enthusiastically, Ramizi and Ermali formulated the mission statement for their business: "Based on the natural opportunities offered by Tropoja chestnut forests, we will trade by mobilizing the free capacities of Tropoja human resources for the collection of chestnuts". Soon, they needed to resolve two major problems: (1) how much processing to perform after the chestnuts had been picked up, and (2), how and where to sell them.

Initially they agreed to sell only fresh chestnuts to Italy. Since the results of the first season were very encouraging, they decided to invest further into the processing of dried chestnuts and established a calibration, sterilization, and selection line.

This development of the company contributed largely to the increased exploitation of chestnuts in Albania. It made the sector better organized, and enabled value-adding activities. Nowadays, AMLA holds a market-leading position in Eastern Europe. It exports 600 tons of chestnuts per year to Italy, France and Switzerland, while the estimated demand is up to 2,000 tons. A new stream of requests is coming from England, Germany and other countries in Western Europe. The chestnut market is increasing at about 8 % a year. In short, the company's supply does not meet the demand for its products.

Domestically AMLA has no competition; however it faces some competition from other countries endowed with chestnut forests (Greece, Turkey, Kosovo, Serbia and Hungary). Nevertheless, due to increasing demand battles with competitors are not fierce. Moreover, the small distances between Albania and international markets gives the company an obvious advantage.

The production capacity of the chestnut forests in Albania is 10,000 tons per year, while the world's total annual production is about 1 million tons. The challenge of the company is to organize the chestnut gathering and production capacities well so as to better meet the rising demand. In 2007, the company certified 1,800 ha of chestnut forest with the European Office.[1] This was an important milestone for the company.

Over the last few years the production capacity of AMLA has been increasing by more than 50 % annually. Its main customers are European chestnut processing companies, which perform "deep" processing of fresh and dry chestnuts. AMLA is developing close cooperative relationships with them all. The high quality of the Tropoja chestnuts, on which the company's competitive advantage is built, can be sustained by improving the conservation methods. Chestnut quality depends a lot on their physical characteristics.

Lately, the technology for chestnut production has evolved considerably in three areas: forest management, harvesting, and processing. One of the main objectives of the owners is technological innovation and improvement of the manufacturing process in order to increase the economic efficiency of the company. Though the company currently employees only 30 full-time employees, there are about 2,000 other seasonal workers engaged in gathering chestnuts.

Mr. Jahaj takes a wide view on AMLA's business activities regarding sustainable rural development. He is aware that more than a third of Tropoja's population lives below the poverty line. The environmental conditions are particularly difficult, the climate is severe, and infrastructure is weak. Some villages are inaccessible for months during winter. Hence, Mr. Jahajfeels he needs to help the community: "Poor families are especially dependent on chestnuts. It is our duty as businessmen to contribute somehow to the development of our area. Ermali and I do not see the company just as a source of profit. I was born and raised in Tropoja. This city has always been one of the poorest and forgotten areas of Albania. These people have spent most of their lives tending the chestnut forests, and now they are their main source of income".

Mr. Jahajhas a high commitment to the sustainable management of the forests, as well as to raising the standards of living in this local community. Accordingly, he plans to invest in a chestnut processing factory in Tropoja, which will mark a turning point from chestnut gathering to chestnut processing, creating employment and income for the region. Next, he sees an opportunity to increase the forest area by 300 ha. A major constraint is the financing of these investments, specifically because Tropoja is considered a high risk area by the banking sector, which is not willing to provide favourable loans for AMLA's growth opportunities.

The main lesson from AMLA's success story is the possibility to establish synergies between business and society, because it is "important to create better conditions of life for our fellow citizens, especially in disadvantaged areas. This

[1] Bio Inspectia AG Bio Suisse Council Regulation EEC 2092/91.

will help create a climate of peace and security and will discourage emigration", Mr. Jahaj says. The developed world can learn a lot from companies like AMLA.

2.3 Xherdo

Overview

Address:	Str. Nikolla Lena, No.138, Tirana, Albania. Factory in Maminas, Durres
Tel./Fax:	+355 42265925
Mob:	+355 692060915
Email:	xherdo@yahoo.com Web: http://www.xherdo.biz

Company Information

Industry:	Essential oils and medicinal plants processing
Year of establishment:	1991
Sales revenue in 2010:	€3 million
Sales revenue in 2000:	€940,000
Average number of employees in 2010:	120
Brain(s) behind the company:	CEO and founderXhevitHysenaj

2.3.1 Nature of Market Leadership

A leading provider of essential oils and processed medicinal plants in Albania, with 80 % of market share in essential oils, and 20 % in processed medial plants. Germany, France, Italy, United States, and Greece are the main export countries in an ever-growing market.

2.3.2 Nature of Competitive Advantage

The company's competitive advantage is built on:

- Tradition: In this market, tradition is an important factor.
- Quality: The demand for quality products, satisfying global market requirements, is growing.
- Quantity: Currently, demand exceeds supply. Therefore, expanding capacity should be seen as an opportunity.
- Exclusive focus on bio products.

2.3.3 Core Lessons Learned on the Path to Business Success

1. Always look at the bright side and turn problems into motives to achieve goals.
2. The leadership must be authoritarian in principle, but flexible in the details.

2.3.4 XHERDO: Hidden Champion

Xherdo has been in the business of collecting and marketing medicinal herbs since 1991. In 1993, the first exports of medicinal plants to Germany were made. The venture was incorporated in 1995, and an investment was made in a steam distillery for essential oils for export to Austria. In 2007, Xherdo invested 1.5 million Euros in a 4,500 m^2 factory of medicinal herbs and essences (essential oils).

In parallel with that investment, a 2.5 ton order came from the United States, requesting thyme, oregano, and juniper essential oils. Nowadays, XHERDO's processing capacity is 3,000 tons of medicinal plants, of which around 1,500 tons are used for the production of natural oils and essences. The company employs 300–400 seasonal workers in summer and has sales over the four continents, in Austria, the United States, Canada, Italy, Germany, Spain, Switzerland, UK, Holland, Belgium, Morocco, and Malaysia. With an increase in the number of big clients, the company became less dependent on single customers. More precisely, 50 % of its revenues are now created by three big clients. Relations with clients are harmonious and very professional, just as the company enjoys very loyal customers.

Though the company prospers, the nature of the business is anything but easy according to Mr. Hysenaj, "To meet market demands we must have standards, to meet standards we should have the appropriate technology, to have the appropriate technology we need financing. As long as we lack expertise and knowledge, we cannot achieve competitive costs. Yet knowledge cannot be gained without experience and experience cannot be accumulated in just 20 years".

Albania was exporting herbs and essence seven in communist times. The country's nature is characterized by high biodiversity in terms of species, ecosystems, and habitats. About 30 % of all known European plant species are found in Albania, whereas 27 species and 150 subspecies are endemic. However, there has been considerable degradation of the environment and loss of biodiversity. After 1990, the production of medicinal plants and their essences declined, and so did exports. This was mainly the outcome of the urbanization process. Since 1995 there has been a resurgence of the market due to better organization of herb collection activities within the industry. Traders and processors began to oversee the whole production, from collection of plants to extraction of essences. Nowadays, the industry of aromatic and medical plants occupies the most important place in Albanian agriculture and food exports, accounting for 40–45 % of the volume of agricultural exports. The industry is developing and growing slowly, yet steadily. In the past 4 years, many Albanian companies have invested several million euros in this sector in advanced processing technology, storage, and marketing.

Xherdo is the strongest domestic company in the area of production of herbal essences, and the most advanced in terms of experience, technology, and marketing. However, competition, though scattered, cannot be underestimated. Currently Xherdo covers 20 % of the domestic market for medicinal plants and 80 % of the market for essences. Regional competition is tougher because it has longer experience in herb processing and extraction. In order to differentiate itself from the competition, the company is deliberately focused onbio-products. Mr. Hysenaj says: "Our products are very difficult to replace since they are 100 % natural unlike most of those sold across the world. China and India produce artificial essences and they are not competitive with natural products. In general, the industry of medicinal and aromatic plants must find again its place and be treated as an essential branch of the food industry. It must also meet world market standards. This is an exciting time for Xherdo".

To meet these world standards, the company and the owner-founder invested in organic products certification. In addition to four ordinary distilleries, Xherdo set up a new distillery solely for the production of aromatic essences. Mr. Hysenaj emphasizes that the processing of medicinal herbs and the export of products with added value require a work algorithm and a legitimate technological process. Unfamiliarity with these two points explains why many small businesses in Albania have launched themselves into this field but have run aground because they have not been able to obtain certification and have not reached the required standards.

Both the company and the owner-founder are heavily involved in many associations and fairs. First, Mr. Hysenaj is the chairman of the EPCA (Essence Production and Cultivators Association) for medical plants in Europe. In 2010 he won the International Quality Summit Awards in the platinum category in New York. The company is a member of IFEAT (International Federation of Trade of the Essences and Aromatics), IFOAM (International Federation of Organic Agricultural Movement) and AMAPSEEC (Association of Medical-Aromatic Herbs of Eastern European Countries). Savvy investments in attainment of certifications for bio-products, participation in international associations, trade fairs and conferences, have opened many lucrative business opportunities.

Currently, the company aims to expand into the processing of tea and spices, and processing (recycling) of technological wastes into shampoo and organic fertilizers. In particular, the company's goal is to distil aromatic waters (herbal distillates) for producing shampoos and bio-lotions, as well as to make full use of the wastes of processing. Not satisfied with the current achievements, Hysenaj sees the possibility of opening a cosmetics line.

Hysenaj is more than a businessman; he is an innovator. While developing his business, he realized that larger essential oil distilling facilities were needed to increase production, improve quality, and make the process more efficient and cost-effective. At the time, affordable distillers were of unacceptably low quality. Sustainability, efficiency, and economics made it clear to Hysenaj that the best thing to do was to adapt the technology himself in a way that would fit his company's needs as well as further empower Albania's agro-processing industry.

Xhevit Hysenaj was born in Tropoja, a district in the very north of Albania, in 1960. Once he completed his higher education in finance at the University of Tirana, Hysenaj began fighting a battle to secure the job he thought he deserved. He was always convinced that he had all the necessary skills to have a management position in public administration or an enterprise. "I always believed," says Hysenaj, "I had much more skills than those who commanded me. In addition, I have always liked to be my own boss".

Mr. Hysenaj is a risk-taker, but firm in his vision. Although he is in a simple business, it could not possibly have grown so quickly without technology. He shares this viewpoint: "I don't know any other way to lead than the way I do. Of course, I've never really thought about it as leadership. I just want to be part of a great group of people that work hard and are contented". Hysenaj acts quickly in his day-to-day management and decision making. He typically responds very fast to new items and requests because, as he says, "I know something else will happen and call for my attention". Next, Hysenaj believes members of a small organization must have a sense of identity, ownership, and purpose. In turn, these feelings foster commitment, conviction, innovation, and interest in long-term success. Last but not least, Hysenaj is very worried about the preservation of Albania's biodiversity. Due to industrialization, over-exploitation, inappropriate harvesting, grazing, and fire, the existence of many of the wild plants is threatened.

2.4 Mare Adriatic

Overview

Address:	Shelqet – VauiDejes, Shkoder, 1000 Albania
Tel:	+355 26622146
Fax:	+355 26622146
Mob:	+355 692095644
Email:	mare.adriatik@yahoo.it
Web:	http://www.mareadriatik.com

Company Information

Industry:	Fish processing
Year of establishment:	1995
Sales revenue in 2010:	€1.08 million
Sales revenue in 2000:	€260,000
Average number of employees in 2010:	150
Brain(s) behind the company:	CEO and founder Mark Babani

2.4.1 Nature of Market Leadership

Mare Adriatic is one of the largest Albanian companies that processes anchovies and sardines from the Adriatic Sea and exports them throughout Eastern Europe.

2.4.2 Nature of Competitive Advantage

Years of experience in the industry, low labour costs in Albania, and potentially an array of international clients for salted anchovy fillets are the main advantages of the company.

2.4.3 Core Lessons Learned on the Path to Business Success

1. If you are in the food-processing business, focus on the quality of the product and invest in processes that will allow you to certify your product as BIO-products.
2. Rely on self-financing.
3. Add value to your product along the industry value chain; appropriate a greater portion of the pie for yourself.

2.4.4 Mare Adriatic: A Hidden Champion

Mare Adriatic is the largest Albanian company processing anchovies and sardines from the Adriatic Sea; whose quality is gaining a reputation over the border and thus resulting in rising exports. Mare Adriatic was conceived in 1995 as a family business by Mark Babani after he had established a partnership with a Greek company in the business of refining and conserving different kinds of fish. Mr. Babani first acquired experience in importing and exporting conserved salt fish in nearby countries, and then tapped into the Albanian sea-food potential. Albania, with 362 km of coastline along the Adriatic and Ionian Sea, has a well-established fishing and sea-food processing industry. With increasing standards of living in Albania, the demand for more "luxury" sea-products has been increasing steadily and helped the company attain enough resources to start expanding into international markets. Small salted anchovy fillets are usually used in restaurants and at home as a principal plate or a starter. After building up a distribution network in international markets, the company re-oriented its sales from domestic to foreign markets where the prices, and hence the profit margins, are higher.

Nowadays, Mare Adriatic is the largest producer of salted anchovies in Eastern Europe. It processes (complying with all EU food-processing standards[2]) over 8 tons of anchovies per day and employs on average 140 people. They are hired from the region. It should be noted that the region in question is very poor and there are scarce employment opportunities. Workers hired by Mr. Babani are very grateful to him, and at the same time very faithful and diligent at work.

Powerful competitors are companies in Morocco and Southern Italy; however, Mare Adriatic is beating them with relatively better cost positions due to lower labour costs, and 20 years of experience in the business. Because the fish processing business is labour intensive, lower labour costs are a strong competitive strength. However, the barriers of entry remain relatively low, and thus the threat of novel rivalry is high. The company aims to position itself in the eyes of the customers as a bio company. Babani says,"We are very careful to maintain quality. Our products are 100 % bio."

Though in a labour intensive business, Mr. Babani has invested a lot in technological updates. Next, he is aware that processing the product increases its value

[2] The company has acquired the License of European Community 30/AL CEE to be allowed to export its products into these markets. It has also acquired the Certificate ISO 9001:2000 and HACCP.

about four times, compared with raw materials. The company is now building a new plant for vacuum-salted anchovy fillets, where the market demand is growing. Innovation is mainly focused on the more efficient technologies of fish-processing as well as in branding and novel ways of delivering value to customers. The company is in close relations with core wholesalers to better tap into their needs and interests.

The leadership story of Mark Babani is similar to personal success stories of other Albanian HCs. In 1991 he migrated to Sicily where he worked in a processing plant of anchovies and learnt the business. He then came back to his homeland in 1994 to open such a factory with the help of the owner of the Sicily plant. After 2 years, the Italian co-owner died, and Mark was left alone wondering what to do. "I felt thrown in the murky sea, where I had to swim".

Mark Babani is a sole shareholder. The finances of the company are firm, decision-making is highly centralized, the leadership style is democratic, and he treats his employees as company clients.

Conclusion

Almost all enterprises in Albania can be defined as micro and small. Most enterprises are in trade because barriers to entry are low. Only 20 % of enterprises are in industry, and more than half of all enterprises are concentrated in Tirana.

The adverse environment for small to medium enterprises is due in part to a series of crises which affected the country, starting with the collapse of pyramidal schemes in 1997. The biggest constraints to growth and formalization of SMEs are the failure to implement laws in a consistent and reliable manner, an undeveloped capital market, poor infrastructure, unresolved property rights, and an underdeveloped judiciary system.

In these conditions, it was difficult to identify the real HCs that fulfil the conditions of Simon's methodology. The examples mentioned above and a lot of other businesses operating in Albania, can be considered potential HCs.

Potential HCs in Albania started as micro or very small firms. They started with little capital, mostly from family savings. In the early stages they had problems with credit from banks; today they are self-financed companies and are even more aggressive about increasing their business.

So, the above mentioned companies are only potential HCs—they may become HCs if they strategically move into industry value chains where value-adding increases.

Most of the HCs have not taken very long to achieve the growth they have, although the paths they have taken are not all the same. For the four companies, it was their participation in international trade shows that opened the road for their products. Based on the opportunity they saw, they had very ambitious goals from the beginning.

All companies in the study chose to invest their energy in a business or sector where they felt they would have a comparative advantage (bio-products or artisanal work). They are all distinctive in their fields.

Up to this point the companies have been competing mainly on their cheap workforce; the way ahead seems to be integration into industry value chains. Currently all Albanian companies seem to be experimenting with industry value chains; most have considered moving into higher value luxury consumer goods (masks, fish, chestnuts, etc., where price mark-ups are high).

Another key success factor of these entrepreneurs has been their commitment to continuously update their technology. They consider the competitive advantages of their products to be quality, their bio origin, and competitive prices based on low-cost labour.

Other common features of these Hidden Champions are their close links with clients (they generally work with one to three major customers). They have a commitment to growth and continuously update their managerial knowledge. They are people-oriented and place an emphasis on teamwork.

In conclusion, we hope the above case studies will motivate other entrepreneurs with growth-potential enterprises to take courage and action for continuing their growth.

Reference

World Bank. (2013). *Data; countries and economies*. http://data.worldbank.org/country

Hidden Champions of Belarus

Pavel Daneyko and Pavel Golenchenko

Overview

Official name:	Republic of Belarus
Type of government:	Presidential Republic
Population in 2011:	9,481,200
Land area:	207,6 km^2

History

1915/1918	The present-day Belarusian territory is the scene of bloody battles between German and Russian forces.
1918	(March 3rd) The Treaty of Brest-Litovsk is signed, marking Russia's exit from World War One.
1919	The Soviet Socialist Republic of Byelorussia is set up.
1921/1928	The Riga Peace Treaty results in the partitioning of Belarus between the Belarusian Soviet Socialist Republic and Poland. New Economic Policy (NEP) introduced across Belarus.
1921/1930	The Polish part of Belarus is subjected to Polonization.
1922	The Belarusian SSR becomes a part of the Union of the Soviet Socialist Republics (USSR).
1936/1940	The Great Purge. More than 86,000 Belarusians suffer political oppression and over 28,000 are sentenced to death at the Kuropaty camp near Minsk.

P. Daneyko (✉)
IPM Business School, Minsk, Belarus
e-mail: daneyko@research.by

P. Golenchenko
Adizes, Institute Carpinteria, CA, USA

P. McKiernan and D. Purg (eds.), *Hidden Champions in CEE and Turkey*,
DOI 10.1007/978-3-642-40504-4_10, © Springer-Verlag Berlin Heidelberg 2013

1939	(September 17th) The Red Army moves into West Belarus.
1941	The start of the Great Patriotic War in Belarus. The Germans occupy all of present-day Belarus.
1945	(May) The Great Patriotic War of the Soviet peoples against the Nazi aggressors ends. Belarus becomes one of the founding members of the United Nations Organization.
1954	Belarus joins UNESCO.
1986	(April) Chernobyl Nuclear reactor disaster.
1990	Belarus declares its national sovereignty. The BSSR is formally renamed the Republic of Belarus.
1991	The USSR collapses; Belarus is proclaimed an independent republic.
1994	The first presidential elections are held and Alexander Lukashenko is elected president of Belarus.
1996	Belarusian Referendum results in the amendment of the constitution that strips parliament of key powers.
1997	Signing of the Union of Belarus and Russia.
2001	President Alexander Lukashenko is re-elected in elections described as undemocratic by Western observers.

1 Introduction: Context

With a population of nearly ten million, Belarus, was one of the most rapidly developing Soviet republics. During the 1970s and 1980s the value of fixed assets in the country grew 4.1 times, while the average growth index within the former USSR was 3.4. Between 1985 and 1989, the Belarusian economy grew at an average rate of 5.2 %, outstripped only by Moldova with its 5.7 %. This obviously increased the country's GDP per capita. At the time of restoration of Belarus's independence, the country's growth rates were only lower than those of Latvia, Estonia and Russia (Easterly 1995) (Exhibit 1).[1]

The structure of the Belarusian economy was predominantly industrial. In 1989, industry accounted for 49 % of the country's GDP. This was the second highest percentage in the Soviet Union after Armenia's (55 %). At the same time, industrial production was targeting external markets, both within and outside the socialist bloc. In 1990, the export share in Belarus's GDP was 50 %—higher than in the other Soviet republics. At that time, 5.5 % of exports went to countries outside the Council of Mutual Economic Assistance (CMEA) area of centrally planned economies (De Melo et al. 1997).

[1] *Source*: World Bank, http://data.worldbank.org/country

Exhibit 1 Belarus

	1999	2000	2001	2002	2003	2004	2005	2006	2007	2008	2009	2010	2011
GDP per capita (current $US)	1,210	1,273	1,239	1,471	1,805	2,356	3,090	3,798	4,667	6,328	5,176	5,818	5,820
GDP per capita growth (annual %)	3.75	6.12	5.09	5.52	7.60	12.01	9.99	10.49	8.99	11.40	1.16	7.89	5.49
Long-term unemployment (% of total unemployment)	n/a	n/a	n/a	n/a	n/a	n/a	n/a	n/a	n/a	n/a	n/a	n/a	n/a
Foreign direct investment, net inflows (% of GDP)	3.66	0.93	0.78	1.69	0.96	0.71	1.01	0.97	3.99	3.60	3.81	2.52	7.26
GDP (current $US m)	12,138.49	12,736.86	12,354.82	14,594.93	17,825.44	23,141.59	30,210.09	36,961.92	45,275.71	60,763.48	49,209.52	55,211.85	55,132.08
Exports of goods and services (current $US m)	7,186.39	8,815.28	8,246.55	9,286.39	11,614.41	15,709.98	18,064.97	22,199.81	27,592.40	37,027.90	24,865.45	29,966.73	48,456.64
Exports of goods and services (% of GDP)	59.20	69.21	66.75	63.63	65.16	67.89	59.80	60.06	60.94	60.94	50.53	54.28	87.89
Merchandise exports (current $US m)	5,909.00	7,326.00	7,451.00	8,020.90	9,945.60	13,773.70	15,979.00	19,734.00	24,275.30	32,570.80	21,304.20	25,283.50	40,409.20

(continued)

Exhibit 1 (continued)

	1999	2000	2001	2002	2003	2004	2005	2006	2007	2008	2009	2010	2011
Merchandise exports to high-income economies (% of total merchandise exports)	18.42	19.98	20.31	26.39	32.07	34.74	42.37	44.50	39.38	36.13	35.06	26.83	n/a
Merchandise exports to developing economies in Europe & Central Asia (% of total merchandise exports)	69.84	72.18	71.47	65.47	61.79	58.61	49.51	48.92	53.70	53.78	54.34	60.33	n/a
Ores and metals exports (% of merchandise exports)	0.75	0.75	0.89	1.33	0.98	0.73	0.53	0.49	0.66	0.50	0.60	0.71	0.61
Agricultural raw materials exports (% of merchandise exports)	3.49	3.62	3.37	3.71	3.58	3.09	2.51	1.86	1.92	1.29	1.55	2.04	1.52
Food exports (% of merchandise exports)	7.46	6.75	8.01	7.68	8.26	8.35	8.25	7.49	7.26	6.71	10.68	12.64	9.40

Fuel exports (% of merchandise exports)	9.06	19.79	17.60	20.08	21.86	26.74	34.63	38.18	34.92	37.31	37.27	27.94	36.17
Manufactures exports (% of merchandise exports)	74.95	65.12	67.75	63.28	62.00	58.04	52.08	50.40	53.32	52.47	47.81	53.16	49.27
High-technology exports (% of manufactured exports)	3.54	3.83	4.08	4.29	3.76	2.85	2.70	2.79	2.77	2.43	3.13	3.04	n/a

Source: World Bank (2013)

Short of natural resources, Belarus mainly served as an R&D and production centre for the Soviet Union, and the majority of industries manufactured military applications. Vehicle engineering, electronics, optics and precision mechanics, as well as the chemical industry, were the most important export sectors. Their creation was made possible by the development of technical sciences and education, as well as a large number of research organizations. A major source of relative competitive advantage was the human factor, both in terms of cheap labour and high level of engineering competencies.

Since the time of the Soviet Union's collapse, Belarus has not implemented any substantial economic or political reforms. Up until 2006, the Belarusian authorities considered the private sector a necessary evil. Private companies experienced continuous discrimination: state-controlled pricing, high taxes, constant check-ups by numerous controlling bodies, limited access to public and private resources, and more. Belarusian courts supported the state-owned enterprises. Privatization in Belarus was shut down in 1996. According to the EBRD estimates, private enterprises generate around 30 % of GDP.

The Customs Union between Belarus and Russia, created in 1996, ensured big market opportunities for Belarusian businesses. Besides, the Belarusian private sector has always been highly visible in Ukraine, the Baltic countries, and Poland.

For the last 4 years, Belarus has been undergoing market-based reforms to promote private sector growth. In the *Doing Business 2010* survey, conducted by the World Bank in 2009, Belarus rose from 115th position in 2007 to 58th, and is in the fourth place in terms of number of implemented reforms. Belarus is now developing a new economic model that offers fairly liberal conditions for the private sector, but still preserves its Soviet economic legacy in the form of state-owned enterprises enjoying certain advantages over private ones.

Obviously, there are certain factors that hobble the Hidden Champions (HC) of Belarus: a weak financial system, uncontrolled corruption, and bureaucracy. Still, the level of corruption is lower than in other CIS countries, and Belarus can boast an advanced educational system generating a knowledgeable workforce.

Because of the long-term discrimination against private business in Belarus, companies are naturally unwilling to advertise their activities and allow outsiders to access their data. This is evident from the fact that of all the companies that took part in the HC survey, only one has revealed its real name.

In a certain way, Belarusian anti-reform politics and the institutional environment of the 1990s favoured the emergence of HCs. Firstly, the privatization shutdown dramatically narrowed entrepreneurial opportunities in Belarus, compared with those of Russia and Ukraine. Therefore green field was the only way of doing business. Secondly, the domestic market was very unstable. Pricing was strictly regulated by the state and businesses were burdened with multiple administrative check-ups. Statutory acts were introduced post factum and the tax system was onerous. Currency crises regularly hit the country. Thirdly, the production volumes and research capabilities in Belarus were such that the local market was not able to fully accommodate them; consequently, export was a very logical recourse. And lastly, a shadowy company was the cherished goal of Belarusian entrepreneurs because it did not attract too much attention from governmental agencies trying to squeeze the last ruble out of private businesses.

Under these circumstances, two successful business models eventually emerged in Belarus. The first involves getting access to different rent sources through close cooperation with the state. The second model, adopted by our HCs, is export-oriented. A larger share of their production is sold abroad, which allows companies to protect themselves from regular currency crises, optimize their tax burden, and implement aggressive growth strategies.

Businesses applying the second model maintain a distant relationship with the state. Implementation of a tacit social agreement with the authorities (e.g. employment and export growth boost) reduces state pressure on business. Despite the success of these companies and their relative independence of the national economy, they prefer to stay under cover; hence they did not completely reveal their business logic and leadership styles during the interviews. Their success stories are not presented in such depth as those of others.

In general, HCs in Belarus are all strong leaders in the CIS region. These regional leaders can be divided into three major groups. The first includes companies manufacturing products that never existed in the former USSR, such as aluminum blinds. These businesses have been pursuing approximately similar development paths. Initially, they were engaged in importing and delivering their products to the markets of Russia, Ukraine and Belarus (RUB). Later they launched their own production in free economic zones. Production technologies were cheap and freely available in the market. Locally based manufacturing allowed a significant price reduction because of the absence of customs duties and availability of low-cost resources. According to our estimates, businesses made such profits that they were able to offer locally made products that were approximately 15 % cheaper than imports of similar quality. Such a difference in value would induce an aggressive penetration into the RUB market, allow tight control over the distribution system, and create a strong entry barrier for competitors.

The second and third groups of Belarusian HCs include companies that created their own products based on competencies that already existed in the country. In particular, the second group consists of companies that have used their expertise in launching engineering enterprises. The third group includes firms creating products based on R&D performed by Soviet research institutions. After studying the demand for locally manufactured products, they quickly turned to foreign markets.

The leaders of all companies described in the survey are engineers sharing many characteristics, such as a strong interest in production structure and processes, R&D, and a vivid entrepreneurial spirit.

Since only one company has given us permission to use its real name, we have assigned code names to the rest of them to protect their privacy.

Name	Market leadership definition	Revenues 2010 (in M€)	Revenues 2000 (in M€)	Average employees 2010
"Excavators"	First in production of truck excavators in CIS region	18	2	150
"Document scanners"	First in production of passport scanners (50 % of the CIS market and a significant market share in the European Union, Middle East and Africa)	10	2	170
"Radiation meters"	Global leader in production radiation measurement with main markets USA and EU	10.5	<1	160
"Shutters"	First in production of aluminum shutters (blinds) in RUB region	n.a.	n.a.	n.a.
STiM	First in production of two complementary products road marking machines and road marking paints in CIS region with market leadership also in Poland	20	0.8	700
"Lids"	First in production of aluminum lids in CIS region with strong presence in CEE region	50	3	1,436

Source: Authors of the chapter

2 Six Case Studies

2.1 "Lids": Hidden Champion

Every time you remove a lid from a bottle of finely distilled Russian or Ukrainian vodka, you are very likely to be holding a lid made in Belarus. "Lids" is a producer of different types of plastic and aluminum caps for alcoholic beverage containers. Literally, the name of the company means "alcohol packaging". The production technologies for "Lids" plastic seals are patented, and R&D has invented safe new types.

The company utilizes a hydro-seal system; there is no moving valve or ball inside to impede bottle refill. Tamper-proof evidence is accompanied by a typical click sound. The blades of the tamper-evident collar are fixed firmly onto the cap, preventing spillage into served food. "Lids" also manufactures aluminium pilfer-proof devices of different dimensions for sealing almost all types of glass bottles.

The company positions itself as the absolute leader in its field, offering a wide product portfolio and most advanced designs. "Lids" also enjoys the biggest revenue compared to its counterparts in the local market. The company's sales revenues have been growing rapidly—from 3 to 50 million euros for the last 10 years—, mainly because of the rapid development of the Russian and Ukrainian markets.

"Lids" has expanded its production capabilities and has managed to stand up against Chinese competitors by continuous product innovation. Its current export share is reaching 90 %. The company maintains close relationships with its customers, contributing to the development of their respective brands by offering exclusive cap designs to the most important clients.

"Lids" has two sources of competitive advantage: process and product engineering, plus an impeccable customer service system. The company spends 5 % of its revenue on R&D and currently holds 67 patents.

The leader of the company is a highly motivated person, always seeking new possibilities and eager to grow professionally. His passion for what he is doing, and how he is doing it, greatly contributes to the company's success.

As of today, the company is an indisputable leader in the CIS markets, chiefly Russia, Ukraine, Belarus, and Kazakhstan. It also has a strong presence in Central and Eastern Europe, and will continue to expand by focusing on the production of value-added seals. Western Europe also makes an attractive marketplace; therefore we can expect the company to look into that opportunity as well.

Three core lessons learned on the path to the business success are:

(1) Choose the niche where your product can be protected from competition by innovative solutions and advanced process technologies. At the same time, be a paranoiac, attacking your competitors and strengthening your position by constant introduction of innovations.
(2) Expand your portfolio to serve your clients better.
(3) Invest in your critical assets: personnel, products, and customer relationships.

2.2 "Blinds (Shutters)": Hidden Champion

Most aluminium shutters (blinds) used anywhere in the RUB region are produced by this company. Today, it is rapidly diversifying its portfolio, building a product line around its core competence in aluminium processing. Blinds remain the main product offered by the company in the RUB market.

The company was founded in 1992 by a young officer who resigned from the USSR army after the collapse of the Soviet Union. The company launch was triggered by the appearance of Latvian aluminium shutters in the USSR. The new product, totally unknown in the Soviet Union, quickly conquered the local market.

The company successfully promoted the product in Belarus, Ukraine, and Russia. In 1998, a company manufacturing shutter parts was established in a free economic zone. It enjoyed the advantage of exemption from customs duties as the production facilities were based in Belarus, and reduced costs (cheap aluminium, electricity, labour force, etc.), which allowed the company to set prices 15 % lower than those of its competitors. This ensured rapid expansion into the Russian, Ukrainian and Belarusian markets, where the company's share reaches 80 %. The company developed quickly and steadily.

In 2001, sales amounted to slightly more than 30,000 euros. Within 10 years, they grew more than tenfold. The product portfolio was widened significantly; the company started producing aluminium goods used in construction and building equipment, such as aluminium gates, aluminium structures for building windows, and more. These additional products ensure the company's biggest overall share of RUB markets; however the share is smaller in the case of aluminium shutters. Today, the company owns five factories, each manufacturing a specific product.

During the recent crisis, the company quickly won the European Union markets and is now successfully fighting local competitors and consistently increasing its share. One of the engines of the company's success is the unique characteristics of the founder's personality. Having a military engineering background, he has a solid knowledge of many technological processes involving aluminium. Additionally, he is successfully introducing up-to-date tools of business management, and has created an effective motivation system. Employees who have previously worked for the company are in high demand in the labour market in Belarus. At the same time, the employee turnover rate is only 3 %. Staff members are proud of their company, and very loyal.

"Lids" and "Blinds" teach us the same lessons: A good strategy to succeed as a niche market leader in the CIS region is *imitation:* copying of imports that are relatively simple from a technological perspective. Because of this simplicity, you can quickly acquire technological knowledge. Your products will differ little in quality from those of foreign competitors; still, they will be cheaper because of the lower customs duties, and labour and transportation costs.

2.3 "Excavators": Hidden Champion

The company was founded in 1997. It produces excavators on truck chassis, designed to carry out repair works on extended objects. The main buyers are various pipelines and companies serving power lines. "Excavators" is the main supplier of this type of machine in the CIS.

The company employs 150 people involved in design and production. Its corporate clients are in the oil and gas sectors, power transmission line service, and construction or repair works on remote sites. Annual sales reach 20 million euros. In 10 years, sales volumes grew nearly 10 times. To date, 75 % of the company's products are exported. The only competitor, based in Slovakia, is a part of a large corporation.

Five years ago the founder of "Excavators" left his post as CEO, but continues to play an active role in the company's management, although he has started a number of other niche business projects of his own. The company remains highly competitive because of its low prices, ensured by efficient production and design. Small companies find it difficult to penetrate the market, while its size is not attractive to big firms.

To sum up: If you are operating in a capital-intensive industry with a technologically complex product, foreign or big competition will have difficulty beating you as long as you maintain sufficient product quality. Still, this strategy will be successful only when certain conditions are met: your product should be exempted from customs duties and labour, raw material, and transport costs should be low. These advantages may not last forever. Therefore, as soon as they are gone, you should exit the business.

2.4 STiM

Overview

Address:	111 Katin Bor, 224025 Brest, Belarus
Tel:	+375162299083
Email:	contact@stim.by
Web:	http://stimby.net

Company Information

Industry:	Manufacturing of machinery and equipment
Year of establishment:	1997
Sales revenue in 2010:	€5 million (from machines), €20 million (from paints)
Sales revenue in 2000:	€800,000 million
Average number of employees in 2010:	700
Brain(s) behind the company:	The CEO, the deputy director, the finance director

2.4.1 Nature of Market Leadership

The company offers two types of products: road-marking application machines and marking paints, with market shares for machines as follows: CIS—80 %, Poland—35 %, Baltics—30 %, Belarus—60 %; and the following market shares for paints: CIS—40 %, Baltics—30 %, Poland—40 %, Belarus—60 %. The company is an indisputable leader in both segments as it has the largest turnover in the CIS region.

2.4.2 Nature of Competitive Advantage

The owner of the company believes that STiM's success stems from the fact that the company produces both paints and machines: "We understand how the machine works with paint and how the paint behaves". The company positions itself as a technical expert in road marking, and organizes seminars on the subject for the heads of public utilities and community service companies. Ensuring high-quality standards and relatively low prices, the company successfully competes with Western European firms.

2.4.3 Core Lessons Learned on the Path to Business Success

1. Endorse innovations, invest in new technologies, and be one step ahead of your competitors.
2. Study your market segment constantly and tirelessly.
3. Do not underestimate the importance of motivation for your staff. Reward them for their excellent performance.
4. Know your product and ensure its superb quality at all times.

2.4.4 STiM: Hidden Champion

STiM (Construction Machinery and Equipment) is as old as "Excavators". Most of the roads in RUB are marked by the machines and paints produced by STiM. This family-owned company was founded in 1997. It produces two complementary products: road-marking machines and road-marking paints. The company's turnover in 2010 amounted to approximately 25 million euros, of which about 5 million were earned through sales of road-marking machines. In 10 years, turnover has increased more than 20 times. The company dominates the machine production market in the CIS and Baltic States, and holds a leading share in the Polish market.

The company pays close attention to the quality of its products. Each machine undergoes a full inspection, run-in period, and test cycle at the vendor's facilities prior to its sale. Vehicle operators are rigorously trained.

To sum up: "Lids", "Blinds", "Excavators" and STiM teach us similar lessons: Specialize in a narrow product group that is profitable but represents only a side product for big global MNCs. They will not pay much attention to that product category. If you are operating in a capital-intensive industry with a technologically complex product, large foreign or domestic competition will have difficulty beating you as long as you maintain the quality of the products at a sufficient level, and have lower material, labour, and transportation costs, and lower taxation. The alternative is to make large investments in R&D capabilities.

2.4.5 "Radiation Meters": Hidden Champion

If you pass by a US police officer, there is a high chance that you will see a tiny radiation measurement gadget, manufactured by "Radiation Meters", attached to his belt. The company also produces highly sensitive radiation meters.

The company was founded in 1992 by an engineer of a Soviet research institute. Several years ago, the company founder died and the firm was inherited by his daughter, a very successful architect. Today the family shares the company ownership with the staff, and actively uses this co-ownership as a strong motivating factor for key employees.

The company produces very small and sensitive devices for measuring radiation, and promotes itself as a technology leader in the market. After the Chernobyl disaster, much attention has been paid to radiation problems; therefore the company has been most active in the Belarusian market. However, to date 99 % of its products are intended for export. The most attractive markets for the company are those of the US and the EU. More than 10 % of the sales revenues are used for R&D.

The company owns nine patents, and several are currently being registered. The company remains highly competitive because of its attractive quality-price ratio, as well as the flexibility of its customer service. This flexibility is ensured by the close cooperation of the company's software and hardware developers.

2.4.6 "Document Scanners": Hidden Champion

When crossing the border and presenting your passport to the border police, you can expect that the officers will use scanning devices produced by this company. The company was founded by two engineers from a Soviet research institute in 1992. It was the year of reforms in the former Soviet Union. Banks had just begun to sell foreign currency to the public. This caused an explosive demand for devices determining the authenticity of the currency. This company started producing such detectors.

The founders themselves designed and assembled the first devices. Having mastered a wide range of gadgets for determining the authenticity of currency, the company switched to the development of passport scanners. Simultaneously, a global electronic passport database was created. Today the company exports 80 % of its products. According to its management, it holds more than 50 % of the CIS market and a significant market share in the European Union, Middle East, and Africa.

The company is successful not only because it offers lower prices. The managers believe that the leading technology of their products is well ensured; the firm owns 31 patents. The company is also extremely flexible in its customer service policy. Its executives believe that the success of "Document Scanners" also stems from the close collaboration of software and hardware developers. They also say, "It is only us who own and produce the equipment for creating passport database and scanning devices". The company is owned by its first shareholders who are still actively involved in developing new products.

"Radiation Meters" and "Document Scanners" teach us the same lesson: Keep an open mind so that you can see opportunities in the problems that you may encounter. If dealing with the Chernobyl accident or money counterfeiting, as long as you possess entrepreneurship skills and expert knowledge, you can try to come up with a solution. Soon you might be knowledgeable and powerful enough to offer these solutions to the whole world.

Conclusion

Belarusian HCs are perhaps more dissimilar than similar to Simon's HCs. In terms of similarities, they are led by strong, visionary, passionate leaders, who carry strong expert knowledge and are entrepreneurial in character. The majority of the leaders of Belarusian HCs exhibit entrepreneurial drive. Those of the 1990s may have been influenced to a significant extent by institutional circumstances, including deliberate state discrimination against the private sector through state-controlled pricing, high taxes, constant check-ups by numerous controlling bodies, and limited access to public and private resources.

In general, HCs in Belarus manufacture technologically complex, as well as simple, products. Their strategic behavior and level of resemblance to Simon's HCs depend to a large extent on their products.

The technologically simple products—those of "Lids" and "Blinds"—did not follow a strategy strictly defined by a narrow product focus and growth through internationalization. Both started their success stories by imitating foreign products and leveraging three local advantages: lower labour costs, favourable taxation, and lower transportation costs. Their strategy can be described as use of the favourable tax regime of the CIS region, and growth through product differentiation. Usually, the new product categories added to the portfolio are technologically simple, but well aligned with the needs and demands of their target customers.

Those that have the technology and knowledge that are necessary to produce more complex products are more likely to follow a classical HC strategy. First they focus narrowly on a specific product and customer group; then they expand abroad. They usually focus on exotic products—those that big MNCs might also offer but view as minor to their business. In this way they avoid tough battles for market share in the region. This international strategy has proved to work well for the HCs. However, they are so narrowly specialized that even growth through internationalization may be limited. The question is what they will do next to create growth.

References

De Melo, M., Denizer, C., Gelb, A., & Tenev, S. (1997). *Circumstance and choice: The role of initial conditions and policies in transition economies* (World Bank Policy Research Working Paper 1866).

Easterly, W., & Fischer, S. (1995). The soviet economic decline. *World Bank Economic Review, 9* (3), 71–341.

World Bank. (2013). *Data; countries and economies.* http://data.worldbank.org/country

Hidden Champions of Bosnia and Herzegovina

Nenad Brkić and Denis Berberović

Overview

Official name:	Bosnia and Herzegovina
Type of government:	Parliamentary Democracy
Population in 2011:	3,752,228
Land area:	51,000 km^2

History

1918 Bosnia and Herzegovina joins the Kingdom of Serbs, Croats and Slovenes.
1929 The kingdom becomes known as Kingdom of Yugoslavia.
1941 Bosnia and Herzegovina becomes a part of the Independent State of Croatia, a country supportive to Hitler with a fascist puppet government.
1945 After a bitter resistance campaign by partisans under Tito, Bosnia and Herzegovina becomes one of the six constituent republics of the Socialist Federative Republic of Yugoslavia.
1980 Tito dies. The slow disintegration of Yugoslavia begins as individual republics assert their desire for independence.
1992 (March) Bosnia and Herzegovina declares its independence from Yugoslavia. 2 months later, Yugoslav aggression on Bosnia and Herzegovina starts. The term "ethnic cleansing" becomes known worldwide as Bosnian Serbs begin to oust non-Serbs from parts of Bosnia and Herzegovina. This is done with political, financial, military and human

N. Brkić • D. Berberović (✉)
Department of Marketing, School of Economics and Business, University of Sarajevo, Sarajevo, Bosnia and Herzegovina
e-mail: denis.berberovic@efsa.unsa.ba

P. McKiernan and D. Purg (eds.), *Hidden Champions in CEE and Turkey*, DOI 10.1007/978-3-642-40504-4_11, © Springer-Verlag Berlin Heidelberg 2013

support from Serbia and Montenegro. The aggression is finalized by the genocide of Bosnian Muslims in Srebrenica.

1995 The war ends, leaving a devastated country. Bosnia and Herzegovina suffered the greatest human and material casualties in the Balkan wars.

2002 Bosnia and Herzegovina becomes a member of the Council of Europe.

2008 Bosnia and Herzegovina signs the Stability and Accession Agreement with the EU.

2009 Bosnia and Herzegovina enters a visa-free regime with the EU.

1 Introduction: Context

Bosnia and Herzegovina (B&H) is situated in Southeastern Europe, on the western side of the Balkan Peninsula. It was a member state of Yugoslavia until it gained independence in 1992.

Yugoslavia was established in 1929, as a kingdom of Croats, Serbs and Slovenes. It was the fulfilment of a centuries-old dream of uniting Slavic nations in Southern Europe.[1] The idea had its promoters not only in all Slavic nations in the Balkans, but also in major European political circles. In 1945 the kingdom was abolished, and after certain territorial changes, the communist state of Yugoslavia was created.

The kingdom of Yugoslavia encompassed B&H, although the latter's politicians did not have any political impact in the country. B&H had already had a long experience being ruled from outside. After four centuries of Ottoman rule, the country was taken over by the Austrian Crown for almost 60 years.

Prior to the Second World War, B&H was an agricultural country with only a few attempts by the Austrian rulers to industrialize it. Industrialization came with the communist rule. The communists further introduced a planned economy, which means that each member-state economy was given a distinct role. As B&H is rich in resources, the country served mainly as a resource base to most other states in Yugoslavia (Serbia, Slovenia, and Croatia). Resources were mainly exported to other member countries; and in exchange, final products were exported from them back to B&H.

Another characteristic of Bosnia's economy has been its orientation towards the military industry. Because B&H is mainly mountainous and in the central part of former Yugoslavia, the communist government situated all its military factories in barely reachable territory. Because of this, and the fact that B&H had never really managed its own economy, advanced industries did not get an opportunity to develop.

The size of the country is 51,000 km^2. According to latest estimates, the country is inhabited by 3,752 million people. B&H is politically decentralized, with two

[1] The name Yugoslavia means "State of South Slaves" in the Slavic languages.

Exhibit 1 Core economic indicators

	1999	2000	2001	2002	2003	2004	2005	2006	2007	2008	2009	2010	2011
GDP per capita (current US$)	1,301.07	1,490.64	1,533.73	1,761.50	2,212.70	2,650.59	2,895.54	3,279.07	4,043.52	4,913.22	4,534.06	4,427.35	4,820.67
GDP per capita growth (annual %)	5.91	2.86	2.88	4.53	3.81	6.14	5.01	6.18	6.91	5.56	−2.74	1.00	1.93
Long-term unemployment (% of total unemployment)	n/a	n/a	n/a	n/a	n/a	n/a	n/a	n/a	n/a	n/a	n/a	n/a	n/a
Foreign direct investment, net inflows (% of GDP)	3.77	2.65	2.06	4.03	4.56	7.08	5.70	6.82	11.81	5.42	0.81	1.98	2.10
GDP (current $US mil)	4,685.73	4,685.73	4,685.73	4,685.73	4,685.73	4,685.73	4,685.73	4,685.73	4,685.73	4,685.73	4,685.73	4,685.73	4,685.73
Exports of goods and services (current US$ mil)	1,295.32	1,579.69	1,632.28	1,619.40	2,535.23	3,231.70	3,519.20	3,519.20	3,519.20	3,519.20	3,519.20	3,519.20	3,519.20
Exports of goods and services (% of GDP)	27.64	28.69	28.39	24.35	30.29	32.24	32.14	36.66	43.33	41.06	31.67	35.78	42.28
Merchandise exports (current $US mil)	751.00	1,069.00	1,032.00	1,005.29	1,340.00	1,792.67	2,400.00	3,323.00	4,151.97	5,021.08	3,953.92	4,803.11	5,850.62
Merchandise exports to high-income economies (% of total merchandise exports)	91.72	90.28	94.78	94.93	96.78	94.24	90.73	90.38	93.31	93.30	92.27	90.34	n/a
Merchandise exports to developing economies in Europe & Central Asia (% of total merchandise exports)	5.55	6.57	2.94	2.60	2.11	4.28	4.31	5.18	4.75	5.30	5.81	6.51	n/a
Ores and metals exports (% of merchandise exports)	n/a	n/a	n/a	n/a	14.14	13.02	17.85	16.64	15.31	12.91	9.49	12.23	12.89

(continued)

Exhibit 1 (continued)

	1999	2000	2001	2002	2003	2004	2005	2006	2007	2008	2009	2010	2011
Agricultural raw materials exports (% of merchandise exports)	n/a	n/a	n/a	n/a	9.97	11.55	9.76	8.31	8.17	6.81	6.15	5.89	6.17
Food exports (% of merchandise exports)	n/a	n/a	n/a	n/a	3.55	4.38	5.77	4.93	5.39	5.97	7.69	7.32	6.81
Fuel exports (% of merchandise exports)	n/a	n/a	n/a	n/a	4.48	7.80	8.77	8.03	7.73	9.65	13.11	14.96	13.83
Manufacturing exports (% of merchandise exports)	n/a	n/a	n/a	n/a	41.19	47.19	57.56	62.06	63.32	64.00	60.74	56.98	57.72
High-technology exports (% of manufactured exports)	n/a	n/a	n/a	n/a	1.76	1.88	2.04	2.17	2.14	4.14	3.28	2.58	n/a

Source: World Bank (2013)

entities and one district. One of the entities is further decentralized into ten cantons. In spite of the 2009 world recession, the country's export figures of B&H have been steadily rising, doubling from 2003 to 2010. Analyses reveal that an average Bosnian company exports much more than an average Albanian company (Agency for Statistics of Bosnia and Herzegovina 2011). Major economic indicators are shown in Exhibit 1.

Today, Bosnia's economy is struggling with major issues such as recovery from the war, transition from planned to market economy, corruption, and an ineffective legal system.

After years of expansion and relatively high growth rates, B&H experienced economic contraction due to the 2009 world recession. The economy has not recovered since. The consumption drop caused a decrease in employment rates, which led to further erosion of consumption. Fiscal prudency did not allow a high debt rise. A significant increase in exports and a decrease in imports helped to lower the current account deficit and the GDP rate decrease. The economy of B&H has a high degree of openness, placing the country in a group of small open economies. B&H is struggling with low competitiveness and attractiveness to foreign investments, which are seen together as a major growth generator, since domestic investments are rare. Cuts to high public spending and increased domestic investment may be additional stimuli for economic growth, but this is not likely to happen before a constitutional, i.e. organizational, change of the state. Currently, B&H is trying to recover by stimulating the increase of exports. Credit for the business sector has expanded due to a drop in interest rates. However, this has not had a significant impact on investments (Central Bank of Bosnia and Herzegovina 2011a).

Constitutional rearrangement and attempts to deal with other issues—demographic (population decrease) or ecological—are on hold due to the lack of political will to make the state more efficient. After the elections in 2010 the new government is expected to solve the strategic problems that the country faces. B&H's EU accession is expected to accelerate only when these political issues are settled (Central Bank of Bosnia and Herzegovina 2011b).

Up to this point, there has been no research on Hidden Champions (HCs) in B&H. The following section includes five studies of HCs situated in different regions of the country, mostly in rural areas. Some of them are regional leaders and some are start-up companies with an emerging competitive advantage (Exhibit 2).

Exhibit 2 Hidden champions from Bosnia and Herzegovina

Name	Short market leadership description	Revenues 2010 (€m)	Revenues 2000 (€m)	Employees 2010
Plastex	Flexible packaging, klip-klap, region, corporate clients	1.6	0.77	45
Lumen	Candles, regional, corporate, and individual clients	4	1.5	51
Alma Ras	Underwear, regional, corporate, and individual clients	5.5	0.3	430
Feal	Leader in aluminium production and processing in South-Eastern Europe	65	10	450
IM Group	Bluetooth device, global corporate clients	n/a	n/a	12

Source: Authors of the chapter

2 Five Case Studies

2.1 Plastex Ltd.

Overview

Address: Gračaničkih gazija bb, 75320 Gračanica, Bosnia and Herzegovina
Tel: +387 (0)35704890
Email: plastex@plastex.ba
Web: http://www.plastex.ba

Company Information

Industry:	Production, trade and services of flexible packaging
Year of establishment:	1986
Sales revenue in 2010:	€1.6 million
Sales revenue in 2000:	€770,000
Average number of employees in 2010:	45
Brain(s) behind the company:	Founder and owner Sead Terzić

2.1.1 Nature of Market Leadership

Plastex holds a leading position in the Central and Eastern Europe market with a product called *klip-klap*; a promotional requisite used in sports, music, political, humanitarian or any other kind of event where promotional products are needed.

2.1.2 Nature of Competitive Advantage

Plastex has a system of continuous quality improvement (Eisenhardt and Galunic 1999). This does not apply to core products only, but to the whole offer as such. It means that product prices, distribution, information systems, communication, general cooperation with suppliers, and supportive services to their clients, are being constantly improved.

2.1.3 Core Lessons Learned on the Path to Success

If you have a technically simple product with a low unit price, but with a similar quality to products from distant, low-cost labour regions like China, you can outperform competitors due to greater proximity to the market and lower transportation costs. However, this is not the only necessary condition. Three other issues are important:

1. Owner's constant intention to realize the vision of success.
2. Continuous desire for improvement and innovation.
3. Establishing and maintaining high-rated relations with customers.

2.1.4 Plastex Ltd: Hidden Champion

Plastex was established in 1986. The company is situated in Gračanica, a town in northern B&H. This area has been known for years for its entrepreneurial inhabitants. The number of Plastex employees has grown steadily over the years, reaching a total of 45 at the end of 2010. The company's turnover has grown from €0.77 million to €1.6 million in the last 10 years. Plastex started its exporting activities in 2006 and generated approximately 3 % of its sales revenue from activities in Southeast Europe. However, its export sales revenue decreased to 1 % in 2009. The company board gives two explanations for this: First, the recent recession, which heavily hit its markets abroad; and, second, the political environment in B&H, which is not supportive to private business activities.

Plastex holds a leading position in CEE klip-klap sales. It is still developing a demand for this product, as it was previously unknown to the market. The company is doing well as the flexible packaging industry is in its growth stage.

The main industry competitors are from within B&H. However, there is no other company that produces klip-klap. According to Mrs. Hodžić, daughter of the owner and chief financial officer (CFO), the closest known competitor is based in China. A major threat from competitors is the fact that their product ranges are very similar. This is because of the similarity in technologies they use, making it difficult for companies to diversify the products they have on offer. Some competitors target the same clients, which is why Plastex focuses more on market niches.

Three major clients generate approximately 20 % of Plastex's total revenue. This can be explained by the corporate 90/10 rule. The company has focused on small to medium corporate clients who create 80 % of the company's revenue. Plastex has a client retention rate of 90 %, and refuses to do business with the remaining 10 % as they are viewed as "bad clients". The reason for avoiding business with big companies is their "business arrogance", as Mrs. Hodžić put it. These companies are big spenders and big clients, but being aware of their significance, their payments are irregular and they often seek compensation from Plastex. Hence, in order to stay liquid, Plastex focuses on more accountable clients—i.e., the SMEs.

Leadership is seen as the company's most important competence. The CEO (and owner) is a strong and decisive leader with a clear vision. This is what Mrs. Hodžić says about her father, and how he came up with the idea to start a business: "Ever since he was a child working on his family's estate, he dreamt of having his own business, being his own boss. He didn't want to work for his dad or somebody else. This is what drove him in starting his own business and looking after it the whole time. The turning point was when I was a child. I asked him to buy me something but he couldn't do it and that made him feel bad. It was then that he decided that the moment was right to start his own business." He does not lack in entrepreneurial intuition or continuity in leading. Finances do not represent a restraint on further development. Employees are satisfied and highly motivated. CRM is believed to be one of the key competencies because the company has loyal customers who often express their high satisfaction with the excellent relations they have with Plastex.

B&H is a collectivistic society (Cateora and Graham 2005). Among other things this means that interpersonal relations are of great importance. This is no different in business interactions, which is why Plastex puts great emphasis on developing good interpersonal relations with its business partners. Showing an understanding for partners' problems, and even helping in situations where it is possible, results in strengthening connections and client satisfaction.

The main product that defines Plastex as a HC is klip-klap. This product is the result of an innovative process. Interestingly, this innovation has not sought high investment; rather, it originated by accident, which is in line with Kirzner's theory of entrepreneurship. This is not a surprise, as the company invests only 2 % of its revenue in innovation. The main driver of the innovation process is customers' needs in conjunction with internal technological competencies, although the latter has dominated the process. The reason for this is the fact that klip-klap was not known in B&H before it was produced by Plastex. Plastex finances its R&D from its revenues. The average ROI is 20 %. However, there is no clear selection process for innovative ideas.

Mrs. Hodžić finds profits, cost savings, and corporate growth satisfactory. Having in mind the problems the recession brought with it, the CFO still believes that Plastex has done well in comparison to the rest of the industry. She is optimistic about the future and believes that the industry is becoming increasingly attractive to new entrants. Plastex's ROI has been between 15 and 20 % over the last 10 years. The company has no financial difficulties and finances do not pose a growth obstacle.

2.2 Lumen Ltd.

Overview

Address:	Dubrava bb, 88344 Drinovci, Bosnia and Herzegovina
Tel:	+387 39672770
Email:	info@lumen.ba
Web:	http://www.lumen.ba

Company Information

Industry:	Production and trade of candles and decoration articles
Year of establishment:	1986
Sales revenue in 2010:	€4.0 million
Sales revenue in 2000:	€1.4 million
Average number of employees in 2010:	51
Brain(s) behind the company:	Founder and owner Miro Vekić

2.2.1 Nature of Market Leadership

Lumen operates mainly in the candle market. Although this company manufactures different objects for decoration, its star product is the candle—mainly for religious, romantic or catering purposes. Lumen considers itself to be a market leader on the basis of both revenues and sales volume.

2.2.2 Nature of Competitive Advantage

Strong leadership and entrepreneurial vision are the most important competencies (Fine et al. 2002). Furthermore, strongly motivated staff and the overall local image of the company play vital roles. Financial strength, know-how gained from the world's best candle producers, and IKEA, were also mentioned as essential to Lumen's success.

2.2.3 Core Lessons Learned on the Path to Success

1. Even in a simple "candle" business, do not discount the role of educated employees. Thus, educate your employees continuously.
2. Be in a constant search of how you can improve the production process. Even small improvements could make a huge difference.
3. Many well-functioning business and product solutions have been already discovered by your partners. Gain that know-how from your corporate clients and suppliers.
4. Use big globally renowned clients (like IKEA) to attract new clients.

2.2.4 Lumen Ltd: Hidden Champion

Lumen is a candle-producing company situated in the southern part of Bosnia and Herzegovina. Mr. Miro Vekić, the owner and CEO of the company, started his entrepreneurship in 1986. He began his private business by buying a 20-year old candle producing machine; he set up the machine in his private garage and started manufacturing. Today the company has 51 employees. Its revenues have increased from €1.5 million to €4 million in the last 10 years. During the same period, the company generated 15 % of its revenues abroad, which have increased to a current 30 %. While this research was being undertaken, Lumen was involved in negotiations for a business arrangement which, if concluded, would increase the export revenues to 45 %. Within B&H the company has its own sales representatives. Lumen is one of the few worldwide candle producers for IKEA. As for the region, Lumen exports to independent retailers.

Lumen operates mainly in the candle market. When you go to a restaurant or buy a set of elegant candles to prepare for a romantic dinner, you will come across candles produced by Lumen. Although this company manufactures different decorative objects, its star product is the candle—for religious, romantic, or catering purposes. Lumen considers itself the market leader on the basis of both revenue and volume of sales.

Mr. Vekić has identified three major competitors; Meteor and Iskra Zelina from Croatia, and Ilirija from Slovenia. These companies have traditions much longer than Lumen's, and they are part of bigger production entities. The only similarities that Lumen shares with its competitors are the products they offer and the structure of ownership. And it is the latter that Mr. Vekić sees as Lumen's advantage in relation to its competitors. He believes that the recent privatization processes in Slovenia and Croatia has weakened the competing companies. Furthermore, despite the privatization, his view is that these companies did not experience a significant orientation towards the market.

According to Mr. Vekić, product quality, price, efficiency, distribution, and cooperation with the distributors are of high relevance to his customers. He further believes that the existence of patents and pre-sales service is not important to his clients. This seems plausible, taking into consideration the simplicity of the product in focus.

A strong leadership and entrepreneurial vision are the company's most important competencies. Furthermore, its strongly motivated employees and overall image, especially within the local community, are its major strengths. Financial strength, the know-how gained from the world's best candle producers, and IKEA, were also mentioned as essential to Lumen's success. Continuous improvement of the production process, and both the widening and the deepening of the product mix, leads to the conclusion that Lumen does innovate consistently.

When it comes to candles, world standards are very strict—each candle has a certain amount of time to burn; it has to have a certain weight; the wax must not drip; the candle should not smoke, and so forth. All these quality standards have helped Lumen not only to beat its regional competition but to foster market evolution and boost demand. These quality standards have made Lumen famous in the region.

Lumen invests 10 % of its revenue in innovation. But the company does not invest as intensively in widening the product mix as it does in deepening it. And without continuous technological development and human resources advancement through educational programmes (given by Lumen's suppliers and consultants), product evolvement would not be possible. The innovation process is generated mostly by market needs. Stakeholders involved in this process are suppliers who offer educational programmes, and clients who have strict specifications for the products they wish to purchase. Lumen is therefore constantly enhancing its products.

It has already been mentioned that Lumen has current annual revenue of €4 million. This can be traced back to the growth of both market and prices, although total revenue has decreased. The competition has become tougher. Mr. Vekić is happy with Lumen's growth, with its current capacity utilization, and the company's market position. Although less satisfied with current profits and cost savings, he is happy with the achieved results in the last 10 years. He believes that his company will face tougher times in the future but has no doubt it will be easier to achieve strategic objectives. This can be explained by the comfortable financial situation the company is in; finance does not impose restrictions on Lumen.

However, one might wonder whether it will be possible to compete on costs in future. Finding a world-class client such as IKEA has certainly been a winning card. By collaborating with such a demanding buyer Lumen has learned a lot. This arrangement has further improved the product and also the company's business model. Yet in order to gain long-term success, Lumen might think of building its own brand; something that the following case study will elaborate in depth.

2.3 Alma Ras Ltd.

Overview

Address:	Olovske luke bb, 71340 Olovo, Bosnia and Herzegovina
Tel:	+387 32823050
Web:	http://www.alma-ras.com

Company Information

Industry:	Manufacturing and trading of underwear apparel
Year of establishment:	1998
Sales revenue in 2010:	€5.5 million
Sales revenue in 2000:	€300,000

Average number of employees in 2010: 430
Brain(s) behind the company: Rasim Memagić

2.3.1 Nature of Market Leadership

Alma Ras holds a leading position in the underwear market in Bosnia and Herzegovina. Yet, this is not considered important, as most of the company's production is exported. Alma Ras is currently expanding its business, with a special focus in Russia and Turkey.

2.3.2 Nature of Competitive Advantage

Continuous improvement of rather small and per se unimportant elements of the business will make the company stronger (Johnson et al. 2008). This management style does not include big, world-changing moves; small improvements of business activities have made Alma Ras what it is today. Mr. Memagić argues: "People often ask what the key to our success was. But there wasn't a key to success. You see, it's all about details. It's the small pieces that need to be put together to gain success. This is what will drive the company in the future: devotion to work, devotion to becoming excellent. For instance, improvements in sales are based on constant educational programmes and giving the sales force instructions on how to do the job in the best possible way".

2.3.3 Core Lessons Learned on the Path to Business Success

1. Being in a low-cost labour country, position yourself as a contractual manufacturer for labour-intensive, technologically noncomplex goods like textiles.
2. Work on constant improvement of details within the production process, customer relations, managing HR, and so forth.
3. Acquire know-how from OEMs. In fact, being an OEM supplier might be the perfect learning method.
4. After you have acquired enough knowledge, your own experience in the business builds and when you have considerably improved your production processes, build up your own brand and leverage it to regions that are more price-sensitive.

2.3.4 Alma Ras Ltd: Hidden Champion

Alma Ras was established in 1998. The business was started by the Memagić family in Olovo, a town near the capital of Bosnia and Herzegovina. With decades-long experience in the textile industry, a few machines, and six employees, the company started producing underwear. Today it has three production facilities in B&H and 630 employees. Only recently, a fourth production facility was set into motion, creating another 200 jobs. Alma Ras cooperates with global underwear producers such as Dolce & Gabbana and Triumph, having most of its production exported. A few years ago the company started building its own corporate brand and developing its own retail system, slowly evolving from the position of an OEM supplier to a company with its own brand.

Alma Ras holds a leading position in the underwear market in B&H. The underwear or pyjamas that you wear these days might have been produced by Alma Ras. This would not be unusual as most of its output is exported. The company is expanding its business in the regional market as well, and has plans to enter markets in Russia and Turkey in the near future. At the moment, Alma Ras is pressing into markets where an OEM is not present, developing its own sales subsidiaries in most of the mentioned markets. After strengthening its own brand it might think of directly competing with its OEM clients. The market itself has grown intensively over the past few years. Both prices and sales have risen. Obviously these trends have boosted profits.

However, Mr. Memagić claims that the competitors that were founded during the socialist period (hence state-owned and privatized in the years after the partitioning of Yugoslavia) are steadily losing ground. Companies that were once managed by the state are not able to respond quickly to market needs or to competitors' moves. Thus, Alma Ras builds its market share by taking customers from these competitors.

Alma Ras started its business by doing jobs for global underwear brands. At the beginning, 100 % of its production was directed to global partners such as Dolce & Gabbana and Triumph. Today, approximately 65 % of its production output goes to these clients, while the rest is sold under the Alma Ras brand in Southeast Europe. Three key customers generate 25 % of its total revenue.

One of the company's key competencies is its flexibility in business negotiations. Customers appreciate this, especially in the textile industries where fashion trends change almost weekly. Some of its other main strengths are its knowledge of the market, employee motivation, and loyaltys Alma Ras now possesses. In addition to this, strong relationships with customers have strengthened the company. From these partnerships, Alma Ras has gained knowledge about business, technology usage, production processes, and marketing. Now it applies this knowledge to build a brand of its own; yet previous knowledge and experience play an important role.

The company produces its underwear from high quality material, paying special attention to distinct product elements. Another characteristic of Alma Ras is its product pricing. The company offers high value at affordable prices.

The company invests 2 % of its overall revenue in innovations. But Alma Ras does not innovate with products only; innovation permeates its whole business model. The greatest challenge is to introduce these changes to employees. Mr. Memagić claims that this will be the toughest thing to do in the future. Alma Ras is going through an essential reorganization of the company's structure and the business as a whole. Once it is complete, Mr. Memagić believes, the company will be able to expand further.

In 2000, Alma Ras had revenue of €0.3 million, which rose by a factor of 18 to €5.5 million in 2010. When it comes to performance indicators, Mr. Memagić is mostly satisfied with capacity utilization and the steadily improving market position, although he believes profits and employee satisfaction can be enhanced. Mr. Memagić is least satisfied with cost savings. But despite a few concerns, he is very happy with the general results that Alma Ras has achieved so far. He claims that the company has had much greater success than other industry players. This is the outcome of cooperation with a world-class company and the executive vision for Alma Ras to build its own corporate brand. Nevertheless, he believes that the underwear business will be much tougher in the future. While there was capital investment in a new factory in the recent recession, the CEO reveals that some other projects had to be stopped due to a lack of financial resources.

Alma Ras is making a transition from a cost-based to a brand-based company. Several lessons have emerged from this case. First, the company already had a solid knowledge of textile production technologies based on previous experience. Mr. Memagić claims that Triumph's managers were amazed by some of the processes Alma Ras was implementing when their cooperation started. Second, it has refreshed its knowledge by collaborating with a world-class company. Although Alma Ras competed on lower costs, the management was aware that this was not a long-term solution. Hence it is gradually building its own brand. Finally, the company's management has been taken over by young managers willing to take risks and make the necessary strategic changes such as heavier investments in marketing, reorganization, developing the company's own retail system, and so forth.

2.4 Feal Ltd.

Overview

Address:	Trnska cesta 146, 88220 Široki Brijeg, Bosnia and Herzegovina
Tel:	+387 39704269
Email:	http://www.feal.ba
Web:	info@feal.ba

Company Information

Industry:	Manufacturing, trading, and projecting of aluminium profiles
Year of establishment:	1976
Sales revenue in 2010:	€65 million
Sales revenue in 2000:	€10 million
Average number of employees in 2010:	450
Brain(s) behind the company:	Tonćo Barbarić

2.4.1 Nature of Market Leadership

The company has held a leading position in Southeastern Europe for 6 years, with increasing business activities on the EU market. Although there are no precise indicators of market shares, the board's rough estimate is that Feal holds more than 50 % of the aluminium market in the SEE region.

2.4.2 Nature of Competitive Advantage

As suggested by Eisenhardt and Sull (2001) Feal offers system design and production at one place. System design of aluminium products, such as windows and doors, is an important element of aluminium construction and processing. It implies flexibility and a customized approach, which is highly valued by Feal's clients. Thus flexibility and a full service offer (production and design) are seen as distinctive competencies by the company's top management. Long-term relations with customers, extensive knowledge of the market and customers' needs, the CEO's strong personality, employee qualifications, and financial strength are also important competencies.

2.4.3 Core Lessons Learned on the Path to Business Success

1. Design all-round offers.
2. Continuously help customers through various suggestions and expertise.
3. Never stop improving and correcting your own production process.
4. Always strive to meet and exceed customer expectations.

2.4.4 Feal Ltd: Hidden Champion

Feal operates in the market of aluminium production and processing. Buildings that you live or work in could not stand without the type of products that Feal manufactures. The train you perhaps travel in would have problems stopping without Feal's products. The company has held a leading position in Southeastern Europe for 6 years, with increasing business activities in the EU market. Although there are no precise indictors of market share, the board's rough measure shows that Feal holds more than 50 % of the aluminium market in the region. These estimates are based on sales and revenue figures.

Feal was established in 1976 by the state government. In 2000 the company was privatized. Today, Feal is a middle-sized company with around 450 employees. In 2000, Feal's revenue was ten million euros, of which approximately two million euros was generated by export activities. With an annual growth of 30–40 %, Feal's revenue increased to 65 million euros by 2010; with exports providing 52 million euros. This high growth rate is based on several factors. First, Feal has gained great knowledge through a long experience in aluminium production. After the company's privatization, the decision making process became much less bureaucratic, making the company more receptive to market needs. This opened up great opportunities, as Feal had the chance to respond to the market, and it did so by expanding its product mix and taking aluminium products to new market segments. Finally, the executive board believes that Feal's competitive advantage is the major reason for its success.

The company is mainly export oriented. It is a heavy investor in both technologies and processing. While prices in the market have been constant in the last 10 years, the market size has increased, resulting in a significant rise in revenue.

Feal's main competitors are Alumil from Greece, TLM from Croatia, and Impol from Slovenia. Technologies and the owner/management structure are the main similarities between these competitors. However, there is an important dissimilarity between Feal and its competitors. While these companies are mainly focused on production, processing, or designing of aluminium products, Feal includes all three services in its offer. By creating an all-round service, the company increases its flexibility and ensures a customized approach to its clients. It further helps customers to articulate their ideas clearly. This often results in high customer satisfaction, which leads to further business arrangements and recommendations to other clients. In this way, Feal has utilized a great portion of the industry value chain and this has led to a great business success. It seems that the company's success has increased with the strengthening of control over the value chain. In comparison to its competitors, Feal offers the highest quality product on the market at the most competitive price, along with the highest quality pre-sale and post-sale services.

Major customers create 25 % of this company's overall revenue. The product is very important to the client, which is the reason why extensive information is usually needed before a sales closure. Most relevant to customers are product and service quality, as well as keeping delivery dates. Other factors, such as price, pre-purchase and post-purchase services, information systems, distance, and cooperation with clients, are also extremely relevant. These strengths help Feal create long-term advantages and relationships with its clients. On the other hand, advertising and patents do not seem to be important to Feal's customers.

As Feal's products are used mainly in the construction industry, it follows that the products are often used for a longer period of time; sometimes even decades. Therefore durability is certainly one of the quality dimensions. In order to achieve this, high-tech machines are employed and the manufacturing process is in general highly capital intensive. Product quality, price, efficiency, after-sales services, and keeping delivery dates, are also seen as competencies that enable Feal to gain greater success than its competitors.

Feal invests 2 % of its revenues into innovating processes. The company owns no patents. Given the nature of its products—i.e., the specific requirements each client has—the board of directors believes that patents would not improve the company's business model. The innovations that Feal introduces are mainly based on customers' inputs and requirements.

The value of Feal's equity has been steadily increasing over the last 10 years. Beside the already mentioned financial indicators, which imply strong growth in the past period, senior management appears to be mostly satisfied with the company's profits. However, there may be room for improvement of some indicators: growth of the company, capacity utilization, and especially cost savings. During the recession Feal has done much better than the rest of the industry, and its overall achievements are far above the industry's and the national economy's average.

Finances do not constitute a growth restraint. Major challenges of future growth are a lack of government support in securing a friendly business environment and macroeconomic changes in international markets.

From this case it can be seen that, despite obstacles coming from the government or the national and international economic environment, a company, can expect business success if it has a particular competitive advantage. Feal's overall service offer to customers—design of aluminium products, manufacture within modern facilities, and advisory role in assembly—is such an advantage.

2.5 Invento Media Group Ltd.

Overview

Address:	Vrbanjuša 134, 71000 Sarajevo, Bosnia and Herzegovina
Tel:	+387 62437460
Email:	info@invento.ba
Web:	http://www.inventomediagroup.ba

Company Information

Industry:	Manufacturing, trading, and projecting of Bluetooth advertising solutions
Year of establishment:	2008
Sales revenue in 2010:	n/a
Sales revenue in 2000:	n/a
Average number of employees in 2010:	12
Brain(s) behind the company:	Sanjin Džonlić

2.5.1 Nature of Market Leadership

Invento Media Group (IMG) is the only company in the world that offers a Bluetooth device with a range of over 500 m. When it entered the market, IMG immensely improved the efficiency of its clients' resource usage.

2.5.2 Nature of Competitive Advantage

For IMG, the most important business know-how lies within their innovations. Investments in that field exceed 30 % of total revenues. The offering of a new product with supporting software solutions, as well as pre-sales and after-sales consultations with business clients, are the major features of this company. The loyalty of its employees and their motivation to develop the product further are additional key strengths. Finally, the flexibility of the company's offer, i.e. the customized approach to each client, also represents a most important business competence.

2.5.3 Core Lessons Learned on the Path to Success

1. Design all-round service offers.
2. Continuously help customers by all kinds of suggestions and expertise, and provide customized software to each client.
3. If you are in the business of continuous product customization, you are in fact in the business of innovation. Your innovations are the key driver of success.

2.5.4 Invento Media Group Ltd: Hidden Champion

IMG was established only recently, in the year 2008. The company deals with devices that enable Bluetooth communication. The next time you go to a shopping mall and receive a discount notification on your cell phone, keep in mind that this might have been sent out by IMG's Bluetooth device. This new media communication channel is increasingly being used by companies seeking on-site communication with their potential or existing clients (O'Reilly et al. 2009). IMG is a start-up company that has grown immensely since its beginning. The company has two employees and ten part time workers. It is owned by four persons. The company grew 266 % in its first financial year and 1,000 % in the next! The reason for this stunning growth is the immense expansion of the client base. The profit was completely reinvested. The main part of Invento's revenues is generated by exports. In the first year exports accounted for 50 % of the company's revenues, while today this number has grown to 85 %.

Invento Media Group is the youngest HC of Bosnia and Herzegovina. Although it started its business only recently, the company already has connections and negotiates with potential clients from all over the world. IMG's managers suggest that technical performance is the indicator that defines a leading position in the market. Theirs is the only company in the world that offers a Bluetooth device with coverage of 500 m or more. IMG is export-oriented, with 85 % of its business now generated by export activities.

When it comes to competition, there are few companies that compete with IMG in the same market. They also offer Bluetooth devices, but IMG believes that their own devices are far superior, in both software and hardware solutions. In the last few years the market has significantly increased, with a growing number of companies seeking innovative uses for Bluetooth communication. IMG's competition offers less expensive products but with a lower performance.

The purchase of this product is usually very important to IMG's clients. They are usually corporate clients—for example, shopping malls that would like to directly inform their customers about discounts or special offers—or companies that would like to maintain regular communication with their clients, such as pharmaceuticals that send out regular bio weather notifications. Currently the top three clients generate 60 % of the company's revenues. Since IMG is selling a new product, customers often need detailed information about its installation, usage and servicing. Hence, cooperation with supply is very important to IMG's clients, and so are the quality of the product and the information systems that support its usage. On the other hand, other factors, such as price or location of the production facility, are less relevant.

IMG's high-tech product is not highly capital-intensive, even though it is technologically intensive. Compared to its few competitors, IMG offers a high quality product with an appealing price for its customers. The already mentioned pre-sales and after-sales services constitute an important part of the overall offer.

The innovation process of IMG is stimulated by impulses from the market. Still, as the product is high tech, innovative ideas are generated within employee circles. Ideas about how the product could be improved, what additional features it could include, and so forth, often emerge during regular discussion sessions. About 50 % of innovations are derived from analyses of ideas, wishes, and needs of current and potential clients. Approximately 25 % of innovations are adequate responses to competitive innovation, and 25 % are generated internally.

Even though finances do present a constraint for IMG, the management believes that future objectives will be easier to achieve because the business they are in is very attractive and lucrative if the company keeps customer satisfaction high. IMG does not have a problem in this respect. Most of its customers are loyal. IMG has done much better than other companies during the recent recession.

A major challenge that IMG faces is financial sustainability. In addition to this, the bureaucratic burden placed on start-up companies will certainly threaten IMG's expansion. As IMG's managers are technologically educated, a lack of specific managerial knowledge might also challenge IMG's future.

IMG is a pioneer of the technologically advanced companies emerging in the Bosnian economy. This carries different challenges, some of which have already been discussed; yet it also shows that the B&H economy is moving towards more technologically advanced businesses.

Conclusion

Compared to Simon's HCs, Bosnian HCs reveal some typical characteristics. First, these are companies from rural areas that have a distinct importance for the region they do business in. They are usually family-owned and run. Most of the Bosnian HCs are companies that have started as small entrepreneurships and over a short period have grown to medium-sized companies.

Another important similarity is the necessary innovativeness of these companies, as suggested by many authors (Yoffie and Kwak 2002; Yoffie and Cusumano 1999). It is usually related to technological advancement; innovative products are often expected to be high-tech products with the latest technological achievements. But this is rather a narrow perception of innovation. A broader definition implies improvements in both products and processes. Products do not have to be high-tech. This broader view of innovation applies in the case of Bosnian HCs. These companies work regularly on the improvement of business processes, such as production, sales, customer relationships, and more, so as to improve their businesses. Yet they are innovative because they seek new ways of achieving their objectives; they search for unusual paths to organize their work and do business. And most important, they all truly believe that these improvements are the reason for their successes.

According to Simon, HCs usually do not experience any serious difficulties in times of economic contraction. None of the Bosnian HCs saw the recent recession as a drawback. On the contrary, Alma Ras, for instance, started a new capital investment and opened 200 new jobs. All the other companies also saw the recession as an opportunity and expanded further.

Most Bosnian HCs are export-oriented, and confirm the international marketing theory. With their exports they focus on markets similar to the domestic one. Yet it seems as if most Bosnian HCs are now beyond this phase, exporting to distant and less similar markets. Feal is increasing its exports to the EU, Lumen has been exporting to the Union for years, and Alma Ras is soon to take its products to Turkey and Russia.

Another important attribute of HCs is the offer of high quality products. All Bosnian HCs argue that their products are of the highest quality. The feedback provided by their customers reveals that these companies build their long-term relationships with their customers on the quality of the product. Most of the managers we interviewed said that price does not play an important role for their clients because they are prepared to pay more if the quality is satisfactory. Nevertheless, Bosnian HCs are able to offer somewhat competitive prices because of the economic environment they operate in. As B&H is a low-to-middle income country, costs are usually lower than in developed countries. Therefore Bosnian HCs manage to keep their costs lower despite the high quality of their outputs. This is one of the reasons that countries like B&H attract foreign investments.

Like all HCs, the Bosnian ones are focused on gaining and extending their know-how. Yet, the way it is done in B&H is very specific. When analyzing the success stories of Lumen and Alma Ras, it becomes clear that these companies gained much from the know-how they got from their global partners (IKEA and Triumph respectively). These two HCs, and there is reason to believe that there are more such companies in B&H, use the know-how of their world-class partners to build their own brands. Hence, regardless of the fact that manufacturing for a global company does not bring high profits, local producers still gain something; they get access to know-how that they can use for developing their own brands.

The obstacles these companies face are quite similar. The political environment in B&H is still unstable, which certainly has its effect on the business community. Most interviewees more or less openly suggested they had problems with the political elites and a government that was not supportive to their business, especially with respect to their exporting activities. Despite this, managers agreed that companies can succeed even in difficult times. Another government-related problem is the fact that the bureaucratic system is not efficient and effective. This explains why Bosnian HCs do not have any patents; they did not even try to legally protect their products because they doubt the protection system. It follows that much greater results would have been achieved if companies had a more supportive external environment.

In line with this is an image of B&H that is still very negative. Images from the war in the 1990s are still present and shape a particular perception of Bosnia among business people around the world. Quality products are not expected from such a torn and destroyed country. Feal had been tracked by a potential German client for four years. Only after reassurance that Feal's product solutions accorded to its standards, did the client contact the Bosnian HC. During informal communication between representatives of the German and Bosnian companies, the German client expressed surprise; they had not expected such a high-quality product and complementary services from a Bosnian company. Even though Invento Media Group has offered a revolutionary tsunami warning solution to an Asian government, the company was turned down because the potential partner expressed concerns about IMG's country of origin. Prejudices or not, these perceptions clearly have a negative influence on HCs business activities abroad.

This chapter has explored the major characteristics of HCs in Bosnia and Herzegovina. Further information on the country reveals the state of the national economy, and hopefully helps the reader to understand why high-tech companies and high-tech products are rare in B&H. We discussed what industries Bosnian HCs are in, why they are considered to be HCs, and how they have worked their way up to global markets. Finally, we revealed some common features of their business decisions and activities.

It is obvious that Bosnian HCs are more similar to those of other CEE countries than those of Germany or the Netherlands. Having in mind the current transition from planned to market economy, and the last war, it is reasonable to expect that real, western-like HCs might emerge in the next 20–30 years. However, some major similarities do exist and this has allowed us to identify some potential HCs. They are all small or medium-sized companies that have grown steadily over the years without being decelerated by the recession or some other major economic drawback. These companies exist mainly in the rural areas of B&H; they are family-owned and family-run. The CEOs are innovative in managing their companies, their products, and their operations. These companies are focused on high-quality outputs. As a result they have high client retention rates. During the data gathering process, and especially during the interviews, a very interesting observation was made. Beside the ambitions that are common to managers of successful companies, one could not neglect the passion that the interviewees had for their businesses. The reason that these companies are champions most probably transcends the commonly observed profit and success drive.

References

Agency for Statistics of Bosnia and Herzegovina. (2011). *Foreign trade 2010*. Sarajevo: Agency for Statistics of Bosnia and Herzegovina.

Cateora, P. R., & Graham, J. L. (2005). *International marketing* (12th ed.). New York, NY: McGraw-Hill Irwin.

Central Bank of Bosnia and Herzegovina. (2011a). *Annual Report 2010*. Sarajevo: Central Bank of Bosnia and Herzegovina.

Central Bank of Bosnia and Herzegovina. (2011b). *Bilten 2, 2011*. Retrieved August 12, 2011, from http://www.cbbh.ba/index.php?id=35&lang=bs

Eisenhardt, K. M., & Galunic, C. D. (1999). Coevolving: At last, a way to make synergies work. *Harvard Business Review*, January–February, 89–101.

Eisenhardt, K. M. & Sull, D. N. (2001). Strategy as a Simple Rule. *Harvard Business Review*, January, 107–116.

Fine, C. H., Vardan, R., Pethick, R., & El-Hout, J. (2002). Rapid-response capability in value-chain design. *MIT Sloan Management Review, 43*(2), 69–75.

Johnson, M. W., Christensen, C. M., & Kagermann, H. (2008). Reinventing your business model. *Harvard Business Review*, December, 1–11.

O'Reilly, C. A., Harreld, J. B., & Tushman, M. L. (2009). Organizational ambidexterity: IBM and emerging business opportunities. *California Management Review, 51*(4), 75–99.

World Bank. (2013). *Data; countries and economies*. http://data.worldbank.org/country

Yoffie, D.B., & Cusumano, M.A. (1999). Judo strategy: The competitive dynamics of internet time. *Harvard Business Review*, January–February, 71–81.

Yoffie, D. B., & Kwak, M. (2002). Mastering balance: How to meet and beat a stronger opponent. *California Management Review, 44*(2), 8–24.

Hidden Champions of Croatia

Mislav Ante Omazić and Rebeka Danijela Vlahov

Overview

Official name:	Republic of Croatia
Type of government:	Parliamentary Democratic Republic
Population in 2011:	4,403,000
Land area:	55,960 km^2

History

1918 Shortly before the end of the First World War in 1918, the Croatian Parliament severs relations with Austria-Hungary and The National Council of State decides to unite the country with the new Kingdom of Serbs, Croats and Slovenes.

1929 After a decade of unrest and political tension, the kingdom is renamed Yugoslavia, and the system of government is further centralized under a royal dictatorship.

1939 The Croatian Peasant Party negotiates a partial restoration of Croatian autonomy.

1941 Nazi Germany invades Yugoslavia. A union, named "Greater Croatia", is formed, also comprising most of Bosnia and western Serbia.

1945 Croatia becomes one of the six constituent republics of the Yugoslav socialist federation.

1971 The early 1970s mark the beginning of a protest movement known as the "Croatian Spring", where many students and activists demand greater civil liberties and greater autonomy for Croatia. Although the movement is

M.A. Omazić (✉) • R.D. Vlahov
Department for Organization and Management, Faculty of Economics and Business in Zagreb, Zagreb, Croatia
e-mail: momazic@efzg.hr

P. McKiernan and D. Purg (eds.), *Hidden Champions in CEE and Turkey*,
DOI 10.1007/978-3-642-40504-4_12,

denounced as nationalism, in 1974 a new Yugoslav federal constitution meets some of the demands for Croatian autonomy.

1980 After the death of President Tito, the slow disintegration of Yugoslavia begins as individual republics assert their desire for independence.

1990 The collapse of communism in eastern and central Europe leads to rising support for parties with a nationalist programme and Croatians vote in the country's first free elections in more than 50 years.

1991 Croatia declares its independence. By the end of the year, nearly one-third of Croatian territory is under Serb occupation and the Croatian War for Independence starts. Before the dissolution of Yugoslavia in 1991, Croatia was the second most prosperous and industrialized area (after Slovenia), with a per capita output exceeding Yugoslavia's average by more than 30 %. Economic infrastructure was directly affected by the war in Croatia and sustained massive damage, particularly in 1991 and 1992.

1995 Croat forces retake three out of four areas created by the UN and the war ends with the signing of the Dayton Agreement.

1996 Croatia joins the Council of Europe.

1998 Croatia resumes control over the forth UN area, Eastern Slavonia.

2003 Croatia submits a formal application for EU membership.

2004 The EU agrees to start accession talks with Croatia in March 2005.

2008 The NATO summit in Bucharest invites Croatia to join the Alliance. The European Commission states that Croatia is likely to end accession talks by 2009 and become a member by 2011, but demands tougher action against corruption and organized crime.

2009 Croatia officially joins NATO. Slovenia lifts its block on Croatian EU membership talks after the two countries sign a deal allowing international mediators to resolve their border dispute.

2011 Croatia successfully completes EU accession negotiations, putting it on track to become the 28th member state. Croatia signs a EU accession treaty, paving the way for it to achieve full membership on July 1, 2013.

2012 Croatian voters back joining the European Union in a referendum by a margin of two to one. After the first instance court decision on a political and economic corruption scandal, a former prime minister is sentenced to 10 years in prison.

1 Introduction: Context

Croatia is a small but complex market. Its geography divides it into two distinct areas: the more affluent and tourism-oriented Dalmatian costal region along the Adriatic Sea, and the rural inland Slavonian region, dominated by agricultural and industrial activities. The country's population of roughly 4.5 million is largely homogenous in terms of ethnicity, language and religion, but in the summer months its numbers are heavily increased by tourists from Europe and the rest of the world, making it a global market for products and services. Croatia is a strong democracy with a market economy, but has significant state involvement in a number of industries, and carries a considerable public financial burden from its social welfare policies. Croatia is a developing economy and, despite progress in economic and administrative reforms, some problems remain. These include a judiciary plagued by case backlogs and a lack of expertise, a complex and sometimes non-transparent bureaucracy, and serious corruption issues, both real and perceived. The overall business and investment climate of the country is perceived to be difficult, and requires caution and patience of foreign companies and potential investors. The biggest investment opportunities in Croatia lie in the energy and infrastructure sectors. The new government has pledged to reduce barriers and foster development in key sectors, particularly tourism, energy, infrastructure, and irrigation/environment. Lacking its own financial and technology resources, Croatia heavily depends on foreign investments. Although the economic engine that comes with EU membership has been greatly diminished by the global credit crunch and the struggling euro, Croatia can expect to see some benefits when it becomes the EU's 28th member in 2013.

Once a member, Croatia will gain access to EU funding programs, including being a partner in the Union's budget. The budget—864 billion Euros from 2007 to 2013—covers expenditures in member states for sectors including agriculture, internal policies, administration and compensation.

Croatia has 1,244 islands of various sizes and almost 44 % of its mainland is covered with forests. It is a country rich in natural resources such as unpolluted fertile land, good climatic conditions, natural forest growth, biodiversity, and a plenitude of water resources. It is characterized by a natural and climatic diversity. Furthermore, the country is known for its innovations and innovators, such as Rudolf Steiner who invented organic farming and the Waldorf schools; Slavoljub Penkala, who invented the mechanical pen; Nikola Tesla, inventor of the alternating current generator, transformer and magnetic field; Faust Vrančić, who devised the first parachute; Ivan Lupis-Vukic, constructor of the first torpedo; Ivan (Juan) Vucetic, author of the most flawless system of fingerprint classification; and many others.

The Republic of Croatia is a small, transitional democratic parliamentary republic located in Central/Southeastern Europe. Among 47 European countries, Croatia is ranked 26th with respect to both population and surface. It has a total population of 4,403,000 people (World Bank 2013). The country is at the crossroads of Central Europe, the Pannonia Plain, the Balkans, and the Mediterranean Sea. Croatia has many peculiarities. The first is a diverse territory that includes plains, lakes, and rolling hills in the continental north and north-east (Central Croatia and Slavonia), densely wooded mountains (Lika and Gorski Kotar), and rocky coastlines along the Adriatic Sea (Istria, Northern Sea coast and Dalmatia). Second, the country has a diverse climate: continental in the north and east, Mediterranean along the coast, semi-highland and highland climate in the south-central region, temperate in Istria, and subtropical on the Palagruza archipelago. Four different regions (Dalmatia, Istria, Slavonia, and Zagorje) are characterized by differences in geography, traditional economy, food, folkloric tradition, and dialect. It is one of the most important tourist destinations in the Mediterranean, well-known for its preserved natural resources (eight national parks), cultural and historical heritage (monuments under UNESCO protection), and proximity to many European capitals (Croatian Regions Office 2013).

In an economy traditionally based on agriculture and livestock, peasants comprised more than half of the Croatian population until the first years after World War II. Pre-1945, industrialization was slow and consisted mostly of textile mills, sawmills, brickyards, and food-processing plants. Rapid industrialization and diversification occurred after World War II. Decentralization came in 1965, allowing growth in certain sectors, such as the aforementioned prosperous tourist industry. Profits from the Croatian industry were used to develop poorer regions in the former Yugoslavia, leading to Croatia contributing much more to the Yugoslavian economy than it ever got back. This, coupled with austerity programs and hyperinflation in the 1980s, led to discontent in both Croatia and Slovenia and fuelled the independence movement. Before the dissolution of Yugoslavia, the Republic of Croatia, was the most prosperous and industrialized area after Slovenia, with a per capita output more than one-third above the Yugoslav average. By 1990, foreign remittances contributed two billion US dollars annually to the economy. Privatization under the new Croatian government had barely begun when the war broke out. As a result of the Croatian War of Independence, the economic infrastructure sustained massive damage during the period, particularly in 1991 and 1992 (Vranjican 2005). With the end of the war in 1995, tourism and Croatia's economy recovered moderately. However, corruption, cronyism, and a general lack of transparency stymied meaningful economic reform as well as the foreign investment that was needed. By the end of the 1990s, Croatia faced considerable economic problems such as the damage done to bridges, factories, power lines, buildings, and houses during the internecine fighting, the large refugee and displaced population, as well as the disruption of economic ties and mishandled privatization. Inflation and unemployment rose and the currency (kuna) fell, prompting the national bank to tighten fiscal policy.

In 2000 Croatia's economy turned the corner as tourism rebounded. It expanded in 2002, stimulated by a credit boom led by newly privatized and foreign-capitalized banks, some capital investment (most important in road construction), and gains from small and medium-sized private enterprises. By early 2005, the country's foreign debt declined in growth and was surpassed in size by the foreign debt of the banking sector, prompting further interventions by the National Bank. Western aid and investment, especially in the tourist and oil industries, was doing its part to help further develop the economy. In 2009, economic output was dominated by the service sector, which accounted for 64.4 % of GDP, followed by the industrial sector (27.5 % of GDP) and agriculture (5.09 % of GDP) (World Bank 2011). The industrial sector is dominated by shipbuilding, food processing, pharmaceuticals, and information technology, as well as biochemical and timber industries. Tourism is a notable source of income during the summer. Croatia was ranked the fourth most successful tourist destination in the world in 2010, owing to an expected 7 % increase in international tourist arrivals (ITB World Travel Trends Report 2010/2011). More information is available in Exhibit 1.

Exhibit 1 Core economic indicators for Croatia

	1999	2000	2001	2002	2003	2004	2005	2006	2007	2008	2009	2010	2011
GDP per capita (current US$)	5,068	4,862	5,192	5,974	7,690	9,237	10,090	11,229	13,376	15,694	14,044	13,461	14,180
GDP per capita growth (annual %)	−2.19	6.75	3.33	4.88	5.37	4.15	4.21	4.98	5.15	2.13	−6.84	−1.16	0.24
Long-term unemployment (% of total unemployment)		53.40	55.90	63.40	59.30	53.60	58.40	60.10	61.50	63.00	56.20	44.40	n/a
Foreign direct investment, net inflows (% of GDP)	6.29	5.16	6.86	4.15	6.00	2.63	3.96	6.93	8.45	8.70	5.51	1.43	2.02
GDP (current US$m)	23,078	21,518	23,052	26,525	34,143	41,004	44,821	49,855	59,336	69,586	62,203	59,472	62,493
Exports of goods and services (current $USm)	8,430	8,970	10,011	10,856	14,534	17,604	18,982	21,359	25,090	29,271	22,766	23,407	26,110
Exports of goods and services (% of GDP)	36.53	41.69	43.43	40.93	42.57	42.93	42.35	42.84	42.28	42.06	36.60	39.36	41.78
Merchandise exports (current $USm)	4,303.00	4,432.00	4,666.00	4,903.58	6,186.63	8,024.16	8,773.00	10,377.00	12,364.30	14,111.70	10,473.80	11,806.20	12,289.00
Merchandise exports to high-income economies (% of total merchandise exports)	73.31	74.17	72.12	70.78	74.45	70.58	69.97	71.79	68.00	66.66	68.19	68.23	n/a
Merchandise exports to developing economies in Europe & Central Asia (% of total merchandise exports)	16.86	17.93	19.35	22.41	22.12	23.47	24.23	17.72	25.83	27.44	26.56	23.37	n/a

(continued)

Exhibit 1 (continued)

	1999	2000	2001	2002	2003	2004	2005	2006	2007	2008	2009	2010	2011
Ores and metals exports (% of merchandise exports)	2.23	3.02	2.66	2.59	2.27	3.40	3.78	4.38	4.59	4.29	3.63	4.51	5.14
Agricultural raw materials exports (% of merchandise exports)	4.71	4.54	4.06	4.29	4.16	3.61	3.40	3.29	3.54	3.32	3.61	3.61	3.85
Food exports (% of merchandise exports)	9.50	8.89	9.78	11.12	12.16	9.02	10.46	11.36	10.46	9.76	12.79	11.31	11.38
Fuel exports (% of merchandise exports)	7.76	10.98	10.22	9.36	9.64	11.34	13.90	15.10	12.76	12.70	12.94	12.33	12.28
Manufactures exports (% of merchandise exports)	75.64	72.54	73.21	72.51	71.63	72.47	68.26	65.60	68.32	69.63	66.40	67.80	66.85
High-technology exports (% of manufactured exports)	8.28	8.68	10.25	12.15	12.25	13.02	11.40	9.85	8.21	8.35	9.76	9.15	n/a

Source: World Bank (2013)

Exhibit 2 Hidden champions from Croatia

Name	Short market leadership description	Revenues 2010 (€m)	Reveneus 2000 (€m)	Employees 2010
Bodren	Leader in production high quality ice wines in the region and the only one with six gold, three silver and two bronze medals at Decanter in 4 years in a row	0.128	0	1
DOK-ING	Leading position in the world in production of mining remote controlled vehicles	26.3	0.55	117
Durante M2	Leading position in selling joint slabs in Western Europe		0	3

Source: Authors of the chapter

Croatia weathered the global financial crisis reasonably well, but still faces significant challenges largely due to its external imbalances and high foreign debt. This presents long-term problems for the financial sector because of to the higher cost of borrowing to cover the current account deficit. The country is preparing for membership of the EU. In February 2005, the Stabilisation and Association Agreement with the EU officially came into force and by the end of 2009 Croatia had closed 17 EU accessions chapters. The remaining 16 were completed by the end of the first half of 2010. In June 2011, the country successfully completed the EU accession negotiations, putting it on track to become the 28th member state in mid-2013.

Three companies will be presented in our Croatian Hidden Champions (HCs) chapter. First, DOK-ING Ltd., a company established during the Croatian Homeland War to manufacture a mine-clearance product that helped people at that time, but became much more over the following years. This case perfectly illustrates one of the principle characteristics of a HC: where others see a danger, a real champion sees an opportunity. Therefore DOK-ING is a real HC.

The second case, Bodren Ltd., involves a specialized sweet wine producer. Even though Croatia has a long history of producing wine, and around 700 different wines are made today, Bodren's produce is quite different from everything else and more daring than most of the wines ever produced in this country. This case is a typical example of the initial phase of a future champion, and is therefore placed in the category of potential HCs.

The third study, Durante M-kvadrat Ltd., is one of four specialized producers and distributors of joint free slabs, a product that could fundamentally change the construction industry across Europe. This case perfectly describes another characteristic of HCs: a champion builds new roads. Since the company has just started its business, it is classified as a start-up. These Croatian HCs are listed in the table above (Exhibit 2).

Although we are certain that there are more HCs (primarily involving software development, organic food and services) in Croatia, we may have failed to identify some of them whereas others preferred to remain hidden. Some of the companies that we interviewed turned out not to be champions in the end.

2 Three Case Studies

2.1 DOK-ING Ltd.

Overview

Address:	Kanalski put 1, 10000 Zagreb, Croatia
Tel:	+38512481300
Email:	info@dok-ing.hr
Web:	http://www.dok-ing.hr

Company Information

Industry:	Engineering and manufacture of remote controlled machinery
Year of establishment:	1991
Sales revenue in 2010:	€26.3 million
Sales revenue in 2000:	€550,000
Average number of employees in 2010:	117
Brain(s) behind the company:	Founder and owner Vjekoslav Majetić

2.1.1 Nature of Market Leadership

A world leader in the production of remotely controlled machinery for underground mining, and a global technological leader in the production of remotely controlled machines for use in specific conditions considered dangerous for humans (mine fields, fire disasters, etc.). Over the last 2 decades, the company has created a set of new market niches where this machinery can be used: mining industry, human-rescue operations, and more.

2.1.2 Nature of Competitive Advantage

The main source of the company's competitive advantage is its superior expert knowledge gained though continuous innovations in machines as a whole and their related features; for example, drive systems that operate on batteries. Newly developed technical solutions are patented. In some novel market niches that the company has created, such as the mining industry, there is still no competition.

2.1.3 Core Lessons Learned on the Path to Business Success

1. Continuously innovate and try to find new solutions in response to customer needs. Whether it is a big improvement or just a slight change from the previous model, it is always best to be one step ahead of your competition.
2. Patent all the solutions to be certain that they will be protected for some time, during which it is important to try to find better ones, This will protect your product from being copied and sold at a lower price.

3. A leader has to be a dreamer. Anything is possible; you just have to find a way to develop it and produce it.

2.1.4 DOK-ING Ltd: Hidden Champion

Among Croatian SMEs, DOK-ING Ltd. is definitely one of the most admired. It was founded in 1991, the same year that Croatia declared its independence. Like the country itself DOK-ING went through many ups and downs until it was recognized as a global leader in the production of unmanned multi-purpose vehicles. Interestingly, the company was initially started in order to sell, install, and service satellite television and video systems, and other technical devices used by the Croatian police. As the war in Croatia escalated, the owner was unsettled by the increasing prevalence of landmines being seeded throughout the country. During the Homeland War from 1991 to 1995, an estimated 2,000,000 mines covered almost 8 % of Croatia. Therefore, the owner of the company, Vjekoslav Majetić, wanted to protect those men who were working in dangerous environments, and enable safe operation in specific life-threatening jobs. This motivation determined the direction of further development of other machines whose common feature was, and still is, remote control. In 1996, to address the need for landmine management and removal, DOK-ING's owners began to research and develop a remotely controlled anti-mine vehicle (AMV) that could locate and detonate landmines. Since then, DOK-ING has improved the design and performance of its AMV, and introduced additional anti-mine, fire-fighting, and underground mining vehicles.

In the first 10 years, the company focused on the development of machinery for humanitarian demining and demining operations in Croatia after its Homeland War, but soon the product became recognized and growth in exports was rapid. Today they export 92 % of everything produced, creating 86 % of revenue from the top three customers outside Croatia. Their product requires the establishment of long and close relationships with customers who have an ongoing need for spare parts, maintenance, or adjustments to the product to suit the user. As a result of extensive investment in the company's technical solutions, customers receive products with a high level of technological and working capacity. Mr. Majetić emphasized that he had built the company around the ability to innovate and quickly respond to customer needs. Therefore the company invests every year around 20 % of their average income in research and development; at the moment it has nine registered patents and seven in the process of registration. DOK-ING Ltd. employs 117 highly motivated workers and is in its maturity phase.

Since its establishment, the company has produced numerous innovative products, such as the XD concept electric car, an explosive ordnance disposal (EOD) robot, a light flail mine clearance system MV-1, the MVD extra low profile dozer for the mining industry, a medium fire-fighting system JELKA-4, and a heavy fire-fighting system JELKA-10. The JELKA-10 is primarily applied in closed facilities and plants where there is a danger of chemicals, explosives, and radioactivity. Its coatings provide an adequate level of defence during action in areas of very high temperature. With these products, the company has acquired a leading market position, and in some areas, such as the mining industry, even a monopolistic one. DOK-ING has a worldwide reputation since its products are used by a long list of international agencies: (1) armed forces (US, Sweden, Croatia, Ireland, Lithuania, Sri Lanka, Colombia, Australia, Libya and Nicaragua); (2) government agencies (Croatia's Mine Action Centre, Iraq's National Mine Action Authority, Azerbaijan's National Agency for Mine Action, and Sri Lanka's Ministry of National Building); (3) humanitarian organizations (Norwegian People's Aid, Swiss Foundation for Mine Action and United Nations World Food Programme); (4) commercial companies (Mechem Consultants, RONCO Consulting Corporation and REASeuro Worldwide); (5) Croatian private demining companies (DOK-ING Demining, DIZ-EKO, AVANGARD, Enigma, TITAN and ISTRAŽIVAČ); (6) the fire-fighting industry (Ministry of Russian Federation for Civil Defence, Emergencies and Elimination of Consequences of Natural Disaster); and (7) the mining industry (Anglo Platinum).

The MV-4 and its larger version, MV-10, are now the best-known demining machines and are used in over 25 countries. DOK-ING's demining machines are located on all continents, and the most important customers are the armed forces of several countries and NATO member states, international humanitarian organizations, and commercial companies.

One particular business venture was the beginning of something entirely new in the development of DOK-ING. It involved cooperation with business partners in South Africa on the development of a machine used to push ore in platinum and chromium mines, and it became the impetus for something novel: the development of a remotely controlled bulldozer for underground mining. The urge for constant development, the exceptional expertise and experience with manufacturing machines for special purposes, a belief in its own abilities, and the vision for future manufacturing techniques and technology, are additional reasons that this company has entered the challenging area of mining equipment development. The first machine for South Africa required a very low profile, which allowed a significant increase in profitability in the excavation of the ore. During work, the machine is very stable, with good performance characteristics, and is one of the best in its category. Today the company is investing a great deal of energy in the development of all "removal" machinery on a new technological platform. With these advanced tools and other equipment, its mining program represents the backbone of the company's production.

The new ULP bulldozer is just the beginning of a new generation of machines for underground mining. A major feature of this machine is the alternative power source for the drive system; in this case the drive works on battery cells. The significantly reduced height allows for much lower excavation profiles, which provides several benefits: a reduction of excavation waste by 25 %, an increased percentage of total platinum in the excavation, reduced energy costs, a significant reduction of investment in equipment, ventilation, air conditioning, and so forth. All of this results in increased profitability.

The adopted techniques and technologies have encouraged the development of new mining prototypes (a drill rig and a roof bolter) with similar characteristics, as well as the development of a new loader and a machine brush (sweeper), which will complete a fleet of machines based on this new technology. This represents a detachment from conservative technology and the current generation of machines.

DOK-ING's innovations have a secure position in domestic and international markets and are a credit to the skilled and professional workforce. Above all, they are a great credit to its owner and founder, Vjekoslav Majetić, the originator of many of the innovations and technical solutions implemented in the company's products. For his work, Majetić has received many valuable awards at the regional, national, and international level.

Lately, the company has been involved in another project that has aroused great interest in the domestic and international markets. It has developed and presented a prototype for a new urban electric car, which, with its technical solutions, features, and modern equipment, attracts great attention. And it seems that this is just the beginning. Majetić and his team are constantly raising the bar and setting new challenges that take them to new spheres and towards products in all imaginable areas:. air, water, or earth. It seems that there are no boundaries to the expansion of this company. Its employees generate new ideas every month, and they quickly become a reality.

So, what are the specific lessons that DOK-ING has brought to us? If you have an idea and committed leadership, anything is possible, no matter how unimaginable it might sound. You just have to find a way to motivate your people to develop and produce it. In short, this is a story about a talented individual who had a vision and was able to rally other talented people to realize it.

2.2 Bodren Ltd.

Overview

Address:	Rusnica 64, 49231 Hum na Sutli, Croatia
Tel:	+385098/378688
Email:	bodren@kr.t-com.hr
Web:	http://www.uhdmo.hr/bodren/

Company Information

Industry:	Wine production
Year of establishment:	1999
Sales revenues in 2010:	€128,000
Sales revenues in 2000:	n/a
Average number of employees in 2010:	1
Brain(s) behind the company:	Founder and owner Boris Drenški

2.2.1 Nature of Market Leadership

First in the region in sweet and ice wine production. This market consists of a group of opinion-makers and customers who have a profound and aesthetic taste in sweet wines that are difficult and risky to produce.

2.2.2 Nature of Competitive Advantage

The core of the competitive advantage for this company is the owner's constant strive to develop new tastes in wine, and his great attention to the high quality of his products. Their quality has been attested by six gold, three silver and two bronze Decanter medals (from 2008 to 2011), and a gold medal in Vienna (2009). Mr. Drenški's wine is among the top 10 for the Regional Trophy in Eastern and Southeast Europe in the category of sweet and organic/biodynamic wines.

2.2.3 Core Lessons Learned on the Path to Business Success

1. Never be fully satisfied with the product you have, and always strive to improve it. This argument is especially important if you produce luxury goods like sweet and ice wines. To establish, prove, and promote the quality of your product, go for international quality competitions; win awards and leverage them in your business.
2. Such awards will considerably increase the customers' willingness to pay; hence they allow you to charge higher prices.
3. Next, when the quality of the product is recognized, you will be able to penetrate the target market. Once the brand is established, it is better to produce smaller amounts of product of higher quality and manage your individual supply and demand curves.
4. The production process is the most important part. Pay maximum attention to the conditions that the product is produced in and the methods used.
5. Stay an entrepreneur with a strong vision and work hard to achieve it, while combining creativity, persistence, passion, achievement, commitment, and utter belief in the ideas that you have.

2.2.4 Bodren Ltd: Hidden Champion

An originally whimsical endeavour has turned into a success story. Our second champion produces something quite unusual for its region. Wine production was first seen here some 6,000 years ago. But it was not until 1857 that Louis Pasteur correctly described the science behind fermentation and wine production processes. Because crushed grapes contain all that is needed to create wine, ancient wine producers simply allowed nature to take its course. As time went on, people realized that by intervening at certain times, they could make a wine with more predictable characteristics. Bodren Ltd. is a small producer of ice and sweet white wines, located in Hum na Sutli, Rusnica in Zagorje region. Although this company is not a typical HC, it has the quality and characteristics needed to become one as it grows and develops its business model. The company was founded in 1999 and has only one full-time employee; family and friends usually help with the business. Bodren Ltd. is classified in the food industry and at the moment is in its growth stage.

Croatia is known for the quality of its wines and is divided into two distinct wine regions—continental and coastal—with Herdner12 sub-regions (Hernder Estate Wines 2011). The continental region numbers about 300 wine-makers who operate with an official stamp of origin. Guests can taste their products in catering facilities, wine cellars, and along wine roads. Of course they can also buy their wines in stores. Although it is quite uncommon for Croatia, and this region as a whole, Mr. Drenški chose to produce ice wine, a particular type of sweet or dessert wine. Grapes that have frozen while still on the vine contain sugars and other dissolved solids that do not freeze as water turns to ice, resulting in a smaller amount of more concentrated and very sweet product. There is no universal definition for sweet wines, so the ones that Bodren currently produces are defined according to Croatian national law on wine. These wines are made in exceptional years; their special quality is achieved through special ripening, harvesting, and processing methods. They must be produced from grape varieties recommended for a particular sub-region or vineyard. In short, makers of sweet wines want their products to contain high levels of both sugar and alcohol; the latter being obtained from the former. There are several main types of sweet wines: late harvest, selection harvest, selection harvest berries, dried berries selected harvest, and ice wine. These are considered to be the highest quality wines. Ice wine is an aromatic wine with a distinct sweet-sour flavour traditionally obtained by harvesting and pressing grapes frozen at a temperature of at least −7 °C. It contains at least 127° Oechsle (Ice Wine, 2011), which is a measure of the amount of sugar in the must. Fermentation lasts from 6 to 10 months. White varieties tend to be pale yellow or light gold in colour when they are young and can maderizee (acquire a deep amber-golden colour) as they age.

Canada and Germany are the world's largest producers of ice wines. The rest comes from Australia, Austria, Czech Republic, France, Hong Kong, Hungary, Israel, Italy, Luxembourg, New Zealand, Slovakia, Slovenia, Sweden, the United States, and now Croatia. Unrelated to the country of origin, every producer has its own distinguishing production that results in a different taste and characteristics of the wine. This enables clients to choose what suits them best. Due to the labour-intense and risky production process, resulting in relatively small amounts of wine, ice wines are generally quite expensive. To produce 0.2 L of sweet wine it is necessary to harvest around 40 kg of grapes. Consequently, prices for this type of wine are rather high. Bodren charges around 35 euros for a 0.25 L bottle and around 45 Euros for a 0.4 L bottles. These prices are similar to those of the competition.

It is very interesting that before entering the business, Mr. Drenski had never produced wine. He had to read all available books on the production of sweet wines. He went to all wine fairs, communicated with those already in the branch, and created his own philosophy of doing something that nobody else in the region dared to do. As many other great stories, this one started as a hobby and Mr. Drenski never stopped working in a public company. In the beginning, he had 1,000 grape vines that he kept for ice harvest. His vineyards are about 300 m above sea level and are well exposed to sunlight. As a result, the grapes contain a high percentage of sugar. This was a very risky enterprise as no one knew if the conditions would be good enough for a harvest. On top of everything, Mr. Drenski's region is stereotyped as producing low quality wines. Therefore, only someone with a strong vision could do what Mr. Drenski did. Even today, after winning many international awards, he thinks that he can do better and is never completely satisfied with what he has done. Now, with the help of family members and friends he cultivates around 2 ha of land, with 7,000 grape vines, in six locations. As all visionary entrepreneurs, he thinks about expansion and has taken some concrete steps. He has bought an additional 4 ha of land where he plans to plant 15,000–20,000 new grape vines. Mr. Drenski has further expansion plans but will stay within his exclusive limits: he will not undertake mass production, nor will he distribute to retail chains. His target markets are those opinion-makers and customers who have a profound and aesthetic taste for sweet wines. But as a growth strategy, an equally good option for him would be to find just one buyer that is large enough to buy the whole series yearly so that he can concentrate on what he does best: produce new varieties.

From 1999 to 2008 Bodren produced less than 2,000 bottles annually for undefined markets. Although the firm was established in 1999, 2008 can be considered the year when the company was really born. Since then it has blossomed. In 2008 Mr. Drenski signed up two categories of his wines (Rhine Riesling, harvest 2006; and Chardonnay, harvest 2005) for the Decanter World Wine Awards in London and won gold medals for both. Decanter is one of the world's most influential wine magazines, sold monthly in 97 countries. Decanter World Wine Awards was founded in 2004 and gained a reputation as one of the most respected and influential wine competitions. The international recognition of this wine grown in Hum na Sutli was preceded by a rating process lasting many months, during which scores were given by professionals from different backgrounds: oenology, hotel management, catering, dealers and consumers. This exceptional recognition has put the dessert wines from Croatian Zagorje into a small and distinguished group of the 12 best in the world. The recognition is even more valuable in light of the fact that the medals were won in an exceptionally strong international competition of 9,400 wines from around the world.

After the Decanter Awards, Bodren's production increased more than twice. Its market is still not formally structured and defined. Although everything produced is sold, Mr. Drenski invests a lot of energy in that process, and cannot concentrate on the production of new varieties. In 2009 he signed up again for the Decanter Awards, this time with four types of wine, and got all four gold medals in the price category of up to 35 lb sterling. That year the awarded wines were Château Bezanec Chardonnay, harvest 2007; Cóuve, harvest 2007; Pinot Gris harvest 2006; and Rhine Riesling, harvest 2007. This puts Mr. Drenski in the category of the most successful regional producers, and adds a global dimension to his business. Even in 2010, a year of crisis, Bodren set new standards in Croatian wine quality by experimenting with new varieties and combinations of them, and winning two silver medals and one bronze medal from Decanter. Furthermore, in 2011, for the fourth year in a row, Decanter awarded Bodren one gold medal, two silver medals, and one bronze medal for its wines. The gold medal went to a wine made from *pinot gris* and *pinot blanc*, a completely new variety protected under the name Bodren.

Mr. Drenski is aware that international recognition begins with a small first step on the ladder that leads to the profession's pinnacle. It is a journey, not a moment of success. Driven by passion, he has another challenge on his mind. This time he wants to produce red sweet wines. His new vines will be *merlot, cabernet sauvignon, zweigelt* and *pinot noir*. On top of that, he wants to redesign his bottles and market them in packaging never seen before in his industry. He wants to revolutionize the wine business in the region and show others that there is a way to success if you believe in your dreams. With 10 of its cultural traditions on UNESCO's heritage list, Croatia has the highest number of recognized intangible world heritages in all Europe. With Mr. Drenski's previous achievements and his future plans Bodren can soon become another authentic Croatian cultural heritage.

So what is the lesson that Bodren can teach us? This story is all about what inspires people to abandon certainty and pursue their vision through creativity, persistence, passion, achievement, commitment, utter belief in their ideas, and whatever else is needed in entrepreneurship. In short, this is a story about resonance between man, art and nature.

2.3 Durante M-Kvadrat Ltd.

Overview

Address:	Dankovečka 9, 10000 Zagreb, Croatia
Tel:	+385 915317991
Email:	durantem2@yahoo.com

Company Information

Industry:	Manufacturing and service-trading cooperatives; Agents involved in the sale of various products (licenced for the production and selling of joint free slabs—contemporary floor systems without dilatations used in the construction industry)
Year of establishment:	2008
Sales revenue in 2010:	€800,000
Sales revenue in 2000:	n/a
Average number of employees in 2010:	3
Brain(s) behind the company:	Owner Marko Jelušić and partners Renata Jelušić and Branka Merdita

2.3.1 Nature of Market Leadership

This is the only licenced company for production and distribution of joint free slabs in Europe. Its market power has been increasing since its conception. The product is patented in Australia. There are only four licenced producers and sellers in different parts of the world, therefore there is no direct competition between them.

2.3.2 Nature of Competitive Advantage

Among the competing companies that have the licence for the production and distribution of joint free slabs in Europe, Durante M-Kvadrat is the only one with advance payment as a method for securing the company's capital in products and money in these turbulent times. This creates big financial savings for the investor. The company is building up a market reputation and a distinctive market position through quality awards. In particular, an Award for Excellence from the Concrete Institute of Australia in 2001, and a Choice Award from the American Concrete Institute in 2008, have confirmed the quality of the company's products.

2.3.3 Core Lessons Learned on the Path to Success

1. Believe in the product that you are selling. It will not be easy to change old, settled ways, but that is not a reason to withdraw. With the right branding and recognition of the product's quality, you will be able to position your product.
2. Patents are important to protect you from the competition. Being a licenced producer and seller of the product makes it considerably easier to do business. But this is just the beginning. To be a true champion, the leader has to be an innovator and continuously develop his or her products.
3. Make sure that you produce quality products, if possible from recycled materials. And make them as simple as possible to install so as to be user-friendly and therefore rapidly accepted by customers.

2.3.4 Durante M-Kvadrat: Hidden Champion

The youngest company among our Croatian champions is Durante M-Kvadrat, established in 2008 as a cooperative consisting of three members and licenced for the production of joint-free slabs, a contemporary floor system without dilations, used in the construction industry. In 2010 they started production in a small plant in Zagreb. Like Bodren, Durante M-Kvadrat is not a typical HC but is close to becoming one in the future. The main company activity is production-service-trading, i.e. trade with various products.

Joint Free Slabs is a patented system for concrete slab construction using an innovative method of allowing for concrete shrinkage. In traditional slabs, control joints are installed for this purpose. Joint Free Slabs Pty Ltd developed a crack inducer grid that eliminates the need for any control joints. The product is built with teardrop-shaped tubes that create micro fissures relieving stress and major cracking. The tubes are connected using a four-sided connector, which also acts as a holder for reinforcing bars. The tubing is built of hard, flexible, high-quality PVC, and the connector is made out of polypropylene. Tubes are assembled into a one-metre grid pattern on site and their primary purpose is to induce a closely spaced network of fine cracks throughout the entire length and breadth of the slab. High-quality recycled materials are used in the manufacture, which can bear the pressure of moving construction machines and concrete spilling out of the pump, and can also resist the temperature peak while the concrete solidifies. The product meets every European and international eco-standard for these kinds of materials. The durability of the product is even longer than the durability of the building itself, and the efficiency of the system is long lasting. The functionality of the system is guaranteed, no matter who installs it or makes the concrete panel. The goal in manufacturing is to use as much recycled materials as possible and to take care of the off-cuts after the system has been installed. The advantages of the product in comparison to its competitors are the simplicity of setting up the panel (which can be done by an unqualified worker), the ideal positioning of the reinforcing bars, the single layer of armouring, the small cross-sections of the concrete panel, and the decrease of forces in the lower cross-section of the concrete panel. There is no need for a concrete finishing layer, and no need for maintenance of the panel.

With this system, vast areas of slab can be constructed much faster than is possible using traditional methods, and there is the potential for sizeable direct savings in both construction cost and time. Moreover, the aesthetics of the finished floor are superior and the cost of ongoing maintenance is significantly reduced. Without the need for control joints, the required thickness of the concrete is also significantly reduced. This product received an Award for Excellence from the Concrete Institute of Australia in 2001 in recognition of "construction techniques and innovation that contribute to the understanding and use of concrete". And in 2008, it won a Choice Award at the *World of Concrete* event in Las Vegas.

The idea of joint free slabs came to the mind of one of the company founders, Mr. Marko Jelusić, while talking about products that still did not exist on the European market. That was the reason for making contact with the product innovator who sells on the Australian market. After 3 years of negotiating, Mr. Jelusic got an authorization to sell the product and was the second in the world to get a licence from the product developer. He also went one step further at the very beginning, and issued the product only with advanced payment as a method for securing the company's capital. This created big financial savings for the investor in construction. There is still a long journey ahead. Making the product commonplace requires patience and determination to invest for a longer period of time. The company is very young and still in its growth stage; therefore the journey is just beginning.

Mr. Jelusić's targeted markets are four main groups of customers in Croatia and Europe who are directly involved in all kinds of building construction: investors, architects, structural engineers and contractors. Their own clients include owners of private houses, scrap metal merchants, warehouses for various goods, food companies, food and drink distributors, sports complexes, shopping centres, and agencies for traffic infrastructure. There appears to be no limiting factor for the business of a joint-free concrete panel system. Its efficiency leads to broader use. This system has no competition in Europe because there are only four licenced producers and sellers in the world, and they enjoy the full protection of the patent's owner, Mr. Bob Warwick. A leading advantage of this cooperative is the constant education and getting to know the four targeted groups as much as possible. They always search for the most efficient way of delivering goods in agreement with the customer, without charging the real costs.

The crisis that hit the world, including Croatia, shook the construction sector. However, because of its advanced payment system, quality of products, and cheaper prices, this company was not affected in any way. In addition, the company currently operates at a profit, and has no debts towards other business subjects or the state, and no unpaid claims. Its net sales increase was 25 % in 2009 and 7 % in 2010.

The international expansion of the business has already gone through several phases. First there were trips to arrange special offers. At present these arrangements have clear goals. Two branch offices are to be opened in Russia and Germany. Many new ideas are developed every day. One of them is cavitation; a very powerful, stable, harmless, eco-approved, simple and cheap system for warming up spaces and heating water. The minimal ratio of the invested and gained energy is 1:2.8. It is a system that can cover up to 6,000 m^2 of space, and can be connected into a series. Slowly but surely, this company is enhancing quality through innovation, a constant search for improvement, and care for nature.

Although Durante may not be a typical HC, and at the moment is not focused on developing its unique product or service, its charismatic leader certainly wants to become a champion in the near future. By using the distribution of a patented product along with a system of advanced payments, this company is creating the capital and network to start its own innovation testing and production. In short, Mr. Jelusic has just started to dream his lofty dreams, which will soon become reality.

Conclusion

These HCs stand out for the clear strategy that they have, as well as their sustainable leadership, superior customer service, more professionally managed finances, and a higher investment in R&D than others. Because of their trading volumes, these companies are the true forces behind globalization. They are role models for others because although they seem normal in their core, they reach top positions in their chosen market niches (Witt 2010). If these three Croatian companies were compared to those identified as champions by Simon, several conclusions would follow: HCs in Croatia produce world-class products, efficiently designed according to the wishes and needs of the targeted market niche. Apart from Durante, they charge premium prices. They have their own ways of distribution that bring them closer to their customers. The leaders of all three companies are visionaries who constantly generate new ideas. They are passionate and charismatic, capable of motivating their workers and charging them with the same enthusiasm. Their success is not simply pure luck; it stems from the ambitious goals that they set themselves and the hard work and determination to reach them. Luck is a "by-product of the desire for perfection" (Simon 2009); these HCs are not waiting for it to come by itself.

DOK-ING fits perfectly into Simon's HC frame: it is a company that produces innovative, high quality machinery for a specific market niche, it has a leading position in the world, invests increasing amounts in R&D each year, and is constantly improving distribution and its maintenance services so as to get closer to the customers.

The other two companies differ slightly. Bodren produces the highest quality wines recognized by experts in the field, and has many awards as proof, but it is still quite a small company searching for its place in the market. But with the vision that the owner has, the effort he invests in making it a reality, the constant improvement of the product, and the strong promotion for chosen clientele, this company is on its way to become a real HC in the future.

Durante M-Kvadrat produces an innovative, patented building product, but it is not the company's invention. Its position in the market is secured with the licence it has, and therefore does not have any direct competition. It is a new company just establishing its market. It has ideas and a plan to finance them with current profits. Like Bodren, this company is gradually fulfilling Simon's criteria for German HCs.

There are many similarities and differences between all HCs in Croatia. But when compared to those in Germany, a common characteristic is their strong leadership. They all have visionary leaders with a clear vision of what they are doing, how they are doing it, and where they see their companies in the future. They lead and motivate others, and transfer their own enthusiasm to them. These are people who knew where they wanted to be, and have managed to find the way and the courage to get there when the opportunity presented itself. They are the brains behind it all. They are the reason that we can talk about champions.

References

Croatian Regions Office. (2013). *Croatia*. Retrieved May, 2013, from http://www.croatianregions.eu/en/3

Hernder Estate Wines. (2011). *Characteristics of the ice wine*. Retrieved May, 2011, from http://www.hernder.com/content/article.cfm?RecordID=21

Simon, H. (2009). *Hidden champions of the twenty-first century*. Berlin: Spinger.

Vranjican, S. (2005). Dostignuća i promašaji gospodarskog razvoja Hrvatske u proteklom stoljeću. *Revija za socijalnu politiku, 12*(3–4), 333–344.

Witt, A. (2010). *Internalisation of hidden champions*. Hamburg: Management Laboratory.

World Bank. (2013). *Data; countries and economies*. http://data.worldbank.org/country

Hidden Champions of Estonia

Rein Riisalu and Anu Leppiman

Overview

Official name:	Republic of Estonia
Type of government:	Parliamentary Democratic Republic
Population in 2010:	1,340,161
Land area:	45,227 km^2

History

Twelfth century	An administrative division had developed in which the ethnical borders of today's Estonia can be recognized.
1208/1227	The invasion of German and Danish crusaders (the Christianization).
1227–1918	Estonia divided between German, Russian, Swedish, Danish, and Polish-Lithuanian rulers.
1918	(February 24th) Estonia declares its independence.
1918/1920	Estonian War of Independence: Soviet Russia against the Republic of Estonia.
1920	(February 2nd) Soviet Russia recognizes the Republic of Estonia (Tartu Peace Treaty)
1921	Leading countries in the world recognizes Estonia *de jure*; Estonia becomes a full member of the League of Nations.
1940	The Soviet Union occupies Estonia; a pro-Soviet puppet government is formed; Western countries do not recognize the changes carried out by force in the Baltic countries.

R. Riisalu (✉) • A. Leppiman
Department of Business Administration, Tallinn University of Technology, Tallinn, Estonia
e-mail: rein.riisalu@ttu.ee

P. McKiernan and D. Purg (eds.), *Hidden Champions in CEE and Turkey*,

DOI 10.1007/978-3-642-40504-4_13,

1941/1944	Invasion by Nazi Germany and the Red Army during WWII; reoccupation by the Soviet Union.
1980s	The Estonian independence movement (described as the Singing Revolution).
1991	(August 20th) The Estonian Supreme Soviet proclaims Estonian independence, thus restoring the Republic of Estonia; within a few years all countries in the world (including the former Soviet Union and Russia) recognize Estonian sovereignty.
2004	Estonia achieves full membership of NATO and joins the EU.
2011	(January 1st) Estonia adopts the single European currency, the Euro.

1 Introduction: Context

Estonian initiatives are better known in the world than Estonia as a country. The following two examples help explain. Probably the most famous initiative related to Estonia is Skype. Skype software, as an Internet peer-to-peer communications application, was invented and developed by Estonians Ahti Heinla, Priit Kasesalu, Jaan Tallinn and Toivo Annus in Estonia. Together with entrepreneurs Niklas Zennström (Sweden) and Janus Friis (Denmark), they launched the first version of Skype on 29 August 2003, and by the following October over 1 million people had downloaded the software. In September 2005, 100 % of the shares of Skype Technology SA were acquired by e-commerce company eBay for 2.6 billion US dollars, and in April 2006, the number of registered users of Skype reached 100 million.

Today, most of the development team and 44 % of the overall employees of Skype are still located in Estonia. At the end of 2010, it is estimated that the number of Skype accounts totalled more than 660 million and there were approximately 145 million active users. According to TeleGeography Research, in 2010 Skype had a 13 % market share in the international call market. On 28 March 2011, Skype reached 30 million concurrent users online for the first time. On 10 May 2011, Microsoft Corp. acquired 100 % of Skype for 8.5 billion US dollars.[1]

The second example involves two Estonians named Toomas Trapido and Rainer Nõlvak, who in the autumn of 2007 initiated the idea to clean up illegally dumped waste across Estonia—in 1 day! Within a few weeks several people joined the initiative group and created a "Let's Do It" team. From October 2007 to April 2008, with the help of hundreds of volunteers, the team geo-mapped about 10,000 tonnes of waste strewn all over Estonia. On 3 May 2008, more than 50,000 people gathered voluntarily and cleaned up all the waste from forests and roadsides within 5 h.

[1] The data in this paragraph and the next are from various Internet sources.

During the following years, the same idea and model were introduced in Latvia, Lithuania, Portugal, Slovenia, Ukraine, Romania, Bulgaria, Moldova, Cambodia, Finland, Brazil, Russia and the CIS. A "World Clean Up" day took place on 24 March 2012. The vision was to have "a wave of 1-day countrywide clean-up sweep across the world, resulting in millions of tons of gathered waste, cleaner nature, as well as renewed and deeper connections between people, communities and nature". The target was to involve 100 countries and 300 million volunteers in World Clean Up 2012. Both initiatives are disproportionately large compared to the size of Estonia. The country Estonia has a population of 1.34 million and is the fourth smallest EU member after Malta, Luxembourg and Cyprus.

The first signs of human activities on the territory of Estonia date back more than 11,000 years. However, during most of the last 1,000 years, foreign powers have ruled the Estonia and its people. Estonia was an independent country from 1918 to 1940. Between 1940 and 1991 it was part of Soviet Union, and the restoration of independence took place in 1991.

As all ex-Soviet countries and their allies, independent Estonia had to make a decisive shift towards a market economy. Entrepreneurship, privatization and foreign investments were some of the keywords in the 1990s. All this has shaped the landscape of the Estonian economy and provided a basis for bringing hidden champions (HCs) to the fore.

After joining NATO and the EU in 2004, and adopting the euro in 2011, Estonia has been fully recognized as a business society following Western principles. Yet, Estonia is still far below the EU average in terms of living standards. Main foreign trade and other economic indicators are presented in Exhibit 1. Clearly, GDP per capita grew significantly over the 1999–2009 period (average growth rate: 4.38 %). Long-term unemployment decreased and exports more than tripled; the most significant export increase was in fuels (shale oil). Based on the progress in the past decade and its current position and policies, Estonia believes it will develop in the near future faster than the EU27 average.

The Estonian HCs owe their success to certain key people who discovered how to use the strengths of their companies, and the opportunities that the environment offers. However, the government of Estonia has played a crucial role in creating a business- and living-friendly environment that gave fruit in several successful companies with strong competitive positions in narrow niches in international markets. When searching for HCs among them, we identified six talent pools that produce such companies in Estonia: (1) trading and travelling, (2) hard technologies, (3) traditional development, (4) former exiled Estonians, (5) ambitious young entrepreneurs, and (6), new technologies. The first four pools have to do with historical advantages and disadvantages that are characteristic of countries like Estonia. The latter two are new-wave pools, which generate achievements by entrepreneurial and creative people who start out in today's business environment. This does not mean that success has been easier in the first four pools. Restructuring the old system and finding one's unique path to the future has required a series of correct decisions, brilliant execution, and some luck. Many have tried but only a

Exhibit 1 Core economic indicators

	1999	2000	2001	2002	2003	2004	2005	2006	2007	2008	2009	2010	2011
GDP (current US$, mio)	5,709.01	5,675.17	6,237.91	7,318.19	9,840.74	12,025.94	13,905.51	16,798.53	21,993.65	23,781.59	19,117.64	18,845.66	22,154.72
GDP per capita (current US$)	4,150.04	4,143.93	4,572.91	5,386.39	7,270.28	8,912.79	10,330.24	12,503.12	16,392.72	17,738.52	14,264.01	14,062.23	16,533.37
GDP per capita growth (annual %)	0.49	10.19	6.70	6.99	8.17	6.68	9.11	10.31	7.64	−4.08	−14.05	3.34	8.29
Total unemployment (% of total labor force)	11.6	13.1	12.4	9.4	10.7	10	7.9	5.9	4.7	5.5	13.8	16.9	12.5
Long-term unemployment (% of total unemployment)	48.9	46.3	48.3	52.9	45.9	52.2	53.4	48.2	49.5	30.9	27.4	n/a	n/a
Foreign direct investment, net inflows (% of GDP)	5.35	6.82	8.70	3.89	9.34	8.03	22.49	13.17	15.59	7.88	9.76	10.89	1.97
Exports of goods and services (current US$, mio)	4,021.68	4,800.88	4,979.55	5,190.85	6,808.83	8,787.90	10,807.12	12,212.56	14,751.63	16,896.33	12,436.84	14,968.95	20,273.61
Exports of goods and services (% of GDP)	70.44	84.59	79.83	70.93	69.19	73.07	77.72	72.70	67.07	71.05	65.05	79.43	91.51
Merchandise exports (current US$, mio)	3,017.00	3,830.00	4,015.00	4,336.00	5,622.00	5,932.48	7,715.75	9,691.94	11,009.94	12,457.82	9,047.79	11,597.09	16,760.24

Merchandise exports to high-income economies (% of total merchandise exports)	71.61	77.77	70.00	68.67	69.62	77.60	74.42	67.74	63.45	64.47	66.64	65.37	n/a
Merchandise exports to developing economies in Europe & Central Asia (% of total merchandise exports)	26.24	20.13	23.60	25.71	27.41	20.83	23.23	25.65	30.39	31.00	27.14	30.69	n/a
Ores and metals exports (% of merchandise exports)	5.07	5.48	2.70	2.43	2.50	2.56	2.52	3.21	3.19	4.11	2.19	3.09	2.74
Agricultural raw materials exports (% of merchandise exports)	11.87	9.19	8.11	8.11	8.16	6.91	5.99	5.07	5.55	4.37	4.31	5.13	4.11
Food exports (% of merchandise exports)	11.02	8.02	10.07	11.72	10.64	9.32	8.08	7.53	9.29	9.23	10.15	9.90	8.92

(continued)

Exhibit 1 (continued)

	1999	2000	2001	2002	2003	2004	2005	2006	2007	2008	2009	2010	2011
Fuel exports (% of merchandise exports)	4.51	4.47	3.91	5.32	4.22	4.54	7.22	15.52	12.32	11.70	16.24	15.58	16.80
Manufactures exports (% of merchandise exports)	67.51	72.82	75.21	72.42	74.48	73.28	70.05	63.49	64.70	66.23	62.39	62.45	63.01
High-technology exports (% of manufactured exports)	13.50	29.93	19.28	11.86	12.66	14.00	14.66	12.63	5.80	5.40	5.68	9.02	n/a

Source: World Bank (2013)

few have reached the top. Let us consider each of the six pools and analyse their economic and historical roots that gave a burst of energy to the HCs.

First, trading and travel is an important pool of regional HCs. Why so? Estonia is located on the Baltic Sea, which for several centuries has played an important role as a trade route in northern Europe. During the Cold War, the Baltic Sea was a part of the border between East and West; and Tallinn, the Estonian capital, was one of the few gates in this border. In 1965, the sea route between Helsinki (Finland) and Tallinn was reopened, but only one ship travelled it until the end of the 1980s. Leaving the Soviet Union was quite complicated in those days; therefore the main passengers were Finns and other West Europeans. Estonian sailors got valuable experience serving the passengers on this route. This experience has contributed to the development of the fourth largest ferry company in the world, which now has about 50 times more passengers than 20 years ago.

Second, the natural resources of Estonia, viewed as hard technologies, gave birth to the second pool of HCs. Though Estonian territory is only 45,000 km^2, and is generally poor in mineral resources, it is endowed with oil shale. Estonia started using oil shale commercially in 1920s for producing fuels and shale oil. Oil shale products comprised 9.5 % of Estonia's total exports, although many countries were mining oil shale at that time. The world reserves of oil shale are larger than those of crude oil. The use of oil shale worldwide decreased significantly after WWII because crude oil and coal had higher calorific value and were much cheaper to obtain. To provide energy to the northwest portion of the Soviet Union (including Leningrad), the leaders of Soviet Union decided to utilize Estonian oil shale. Many investments were made; huge power plants fuelled by oil shale were built, and Estonia became the world's largest oil shale producer after the 1960s. Although production volumes have decreased by more than half from their peak in 1980, more than 80 % of oil shale used in the world today is mined in Estonia. The oil shale industry was revived in the 2000s, when oil prices remained high. The ultimate business secret and entry barrier today is the technology, i.e.,—how to make gasoline and oil shale products from oil shale in the most cost-effective and environmentally friendly way. Estonia is leading in these technologies.

Not all oil shale processing plants were reopened after WWII. The Soviet Union started processing uranium in a former Estonian oil shale plant. This was a closed military site called "Factory No. 7". In 1970, this company started producing rare earth metals and rare metals. After 1990, the processing of uranium was halted. Today, the company is only one of two rare earth processing facilities in Europe—it is one of the world's leading producers of pure niobium and tantalum. By selling the majority of the shares to a US competitor in April 2011, the company secured a steady and secure supply of rare earth feed stocks.

Third, Estonia has an international competitive advantage in traditional development (agriculture), for example in breeding quails. Estonia started that activity in the 1970s, and by 1988 had developed an internationally recognized Estonian breed of quails. Today, Estonia has the largest quail farms in Europe. Japan has the world's largest quail farms, where of course they raise their own indigenous breed of quails.

Exhibit 2 Estonian hidden champions

Name	HC pool Main business field Market position	Revenues 2010 (in M €)	Revenues 2000 (in M €)	Average employees 2010
Eesti Energia (Enefit)	Hard technologies Oil shale industry #1 oil shale industry in the world and #2 shale oil producer in Europe	796.2	275.9	7,353
Järveotsa Vutifarm	Traditional development Quail farms #1 quail farms in Europe	0.4	0.1	12
Kiviõli Keemiatööstus	Hard technologies Oil shale industry #3 shale oil producer in Europe	26.6	7.7	647
Krimelte	Ambitious young entrepreneurs Construction materials #1 insulating foam producer in CEE	67.5	4.7	200
Molycorp Silmet	Hard technologies Rare earth metals and rare metals industry #1-2 rare earth metals industry in Europe	34.2	29.7	494
Playtech Estonia	New technologies IT Leading software developer for unified software platforms and content for the remote and land-based gaming industry in the world	15.8	n/a	408
Tallink Grupp	Travelling and trading Maritime transportation #1 mini-cruises ferry operator in the world and #1 duty free & retail shop on ferries in the world	813.9	130.4	6,612
Viru Keemia Grupp (VKG)	Hard technologies Oil shale industry #2 shale oil producer in the world and #1 shale oil producer in Europe	125.5	48.3	1,406
Wendre	Former exile Estonians Textile industry Leading beddings manufacturer in Europe	76.3	11.3	745

Source: Authors of the chapter

The fourth pool from which HCs originate are former exiled Estonians, endowed with expert knowledge and networks, developed through years of living abroad. In particular, during WWII, thousands of Estonians fled the country and restarted their lives in Western Europe, America, or Australia. After the restoration of independence, many of them or their children moved back to Estonia bringing their know-how, relationships, and capital to privatized companies. Their roots distinguished them from other foreign investors (the latter have also played a remarkable role in developing Estonian business and society). The most successful story from this pool comes from the textile industry—a businessman born in an Estonian family in Sweden has become a leading European beddings manufacturer in Estonia in only 15 years.

The fifth pool of HCs is made up of ambitious young entrepreneurs. Democracy and a market economy allowed everyone to start with his own business. The Soviet era had destroyed the traditions of family businesses and former entrepreneurs. On one hand there was a lack of knowledge and experience; on the other, there were few constraints. Most members of the new business generation created companies that resembled those of Western Europe—especially in the service sector, which was underdeveloped during the Soviet era. After securing positions of market leadership in Estonia, and in some cases, remarkably, securing market share in other Baltic countries, the founders sold their companies to large Scandinavian, or even global, companies. There are a few exceptions; those who were not satisfied with their leading position in the local market. They set out to be players on the world stage. One example comes from the construction materials business—an Estonian company is among the world's top five producers of insulating foam.

Lastly, the most transformative pool of HCs in Estonia involves new technologies—a challenge worldwide. The recent past has proved that it is possible to build a billion-dollar company within several years. Skype, which is already an IT software champion, is not the only success story in Estonia. Playtech—the world's largest software developer for unified software platforms and content for the remote and land-based gaming industry—also comes from the IT sector and is somewhat similar to Skype. The original IT competence came from Estonians, and the business competence was supplied by foreigners. Today, the company has expanded and opened new offices in several countries. It seems that the classic HC concept does not fit new technology initiatives. These teams have been international since the beginning, and the companies are not HCs just in one particular country.

As can be seen in Exhibit 2, Estonian HCs are diversified; some with strong global leadership, others with regional leadership. Some of them have revenues close to one billion euros, others have less than 1 million euros. Despite this diversity, all of them command a significant competitive strength in international markets. Two companies (Tallink Grupp and Eesti Energia) of the nine identified in Exhibit 2 are described in detail in the next part of this chapter.

2 Two Case Studies

2.1 Tallink GRUPP[2]

Overview

Address:	Sadama 5/7, 10111 Tallinn, Estonia
Tel:	+372 6409800
Email:	info@tallink.ee
Web:	http://www.tallink.ee (customers), http://www.tallink.com (investors)

Company Information

Industry:	Sea and coastal passenger water transport services
Year of establishment:	1989
Sales revenue in 2010:	€814 million
Sales revenue in 2000:	€130 million
Average number of employees in 2010:	6,612
Brain(s) behind the company:	CEO Enn Pant

2.1.1 Nature of Market Leadership

Tallink Grupp is the number one mini-cruises ferry operator in the world, and the number one duty free & retail shop on ferries in the world by revenue. Northern Europe has the world's greatest passenger volumes in maritime transport. The nature of market demand in the northern Baltic Sea differs from the rest of Europe, where fast transfers (shuttles) dominate. Helsinki, Stockholm, Tallinn, and Riga are the capital cities and attractive short-break destinations. When taking mini-cruises, the passengers often overnight on the ferries and spend a lot of money in the restaurants and shops. Finland's Åland Islands in the northern Baltic Sea are exempted from the EU's VAT rules, and therefore ferries that stop over at the islands can offer tax-free sales.

2.1.2 Nature of Competitive Advantage

Tallink Grupp achieved a tangible advantage in the eyes of the customers by introducing state-of-the-art and cost-effective ferries in 2000s. Today, Tallink Grupp is the number two ferry operator in the world in terms of the gross tonnage of its ferry fleet, and number one in terms of its number of beds. Tallink Grupp's

[2] The content is based on an interview with Andres Hunt, the Vice Chairman of Tallink Grupp on 1 December 2010, Tallink Grupp's corporate factsheet and financial reports of Tallink Grupp (http://www.tallink.com).

main strengths include knowledge of the market, professional marketing, qualified employees, the atmosphere in the company, the decision-making processes, and last but not least, the continuity of leadership. Capital intensity and a fleet of ferries specific to the market, on the one hand, and knowledge of the market and the established distribution of the market, on the other hand, create barriers to the entry of new players. The living standard of people on the east coast of the Baltic Sea is increasing and business volumes still have the potential to go up in the Baltic North.

2.1.3 Core Lessons Learnt on the Path to the Business Success

1. The business environment is a strategic window—for some period it is closed (in this case during the Cold War) but those who are patient, prepared, and bold, can reap great benefits when it opens.
2. Customer behaviour is always local but meeting the clients' needs is always universal.
3. By focusing on a narrow regional market niche (i.e. oasis), instead of trying to play globally, you can become the world's top player in a particular service sector while the world's market concentration is low.

2.1.4 Tallink Grupp: Hidden Champion

Many business people have visited Frankfurt Airport or Paris Charles de Gaulle Airport and probably spent their time and money shopping there. Did you know that the Estonian maritime company Tallink Grupp made the same amount of revenue in duty free & travel retail shops as the airports in Frankfurt or Paris in 2010, and that this is more than what was earned at London's Gatwick or Beijing's BCIA? Focusing on niche maritime mini-cruises in the northern Baltic Sea, Tallink Grupp has become the world's largest mini-cruise ferry operator in terms of revenue, and the world's largest duty free & retail shop on ferries.

In 1989, a company named Tallink was founded as a Finnish-Soviet joint venture. It was the so-called perestroika era and many cases of this type of cooperation with foreign partners were initiated. The original business idea of Tallink was to transport tourists between Helsinki (Finland) and Tallinn (Estonia). One founder, the Estonian Shipping Company (ESCO), already had experience serving that route since 1965. In 1993, when the Finnish partner sold its shares, Tallink became a fully Estonian-owned company. Since the end of 2001 the company's official name has been Tallink Grupp. Today it is a NASDAQ-OMX listed company (TAL1T). Forty percent of its shares are owned by a single large Estonian shareholder who has representatives on the company's management board; another 40 % belong to foreign investment funds and banks; and 20 % are held by small shareholders.

Northern Europe has the world's greatest passenger volumes in maritime transport, with more than 70 million passengers in 2009. The nature of the market demand in the northern Baltic Sea differs from that in the rest of Europe, where fast transfers (shuttles) are dominating. Helsinki, Stockholm, Tallinn, and Riga are capital cities and attractive short-break destinations. When taking mini-cruises, the passengers often overnight on the ferries and spend a lot of money in the restaurants and shops. Finland's Åland Islands in the northern Baltic Sea are exempted from the EU's VAT rules. Therefore, ferries that stop over at the islands can offer tax-free sales. For example, 55 % of Tallink Grupp's total revenues come from restaurants and shops, and less than 30 % from ticket sales.

In 2010, the total turnover of Tallink Grupp was 813.9 million euros, including 450–500 million earned in mini-cruises. The average annual turnover growth in the past 10 years has been 20 %. In 2010, 8.4 million passengers travelled by Tallink Grupp's ferries. The average number of employees in 2010 was 6,612. According to the ShipPax Market 2010 report Tallink Grupp was the fourth largest ferry operator in the world in terms of revenue. It had the second largest gross tonnage and the largest number of beds.

Since the market demand and business environment in the Baltic North are unique, the main competitor comes from the same region—the Finnish ferry operator Viking Line. Until the mid-2000s, Viking Line was the largest ferry operator in the Baltic North. In 2006, Tallink Grupp acquired Silja Line (Finland), which had been Viking Line's competitor for ages. This strategic move strengthened Tallink Grupp's position on the route between Estonia and Finland and provided an opportunity to enter into new routes between Finland and Sweden. Although Viking Line and Tallink Grupp have similar business models, successful mergers and organic growth have helped Tallink Grupp to grow into the largest ferry operator in the northern Baltic Sea (its revenue is twice as large as that of Viking Line today, and Tallink Grupp has more than 50 % market share on each main route).

One of the main reasons for Tallink Grupp's success has been the strategic decision, made by the company's management at the end of 1990s, to own outright the fleet that the company needs for operations (It is very common for operators to charter ferries). Vice Chairman, Andres Hunt, explains, "If we believe in sustainable business on our routes, and the ferry operates 12 months a year, it is cheaper to own the ferries, and pay loan interest to the bank, than to rent the ferries from a chartering company, which is also paying a bank interest". So, Tallink Grupp started buying ferries, and in 2000 the management decided to start building new ferries for the company. Tallink Grupp achieved a tangible advantage in the eyes of its customers by introducing state-of-the-art and cost-effective ferries. At the beginning, competitors were rather pessimistic about the ferry building and reacted only after Tallink Grupp had changed the market standards.

Depending on the route, mini-cruises last from 14 to 36 h (for comparison, Tallink's shuttles between Helsinki and Tallinn take only 2 h). The mini-cruise product consists of a set of services, but Tallink Grupp does not have a specific competitive advantage at the product level. Sometimes the entertainment programmes that are offered on board make the difference, but these can easily be copied. Half of the customers are Finns and sales to foreign customers (i.e. export) account for approximately 83 % of total revenue in 2009. Travel agencies, which contribute 40 % of sales (the rest is sold by Tallink Grupp itself), function as distribution channels.

From the customer's point of view, the most important product characteristics are keeping to schedules (departure and arrival on time), information (advertisement), product quality, and price. Tallink Grupp believes that it is slightly better in the first three categories, while Viking Line tends to offer lower prices. Tallink Grupp's main strengths include knowledge of the market, professional marketing, qualified employees, the atmosphere in the company, the decision-making processes, and last but not least, the continuity of leadership.

The current CEO, Enn Pant, has been in charge since December 1996; prior to that the company's management consisted of experienced captains. Today all four members of the Management Board have business and finance backgrounds: "We know how to deal with money!" Vice Chairman Andres Hunt says. As leaders, the management board members are rather similar, although each has a unique approach for dealing with issues. As a team they are good at developing strategies and executing them. Looking back at 10 years of achievement, the leaders of Tallink Grupp are especially pleased with the competitive position and growth of the company. Also, Tallink Grupp suffered less during the last economic recession than business in general.

Looking into the future, Tallink Grupp sees a lot of potential in its current niche. The living standard of people at the East coast of the Baltic Sea is increasing and business volumes may go up without moving to other regions.

What does the Tallink Grupp case teach us? Doing your business in a supportive environment and meeting the clients' wishes are universal success factors, but focusing on a narrow regional market niche (i.e. oasis) at the same time, instead of trying to play globally, may still make you the world's top player in a particular service sector while the level of market concentration is low.

2.2 Eesti Energia AS (Enefit)[3]

Overview

Address:	Laki tn. 24, 12915 Tallinn, Estonia
Tel:	+372 7152222
Email:	info@energia.ee
Web:	http://www.energia.ee, http://www.enefit.com

Company Information

Industry:	Electricity
Year of establishment:	1939
Sales revenue in 2010:	€796 million

[3] The content is based on interviews with Sandor Liive, CEO of Eesti Energia on 30 December 2010 and Harri Mikk, Member of the Management Board of Eesti Energia on 29 December 2010, as well as on the financial reports of Eesti Energia and the company's web pages (http://www.energia.ee and http://www.enefit.com).

Sales revenue in 2000:	€276 million
Average number of employees in 2010:	7,353
Brain(s) behind the company:	CEO Sandor Liive & Board Member Harri Mikk

2.2.1 Nature of Market Leadership

Enefit is the number one producer of oil shale electricity in the world and the second largest producer of shale oil in Europe. Oil shale is a sedimentary rock that can be found underground; it is a fossil fuel. For about 50 years, Enefit has mined more oil shale than anyone else in the world. The company earns its main revenue from selling electricity and network services (77 %), shale oil (7 %), heat (6 %), and oil shale (4 %). Exports comprise 18 % of total sales. Enefit is the second largest producer of shale oil in Estonia, and therefore in Europe, since Estonia is the only country in Europe where shale oil is commercially produced.

2.2.2 Nature of Competitive Advantage

Although many countries intensively used oil shale between WWI and WWII, it was replaced by crude oil and coal for economic reasons. Estonia continued to develop methods for processing oil shale and today possesses unique technologies that allow oil shale to be utilized in an efficient and environmentally friendly way. The world's reserves of oil shale are about 3.5 times greater than those of crude oil today. The higher the world price of crude oil, the better the perspectives for the oil shale industry.

Shale oil has been a fuel for ships and boiler houses as an alternative to crude oil products. Enefit is now developing a new complex to produce high quality Euro 5 diesel fuel, suitable for road vehicle use. As long as the world price for Brent crude oil is above $60 US dollars per barrel, shale oil fuel is competitive. Launching the shale oil upgrader in 2016 will create new horizons for a company that knows how to work with oil shale. The oil shale business requires technological know-how and the control of oil shale reserves. Enefit has contracts for the use of the latter in the US, Jordan, and Estonia.

2.2.3 Core Lessons Learned on the Path to Business Success

1. Energy security is not just a political issue—in a world where resources are limited, it is also an economic issue. When cheap crude oil runs out, the second best alternative in economic terms will take its place. To establish your competitive strategy, assess how long the dominant product can be sold cheaper than your product and prepare yourself for market penetration. Being hidden but awake may require support from the government.
2. Innovate because your product is never good enough—and some day you may discover that the whole world wants to be your client.
3. Access to resources and technological know-how are extremely important.

2.2.4 Eesti Energia: Hidden Champion

Did you know that Estonia has the second-lowest average electricity price in the EU27? About 90 % of the electricity generated in Estonia is produced from oil shale, a sedimentary rock that can be found underground all over the world. It is a fossil fuel. The Estonian word for "oil shale" is translated as "burning rock". Estonia has been the world's largest oil shale miner and user since the 1960s.

Oil shale mining in Estonia started in 1916. The main reason was the lack of fuels during and after WWI. Several private and state-owned oil shale mining companies were created in the first decades. In Soviet times, all mining was centralized under one company—Eesti Põlevkivi (Estonian Oil Shale).

In 1939, Eesti Energia was founded with the aim of building a countrywide electricity grid to link various power stations in Estonia and achieving an optimal division of electrical power. In the 1940s and 1950s, the leaders of the Soviet Union decided to utilize Estonian oil shale to provide electricity for the northwestern part of the Soviet Union (including Leningrad). Two power plants fuelled by oil shale were built and incorporated into Eesti Energia between 1956 and 1973.

After the restoration of independence, the future of the oil shale industry in Estonia was in doubt. There was intense discussion at the highest levels. Availability of cheaper crude oil products as an alternative fuel, the investment requirements, and concern for the environment were arguments against the oil shale industry, whereas energy security, balance of trade, and jobs were arguments for it. Although there were concerns about the prospects for oil shale, the administrative prices of oil shale and electricity were at a level that Eesti Põlevkivi and Eesti Energia were able to sustain without subsidies and in the closed electricity market the end consumers had to accept the prices.

In 1998, Gunnar Okk joined Eesti Energia as the new CEO. Gunnar Okk built a new management team and started to introduce reforms and modernization measures in the company. In 2003, Eesti Energia acquired 100 % of the shares of Eesti Põlevkivi; thus oil shale mining and electricity generation were united into one concern, 100 % owned by the Estonian state. Since 2005, Sandor Liive has been the CEO of Eesti Energia (he started in the company as financial director and member of the management board in 1998).

In 2010, the total turnover of Eesti Energia was 796.2 million euros. The company earned its main revenue from selling electricity and network services (77 %), shale oil (7 %), heat (6 %), and oil shale (4 %). Exports comprised 18 % of total sales. The 10-year-growth of total turnover has been on average 11 % per annum. Eesti Energia had about 470,000 residential and 26,000 business customers. In 2010, its average number of employees was 7,353. Eesti Energia mined a total 14.0 million tonnes of oil shale geological resource, of which 17.9 tonnes of saleable oil shale was produced in 2010. The Eesti Energia concern utilized 89 % of all that saleable oil shale. Based on these numbers, it is the world's largest oil shale company. It produced 190,000 tonnes of shale oil in 2010, which made the company the second largest shale oil producer in Europe.

Today, oil shale is used commercially only in Estonia, China and Brazil. There are two private competitors in Estonia, VKG Group and Kiviõli Keemiatööstus, but the main focus of these companies is on shale oil extraction, not electricity generation. The Estonian competitors previously depended on oil shale mined by Eesti Energia and only recently have they opened their own mines. The largest competitor in the field of oil shale is Fushun Mining Group Co that operates in China. The main activity of that corporation is coal mining, but according to the latest available data, Fushun also mines more than ten million tonnes of oil shale annually. In Brazil, the large multinational energy company Petrobras also deals with oil shale mining but the volumes are less than three million tonnes annually.

Although historical decisions, government regulation, and support during difficult times have played a very important role in putting Eesti Energia on the oil shale map today, the reasons for this success clearly lie in the continuity of leadership and the company's long-term strategies. Between 2001 and 2010, Eesti Energia has invested about 1,780 million euros (80 % of these investments have been financed from current business cash flows) in the upgrade of the distribution network, construction of new oil shale power plants, upgrade of oil shale mining equipment, construction of wind parks, environmental projects and other activities to provide customers with environmentally sustainable electricity and high-quality liquid fuels. Decisions on investments in projects valued at about 2,500 million euros for the next 10 years have already been made.

As Sandor Liive, the CEO of Eesti Energia explains: "As the leader, I discuss and agree our long-term directions—where we want to move. We have ambitious goals and we want to achieve them. Facing obstacles does not dampen our will; quite the opposite, it increases it. Our key people are like springs—the more you push them, the higher they jump. This is typical of our team, although as leaders and team members, everybody has a different style and background. My main task as the leader of Eesti Energia has been to find the right people with an entrepreneurial spirit for the team and provide them with sufficient freedom".

The gradual opening of the electricity markets in the Nordic and Baltic countries provides excellent export opportunities for Eesti Energia's cheaper electricity; in 2010, almost half of company's revenues and over 60 % of its profits came from the open markets.

At the same time, Eesti Energia's core business—oil shale—faces unlimited opportunities in the future. The reserves of cheap crude oil in the OPEC countries and Russia are decreasing and the market responds with higher market prices. As long as the market price for Brent crude oil is above 60 US dollars per barrel, shale oil fuel is competitive. Extracting shale oil adds more value to the rock than just burning it for electricity generation. Eesti Energia is developing an industry complex, complete with shale oil upgrader to produce high quality Euro 5 diesel fuel in 2016, suitable for road vehicle use.

The oil shale business is a business that requires technological know-how and the control of oil shale reserves. For the extraction of shale oil, Eesti Energia has developed Enefit-280 technology—the first new generation oil plant—and it was put into service in 2012. Eesti Energia is believed to have the world's most efficient oil shale processing technology. Electricity generation by oil shale may gradually be replaced by renewable energy carriers—in the Estonian case, by wind, biomass, and waste. The idea of a nuclear power station is not unrealistic either for the leaders of Eesti Energia.

The world's proven reserves of oil shale are more than 3.5 times larger than the reserves of crude oil today. About 70 % of those are located in the US and significant reserves also exist in about 14 other countries, including Russia, the Democratic Republic of Congo, Brazil, Italy, Morocco, Jordan, and Australia. The hunting season for acquiring the best oil shale reserves in the world has already opened. Eesti Energia has contracts for the use of oil shale in the USA and Jordan. By launching their new diesel fuel refineries and new generation Enefit-280 plants, each using 2.26 million tonnes of oil shale annually to produce 290,000 tonnes of shale oil, 75 million cubic metres of highly energy-efficient retort gas, and 280 GWh of electricity—Eesti Energia will become one of the big champions. The potential is huge: the world consumption of shale oil products currently totals about 0.02 % of the world consumption of crude oil products! As Sandor Liive points out: "The destiny of companies and individuals is shaped by creating dreams or visions and the will to win, the will to make your dreams come true. We enjoy winning!"

What can we learn from the case of Eesti Energia? Energy security is not just a political issue; in a world where resources are limited, it is also an economic issue. When cheap crude oil runs out, the second best alternative in economic terms will take its place. To establish your competitive strategy, assess how long the dominant product can be sold cheaper than your product and prepare yourself for market penetration. Being hidden but awake may require support from the government. You have to innovate because your product is never good enough; and some day you may discover that the whole world wants to be your client. And last, but not least, the access to the resources and technological know-how is extremely important.

Reference

World Bank. (2013). *Data; countries and economies*. http://data.worldbank.org/country

Hidden Champions of Hungary

Miklós Stocker and Péter Szlávik

Overview

Official name:	Hungary
Type of government:	Parliamentary Democratic Republic
Population in 2011:	9,971,727
Land area:	90,530 km^2

History

1920	After the collapse of the Austro-Hungarian Monarchy and the Treaty of Trianon, Hungary loses 2/3 of its territory and more than half of its population.
1940	Hungary joins World War II.
1945	At the end of the war, Hungary loses its regained territory.
1949	Hungary becomes a People's Republic under the influence of the Soviet Union.
1989	Hungary becomes a republic
1999	Hungary admitted to NATO
2004	(May) Hungary is one of the 10 new states to join the EU
2011	(January) Hungary takes over the EU presidency.

Hungary has approximately ten million inhabitants living in an area of 90,530 km^2. According to World Economic Forum data, Hungary is in 46th

M. Stocker (✉)
Department of Business Studies, Corvinus University of Budapest, Budapest, Hungary
e-mail: miklos.stocker@uni-corvinus.hu

P. Szlávik
Budapest Business School, Budapest, Hungary

P. McKiernan and D. Purg (eds.), *Hidden Champions in CEE and Turkey*,
DOI 10.1007/978-3-642-40504-4_14, © Springer-Verlag Berlin Heidelberg 2013

position in the GDP per capital ranking and 52nd position in the Global Competitiveness Index ranking. GDP per capita in Hungary was $ 12,635 in 2009, the average growth rate for the period between 1999 and 2009 has been around 2.6 % (more economic indicators for the country are shown in Exhibit 1).

1 Introduction: Context

For a better understanding of the current economic structure of Hungary, we need to look back a few decades. For most of the past one and half century[1] the country was -part of a larger economic area: first the Austrian-Hungarian Empire, then—after the Second World War—the community of socialist states, and finally the European Union.

Hungary's industry structure changed significantly in the 4 decades following the Second World War. The country was a founding member of COMECON (Council for Mutual Economic Assistance), an economic organization led by the Soviet Union. One of the crucial policies of that organization was the specialization of its members. It meant that selected industries were developed, while others (e.g. automotive) withered. Pharmaceuticals, the chemical industry, food processing, agricultural machinery, bus production, and electronics, had a special focus. We will see that some of the Hungarian hidden champions (HCs) are connected to these industries.

During its economic and political transition, Hungary invited foreign investors and sold many of its leading industrial companies to corporations, such as General Electric, Electrolux or Michelin. The privatization was followed by an period of intense investment during which some of the world's leading companies—General Motors, Philips, Nokia, Samsung, TEVA, and others—established a presence in the country. They were motivated by the country's well-educated, experienced workforce and its industrial tradition, and other factors, such as salary level, infrastructure and investment incentives. In 2009 the contribution of large companies to the added value was 49.7 %, which was 18 % higher than the EU average of 42.1 % (Román 2009).

The last 20 years were also characterized by the development of Hungary's SME companies. These innovation-focused, small and medium-sized enterprises were either established as spin-offs of former state-owned firms or were formed on the knowledge base of these industries. Parallel to traditional industries, new sectors—IT services, biotechnology and green energy—gained importance. There are examples of both types of companies among the HCs that we introduce.

Hungary has a long tradition in the field of innovation. Many famous researchers and innovators have Hungarian origins, for example T. Puskás, J. Neumann, L. Bíró, and E. Rubik. Companies with an innovative focus have always had prestige in Hungary. We will see that the HCs discussed in this study also have

[1] The exception is the period between the two world wars.

Exhibit 1 Core economic indicators from Hungary

	1999	2000	2001	2002	2003	2004	2005	2006	2007	2008	2009	2010	2011
GDP per capita (current $US)	4,713.54	4,542.72	5,175.03	6,535.29	8,247.00	10,084.52	10,936.95	11,173.57	13,534.71	15,364.68	12,634.55	12,863.13	14,043.66
GDP per capita growth (annual %)	3.49	4.50	3.95	4.80	4.15	5.03	4.17	4.06	0.27	1.07	−6.65	1.49	1.99
Long-term unemployment (% of total unemployment)	49.40	48.90	46.50	44.80	42.20	45.10	46.10	46.10	47.50	47.60	42.60	50.60	n/a
Foreign direct investment, net inflows (% of GDP)	6.85	5.97	7.48	4.54	2.61	4.20	7.71	16.60	51.90	48.62	−2.34	−16.07	6.88
GDP (current $US m)	48,255.01	46,385.59	52,720.97	66,389.49	83,538.37	101,925.73	110,321.71	112,533.15	136,102.02	154,233.54	126,631.68	128,631.63	140,029.34
Exports of goods and services (current $US m)	31,180.92	34,605.68	37,950.72	41,991.39	51,297.97	64,565.57	72,753.98	87,487.97	110,657.15	125,946.87	98,254.39	111,324.32	129,199.24
Exports of goods and services (% of GDP)	64.62	74.60	71.98	63.25	61.41	63.35	65.95	77.74	81.30	81.66	77.59	86.55	92.27
Merchandise exports (current $US m)	25,032.19	28,192.45	30,435.54	34,517.32	43,094.22	55,566.72	62,936.38	75,255.38	95,399.82	108,504.15	83,008.04	95,482.61	111,916.66
Merchandise exports to high-income economies (% of total merchandise exports)	91.62	90.93	90.16	89.94	89.59	88.88	85.15	82.50	81.01	79.78	80.84	79.24	n/a

(continued)

Exhibit 1 (continued)

	1999	2000	2001	2002	2003	2004	2005	2006	2007	2008	2009	2010	2011
Merchandise exports to developing economies in Europe & Central Asia (% of total merchandise exports)	6.22	7.22	7.64	7.51	8.32	8.72	11.57	13.53	15.19	16.81	15.55	16.43	n/a
Ores and metals exports (% of merchandise exports)	1.89	2.11	1.91	1.78	1.73	1.90	1.79	1.93	1.70	1.56	1.17	1.60	1.86
Agricultural raw materials exports (% of merchandise exports)	1.15	1.04	0.91	0.90	0.83	0.76	0.61	0.49	0.52	0.54	0.52	0.66	0.74
Food exports (% of merchandise exports)	8.58	7.32	7.78	7.28	7.08	6.58	6.24	5.72	6.44	7.15	7.86	7.45	7.85
Fuel exports (% of merchandise exports)	1.59	1.61	1.56	1.48	1.56	1.82	2.60	2.35	2.80	3.10	2.47	2.76	3.45
Manufactures exports (% of merchandise exports)	85.36	86.28	85.25	86.46	87.16	88.29	85.16	83.96	81.19	80.33	82.19	81.84	80.81
High-technology exports (% of manufactured exports)	22.67	26.53	24.23	24.93	25.76	29.05	25.83	24.12	23.79	23.30	24.94	24.24	n/a

Source: World Bank 2013

strong innovative characteristics. Unfortunately, the level of spending on innovation is well below that of other developed countries.[2]

The average size of the Hungarian HCs is smaller than the world average. According to Simon, a HC's average number of employees is 2,037 (Simon 2009 p.20). In the EU, companies are defined as "large" if they have at least 250 employees.[3] In Hungary, we could not identify a single HC in this category. Hungarian HCs are typically medium-sized enterprises according to their average number of employees.

The Hungarian HCs that we managed to interview are highly innovative companies. It is interesting to note that the typical leader of these companies has a strong personality. Although they have existed for more than 20 years, only two successions have occurred. All of the selected companies have based their operations on the knowledge of world-renowned Hungarians—scientists, engineers or economists. Leadership, motivation, knowledge, and research and development were all important elements mentioned during each interview.

All of these factors are necessary for success, but by analysing these sample companies we should also note that they all identified market opportunities and were brave enough to pursue them. Exhibit 2 provides core business data for the selected HCs, to be followed by a detailed analysis.

2 Four Case Studies

2.1 Cason Engineering Plc[4]

Address:	Velencei út 37, H-2030 Çrd, Hungary
Tel:	+3623522100
Email:	office@cason.hu
Web:	http://www.cason.hu

Company Information

Industry:	Communications, metering, and monitoring technology
Year of establishment:	1992
Sales revenues in 2010:	Around €8 million

[2] According to the OECD Factbook of 2010, it was 0.97 % of GDP in 2008 while the OECD average was 2.28 %.

[3] Besides the number of employees, either the annual turnover is over 50 million euros or the total assets are over 43 million euros.

[4] http://www.cason.hu/CompanyInfo.aspx

Exhibit 2 Core business data for Hungarian hidden champions

Market definition	Revenues 2010 (€m)	Revenues 2000 (€m)	Employees 2010
Industrial system communication (e.g. data collection of Gas distribution)	8	2.3	80+
Pharmaceutical and Biotechnological usage of Cyclodextrin and its derivatives	1.5	1	37
Modular, network integrated technical testing stations for car diagnostics	5	3	100
Professional Data Recovery, Professional Ethical Hacking; Quality Assurance in Traffic Information Systems, Behavioral Analysis of Information systems	6	0.6	100

Source: The authors of the chapter

Sales Revenues in 2000:	Around €2.3 million
Average number of employees in 2010:	More than 80
Brain(s) behind the company:	Ferenc Szakács

2.1.1 Nature of Market Leadership

CASON provides a system solution for the industrial gas distribution and data-monitoring market, where it has the most advanced technology relative to other providers of similar products.

2.1.2 Nature of Competative Advantage

CASON has a huge technological advantage, which differentiates it from its competitors. Its solution is completely different in terms of product and technology. Accordingly, this innovation allows CASON to price its solution at around 1/10 of the price of its competitors.

2.1.3 Core Lessons Learned in the Path to Business Success

1. Create a niche and do not fear the large MNCs.
2. Focus on problem-solving and be highly innovative.
3. Have a vision and well-educated and motivated employees.
4. Push harder if you face contraction in your market.

2.1.4 Cason Engineering Plc: Hidden Champion

Can you imagine a gas leakage in a system several thousand kilometres long? How would you know where to find the leak? How would you calculate the exact quantity of the gas flow? CASON offers wide-area wireless communication with high levels of reliability, which provides you exactly these data. The company offers solutions for the oil and gas industry, electrical energy distribution, and water distribution. With CASON's multi-utility smart solutions, data metering in electricity, gas, or even water networks, can be effectively managed for both residential and industrial consumers.

CASON began its operations in 1992 as a dealer in laboratory equipment and a service provider. In 1994 it turned to automation as its focus shifted from commercial equipment to solving its clients' problems. In the mid-1990s, CASON developed several pieces of equipment in line with its problem-solving mentality, but only began to market them in 2000.

Since 2000 CASON has been a developer-producer company, and in 2002 it entered a new niche of wide-area industrial system communication. Its main activities include development, manufacturing, and sales of specialized hardware devices. The company is also engaged in industrial wireless data communication products; measurement and process control products; design, installation, and operation of industrial process control; and data communication and information systems.

As early as in 2000, CASON won its first innovation award: the Innovation Prize from the Hungarian Chamber of Trade and Industry. It was followed by the Hungarian Innovation Grand Prize in 2005 and the Microsoft Innovation Award in 2010. In 2006 CASON was among the 500 most dynamically growing companies in Europe.

CASON is a HC in the gas distribution data market, where the company has a huge technological advantage, which differentiates it from competitors. Its solution is completely different in terms of product and technology. CASON can price its solution at around 1/10 of the price of its competitors.

Actually, using a strict definition, CASON does not have a direct competitor. In broader terms, they compete with large companies like Siemens, ABB, Iskra or Elster. However, these companies solve customer problems in a different way, with a different technology.

CASON competes mainly in the Central Eastern European and the Western European market but is developing its Arabian and Asian market presence. It has also entered the North American and Russian markets. It became a market leader in the CEE region approximately 5 years ago and is continuously challenging the industry with its newly developed technologies.

CASON has quadrupled its revenue in the past 10 years; however the 2009 crisis hit the company hard and it registered its first contraction in turnover. In 2001 its exports accounted for only 1 % of revenue, but over the 10 following years, that figure rose to 40 %.

The average life time of CASON's products is 5–10 years. The company has yet to experience re-orders because its sold products have not reached obsolescence. Because of this position, CASON needs to find new clients, or identify new projects, year after year. Its major customers account for approximately 30 % of sales. The company's market is characterized by a long sales cycle. According to the CFO, the sales cycle of a significant project is around 2 years.

CASON's products are high-tech, and their development and production are very capital-intensive. The company has already run into capital constraints to growth; therefore it has redefined its business model to achieve higher growth in a potentially huge market. CASON puts an emphasis on three core processes—

development, assembly, and testing,—that seem to be the three most critical business processes in its value system.

In terms of development, CASON has special know-how provided by exceptional and very innovative specialists. This gives the company a cutting edge in the developmental phase of new products. Once the instruments have already been designed and developed, manufacturing does not offer a large proportion of added value as it is mainly repetitive; therefore the company has decided to rely on third party producers instead of investing in its own production facilities.[5] In the next phase of the value system however, CASON puts a huge emphasis on the assembly and testing of parts, as this can assure their high quality.

CASON's solutions are much more effective than those of its competitors because of many factors, such as high-level quality products, flexibility in production, and tailor-made solutions to meet customers' special requirements. To maintain this position, significant research and development efforts are constantly needed. CASON spends 10 % of its annual revenue on R&D. This is a considerable amount, taking into account the fact that this business is very capital-intensive. CASON does not use patents but creates a novel inflation approach instead. The company builds on a path-dependent nature of development where it has a lead on their competitors. When competitors follow and develop CASON's known technology, the company introduces a more efficient one, which gives it an efficiency advantage again. Sometimes CASON even inflates its own technologies in order to further increase the efficiency gap.

CASON could not follow this strategy without the vision of its leader, Mr. Ferenc Szakács, or the company's motivated and well-educated managers and employees. Their innovativeness, loyalty, and knowledge of markets are essential. If CASON can solve its capital constraints, growth opportunities will be almost infinite, and it can become a well-known champion.

What specific lessons can CASON teach us? Create a niche, do not fear the large MNCs, focus on problem solving, have a vision, be highly innovative with well-educated and motivated employees, and push harder if you face contraction in your market.

2.2 Cyclolab Research and Development Laboratory Ltd[6]

Overview

Address:	Illatos út 7, 1097 Budapest, Hungary
Tel:	+3613476060
Email:	cyclolab@cyclolab.hu
Web:	http://www.cyclolab.hu

[5] Contract manufacturing has some good and reliable history in Hungary.

[6] http://www.cyclolab.hu/company1.html

Company Information

Industry:	Manufacturer of basic pharmaceutical products
Year of establishment:	1989
Sales revenues in 2010:	Around €1.5 million
Sales revenues in 2000:	Around €1.0 million
Average number of employees in 2010:	37
Brain(s) behind the company:	József Szeitli, Lajos Szente

2.2.1 Nature of Market Leadership

CycloLab is the only company in the world in the business of R&D and small-scale manufacturing of all-round cyclodextrin.

2.2.2 Nature of Competitive Advantage

The firm has more than 30 years of experience in cyclodextrin research, development and manufacturing. It has seized the cyclodextrin market at the right time and controls its whole value system, keeping other companies away from it. Because of this it has no direct competitors.

2.2.3 Core Lessons Learned on the Path to Success

1. Emphasize knowledge, leadership, research and development, and motivation.
2. Seize the whole value system if you are in a position to do so.

2.2.4 Cyclolab: Hidden Champion

Can you imagine pharmaceutical products that can be absorbed and take effect in your body much faster? With CycloLab's cyclodextrin products, several drugs are enhanced in this way. CycloLab can also develop solutions for lowering toxicity or even extend patent- protection. The company also develops solutions for the food, cosmetics, environmental applications, and agrichemical industries.

The foundation of the company goes back to 1992 when a leading Hungarian pharmaceutical, Chinoin, established CycloLab as its subsidiary. Prior to that, the company's team had worked as an organizational unit of Chinoin and had therefore gained significant experience. Around 1995 the company was taken over by the management through a successful management buy-out program. CycloLab was an independent company until 2008 when a Swiss company gained majority ownership, while the management remained a minority shareholder.

CycloLab was founded by Professor József Szejtli (Ph.D., D.Sc.) who acted as chief executive officer, and later as honorary president, until his death. He was author and co-author of over 250 scientific papers, over 200 conference presentations, six books, and over 100 patents. The total number of citations of his papers and books is over 5,000. He was awarded several national and international awards (e.g. the Moet-Henessy award), and in 2003 won the Széchenyi prize, the highest science award in Hungary.

The company has also won some prestigious prizes, such as the Millenium Award of the Hungarian Patent Office in 2007, and the Hungarian Innovation Grand Prize in 2008. CycloLab has ISO (International Standards Organization) 9001:2000 qualifications and uses the cGMP (current Good Manufacturing Practices) quality system, both of which are fundamental requirements in this industry.

CycloLab can be defined as a HC as it is the only all-round cyclodextrin R&D and small-scale manufacturing company in the world. The firm's key personnel has more than 30 years of experience in cyclodextrin research, development and manufacturing, and continues the legacy of its high-profile founder, Professor Szejtli.

CycloLab has a very specific market and usually serves 80–100 % of world demand. These figures suggest an attractive business position; however this market is difficult because it is an extremely small niche. There are products for which the world's whole annual demand is only 2 g. In addition to its own production, CycloLab usually sells its research, development and manufacturing capability, which can support clients in patent-protection extension of existing drugs, or enhance drug attributes such as water solubility, stability, taste, lower toxicity, and more. Because of this service approach, CycloLab collaborates well with large pharmaceutical companies that produce original or generic medicine.

CycloLab has been a leader in its market segment for around 20 years. However, its presence cannot enlarge the market. The company has always had significant export activities. Ten years ago their proportion was 90 % while nowadays it is around 80 %. It is very interesting that local clients usually have an international parent company with whom CycloLab used to do, or still does, business.

Strictly speaking, CycloLab does not have any direct competition. Instead, it has strategic partners. When asked to name competitors, the interviewees mentioned some only in a broad sense. Yet, these companies are completely different from CycloLab; therefore they are not direct competition at all. Only university research institutions can compete directly with the company; however they usually do not have the same capabilities or experience. The main difference between CycloLab and its competitors is that the latter simply cannot do what CycloLab can.

Although knowledge, leadership, research, and motivation have been the main aspects behind the success of CycloLab, it is important to note that its timing and holistic approach were also crucial. CycloLab seized the cyclodextrin market at the right time and controlled its whole value system, preventing other companies from entering this niche.

The advertisement for CycloLab is also very interesting as its name spreads with its employees' scientific publications. CycloLab's team has so far published approximately 500 technical/scientific papers including conference presentations, and has filed over 100 patent applications. Although the company has numerous patents, it can use only a few of them actively as patents for longer periods are more expensive and do not pay back their costs.

CycloLab's main product is used instantly.[7] The product is in the growth period of its life cycle. It is interesting that CycloLab's managers do not think of their company as high-tech; however in comparison with others in this Hungarian group it is certainly a high-tech company.

CycloLab has had only two CEOs in its history: company founder, Professor Szejtli and Dr Lajos Szente who took over after his death. In this business, it is very important that the CEO have a scientific reputation because only this can make both the CEO and the company legitimate. The fact that even the CFO holds a Ph.D. in genetics, emphasizes the company's scientific orientation. According to its main profile, CycloLab spends around 80 % of its revenue on research and development.

CycloLab has been growing organically throughout its history; its equity has risen year by year, and today its percentage exceeds 90 %. Although the company has not suffered capital constraints to growth, the small size of the market has been a heavy impediment. Despite all research efforts, CycloLab has not been able to enlarge the market significantly.

What specific lessons does CycloLab teach us? Emphasize knowledge, leadership, research and development, and motivation, and seize the whole value system if you are able to do it.

2.3 Energotest[8]

Overview

Address:	Gomba utca 4, H-2330 Dunaharaszti, Hungary
Tel:	+3624501150
Email:	energo@energotest.hu
Web:	http://energotest.hu/fooldal

Company Information

Industry:	n/a
Year of establishment:	1989
Sales revenues in 2010:	Around €5 million
Sales revenues in 2000:	Around €3 million
Average number of employees in 2010:	100
Brain(s) behind the company:	Tamás Zentai

[7] As the consumers of the drug use it instantly.

[8] http://energotest.eu/index.php?lang=en

2.3.1 Nature of Market Leadership

Energotest is a rising leader in modular, network-integrated technical testing stations in the car diagnostics industry in the CEE region, with indisputable market leadership in Hungary.

2.3.2 Nature of Competitive Advantage

Energotest has redefined the technical testing station industry by developing a testing station with which buyers can produce more revenue by giving more services to their customers. Energotest has also developed modularity and network integration, and constantly develops its mechanical, electronic, and software products. Energotest was able to cut down the prices in the industry through their constant development, which has given the company cost leadership.

2.3.3 Core Lessons Learned on the Path to Business Success

1. There is a trade-off between financial capital and thinking.
2. To be successful, one should develop constantly, step by step, and treat employees like co-workers.
3. Be brave enough to enrich the company's products, and manipulate the profit position in the industry or value stream.

2.3.4 Energotest: Hidden Champion

Have you ever been to a garage to have your car's brakes or emissions tested, or for a regular examination? If you live in the CEE region, there is a great chance that the technical testing station used by your mechanics was a product of Energotest. Besides regular technical testing stations that company also develops unique ones for university research centres.

Energotest's foundation goes back to 1989 when its predecessor, a state-owned company, became near bankrupt and in the restructuring process its leaders found that their garage division was not welcome any more. The leaders of the division and their friends founded Energotest in 1990 with little financial capital, but with plenty of thinking capability and ambition.

Energotest's main problem throughout its history has been its undercapitalization. The company's owners always had to take this into consideration even when faced with other challenges. Energotest's CEO, Mr. Tamás Zentai, has always thought that there was is a trade-off between financial capital and thinking. As the company lacked financial capital, it had to overcome that impediment with more thinking power. Following this rule, Energotest always looked for markets where it could become a leader even with scarce financial resources. First, the company developed a component for technical testing stations, then its own testing product. In the next step, it developed a product group, later a system, and even an integrated system. Today Energotest has a cooperating modular, network-integrated, technical testing station for car diagnostics. Over 20 years the company has developed constantly to reach a radically redefined solution for a known problem in the market. It has not only constantly redefined its product, but also shifted the profit position in the value stream and completely obliterated its former main competitor.

Energotest places heavy emphasis not only on development but also on efficient energy usage and quality. Energotest introduced ISO 9001 in 2001 and the ABAS ERP system and geothermic energy supply in 2006. It has TÜV, NAT and GEA certificates.

Energotest is a HC for its modular, network-integrated technical testing stations in the car diagnostics industry. In a tight market definition, Energotest does not have any significant competitor; however, in broader terms its competitors are MAHA, Bosch-Beissbarth and Snap-on.

Energotest is mainly active in the Central Eastern European market and is developing its Western European and Russian markets. Because of its step-by-step policy, it began internationalization fairly late, only in 2007. Its share of the whole technical testing station market in the CEE region is approximately 15 %.

Energotest has practically obliterated MAHA, its main domestic competitor, as today MAHA has just 1/30 of Energotest's revenue in Hungary. The main factor behind Energotest's success is that it has redefined the technical testing station industry by developing a testing station that allows buyers to produce more revenue by giving more services to their customers. Energotest has also developed modularity and network integration, and constantly develops its mechanical, electronic, and software products.

The latest Energotest testing stations have changed the value stream strategically by creating new profit opportunities for their clients. With Energotest products, clients have a broader, more profitable service portfolio and can provide services that were previously further in the value stream. This seems to be a win-win-win situation; Energotest and its clients are more competitive, and car owners can save time and money. Only the shrinking independent service companies lose; they do not have any influence on the value stream. However, they could integrate if they bought into Energotest's testing stations.

Energotest has also cut prices in the industry and provided more services. It has also formed partnerships with fellow research institutions at universities, which gives them new market opportunities. They entered the Ukrainian and Russian markets mainly through university connections.

The average life span of Energotst's main products is fairly long: 12 years. During this period the company offers its clients a wide range of services, such as maintenance, calibration, software upgrades and training. Although these produce a smaller amount of revenue than the main products, they provide a constant cash inflow. The company's products are in the growth phase of their life cycle; therefore they can easily be sold even in existing markets. Constant development holds the products continuously in the growth phase.

Although development is an important part of Energotest's business and the company holds five or six patents, these are not key elements of their success. As the company continues to develop, it is constantly ahead of its competitors. This allows it to reallocate money and energy necessary for patenting towards new developments, strengthening the path of dependency. Most of the company's innovations are market-driven; however it also develops risk innovations that can provide opportunities in new markets.

Energotest's is a limited liability company. The main owner holds over 70 % of the equity. This proportion has been rising constantly throughout the years. As already mentioned, they usually experience capital constraints but they strive to enhance their capital position and grow conservatively.

Energotest's success is based largely on the leadership style of its top management. Its core values include long-term thinking, collaboration, and responsibility. The development of the co-workers is also top priority. The management treats all employees as co-workers. Mr. Tamás Zentai, founder and CEO, is a thinker and humanist-capitalist who expects performance but also provides feedback and reward in exchange. After 20 years of leadership, he is transferring his CEO position to his selected successor.

What specific lessons does Energotest teach us? There is a trade-off between financial capital and thinking. To be successful, one should develop constantly, step by step, and treat employees like co-workers. Be brave enough to enrich the company's products and manipulate the profit position in the industry or the value stream.

2.4 Kürt Information Security and Data Recovery Plc[9]

Overview

Address:	Szabadság út. 301, H-2040 Budaörs, Hungary
Tel:	+3614246666
Email:	kurt@kurt.hu
Web:	http://kurt.hu

Company Information

Industry:	Information technology and computer service activities
Year of establishment:	1989
Sales revenues in 2010:	€6 million
Sales revenues in 2000:	€600,000
Average number of employees in 2010:	100
Brain(s) behind the company:	Sándor Kürti

2.4.1 Nature of Market Leadership

Kürt is in the business of:

1. Professional data recovery
2. Professional ethical hacking

[9] http://kuert-group.com/ and http://www.kürt.hu

3. Quality assurance in traffic information systems
4. Behavioural analysis of information systems

In particular, Kürt has been the first in CEE in data recovery for the last 21 years, and has held CEE market leadership in the other three market segments for the last 4–7 years.

2.4.2 Nature of Competative Advantage

The core of the company's competitive advantage is supreme technology and an integrated, so-called "tool-people approach", involving considerable moral, educational and work-related investments in people. Because of this, the company has the highest success rate in data recovery and ethical hacking in the market.

2.4.3 Core Lessons Learned on the Path to Business Success

1. Have a strong product and develop it constantly.
2. Think about the long run and reinvest most of your profits (Kürt is a family business and there was never a question about this).
3. Make an ethical workplace where your people enjoy working and they will be motivated and give you the highest performance.

2.4.4 Kürt: Hidden Champion

Can you imagine what you would do if your PC's Winchester were damaged? What would you do without your important data? Kürt's data recovery solutions can recover data even from seriously damaged storage devices, whether broken, soaked, burnt, erased or unreadable. In emergencies, you only have to contact Kürt and it will recover your data. Kürt also helps companies to find potential threats in their information systems and secure them.

Kürt's name became synonymous with IT security and data recovery in the early 1990's. After its foundation in 1989, the company began operations by repairing hard disks and floppy disk drives, and its main asset became the knowledge of its specialists.

Today Kürt has more than 20 years of experience in developing solutions for information security and data recovery. Its past experiences and the work of its highly innovative experts have made Kürt one of the leading data-recovery companies in the world.

Each year, Kürt successfully solves around 2,500 data recovery tasks with its in-house developed technology, which is also sold in many countries across three continents. As early as 1994, Kürt won the Hungarian Innovation Grand Prize, followed by other awards, such as the Award for Business Ethics from the Budapest Klub in 2002, the Innovation Award from the Ministry of Information Technology and Telecommunication in 2003, and the Healthy Workplace Award from the American Chamber of Commerce in 2004. In 2006 Kürt was among the 500 most dynamically growing companies in Europe.

Dr. Sándor Kürti founded the company and is still its chairman. From the beginning, Kürt has been a family business, where the owners are thinking long term, reinvesting 80 % of their annual profit and thriving in an ethical workplace.

We can define Kürt as a HC in four markets, namely:

1. Professional data recovery
2. Professional ethical hacking
3. Quality assurance in traffic information systems
4. Behavioural analysis of information systems

Although the professional data recovery market is in a decline phase, the other three successful markets are in the maturity phase. All of Kürt's 22 years of existence have been marked by constant adaptation and development. If the company continues this approach into the future, it will enjoy long-lasting success, which can be founded on the existing customer base and market position.

Kürt has a dual management style: the founder-chairman and his vice president are responsible mainly for PR and branding while the CEO is responsible mainly for the business focus. The top management consists of six people and the organization is departmentalized by product groups combined with the supporting function in the staff. Most of the top managers hold business degrees. Technical degrees are also common.

Kürt's main sources of competitive advantage include its technological lead and a business model integrating people with their tools. These competitive advantages ensure development; in the IT business, today's technological leads become tomorrow's commodities. Thus it seems that the main driver of the company's competitive advantage is its capacity for continuous development.

In the last 10 years, Kürt has multiplied its turnover tenfold. However, there was a break point in 2005–2006 when the company's main technology became a commodity in the market. Kürt responded well to the challenge and became market leader with three other products within a few years.

IT security and data recovery are usually project businesses; therefore market share can vary significantly year by year. Kürt has 30–70 % market share in CEE, and approximately 20 % in Western Europe. Its main competitors are Kancellar.hu and Ontrac.[10] Occasionally the Big Four consulting companies (KPMG, PWC, Ernst & Young, and Deloitte & Touche) are also in the market. Kürt is currently developing its North American and Middle Easter presence.

Kürt has had an exceptional success rate in data recovery and the ethical hacking business, thanks to its well-educated and experienced experts. Kürt states that its high-tech business is not at all capital-intensive, but is very knowledge-intensive; therefore competence, motivation, PR, and image are the key elements of success. Kürt spends 20 % of its annual revenue on R&D to ensure its lead in technology and competence. It is interesting, however, that patents do not play a role in their success; the company owns only one patent. They regard patents as unimportant, which is usual in the IT business.

[10] Ontrac acquired all of Europe's Data Recovery companies, except Kürt. They tried to acquire Kürt as well; however the family rejected the offer.

As a family business, Kürt has a very high level of equity—70 %—and it has been constantly rising throughout their history. It has not experienced capital constraints to growth, but its growth policy has sometimes been conservative.[11]

What specific lessons does Kürt teach us? To be a HC in the IT business, the company should have a well-defined product, continue to develop its experts and products, build its PR, and reinvest its profit. It should keep finding new market segments as the business environment can change rapidly. Finally, we see that a successful company can be ethical as well.

Conclusion

Hungarian HCs largely correspond to Simon's general concept, although there are some important differences. Most of the lessons that Simon learned from the HCs that he studied transpire for the Hungarian ones, too. Leadership with ambitious goals, high-performance employees, and depth are certainly typical traits of the Hungarian HCs. It is interesting, however, that decentralization is not, as the Hungarian HCs are approximately 20 times smaller than Simon's average in terms of number of employees. It is well known from the management literature that smaller companies are more centralized.

According to Simon's third circle of lessons, innovation, focus, and globalization are important factors. This is true also for the Hungarian HCs, but closeness to customers is less so. The Hungarian HCs are very much technology or science-driven companies. Only Energotest reported that closeness to customers is important to it, and this is because its added value manifests itself in physical terms, in the testing station. In contrast, the added value of the other Hungarian HCs can be distributed easily because it is manifested in knowledge products—a chemical molecule, a programme code, or information—therefore physical closeness is unimportant.

In conclusion, the Hungarian HCs are small, highly innovative companies with a strong, centralized leadership. These companies employ well-educated or scientifically qualified employees and efficiently integrate their knowledge in company products to create value for their customers.

References

Román, Z. (2009). *Statisztikai Tükör* 2009/109. KSH

Simon, H. (2009). *Hidden champions of the 21st century*. New York, NY: Springer.

World Bank. (2013). *Data; countries and economies*. http://data.worldbank.org/country

[11] They would rather not expand than use external financing.

Hidden Champions of Latvia

Arnis Sauka

Overview

Official name:	Republic of Latvia
Type of government:	Parliamentary Democratic Republic
Population in 2010:	2,058,184
Land area:	62,200 km^2

History

1918	After the end of the First World War on November 18, 1918, Latvia is proclaimed an independent state for the first time in its history.
1920	Peace treaty signed with Russia. Some 200,000 refugees return to Latvia. The Latvian economy begins to grow, focusing mostly on the export of agricultural products.
1937	Latvia has repaid all its external debts and deposited 6 tons of gold in various banks in the United Kingdom, Switzerland and the United States, during its economic boom.
1940	(June 17th) Latvia is completely occupied by the Soviet Union. The "Sovietization" of Latvia (i.e. transformation of Latvia into a Soviet republic) begins.
1941	Holocaust on the territory of Latvia: some 70,000 Jews are murdered. Latvians are recruited in the army of the Soviet Union as well as the German SS legion. Some 200,000 Latvians perish on both sides.

A. Sauka (✉)
Business and Management Department, Ventspils University College, Ventspils, Latvia

Business and Management Department, Stockholm School of Economics in Riga, Riga, Latvia
e-mail: arnis.sauka@sseriga.edu

P. McKiernan and D. Purg (eds.), *Hidden Champions in CEE and Turkey*,
DOI 10.1007/978-3-642-40504-4_15,

1944/1945	Renewed Soviet occupation causes mass inflow of inhabitants from other republics of the Soviet Union to Latvia (i.e. mostly Russians, Ukrainians, and Belarusians).
1949	To prevent resistance from the local intelligentsia and workers in the rural areas to collectivism (establishment of the kolkhoz), a large deportation of Latvians is implemented in March, 1949, when 42,125 Latvians are shipped to Siberia and the Far East. Large factories are also constructed during this period. The chemical industry, machinery manufacturing, textiles, production of building materials, pharmaceuticals, electrical and electronic industries are all represented on the relatively small territory of Latvia. In addition to this, there is development in the agricultural sector.
1985	With the start of perestroika, the idea of independence becomes more popular in Latvia.
1991	(August 21) Latvia regains independence (Parliamentary Democratic Republic). The transition from socialism to a market economy starts with the implementation of various reforms, the collapse of most large factories, and a reorientation to a service economy.
1994	Bank crisis in Latvia.
1998	The Russian crisis hits the economy.
2001/2007	Years of rapid economic growth. Latvia, Lithuania and Estonia are labeled the "Baltic Tigers".
2004	(March 27) Latvia joins NATO and the European Union.
2008	Latvia is hit hard by the world financial crisis.
2010	The recovery of the Latvian economy begins with a 3.3 % GDP growth forecast in 2011.

1 Introduction: Context

Latvia, often perceived as being part of a common economic area, the Baltic States,[1] is located in Northern Europe on the coastline of the Baltic Sea. Extending over an area of 64,589 km^2, and bordered by Estonia, Lithuania, Russia and Belarus, the country has approximately 2.1 million inhabitants. The economy of Latvia is dominated by the service sector, accounting for approximately 70 % of 2010 GDP.[2] GDP per capita in Latvia was $ 11,476 in 2009. The main sub-sectors are retail and wholesale trade, real estate, renting, and business activities, whereas manufacturing comprises only approximately 10 % of 2010 GDP. More information on Latvia's core economic indicators are available in Exhibit 1.

[1] Consisting of three countries: Latvia, Lithuania and Estonia

[2] The data in this paragraph are from various Internet sources.

Exhibit 1 Core economic indicators of Latvia

	1999	2000	2001	2002	2003	2004	2005	2006	2007	2008	2009	2010	2011
GDP per capita (current $US)	3,048.98	3,300.93	3,529.94	3,983.02	4,810.67	5,950.13	6,973.16	8,713.07	12,638.15	14,857.89	11,475.69	10,723.36	12,726.35
GDP per capita growth (annual %)	5.55	7.70	8.87	7.22	7.81	9.27	11.19	12.85	10.55	−3.82	−17.55	0.36	6.37
Long-term unemployment (% of total unemployment)	53.80	57.20	59.10	42.30	45.10	44.60	46.00	36.50	26.40	25.70	26.70	45.00	n/a
Foreign direct investment, net inflows (% of GDP)	4.77	5.27	1.59	2.72	2.71	4.63	5.06	8.54	9.43	4.26	−0.17	1.80	5.32
GDP (current $US m)	7,288.52	7,833.07	8,313.05	9,314.78	11,186.45	13,761.57	16,041.84	19,935.05	28,765.69	33,669.37	25,875.78	24,009.68	28,252.50
Exports of goods and services (current $US m)	2,942.24	3,261.83	3,456.35	3,807.39	4,706.24	6,049.61	7,675.88	8,947.72	12,181.12	14,415.86	11,356.22	12,919.97	16,758.17
Exports of goods and services (% of GDP)	40.37	41.64	41.58	40.87	42.07	43.96	47.85	44.88	42.35	42.82	43.89	53.81	59.32

(continued)

Exhibit 1 (continued)

	1999	2000	2001	2002	2003	2004	2005	2006	2007	2008	2009	2010	2011
Merchandise exports (current $US m)	1,723.09	1,868.47	2,000.71	2,285.13	2,892.52	4,009.17	5,161.29	6,154.81	8,308.35	10,144.11	7,702.09	9,532.58	13,160.52
Merchandise exports to high-income economies (% of total merchandise exports)	78.54	80.28	75.45	77.07	78.87	74.35	74.41	66.22	64.02	59.67	58.74	58.30	n/a
Merchandise exports to developing economies in Europe & Central Asia (% of total merchandise exports)	19.63	16.27	18.28	18.32	18.20	20.53	23.47	31.44	33.45	35.87	34.59	36.49	n/a
Ores and metals exports (% of merchandise exports)	4.16	6.04	5.31	5.61	3.96	3.25	3.52	3.97	3.50	4.18	2.79	3.72	4.36
Agricultural raw materials exports (% of merchandise exports)	29.85	29.47	24.87	23.87	25.48	19.42	15.94	14.23	14.37	9.37	9.88	12.16	9.97

Food exports (% of merchandise exports)	6.19	5.66	8.69	10.10	8.84	9.19	11.28	12.32	13.33	15.73	17.33	16.82	14.65
Fuel exports (% of merchandise exports)	2.95	2.47	1.38	1.48	1.38	4.63	8.92	5.20	3.66	3.46	5.08	5.33	7.94
Manufactures exports (% of merchandise exports)	56.63	56.05	59.46	58.66	60.04	61.38	56.59	60.50	61.39	63.22	60.75	58.58	55.54
High-technology exports (% of manufactured exports)	4.06	3.96	3.77	3.87	4.59	4.89	5.31	6.82	6.95	6.95	7.76	7.64	n/a

Source: World Bank (2013)

The dominance of the service sector is a relatively new trend in Latvia, occurring only during the last 20 years or so. Historically, however, Latvia has been known as one of the most industrialized centres in the region. For instance, in the nineteenth century its capital Riga was the third largest industrial city in the Russian Empire, right behind Moscow and St. Petersburg (Švābe 1990). Riga was also one of the most important industrial centres in the twentieth century. There were two main reasons for the heavy industrialization of Latvia and its capital city: (1) its favorable location, and (2), a cheap yet qualified labour force (Bleiere et al. 2005).[3]

In 1918, after the First World War, Latvia was proclaimed a sovereign country for the first time. During this period, the economic focus shifted from industrialization to agriculture. Latvia became well known in the region for exporting agricultural products such as butter, meat, linen and wooden materials—mainly to Western Europe (Jansone et al. 2008). Along with the development of the agricultural sector however, several manufacturing companies were also established in the early twentieth century, Riga's VEF being probably the most important of them. This company was created in 1922 and produced a wide range of products, from radio receivers to airplanes. The world-class photo camera VEF Minox—the smallest camera in the world at that time and beloved by spies—was also made by VEF.

The development of the agricultural and industrial sectors continued after 1934, when Karlis Ulmanis became the president of Latvia. Ulmanis is still remembered as the initiator of the country's economic boom. By 1937, Latvia had repaid all its external debts and deposited approximately 6 tons of gold in various banks in the United Kingdom, Switzerland and the United States (Avots 2004). However, with the start of the Second World War on September 1, 1939, and following the Molotov-Ribbentrop Pact, Latvia fell into the Soviet Union's influence zone. Consequently, on October 5 of the same year, after the signing of a contract of mutual help and friendship with the Soviet Union, the occupation of Latvia began with some 20,000 Red Army troops invading the country. On June 17, 1940, Latvia was completely occupied, and the Sovietization[4] of the country began. This period, until the German army entered the territory of Latvia on June 22, 1941, is remembered as the "Year of Horror".[5] A considerable part (approximately 65,000 people) of the German intelligentsia, the so-called Baltic Germans, left the country. This brain drain was doubtlessly a big loss for Latvia's educational system, culture, and economy as a whole.

In 1945 the Soviet occupation of Latvia was renewed. This was followed by a mass inflow of people from other republics of the Soviet Union, such as Russians, Ukrainians, and Belarusians, aimed at strengthening the position of the Soviet

[3] In the nineteenth century, when the territory of Latvia was part of the Russian Empire, 85 % of the inhabitants of Latvia could read and write (compared to 54 % inhabitants with such skills in the Russian Empire).

[4] i.e. transformation of Latvia into a Soviet republic, which included nationalization of property, terror and repressions, among other things.

[5] On June 14, 1941, alone, more than 15,000 Latvians were deported to Siberia.

Union. Furthermore, to stifle resistance to "collectivization" (i.e. establishment of the kolkhoz) from local intelligentsia in the rural areas of Latvia, the biggest deportation in the history of the country was implemented in March 1949. As many as 42,125 Latvians were deported overnight to Siberia and the Far East (Jansone et al. 2008).

The middle of the twentieth century is also remembered as the time when big factories were constructed in Latvia. Industries involving chemicals, machinery, textiles, building materials, pharmaceuticals, and electronics, were all represented on this relatively small territory. As a result, both labour force and raw materials were imported from other Soviet republics, and Latvia became one of the most highly industrialized regions of the Soviet Union. The traditional agricultural sector was also quite developed at that time, as Latvia supplied most of the largest cities of the Soviet Union with food (Jansone et al. 2008).

With the start of perestroika[6] in the early 1980s, the idea of independence became increasingly popular in all three Baltic States. After the political and economic crises that brought down the Soviet Union, Latvia regained its independence on August 21, 1991. It became a parliamentary republic, and various reforms, including privatization, began with a clear focus on the shift from socialism to a market economy.

Initially that shift was not easy for Latvia. The country experienced a steady decline in economic development, reaching real GDP growth of −34.0 % in 1992. Also, almost all big factories in Latvia—the heritage of the Soviet Union—collapsed during the early 1990s. Although various opinions on this issue exist, one reason often mentioned to explain the loss of these factories is that their main market—i.e. the territory of the former Soviet Union—was virtually no longer accessible (i.e. Balabkins 2002). More plausibly, the main reason for the collapse of the industrial sector in Latvia was the lack of skills necessary to transform factories so that they could operate in a market economy. As a consequence, only a marginal proportion of the heavy industry heritage remained in Latvia in mid-2011; as noted earlier, the country is currently dominated by the service sector. However, a considerable number of Russian speakers, who entered Latvia during the period of the Soviet regime,[7] have remained.

In the later stages of the transition, after joining the European Union and NATO in 2004, Latvia experienced the fastest growth rates in the European Union, reaching GDP growth of 12.2 % in 2006.[8] Yet, this was followed by a sharp slowdown, starting in early 2008, as a consequence of the world financial crisis. In 2009, Latvia's GDP growth fell to approximately −18 %. The depth of the crisis was also enhanced by the greatly increased consumption during the years of rapid economic growth, as a result of easy access to cheap bank loans and over-optimistic

---

[6] Mikhail Gorbachev, the General Secretary of the Communist Party of the Soviet Union, initiated a series of political and economic reforms, collectively labelled as "perestroika" in 1985. Perestroika allowed more independent action at various ministries and is often perceived as a major catalyst for the breakup of the Soviet Union (see http://en.wikipedia.org/wiki/Perestroika for more information).

[7] Latvians comprise only 59.4 % of the total population of Latvia, 27.6 % being Russians, followed by Belarusians (3.6 %), Ukrainians (2.5 %) and Poles (2.3 %) (2010).

[8] The data in this paragraph and the next are from various Internet sources.

forecasts as regards the future growth of the Latvian economy. After the credit bubble burst in early 2008, Latvia had to borrow some 7.5 billion euros from the European Commission and the World Bank, as well as other organizations and governments, to stabilize its financial sector.

The deep recession, among other things, led to a reassessment of the role of entrepreneurship in the country, and a new look at the quantity and quality of Latvian companies as well as the quality of the business environment in Latvia. Despite some positive signs as regards nascent entrepreneurship (Rastrigina 2010), Latvia has one of the lowest numbers of SMEs per 1,000 inhabitants in the European Union.[9] Furthermore, various international reports and indicators, such as the Innovation Union Scoreboard 2010, the Global Entrepreneurship Monitor, the Global Competitiveness Report 2010–2011, and others show that there is also considerable potential to increase the quality of both Latvian firms and the Latvian business environment.

One of the key challenges for the Latvian business environment and economic development seems to be the relatively high level of shadow economy in the country. According to Sauka and Putniņš (2011), the size of the shadow economy[10] in Latvia reached 38.1 % of GDP in 2010, and is almost twice as large as those of the neighbouring countries: Estonia (19.4 %) and Lithuania (18.8 %). Sauka and Putniņš (2011) suggest that strong dissatisfaction with Latvia's tax system and the government in particular, caused by the inconsistency of tax policy and the way the taxpayers' money is spent, is likely to be one of the main factors behind the large differences between the three countries in the size of their shadow economies. Other factors explaining the widespread tax evasion in Latvia include efforts to optimize expenses by avoiding taxes and thus increase the competitive advantage of companies, weak legal enforcement, societal traditions of avoiding taxes, as well as low standards of ethics and morality.

These findings, as well as various international indicators compiled by the World Bank, the EBRD, and other international organizations aiming to measure the quality of institutions, at least partly explain why the competitiveness of Latvian companies scores only 70 in the world ranking (Global Competitiveness Report 2010–2011). It can be argued that improving the way that the government communicates with entrepreneurs, and regaining the trust of entrepreneurs by

---

[9] It is worth noting, however, that the number of SMEs is considerably higher in Riga, the capital city of Latvia, reaching the EU average of approximately 50 SMEs per 1,000 inhabitants (Sauka and Welter 2010).

[10] Here, the term "shadow economy" is used to refer to all legal production of goods and services that is deliberately concealed from public authorities. This definition corresponds to what the System of National Accounts and the Organization for Economic Co-operation and Development (OECD) in their comprehensive 2002 handbook *Measuring the Non-Observed Economy*, refer to as "underground production". It is also consistent with definitions employed by other researchers; e.g., the World Bank study of 162 countries by Schneider et al. (2010).

reducing governmental spending and implementing reliable tax policies, will, among other things, improve the overall entrepreneurship climate in Latvia (Sauka and Welter 2011).

In light of these arguments, emphasizing the role of the external environment, several studies also draw attention to the company-specific characteristics that impede the competitiveness of Latvian firms. A recent study by Sauka (2011), for instance, shows that firms in Latvia are often forced to operate at rather high costs—an outcome of technologies or premises purchased in 2007/2008 at high prices—while at the same time offering low value-added products and services overall. Sauka (2011) also suggests that to become more competitive, Latvian companies should considerably increase the level of innovation, be more active while working with their competitors, and take more calculated business risks.

Furthermore, Latvian companies seem to be remarkably passive in using communication networks—a widely recognized tool used by successful, competitive companies around the world to attract external resources at a low cost, or no cost at all, to achieve a competitive advantage (Simon 2009; Cason, 2009). As reported by Sauka (2011), in general, Latvian companies virtually ignore the potential benefits from cooperation with business laboratories, universities and research institutes, although these are potential sources of innovations and market intelligence. They also ignore municipalities and business promotion organizations, even though companies across the world often use these resources to penetrate new export markets and establish a position in the local market. Thus, the key challenge that many Latvian companies need to address to increase their competitiveness, and perhaps qualify for the title of Hidden Champion (HC) in the foreseeable future, is not only the external environment. They also need more careful planning of internal firm strategies.

In summary, this is doubtlessly a very critical view, aimed at identifying core areas for improvement so as to increase the competitiveness of Latvian companies and Latvia's overall business environment, which in turn should lead to better economic performance. On a more positive note, however, following a steady decline of economic growth as a result of the crisis in 2008, the Latvian economy actually began to recover in 2010 with a 3.5 % GDP growth forecast in 2011 (Eurostat 2011). There are, of course, various reasons for this undoubtedly remarkable achievement, but one of the most important is the steady increase in exports. In 2010, Latvian exports increased by almost 30 % as compared to the previous year. Approximately 70 % of these went to EU countries. The most important commodity groups of Latvian exports are wood and wood products (19.3 % in 2010), followed by metal products, machinery and mechanical appliances, as well as electrical equipment (LIAA 2011).

Furthermore, the industrial sector outpaced the service sector after 2010, which bucked the trend before the crisis. This can be seen as a positive development, not least since most of the current HCs in Latvia are in the industrial sector, focusing on high value-added, innovative products that often require technical skills. In many cases, as demonstrated by the owner-managers of Latvian companies, these skills and knowledge are a heritage from Soviet times—and are not at all easy for competitors to imitate—.

Exhibit 2 Hidden champions from Latvia

Name	Short market leadership description	Revenues 2010 (€m)	Revenues 2000 (€m)	Employees 2010
Aerodium	Pioneers in developing vertical wind tunnel technology that suits wider market needs. Among the world leaders in the respective industry through combining technological expertise, promotional activities and customer service among other things	5.1	n/a	100
BLUE Microphones	Producer of high quality microphones for the mass market. One of the leaders in the U.S. market and often perceived as the 'Mercedes' of microphones	14	0.1	45
MADARA Cosmetics	Emerging leader in the eco-cosmetics market niche in Europe	2.1	n/a	40
A-boards	Producer of high quality kite boards and kite boarding equipment. Through successful distribution and focus on high quality products the company has established a strong position in a very noisy market full of rivals	0.2	0.25	5+
Mammu	Young start-up, social business aimed at creating a major social movement around the world	0.02	n/a	6+

Source: Authors of the chapter

Continuing on a positive note, being a relatively small country, and only 20 years after escaping from the Soviet regime, Latvia can be proud to have internationally successful companies. In this context, following Simon's (2009) classification, one can distinguish between (a) real HCs, such as Aerodium and BLUE Microphones, which have already achieved remarkable success in the international arena, (b) potential HCs, such as MADARA Cosmetics and A-boards, i.e. companies that show clear potential to become leaders in their respective market niches, and (c), start-ups with potential for considerable growth, such as Mammu, a company that seems to be on its way to remarkable success. The main characteristics of all these companies are summarized in Exhibit 2.

To identify the key drivers of success, two real HCs—Aerodium and BLUE Microphones—are explored in more depth in the following sections of the chapter. These sections are then followed by a brief introduction to Latvia's potential HCs: Madara Cosmetics and A-boards, as well as a start-up with growth potential, Mammu. The concluding section summarizes the main similarities and differences between Latvia's success stories, as compared to their counterparts from the rest of the world.

2 Five Case Studies

2.1 Aerodium Ltd.

Overview

Address:	Brivibas street 214 M-2, Riga, LV-1039, Latvia
Tel:	+371 25400010
Email:	info@aerodium-technologies.com
Web:	http://www.aerodium-technologies.com

Company Information

Industry:	Activities of amusement parks and theme parks
Year of establishment:	2003
Sales revenues in 2010:	€5.1 million
Sales revenues in 2000:	n/a (The company did not exist.)
Average number of employees in 2010:	100
Brain(s) behind the company:	CEO and founder Ivars Beitans

2.1.1 Nature of Market Leadership

The company produces vertical wind tunnels and sells its experience in vertical wind tunnels. It holds a 50 % market share in Europe and is currently expanding into the Asian and US markets.

2.1.2 Nature of Competitive Advantage

The company is a pioneer in developing vertical wind tunnel technology that suits wide market needs. It has managed to position itself among the world leaders in the industry by combining technological expertise, product diversification, promotional activities, and customer service.

2.1.3 Core Lessons Learned on the Path to Business Success

1. Introducing a product that is very hard to imitate—due to unique knowledge, substantial financial investments, and time—can allow a company to target wider market segments more openly and help it establish a solid foundation for long term success.
2. Combining technological innovation with clever market segmentation, while at the same time providing a diversified product range, is a business model that has brought success to Aerodium and is perhaps worthy of consideration by other growth-oriented companies.

3. Create unquestionable employee commitment. The employees' passion for the product that they deliver is crucial for success at a global level.

2.1.4 Aerodium Ltd: Hidden Champion

The idea to launch Aerodium occurred to Ivars Beitans incidentally when devices called "vertical wind tunnels" caught his attention. Head of the Latvian Bungee Jumping Association, a stuntman, and a passionate traveller, Ivars simply could not resist the temptation to try them out himself. His technical background made him think that the flying experience that he had greatly enjoyed in various countries could be brought to a new level mainly by improving the technology of the wind tunnels. Knowing that even the best product requires substantial marketing and promotion, Ivars contacted Ansis Egle who was a sports enthusiast and had experience in marketing and promotional activities.

By the end of 2004, when the discussion between Ivars and Ansis took place, Aerodium Ltd. had already been registered and the first wind tunnel had been delivered to Riga. "When we entered the market at the end of 2004, we entered an industry that had already existed for 25 years, since the day French-Canadian inventor Jean St. Germain created the first recreational vertical wind tunnel in Montreal, Canada", Ansis Egle says. The name of the Latvian company also came from Canada. It is called after a company with an already established name and reputation in the world market, Aerodium Canada.

Ansis says, "As in the PC industry, when the PC technology was still developing, in this industry it is common to buy a ready-made product from a supplier, use it as raw material, and then invest in know-how to create your own product". The initial product that Aerodium bought from Aerodium Canada was indeed nothing more than raw material. "If Aerodium Canada had approached a sensitive market like Russia with wind tunnels of the same poor quality as those that they delivered to us, they would have been in trouble. The device simply did not work as it should have. Actually, it did not work at all!"

The fact that it was typical of the industry that products did not deliver their promised value seemed to work in Aerodium's favour. From the very beginning of its existence, the company was simply forced to identify problems and look for technological solutions. "We took this very seriously and started with basic things: aerodynamics and construction. Ivars Beitans's technical knowledge has been invaluable in this regard. He is the inventor of most of the technologies invested in our products!"

"Only a few months later, after arriving from Canada, the wind tunnel looked completely different", Ansis Egle says. Indeed, the technological investment paid off and, following the advertising campaign, the success of the wind tunnel in Latvia surpassed all the expectations of the Aerodium team. "In the summer of 2005, there was a queue of people waiting from early in the morning until midnight every day for an opportunity to fly. These were customers not only from Latvia, but also from neighboring countries, such as Lithuania, Estonia, Sweden, and Finland.

The demand was simply huge!" Ansis says, explaining that this wind tunnel was the first of its kind in Eastern Europe. Thus, Aerodium could enjoy the first mover's advantage to the full extent.

Achieving fast success in the region, Aerodium was looking for possibilities to enter global markets, and was ready for that in 2006, when it won the tender for the Winter Olympics in Torino, Italy. Aerodium's show at the Torino Olympic Games was a big success and attracted lots of attention. "During the closing ceremony, live TV coverage reached 500 million viewers worldwide who saw that flying was possible", Ansis says. "It was indeed a turning point not only for Aerodium but the whole industry as well as nobody had ever had the idea to put a vertical wind tunnel in an entertainment show, and nobody had ever carried out such a performance publicly".

Impressed by the show, many companies tried to enter the market. According to Ansis, "It was like an explosion which lasted for some 2 years and then faded away. The reason for this is that companies simply took this thing too easy. It looks like all you need is an engine and a propeller to make people fly. Actually, huge know-how is required to ensure the successful operation of the device, and lots of technological solutions and patience are required of the producers". Indeed, none of the companies that emerged as a result of the show in Torino were still active after 2008. One of the lessons from this experience seems to be that if technology, or anything else that brings added value to the product or service, is relatively easy to replicate, then exposing oneself to a wider audience is indeed risky and will most probably attract too many rivals already in the early phase of the business start-up. As demonstrated by Aerodium, however, by introducing a product that is very hard to imitate—because of the unique knowledge, substantial financial investment, and time that it takes to produce it—a company can target wider market segments more openly and establish a solid foundation for long-term success.

The key to Aerodium's strategy is innovation, especially when it comes to technological development of the wind tunnels. To be precise, approximately 30 % of the profits are invested back in R&D, which has resulted in a number of patents. Ansis Egle emphasizes the need for innovation: "We are innovating in order to create demand for Aerodium products on the world market. In our business, this is only possible if you have better technology than your competitors. Technology-wise we are indeed very ambitious: if there is an opportunity, we do everything it takes to take advantage of it".

Innovation in technology has led to another competitive advantage for the company: a diversified product range. This is what Ansis says about the company's strategy: "If our competitors arc fine with producing the wind tunnel, setting it up and collecting money, then we want to achieve much more than that. Our strategy is market expansion through segmentation, offering the right product for each market segment". And how do they do that? After Torino, the company realized that big shows involve big investments, which leads to a high price for the customer. Thus, Ivars Beitans thought about ways to optimize the cost structure while at the same time serving customers who cannot access or afford the flying experience in big tunnels. Ultimately, he came up with the idea of the mini-tunnel.

Apart from the mini-tunnel, Aerodium has types designed for specific target markets. As Ansis explains, "In general, the company's revenue stream rests on three market segments. The first are customers who usually buy only once, such as military forces. These are the markets in Pakistan, Saudi Arabia, also Malaysia, Korea, India and Greece. The second segment is show business, and we are very active in various show business events around the world. The third segment is comprised of people who would simply like to enjoy the flying experience. For this we have tunnels in Latvia, Denmark, Bulgaria and other countries". Thus, so far it seems that combining technological innovation with clever market segmentation at the same time as providing a diversified product range is a business model that has brought success to Aerodium and is perhaps also worthy of consideration by other growth-oriented companies.

"Indeed, diversity of products, technological know-how and market segmentation are three elements that form the success formula in our industry: the formula for our happiness", Ansis asserts. The other two are the customers' trust of the brand, and globalization strategy. To gain trust, at the very beginning of their business operation, the company owners were wise enough to establish a network with Aerodium Canada. "With improved technology, we soon started to outperform Aerodium Canada and its owners simply offered to sell it to us", Ansis explains. When it comes to entering global markets, Aerodium has realized that the best strategy for penetrating new markets is forming partnerships with local companies. "Yes, we share our technology and success, but this allows us to understand the market better. And it is much better than having risk capitalists on your neck who have unlimited control of your business. Furthermore, it is clear that we simply cannot enter the market, set up the technology and operate it from a distance".

"Our customers say that one of the things they really like about Aerodium is the service we provide, and this is yet another determinant of our success", Ansis Egle points out. There are many ways in which Aerodium makes sure that every customer feels satisfied with his first flying experience. For instance, Aerodium records customers' flying experiences and delivers a CD to strengthen their memories and enable them to share their experiences with others. "This is the only way that we manage to increase value added for the customer, at the same time making sure that these customers do some marketing for us. This involves relatively low costs and generates great returns". Thus, Aerodium demonstrates that customer satisfaction is not created just by providing an invaluable experience involving high technology. Creating loyalty by further extending this memorable, emotionally rich experience also plays a significant role. To illustrate this further, we can think of an example from the restaurant business. After an unforgettable lunch that has taken the chef hours to prepare, the waiter serves free, good-quality coffee. These are small, often unexpected, pleasures that people value and remember.

Another way to provide the best value for both existing and new customers is, of course, by delivering the right product and service in the right place at the right time. And this is not achievable without good relationships with suppliers. However, managing relationships with suppliers is not an easy task because of the specifics of the product. "We can hardly find two wind tunnels that are the same;

usually each tunnel has its own specificities. This means that it requires new drawings and the technology changes to a greater or lesser degree. In a word, we constantly work with something new that has never been produced. For this reason, we always need to look for new suppliers who can provide the best solutions for each case", Ansis explains, adding that being aware of what competitors do is absolutely crucial at this stage.

Aerodium's chief competitor is the Florida-based firm Sky Venture, an experienced company that has operated in the market since the beginning of the 1990s and currently dominates the North American market. Having some 50 % of the market share in Europe, Aerodium has several competitors in Switzerland and Germany. "Then we had L1 in the US, but they disappeared. All in all, the good news is that our competitors have recently started to seek out contact with us, and in our opinion this only indicates how strong we are", Ansis says.

"You can have great suppliers and detailed knowledge about the competitors, but in the end it is the employees who drive your business and underestimating this factor is the biggest sin any company can commit," Ansis points out. And how do they find the best employees? "Well, they are the ones with a spark in their eyes. This is true for the owners of the company, and the selection of employees is primarily based on their motivation and willingness to achieve something together with us. Aerodium's employees are very much aware that they work on unique products and our common aim is leadership in the world market. Routine? This is hardly possible in our business as things constantly change just as our products change" Ansis adds, confirming findings from previous research that creating the unquestionable commitment of employees who are passionate for the product that they deliver is indeed crucial for success at the global level (i.e. Chaston 2010).

In a relatively short time, Aerodium has grown both financially and in terms of employees. Currently, the company employs people at its branches in Bulgaria, Libya, Denmark and other countries and has the equivalent of some 100 full-time employees around the world. Financially, regardless of the financial crisis, Aerodium's turnover increased by 28 % in 2010 as compared to 2009, and with constant improvements in technology, as well as promotional activities, the company continues to grow.

Aerodium also has a clear idea of how to maintain and increase its market position: "We are looking in the direction of Asian and North American markets," Ansis Egle says, highlighting various activities, such as cooperation with Shaolin monks in China, that are being implemented. "In general, we keep our eyes open and try to take advantage of any opportunity that could help to further penetrate the global arena". This demonstrates a clear pattern of proactive leadership at Aerodium, sensitive to opportunities and quick to adapt to them. Indeed, Aerodium is not planning to stop, and this is reflected in its vision: to create a worldwide movement consisting of enthusiasts who love to fly. "Trust me, the flying experience is a unique feeling and we can offer such a feeling while guaranteeing safety. This means that flying actually qualifies as a sports activity, with championships for amateurs and professionals. If we achieve this in 5–10 years, I will be happy",

Ansis Egle concludes, leaving us with the impression that Aerodium intends to continue flying globally. . . and high, despite the challenges that it is very likely to face while attempting to take advantage of further market opportunities.

2.2 Blue Microphones Ltd

Overview

Address:	5706 Corsa Avenue, #102, Westlake Village, CA 91362–4057, U.S.
Tel:	+818-879-5200
Email:	press@bluemic.com
Web:	http://www.bluemic.com

Company Information

Industry:	Manufacture of consumer electronics
Year of establishment:	1995
Sales revenues in 2010:	€10 million
Sales revenues in 2000:	€700,000
Average number of employees in 2010:	45
Brain(s) behind the company:	Founders Martins Saulesspurens and Bernard Wise (In 2008 the owners, and thus the key decision-makers, changed.)

2.2.1 Nature of Market Leadership

One of the leaders in the US, having 80 % of the market share in a specific product category: high-end microphones.

2.2.2 Nature of Competitive Advantage

The company's main advantage is the high-quality microphone, often perceived as the "Mercedes" of microphones, that it produces for the mass market, and its strong brand name. Once its leadership in high-end microphones was established, the company managed to successfully move down the customer pyramid to gain both revenues and profits without destroying its brand at the high end.

2.2.3 Core Lessons Learned on the Path to Business Success

1. Sometimes positioning a product in an unappealing price category or market segment might provide enough of a time gap to establish oneself before imitations from competitors appear.

2. Product diversification is an important determinant of success at a global level.
3. Knowing the core users of your product and their task-related problems, as well as being able to solve these problems, is one of the keys to attracting and retaining loyal customers.

2.2.4 Blue Microphones Ltd: Hidden Champion

Martins Saulesspurens, the founder of BLUE Microphones, has always been interested in music and technology. Still, his passion for music came first, long before Martins graduated from university as an engineer and started to work for the Academy of Music of Latvia as the director of a sound recording studio. "Jazz music was of particular interest to me, but this was the 1950s and 1960s in Latvia, and access to any jazz records in the Soviet Union was highly restricted". Thus, searching for jazz records, he decided to send a letter to a journal in England, expressing his eagerness to find people who would be interested in exchanging jazz records. As Martins remembers, "At that time, not too many people dared to do such things as any contact with the rest of the world was seen as a threat to the Soviet regime".

The next step towards launching his own business was Martins' first visit to the US back in 1988, just after the Iron Curtain fell and travelling outside the USSR was possible. During his stay in the US, one of his pen pals introduced him to a teacher who was very interested in Latvian music. According to Martins: "This person made a very interesting offer, asking whether my son would like to come to the US to study". To educate his son in the US, Martins had to cover certain expenses; thus, he started to think seriously about how to make money.

"During the Soviet era, the main film studios were all equipped with relatively good microphones, mainly of Austrian origin", Martins says, adding that he was lucky to get free access to microphones that were damaged or simply worn, and thus considered to be of no value. "This is where I could use all my technical knowledge, attempting to reconstruct them and then sell them outside Latvia". Martins managed to sell some of those reconstructed microphones during his first visit to the US: "This turned out to be quite successful, as my first deal in the US was worth about 6,000 US dollars. Thus, not only did I realize that the old junk I had access to, had some value if properly restored, but I also managed to raise some start-up capital for my son's education in the US and for my further business activities".

BLUE Microphones was established in May 1995, and registered across the ocean in the US. Martin says, "I was never really interested in launching a business in Latvia, in particular during the times when the environment was very harsh there". This demonstrates that when business opportunities for a particular business are hard or impossible to realize in one region of the world, it is not a reason to stop pursuing them elsewhere. Back in the autumn of 1995, BLUE Microphones was presented at one of the foremost US exhibitions dealing with sound and technology, leading to very important new contacts and generating sales. In the beginning, Martins was the only owner of the company; however, he cooperated closely with Bernard Wise, better known as Skipper: "He was a professional musician I had known for several years already, and he was busy making music. Skipper was of particular help in the very first years of BLUE Microphones' operations, as he was able to bring in new customers and helped in many other ways". It is no surprise that when Skipper's contract with his former employer, JVC, expired in 1998, he formally joined BLUE Microphones.

During the first 2 years of operations, BLUE Microphones' main products were reconstructed microphones. However, this changed in 1997, when one of the leading recording studios in the US ordered the same microphone that they had bought previously. "Well, we did not have this type of microphone for reconstruction and it was indeed impossible to get it anywhere soon", Martins says, adding that, "since it was an expensive microphone, to keep the customer we literally had no choice but to follow his advice to produce the microphone ourselves". Overall, with the production of its own microphones, BLUE Microphones' sales increased substantially. For instance, the annual turnover of the company was around 40,000 US dollars in 1996, reaching 10 million in 2009 and 14 million in 2010.

Still, Martins emphasizes the importance of the decision to produce the first microphone, which, using his words, "happened almost by accident, but shaped the whole strategy of BLUE Microphones". According to Martins, "Entering the market with the most expensive microphone was the main reason for our success. In fact, the first microphone we produced is still the most expensive in our product range, costing some 5,000 euros per piece. If we compare ourselves with, for instance, the automobile industry, we positioned ourselves as "the Mercedes of microphones" in the market. This means high value-adding, high prestige and also a high price for our product and brand in general". The successful outcome of this strategy suggests that sometimes positioning a product in an unappealing price category or market segment might provide enough of a time gap to establish oneself before imitations from competitors appear.

Indeed, this strategy helped BLUE Microphones not only to get established but also to maintain a good market position. Many companies soon appeared on the market, trying to copy BLUE Microphones, mainly with made-in-China products that had a much lower price. "Well", says Martins, "this was not a problem for us as the value added and prestige that came with using BLUE Microphones was more important than simply a lower price". The reliability of the BLUE Microphones brand name would not, of course, have been possible without innovation and investment in R&D. "In this regard, both my own knowledge and that of Bernard Wise was very helpful", says Martins. Being a musician, Skipper knew exactly what sound engineers require and Martins knew how to implement these requirements technology-wise. They also soon realized that to be successful it is important to diversify the product range, and this, as for many HCs around the world (Simon 2009), became another cornerstone of BLUE Microphones' strategy.

The diversification strategy was to design each microphone for a specific use. "For instance, we offered microphones that are best for female voices, while other microphones were designed for a lower voice; then there were microphones for drums, different kinds of guitars or any other particular instrument", Martins says. Overall, the way BLUE Microphones diversified its products was very innovative in this market, as at that time most of the major producers were trying to offer universal microphones. Martins explains: "Using a universal microphone meant that, when recording music, sound engineers had to adjust the upper and lower levels of the sound to emphasize a voice or instrument. One of our innovations in the market was microphones that did all that with built-in technology: without interruption from sound engineers. Engineers like this a lot!" It is thus only logical to conclude that knowing the core users of your product and what their task-related problems are, while being able to solve these problems, seems to be one of the keys to attracting and retaining loyal customers. This is crucial for virtually any business.

Networking is another success determinant of BLUE Microphones. Martins emphasizes the importance of personal contacts, especially when it comes to the distribution of BLUE Microphones products: "When I made my first visit to the US in the late 1980s, there were many small shops selling music equipment—just like grocers today. This, however, soon changed, with big distribution chains starting to enter the market... Guitar Center, one of the biggest distribution chains specializing in records and musical instruments, opened its doors just a few blocks away from where I lived. I was lucky to meet with one of the managers of this business, and we soon found a common language, which in turn opened doors for BLUE Microphones at Guitar Center". Indeed, in this industry it was very unusual for a retail chain to work directly with a manufacturer, especially a small one. Today, however, BLUE Microphones are among the three best-selling microphone brands at Guitar Centers all over the US.

With its products on offer at Guitar Center, BLUE Microphones had much better chances of moving its products at other major chains as well. This turned out to be crucial for the business, as small shops that specialized in records and musical instruments soon disappeared from the market. "Today, there are some three or four big chains that dominate the entire US market in this industry, and we are present in most of them. This, of course, is a huge competitive advantage", says Martins. The way products were distributed, however, was only one of the major changes that occurred in the industry. There was another change which in fact required a change in the initial BLUE Microphones strategy.

In the early years, the company's main target audience were professional studios, an obvious choice for a company offering high quality microphones starting at 1,000 US dollars apiece. Changes in the market, however, were brought about by new developments in IT and more specifically by the possibility to record in digital format. Martins explains: "Previously, most musicians used the services of big recording studios because they could not afford their own. With the development of technology, creating a recording studio that would have previously required the investment of half a million dollars was now achievable with 40,000 dollars or less". This had important implications for BLUE Microphones as there was simply no serious market for very expensive products.

BLUE Microphones found a simple and very effective solution for this market change: "Now", says Martins, "customers could finally buy 'the Mercedes of microphones' for a lower price while still benefiting from the 'Blue Microphones' brand. And many really appreciated this!" The first BLUE microphone for the mass market was produced in Latvia, but the company could not proceed with this strategy as production costs were simply too high. "It turned out that we had to sell the microphone for 99 dollars and the only way to ensure such a price is to produce microphones in China".. Once BLUE Microphones managed to reach the 99-dollar selling price, the sales of their first mass market microphone progressed very quickly. In fact, not only did the company manage to sell about 100,000 of these microphones but it was also able to remain on the market with the same microphone for more than 5 years. This is indeed a unique achievement considering how quickly IT-related products fade! Arguably, however, all this would have hardly been possible if BLUE Microphones had not managed to reach economies of scale prior to the competition's emphasis shift from quality to price. This is another lesson from this remarkable experience for growth-oriented businesses.

Regardless of the relatively cheap price, BLUE Microphones still positioned itself as a value-added brand, which in turn required investments in R&D. According to Martins, "The best strategy is to become even better, and this is what BLUE Microphones is continuously trying to achieve. All our microphones, regardless of their price, have some unique features, and this is how we maintain the reputation of our brand name even while selling at lower prices. Investment in R&D is simply a prerequisite for growth. As with digital microphones, we have become part of the IT industry, which indeed develops very quickly. Innovations in the production of microphones are also driven by demand from the market, which is in turn influenced by the introduction of new technologies in related fields. This is like a never-ending circle, and we cannot afford to be left out of it". Once again, this emphasizes the crucial importance of being alert to all market opportunities (e.g. Simon 2009), including those created by major changes in the market place, such as changes in distribution patterns or pricing, or those in the industry as a whole as a result of new technology.

Martins and his business partner sold BLUE Microphones to Transom Capital Group in April 2008. Martins is now chief engineer, responsible for the final products, and owns only a small share of the company, but his business partner is president of BLUE Microphones. "Because of this, we cannot talk about BLUE Microphones as our company anymore", says Martins. "Still, the company is moving forward and we are happy to be part of it".

"Speaking of further development, it is of course important to know what our competitors are doing in the market", Martins says, admitting that BLUE Microphones has always had difficulty entering the European market. Two leading companies completely dominate this market; AKG from Austria and Neumann from Germany. According to Martins, customers' loyalty to these brands in Europe makes entry into Europe "more than simply complicated". Partly because of this, BLUE Microphones' principal market since the day the company was established has been the US. Even today, approximately 4/5 of BLUE Microphones' sales are in the US, where the company has some 80 % market share in segments such as USB microphones. Having a turnover of more than 10.0 million US dollars, BLUE Microphones employs some 45 workers. This says a lot about the efficiency of the company.

Overall, and largely because of BLUE Microphones' ability to achieve economies of scale, during the last 2 years the company's growth has been based on mass-market products, including microphones for mobile phones, stage microphones and the like. Partly because of this, Blue Microphones' product promotion strategy has also experienced some changes in recent years. The company no longer uses advertisements in the mass media, instead focusing on gaining market visibility through musicians, TV shows, movies and books. "For instance, BLUE Microphones offers young musicians the opportunity to buy its microphones for a considerably cheaper price. BLUE Microphones products can be seen in movies such as *Star Trek*, and leading TV shows in the US, such as *American Idol,* are using our microphones", Martins says. BLUE Microphones also makes extensive use of PR tools, keeping in touch with journal editors who write on technological developments in the music industry.

"What happens to BLUE Microphones in the future will not really depend much on me or my business partner", Martins says, pointing out that the new owners of the firm now make strategy decisions. "And this, of course, is the way it should actually be", he adds. "Innovations in technology, product diversification, a good network with suppliers and distributors and the passion of the people working for BLUE Microphones has been, and most probably will remain, the main determinants of its success formula", says Martins, concluding that, "These are the reasons why BLUE Microphones has never had any bad year and has only experienced growth since the very beginning when it first entered the market".

2.3 Madara Cosmetics Ltd

Overview

Address:	Sampetera street 2, LV-1046, Riga, Latvia
Tel:	+371 67470243
Email:	info@madara-cosmetics.lv
Web:	http://www.madaracosmetics.lv

Company Information

Industry:	Production of perfumes and toilet preparations
Year of establishment:	2006
Sales revenue in 2010:	€2.1 million
Sales revenue in 2000:	n/a (The company did not exist.)
Average number of employees in 2010:	40
Brain(s) behind the company:	Co-founder and CEO Lotte Tisenkopfa-Iltnere

2.3.1 Nature of Market Leadership

This is a potential Hidden Champion. The company is currently a leader in the cosmetics market in Latvia, and is rapidly increasing its share in the European eco-cosmetics market niche.

2.3.2 Nature of Competitive Advantage

Good quality eco-cosmetic products, produced in-house to maintain quality. A strong brand name.

2.3.3 Core Lessons Learned on the Path to Business Success

1. Ability to spot opportunity in a timely fashion, i.e.—in the case of MADARA Cosmetics -realizing that there is a considerable growth potential for eco-products in the world market. Acting fast to take advantage of such an opportunity is crucial for business growth.
2. Entering a highly competitive market is much easier for a small business if it successfully establishes itself in a market niche.
3. Enter global markets as soon as possible. Focus on quality. Employees and networking matter enormously for a growth-oriented SME.

2.3.4 Madara Cosmetics Ltd: Potential Hidden Champion

MADARA Cosmetics Ltd. was established in 2006 as a high-quality ecological skincare brand targeting the high-price segment. The company is a good example of a business founded in the highly competitive cosmetics market, yet able to successfully establish itself in a market niche, focusing on green/eco products. In a relatively short time MADARA Cosmetics managed to enter more than 30 markets and achieved remarkable financial growth indicators. After a sales turnover of 170,000 euros in 2007 and 550,000 in 2008, the company reached 2.1 million euros in 2010 and expected an increase of 60 % in 2011.

According to the owner and CEO of MADARA Cosmetics, Lotte Tisenkopfa-Iltnere, several factors are keys to this success. First, the green lifestyle of the owners has set a high quality standard for the products that MADARA cosmetics offers: "We not only produce for customers but also use all the products ourselves". Spotting the high and growing demand for eco-cosmetics in Europe, Japan, and Malaysia, and entering these markets quickly with the help of an investor and an established network of local distributors, each of them responsible for a certain market, are important factors that have contributed to the fast growth of the company, and are possible lessons for other growth-oriented SMEs hoping to enter new markets with limited financial resources. The CEO also emphasizes the importance of human capital, namely the professionalism of the MADARA Cosmetics team, as well as constant innovation in products and product design, in achieving success. Overall, MADARA Cosmetics is among the select few Latvian companies on their way to becoming a leader in their market niches. This is their aim at least: to be one of the three top-of-mind brands in Europe in 20 years in the field of eco-cosmetics.

2.4 Aboards Ltd

Overview

Address:	Braslas street 29, Riga, LV1084, Latvia
Tel:	+371 28691000
Email:	aboards@aboards.eu
Web:	http://www.aboards.eu

Company Information

Industry:	Agents specialized in the sale of products
Year of establishment:	2006
Sales revenue in 2010:	€250,000
Sales revenue in 2000:	n/a (The company did not exist.)
Average number of employees in 2010:	More than 5 dealers around the world
Brain(s) behind the company:	Founder Kriss Spulis

2.4.1 Nature of Market Leadership

This is a potential Hidden Champion, estimated to hold 5 % of the global market share in a very competitive market—kite boards and kite boarding equipment—full of competitors.

2.4.2 Nature of Competitive Advantage

Good quality products, a strong brand name, and a high loyalty among kite boarding enthusiasts. This is a very strong community of people with specific interests and lifestyles. By focusing on this specific subgroup of customers, Aboards Ltd. has managed to outperform big OEMs that produce a whole range of sporting equipment but do not fully understand or address the kite boarding freaks.

2.4.3 Core Lessons Learned on the Path to Business Success

1. Focus on a narrow customer segment with specific life-style preferences, not well addressed by OEMs.
2. Entering export markets as quickly as possible is crucial.
3. Building a strong network of distributors is crucial for entering global markets more quickly and economically.
4. Constant innovation, the owner's competence in technology, a clever marketing strategy on an international level, quality control, and logistics contribute to success in a global market.

2.4.4 Aboards Ltd: Potential Hidden Champion

Aboards Ltd. was established in 2006. It specializes in producing good-quality kite boards and kite boarding equipment in a high-price segment. In just 4 years, Aboards achieved remarkable success; despite being in a very competitive market, the company has acquired some 5 % of the world market share. According to the CEO and owner of Aboards, Kriss Spulis, there have been several key success determinants for the company. First, the company's early export orientation was crucial. Today, with the help of local dealers who are in turn responsible for developing the brand in the respective regions, and mainly using the B2B approach, the company exports over 90 % of its production to more than 30 countries on five continents. Not only the distribution but also the manufacturing process is globalized: the firm has manufacturing sites in various countries in Europe, Asia and beyond. Further keys to success have been constant innovation, the owner's competence in technology, a clever marketing strategy at an international level, quality control, and logistics. Finally, regular and hard work is highlighted as a factor that has enabled the company to grow quickly: "To go a long way you need to keep on taking small steps", the CEO of Aboards explains, pointing out that, taking small steps, the company is aiming to go as far as possible.

2.5 Mammu

2.5.1 Mammu: Potential Hidden Champion

Although some Latvian companies are just emerging, they clearly demonstrate a potential to become market leaders in their niche. One such company is MAMMU. Founded in 2010, MAMMU is a social business; it is already a best-case example for the creative think-tank Grameen Creative Lab of Dr. Yunus, who promotes the MAMMU business model worldwide at all major social business events. According to the co-owner of MAMMU, Fionn Dobbin, "The key idea for MAMMU is to support mothers in need by giving them a chance to earn money". With the help of top designers and photographers, mothers in need are involved in manufacturing fashionable scarves—MAMMU's chief product—using green materials. Though only recently established, MAMMU is on its way to becoming a social movement around the world. Currently the company exports its scarves to the US, France, Germany, Denmark, the UK and Luxembourg, and is ready to enter many other countries worldwide.

Conclusion

Being among the best in their industries, HCs are growth-oriented, highly ambitious firms that pursue or have achieved market leadership (Simon 2009). Like MADARA Cosmetics and MAMMU, these companies are never shy about announcing their aims and ambitions, even when relatively young and small. Furthermore, according to Simon (2009), HCs are oriented towards the long term and possess a clear vision and an "inner flame". They are also able to pass on this flame to others. This holds true not only for employees, who, having common values, are often as enthusiastic about reaching the company targets as the owners themselves, but also for customers. Apart from being growth-orientated, the ability to achieve constant, fast and long term growth, even in mature markets or industries, is a factor that distinguishes HCs from firms that merely grow quickly. It is certainly a prerequisite for moving from the "hidden champion" to the "big champion" category (Simon 2009).

In explaining the growth drivers of HCs, Simon (2009) emphasizes globalization and innovation as being of crucial importance. Through innovation, these companies manage to create their own markets or demand for their often high-tech products. Thus not only innovation per se, but also the ability to market the innovation, is considered of major importance. Furthermore, product diversification as a strategy enabling the growth and further penetration of international markets has been highlighted as a very important characteristic of HCs. In this context, technical knowledge, often possessed by the firms' owners, plays a very important role. Neither Aerodium nor BLUE Microphones are exceptions in regard to all the previously mentioned general characteristics of HCs.

Also, the way in which Aerodium and BLUE Microphones bring innovations to global markets corresponds to the general strategies of HCs. A key to success in internationalization efforts is maintaining a close relationship with every market, mainly using the knowledge of local people, who are often distributors or other cooperation partners (Simon 2009). The main reason for the importance of close relationships with the markets is, of course, the ability to handle issues related to mentality, legislation, and other specifics of the particular markets. Such relationships are, however, also crucial when it comes to providing high quality and timely service to the customer, as demonstrated by the case of Aerodium.

HCs are very focus-oriented companies that specialize in their particular market niche or business activity; going "deep, not broad" (Simon 2009). In the case of BLUE Microphones and Aerodium, as well as Aboards, a narrow focus does not, however, mean putting all your eggs in one basket. Even though they are focused, these companies have managed to diversify their product ranges to the extent that they are no longer dependent on a single product or market. All in all, just like Aerodium and BLUE Microphones, HCs concentrate on what they do best, often outsourcing other activities, thus becoming as efficient as possible. Furthermore, replicating the findings of previous studies (see Chaston 2010 for a review), all cases from Latvia demonstrate the great importance of the role of the owner/managers. It is their lifestyle, interests, and hobbies, and—even more important—specific knowledge, that has helped them to launch innovative products and sustain a competitive advantage in the respective market niche.

The pricing and human resource management strategies of Latvian HCs and most regional leaders, along with the influential personalities of their owners, seem to be very much in line with what seems to characterize HCs from other countries. Furthermore, like most HCs around the world, Latvians handle their success strategies with discretion. Thus, it would not be surprising if there were other success factors or strategies, or perhaps a particular combination of these, that have not only brought Latvia's HCs to where they are now but will also enable their future success.

Acknowledgements to Dr. Diana Pauna for her valuable assistance in getting in touch with a number of companies explored in this chapter as well as Valters Beldavs and Bronislava Sauka for their helpful advice on questions related to the history of Latvia.

References

Avots, V. (2004). *Ulmaņlaiki: legendas un fakti*. Rīga: Jumava.

Balabkins, N. (2002). *Tautsaimnieka atziņu ceļš: Esejas un vērtējumi*. Rīga: Terji Deviņi.

Bleiere, D., Butulis, I., Feldmanis, I., Stranga, A., & Zunda, A. (2005). *Latvijas vēstrure 20. Gadsimts*. Rīga: Jumava.

Chaston, I. (2010). *Entrepreneurial management in small firms*. London: Sage.

CSB. (2012). Retrieved March 12, 2011, from http://www.csb.gov.lv

European Commission. (2010). *Innovation Union Scoreboard, 2010*. Retrieved June 5, 2011, from http://ec.europa.eu/enterprise/policies/innovation/facts-figures-analysis/innovationscoreboard/index_en.htm

Eurostat (2011). Retrieved June 15, 2011, from http://epp.eurostat.ec.europa.eu/

Jansone, A., Robežniece, I., & Zelbārte, I. (2008). *90 Latvijas gadi: 1918–2008*. Rīga: Latvijas Nacionālais vēstures muzejs.

LIAA. (2011). Retreived June 5, 2011, from http://www.liaa.gov.lv/eng/trade_with_latvia/foreign_trade_statistics/

Rastrigina, O. (2010). *Global Entrepreneurship Monitor 2009 Latvia Report*. Riga: Stockholm School of Economics in Riga, Baltic International Centre for Economic Policy Studies and SKDS.

Sauka, A. (2011). *Latvijas uzņēmumu konkurētspēja*. Rīga: Nordea un Rīgas Ekonomikas augstskola.

Sauka, A., & Putniņš, T. (2011). *SSE Riga shadow economy index for the Baltic countries 2009 and 2010*. Riga: Stockholm School of Economics in Riga.

Sauka, A., & Welter, F. (2010). *Business insolvencies in Latvia*. Riga: Stockholm School of Economics in Riga.

Sauka, A., & Welter, F. (2011). Mentalities and mindsets - Difficulties of entrepreneurship policies in the Latvian context. In F. Welter & D. Smallbone (Eds.), *Handbook of research in entrepreneurship policies in Central and Eastern Europe* (pp. 83–101). Cheltenham: Edward Elgar.

Schneider, F., Buehn, A., & Montenegro, C. (2010). *Shadow economies all over the world: New estimates for 162 countries from 1999 to 2007 (Policy Research Working Paper Series 5356)*. The World Bank.

Schwab, K. (2011). *Global Competitiveness Report 2010–2011*. Retrieved June 5, 2011, from http://www3.weforum.org/docs/WEF_GlobalCompetitivenessReport_2010-11.pdf

Šterns, I. (2002). *Latvijas vēsture: 1180–1290: krustakari*. Rīga: Latvijas vēstures institutūta apgāds.

Švābe, A. (1990). *Latvijas vesture*. Rīga: Avots.

Hidden Champions of the Republic of Macedonia

Mijalce Santa and Ljubomir Kekenovski

Overview

Official name:	Republic of Macedonia
Type of government:	Parliamentary Democratic Republic
Population in 2011:	2,063,893
Land area:	25,220 km^2

History

1918	After the collapse of the Austro-Hungarian Empire, the present-day Republic of Macedonia becomes part of the Kingdom of Serbs, Croats and Slovenes.
1929	The kingdom becomes known as Yugoslavia.
1941	The present-day Republic of Macedonia is occupied by Nazi Germany, Bulgaria and Italy during World War II.
1945	At the end of the war, the present-day Republic of Macedonia becomes a constituent republic of socialist Yugoslavia.
1991	The Republic of Macedonia held a referendum at which 95.26 % voted for independence from Yugoslavia.
1992	The Republic of Macedonia joins the International Monetary Fund.
1993	The Republic of Macedonia joins the United Nations.
2001	(Spring) Insurgency in the Republic of Macedonia

M. Santa (✉)
E-business department, Ss Cyril and Methodius University, Faculty of Economics – Skopje, Skopje, Macedonia
e-mail: mijalce@eccf.ukim.edu.mk

L. Kekenovski
Economy department, Ss Cyril and Methodius University, Faculty of Economics – Skopje, Skopje, Macedonia

P. McKiernan and D. Purg (eds.), *Hidden Champions in CEE and Turkey*,
DOI 10.1007/978-3-642-40504-4_16, © Springer-Verlag Berlin Heidelberg 2013

2001 (August) Ohrid Framework Agreement signed. The conflict ends.
2003 The Republic of Macedonia officially becomes member of the WTO.
2005 The Republic of Macedonia becomes candidate country for membership of the EU.
2008 Greece blocks the Republic of Macedonia's admission to NATO

1 Introduction: Context

The Republic of Macedonia is a small landlocked country with nice people, tasty food, and a lot of sunny days. Throughout its history, the present-day territory of Macedonia has been a crossroads for both traders and conquerors moving between the European continent and Asia Minor. Each of these transiting powers has left its mark upon the region, giving rise to a rich and varied cultural and historical tradition. For over 500 years, until 1912, Macedonia was under the rule of the Ottoman Turkish Empire. After the Second Balkan War, the territory of Macedonia was divided between Bulgaria, Greece, and Serbia. After that, the present-day area of the Republic of Macedonia was incorporated into the newly formed Kingdom of Serbs, Croats, and Slovenes. After the Second World War, the Republic of Macedonia became one of the constituent republics of the new Socialist Federal Republic of Yugoslavia (SFRY).

The Republic of Macedonia entered the SFRY as the poorest and least developed country. During the SFRY period, the Republic of Macedonia started the process of industrialization and building of its infrastructure. Large industrial capacities were built during this period. The focus of the Macedonian economy was to supply the Yugoslav market with agricultural products, vegetables, fruits, tobacco, steel plates, textiles, and semi-finished products, which were finalized in the other republics and then exported outside Yugoslavia. This dependence of the Macedonian economy on Yugoslav markets had a devastating influence after the break-up of Yugoslavia.

The Republic of Macedonia peacefully gained its independence from Yugoslavia through a referendum on 8 September 1991. However, international recognition of the new country was delayed by Greece's objection to the use of the word "Macedonia" in the name of the country, and as a result the state was admitted to the United Nations under the temporary reference "The Former Yugoslav Republic of Macedonia". Other international organizations adopted the same name.

In spite of 45 years of development, the Republic of Macedonia was still the poorest and least developed country of all the republics in the federation when it left Yugoslavia. Republic of Macedonia declared monetary independence in 1992, and introduced the denar as a national currency. The loss of traditional Yugoslav markets, wars in the region, a blockade from Greece, and an embargo on FR Yugoslavia, are all factors that contributed to Macedonia's deep recession in the first half of the 1990s. Although some economic recovery occurred in the second half of 1990, the war in Kosovo and the conflict in Macedonia in 2001 resulted in new economic decline (US Department of State 2011).

In 2003 the Republic of Macedonia officially became a member of the WTO. The Stabilization and Association Agreement officially came into force in 2004, and in 2005 the Republic of Macedonia became a candidate country for membership of the EU. The country has been a member of EFTA and CEFTA since 2006. Greece blocked the Republic of Macedonia's admission to NATO in 2008 and continues to block the start of accession negotiations with the EU.

In the past 2 decades, the Republic of Macedonia has undergone considerable economic reform and has developed an open economy with trade accounting for more than 90 % of GDP in recent years. The core economic and foreign indicators for the Republic of Macedonia are provided in Exhibit 1.

The key industries in the Republic of Macedonia are manufacturing, trade and agriculture. The top trading partners for exports (at the end of November 2010, in percentage of total) are (NBRM 2011): Germany (20.5 %), Kosovo (13.6 %), Bulgaria (9.0 %), Serbia (8.1 %), Greece (7.6 %), Italy (7.1 %), and Croatia (3.7 %).

An important feature of Macedonian exports is that their structure has been practically unchanged in the whole period and has been dominated by products of low value added. Textiles, metal and non-metal minerals have constantly accounted for more than half of all exports from the Republic of Macedonia.

Nearly 99 % of the companies in the country are registered as small enterprises, employing nearly 55 % of the employees in the private sector. According to the main activity registered, the majority of businesses are in the wholesale and retail trade sector (47 %), manufacturing sector (13.1 %), and the transportation, storage, and communications sectors (approximately 10 %). The largest employer is the manufacturing sector, with 35.6 % of the total number of employees in the private sector (Invest in Macedonia 2011).

The Macedonian economy has so far weathered the global economic crisis better than most countries in the region. The crisis resulted in a collapse of external demand and a sharp drop in private capital flows (World Bank 2011). In this aspect, the Republic of Macedonia has recently been ranked as the fourth "best reformatory state" out of 178 countries ranked by the World Bank. According to the World Economic Forum Competitiveness Report for 2010–2011, the country ranked 79th out of 139 economies (Schwab 2010). This is evidence of steady improvement since the Republic of Macedonia was in 89th place in 2008/2009, and in 84th place in the 2009/2010 report.

The weakest points of the Macedonian economy, according to this report, are the lack of business sophistication and innovation. On these indicators the country ranks 96th and 97th out of 139 economies. The Macedonian economy is placed in the group of efficiency-driven economies (Schwab 2010). Furthermore, it is characterized by a high rate of unemployment—32.0 % in 2010, and a "grey economy" estimated to be between 20 % and 45 % of GDP (World Fact Book, World Bank 2011).

31.7 % in the third quarter of 2010—and a grey economy estimated to account for 20–45 % of GDP (CIA 2011).

The Macedonian hidden champions (HCs) operate in these conditions. What differentiates them from other companies is their business sophistication and

Exhibit 1 Core economic indicators for Macedonia

	1999	2000	2001	2002	2003	2004	2005	2006	2007	2008	2009	2010	2011
GDP per capita (current $US)	1,835.56	1,785.33	1,704.78	1,874.79	2,345.49	2,712.32	2,936.94	3,211.09	3,984.44	4,791.19	4,528.25	4,434.49	4,925.34
GDP per capita growth (annual %)	3.88	4.14	−4.86	0.55	2.53	4.36	4.09	4.77	5.90	4.71	−1.12	1.59	2.87
Long-term unemployment (% of total unemployment)	n/a	n/a	n/a	n/a	n/a	n/a	n/a	84.00	84.80	84.90	81.60	83.10	n/a
Foreign direct investment, net inflows (% of GDP)	2.41	6.00	13.01	2.78	2.48	5.86	2.43	6.52	8.99	6.22	2.79	3.29	4.87
GDP (current $US m)	3,673.29	3,586.88	3,436.96	3,791.31	4,756.22	5,514.25	5,985.81	6,560.55	8,159.83	9,834.04	9,313.57	9,137.54	10,165.37
Exports of goods and services (current $US m)	1,549.09	1,744.33	1,467.33	1,441.82	1,810.36	2,202.26	2,641.81	3,058.68	4,272.55	5,005.22	3,634.12	4,347.69	5,021.47
Exports of goods and services (% of GDP)	42.17	48.63	42.69	38.03	38.06	39.94	44.13	46.62	52.36	50.90	39.02	47.58	49.40
Merchandise exports (current $US m)	1,191.00	1,323.00	1,158.00	1,115.53	1,366.99	1,675.88	2,041.00	2,401.00	3,398.27	3,990.64	2,708.49	3,301.83	4,455.38
Merchandise exports to high-income economies (% of total merchandise exports)	68.81	67.09	69.32	69.34	69.35	67.47	60.29	81.29	64.78	57.66	55.29	55.86	n/a
Merchandise exports to developing economies in Europe & Central Asia (% of total merchandise exports)	7.68	31.69	29.36	29.19	28.75	31.98	33.90	18.15	34.81	41.99	31.30	27.69	n/a

Ores and metals exports (% of merchandise exports)	8.72	8.82	8.34	7.47	4.66	2.22	3.02	4.25	4.57	n/a	3.05	n/a	5.92
Agricultural raw materials exports (% of merchandise exports)	1.69	1.70	1.22	1.14	1.18	1.00	0.78	0.76	0.70	n/a	0.53	n/a	0.64
Food exports (% of merchandise exports)	19.12	14.96	16.37	18.27	16.78	15.26	16.35	16.09	13.69	n/a	18.19	n/a	14.13
Fuel exports (% of merchandise exports)	1.89	4.77	3.76	2.25	5.40	4.68	8.02	9.38	4.92	n/a	1.12	n/a	8.36
Manufactures exports (% of merchandise exports)	66.43	69.41	70.09	70.52	71.52	76.55	71.65	69.43	76.07	n/a	50.87	n/a	70.90
High-technology exports (% of manufactured exports)	0.88	1.24	1.09	1.38	1.35	1.17	1.08	1.11	0.83	n/a	2.95	n/a	n/a

Source: World Bank (2013)
Source: World Bank (2011)

Exhibit 2 Hidden champions from Macedonia

Name	Short market leadership description	Revenues 2010 (€m)	Revenues 2000 (€m)	Employees 2010
Mikrosam	Advanced company that provides innovative composites manufacturing solutions to customers from all over the world. It is estimated to be among top 10 companies in the world	n/a	n/a	70
Ading	One of the strongest players on the market of admixtures and other chemical materials for construction industry in South-east Europe and Middle Asia	12	4.3	100
Vipro	Company offers unique ajvar to international markets. It is estimated to be the biggest global producer of this product	0.05	2	30–90 seasonal
Konti-hidroplast	One of regional leaders in Western Balkan, in production of polyethylene hoses and polyethylene pipes	18	7–8	115

Source: Authors of the chapter

innovation that helps them create additional value through their products and services. Exhibit 2 summarizes the key characteristics of the Macedonian HCs.

2 Four Case Studies

2.1 Mikrosam

Overview

Address: Krusevski pat b.b., 7500 Prilep, Republic of Macedonia
Tel: +38948400100
Web: http://www.mikrosam.com

Company Information

Industry:	Manufacture of other special-purpose machinery
Year of establishment:	1990
Sales revenues in 2010:	n/a
Sales revenues in 2000:	n/a
Average number of employees in 2010:	70
Brain(s) behind the company:	Founder Blagoja Samakoski

2.1.1 Nature of Market Leadership

The company is a leader in integrated solutions for products made from composite materials. These composite materials are increasingly used in various products, from gas tanks to major parts for the new generation of airplanes and satellites. The market for machinery that can create these products is growing rapidly all over the world.

2.1.2 Nature of Competitive Advantage

The core of the company's competitive advantage is achieved by concentrating on three important technology areas: composites production expertise, motion control and process automation, and specialized software development. With the development of highly advanced and integrated solutions and products, Mikrosam has a distinctive product and market position.

2.1.3 Core Lessons Learned on the Path to Business Success

1. Invest in knowledge. If you want to create the most advanced technology and solutions, your people will also need to have the most advanced knowledge. This can be achieved only by strong and long-term investments in knowledge and learning.
2. Create value. If you have a product that brings value to your customers, it will be in demand even in times of crisis.
3. Create a succession team. Nobody lasts forever, but if you create, educate, and train a team that believes in the idea, values, and goals on which the company was created, you can be sure that the company can last.

2.1.4 Mikrosam: Hidden Champion

Mikrosam is a company so advanced that it is the only company in the world offering integrated solutions for the manufacture of products from composite materials. Internationally, it has successfully built and integrated over 130 production lines for customers in 30 countries. In 1990 Mikrosam started working on design consulting, building electronic components and designing machines for production of composite materials. The company soon had to expand from its design office in the city of Prilep, and invested in a large production facility aimed at developing sophisticated, specialized machinery. This decision was made to allow complete control of the machine building process, from conception to delivery, and the start of production at the customer's site. The company offers turn-key solutions that can be delivered anywhere in the world.

Microsam produces advanced filament winding machines, pre-preg making machines using thermo-set and thermoplastics, fibre placement machines, customized composite machining centres, and integrated manufacturing lines. The fibre placement machine is the company's highest achievement. This type of machine is used in the production of major parts for the new generation of airplanes and satellites using composites. Till now, only four countries in the world have had the technology to produce this type of equipment: the USA, France, Spain and the Republic of Macedonia. The fibre placement machine represents an important step in the company's growth trajectory for offering complete turn-key solutions worldwide.

Microsam goes beyond what its competition does. It studies the customers' needs and proposes solutions that will meet and exceed those needs. To achieve this, Mikrosam invests heavily in its employees—the company's most valuable resource. Its 70 employees have access to more than 4,000 books in hard copy and more than 50,000 available in electronic format. Furthermore, all of Milrosam's engineers attend international trade fairs, conferences, seminars and training sessions on issues and themes that enable them to successfully create solutions for customers and compete with the competition.

This has contributed to 20–30 % annual growth in a growing market, and Mikrosam has been an industry leader for approximately 6 years. Now it is expanding into Russia, China, India, Israel and Japan. Exports represent 99 % of the total sales revenue, versus 85 % 10 years ago.

In this specialized market, the main competition comes from companies in the developed world, including the USA, Germany, Switzerland, Spain, and France. Mikrosam believes that it has very good product quality, the best price-to-performance ratio, and the strongest after-sales service. It also can keep its delivery dates. All these factors are highly valued by its customers. Making an offer that combines these characteristics very often makes Mikrosam the first choice for customers. "It is hard to persuade customers that in Macedonia we are developing and producing such advanced high-tech equipment, but when we bring them to see our solutions and facilities, everything goes much more easily," says Dimitar Bogdanovski, sales manager of Mikrosam. This is one big challenge that Mikrosam is working to overcome in its strategy of world-wide expansion.

To keep up with technological developments, market needs, and the realization of its ideas, Mikrosam invests 10 % of its income in research and development. This has resulted in many patents.

For several years, the company has supported its community by organizing free and personal educational services for a selected number of enthusiastic adults through the Mikrosam Academy. The latest endeavour has been the establishment of the first private Institute for Advanced Composites and Robotics with the vision to become a centre for practical research for the common good of the worldwide community. Since 2011, the Institute has provided postgraduate studies in the field of composites and robotics. It is planning to start doctorate studies in 2012.

Overall the company has achieved satisfactory success; it has done better than others during the recession. By offering turn-key solutions, Mikrosam has created vertical integration, a characteristic of HCs that makes it difficult for others to compete.

The future may be harder, but the past has taught Microsam that if you invest in new knowledge, in new technologies, and in your people, and you have a global outlook on the market, success will come. That success will make you a HC.

2.2 Ading

Overview

Address:	Novoselski pat bb, 1000 Skopje, Republic of Macedonia
Tel:	+38922034800
Email:	ading@ading.com.mk
Web:	http://www.ading.com.mk

Company Information

Industry:	Manufacture of articles of concrete, cement and plaster
Year of establishment:	1969 (privatized 1996)
Sales revenues in 2010:	n/a
Sales revenues in 2000:	n/a
Average number of employees in 2010:	100
Brain(s) behind the company:	Management team

2.2.1 Nature of Market Leadership

Ading is a regional leader in the production and sales of admixtures and other chemicals used in a large number of products and materials for the construction industry. The need for materials that have the ability to be used in different conditions and places is creating a growing market for admixture products.

2.2.2 Nature of Competitive Advantage

At the centre of the competitive advantage of Ading is the strong engineering background of its employees, which enables the company to offer high-quality technical support to clients. This, combined with the flexibility typical of a relatively small firm, is the company's strength.

2.2.3 Core Lessons Learned on the Path to Business Success

1. Early identification of clients' needs is one of the most important lessons. If you know what a customer needs, you can prepare an appropriate solution faster than your competitors.
2. You need strong client relations; be there for the customers when they need you. This helps secure repeated business and creates a good image.
3. Provide in-depth services that help clients see the complete picture, and work with them to put the right product in the right place.

2.2.4 Ading: Hidden Champion

In the building industry there is concrete and additives that add value to the concrete. Ading is a joint stock company that produces and sells admixtures and other chemicals for the construction industry. These components add value by becoming ingredients of each construction. Established in 1969, Ading successfully completed its transformation in 1996, and has since become a joint stock company with a strong international orientation. It has 100 employees of which 50 have a higher education. The company has grown while being managed by a strong network of people with experience and detailed knowledge of all the company processes. Furthermore, the "old" management has created and invested significantly in a "young" management team that will succeed them and move the company to new levels.

Ading is producing and selling its own brand on the market. In some markets its brand is actually a synonym for the product. To further meet customers' needs, the company offers a complete solution by offering project design and implementation through its daughter company. All these aspects, combined with expansion into worldwide markets, have contributed to growth in turnover from 4.3 million euros in 2000 to 12 million in 2012. This increase will continue because Ading's products are in a growth phase and development will improve their usefulness.

The competitors in this industry are big companies, such as BASF, SIKA, and KEMA. They are big multinationals with large numbers of different products and offices all around the world. Furthermore, this is an industry where customers need a lot of information about the products, and perceive them as important to them. To compete in this environment, Ading is building strong customer confidence in its products, and establishing long and close relationships with them. To achieve this, Ading relies on technical support, a large number of engineers, and flexibility.

"This is why the products of Ading are sold by highly qualified engineers who have participated since the project phase of the building, and they provide a technical report for it", says Mr. Zoran Petrovski, deputy general manager. This is also related to the culture of the company where engineers are more valued than employees with a business background.

To secure its position, meet the demands of the market, and expand to new markets and products, Ading invests around 3 % of its income in R&D. Furthermore, it reinvests its complete profit. Research can change direction so as to meet a customer's needs. Nanostructures and their use are explored in the products. But according to Mr. Petrovski, there is more to be done. There is a need for better utilization of capacities, higher profits, and lower costs, so that the company can be ready to compete in a more dynamic and competitive industry.

Ading has learned that strong client relations and providing in-depth services creates a base for return business. Getting involved early on with the needs of the customers, and helping them to identify solutions, can help companies secure a competitive position. For a HC, in a niche market, these are important characteristics.

2.3 Vipro

Overview

Address:	Moinski pat bb, 1480 Gevgelija, Republic of Macedonia
Tel:	+3892783068
Email:	vipro@t-home.mk
Web:	http://www.vipro.com.mk

Company Information

Industry:	Processing and preserving of fruit and vegetables
Year of establishment:	1993
Sales revenues in 2010:	n/a
Sales revenues in 2000:	50,000 euros
Average number of employees in 2010:	30–90 (seasonal)
Brain(s) behind the company:	Founder and CEO Viktor Petkov

2.3.1 Nature of Market Leadership

In the niche market of organic food, Vipro's position is even narrower. It produces traditional homemade ajvar sauce, pindzur, pickled, roasted and vacuum-packed vegetables, jam, and paste from peppers and olives. Vipro is a global leader in this niche market, serving the needs of those who have emigrated from the Balkan countries. The increasing trend for people to choose healthy foods and new tastes creates an immense opportunity for the company's products.

2.3.2 Nature of Competitive Advantage

Vipro uses high-quality, fresh raw ingredients, processed without delay, in accordance with strict production standards. Its products are based on traditional recipes that give a distinctive flavour and taste to their products.

2.3.3 Core Lessons Learned on the Path to Business Success

1. Be ambitious. Do not be afraid to raise the bar high. Set ambitious goals and take bold steps to achieve them.
2. Create an appropriate environment in the company. Identify the right human resources and invest in them.
3. Sense the customers' needs before your competition. This will help you create products that fill in gaps in niche markets whose existence nobody suspected.

2.3.4 Vipro: Hidden Champion

Vipro started as a company producing soft drinks, then continued with mineral water. Finally, in 1998, after 5 years of existence, it switched to organic food production and processing of fruits and vegetables. The company started with traditional homemade ajvar and pindzur (vegetable dips or spreads traditionally used on the territory of the Republic of Macedonia); later it started producing pickled, roasted vacuum-packed vegetables, jam, and other products, such as paste from peppers and olives, to meet the different needs of customers. Vipro's turnover has grown from 50,000 euros in 2000 to 2 million at present. Although the company has suffered some negative effects from developments in the region, it strives to expand into new markets, diversify its products, and improve existing ones. To achieve this goal, Vipro is investing in a new factory with increased production capacity. In the medium term this will increase revenues to five million euros, whereas the long-term goal is to achieve a turnover of 20 million. This investment will lay the ground for the next stage of Vipro's growth.

Vipro has also created a smart market-entrance strategy. It is competing in a temporary market. "It consists of people that emigrated from the Balkan countries and Eastern Europe to Western Europe, the USA, Canada, and Australia. The ultimate target is the domestic market, the native population in these countries. The emigrants are our gate to the native populations", says Mr. Viktor Petkov, founder and CEO of Vipro.

In some of the targeted countries, such as Canada and the USA, the company has 50 % of the market. In other countries, its market share is smaller, yet sizeable. This trend has been observed in the past 7 or 8 years. Exports to other Balkan countries have also grown because of changes in life style; people have less time to prepare their own home-made products. Vipro is following this trend, moving its products from a commodity position towards branded-food specialty products. This has resulted in a situation where exports make up 75 % of the total sales revenue.

Since the beginning, exports have been organized through sales agents but Vipro's plan is to have its own offices in the future. The top three customers contribute a maximum of 30 % to Vipro's revenue. The intention is not to be dependent on a small number of customers but to diversify the sources of revenue.

Vipro's main global competitors are from Serbia, Bulgaria and Turkey. But local companies from Macedonia such as Vori, Diem, Bonum, and Trgoinzenering, are also direct competitors to Vipro on global markets. Quality is the most important factor to buyers. To achieve high quality and differentiate its product, Vipro uses high-quality, fresh raw ingredients, processed without delay under strict production standards. These factors, combined with Mr. Petkov's drive "to create something new, to offer the customer more opportunities, and to constantly try to improve the existing products and launch new ones", will ensure Vipro's growing presence on international markets.

Mr. Petkov is generally happy with what the company has achieved but his ambitions are bigger and he expects growth to continue, especially after opening a new factory. His flexibility, good timing, speed, ability to analyze information and make forecasts, and emphasis on teamwork, will enable his company to grow even further and expand into new markets with new products. He will need to use these characteristics to meet the challenges of a not-so-positive regional environment, select products and find high-quality human resources.

Mr. Petkov has learned that he must be ambitious. If you are in his position, you should not be afraid to raise the bar high, set ambitious goals, and take bold steps to achieve them. Furthermore, you should create an appropriate environment in the company and encourage people. And never forget to study the customer's needs before your competition does. If you have learned these rules, you will find it easier to become a HC.

2.4 Konti-Hidroplast

Overview

Address:	Industriska bb, 1480 Gevgelija, Republic of Macedonia
Tel:	+38934212064
Email:	contact@konti-hidroplast.com.mk
Web:	http://www.konti-hidroplast.com.mk

Company Information

Industry:	Manufacture of plastic plates, sheets, tubes and profiles
Year of establishment:	1990
Sales revenues in 2010:	n/a
Sales revenues in 2000:	n/a
Average number of employees in 2010:	115
Brain(s) behind the company:	CEO Boris Madzunkov; Founder and former CEO Dimitar Madzunkov

2.4.1 Nature of Market Leadership

Konti-hidroplast is a strong regional competitor in the market for polyethylene and polypropylene pipes. The market is expanding, and the pipes are used for a number of different purposes: movement of drinking water, gasification, atmospheric water, sewage, drop-by-drop irrigation systems, and transportation of fluids. The need to move water and other fluids in different areas creates a growing market for polyethylene and polypropylene pipes.

2.4.2 Nature of Competitive Advantage

At the core of Konti-hidroplast's competitive advantage is the company's strong entrepreneurial spirit, combined with a strong determination always to implement the latest technologies and innovations in product development and production.

2.4.3 Core Lessons Learned on the Path to Business Success

1. Willpower and goals come first. It is not easy but you need to stick to them. There are a lot of obstacles that can hinder your development and success, but you can carry on with this lesson in mind.
2. Do not focus on short-term gains, but think long-term and invest to achieve your goals. You cannot get rich or become successful very fast; you need to lay down the ground, direct your actions, and put in a lot of hard work for many years. It is important that the business can endure longer.
3. Respect your employees so that your company is successful. The employees are very important, especially in hard times. Treating them well brings a lot of important support and energy during hard times.

2.4.4 Konti-Hidroplast: Hidden Champion

In 1990, Mr. Dimitar Madzunkov, founder and owner of the company, started producing polyethylene pipes for irrigation and transportation of drinking water. In 1993 he changed the name of the company to Konti-Hidroplast: "I wanted to stress the continuity of the company, to indicate that we will always grow", he said. He and his son have managed this. In 2010 his company had more products, and was present on more markets, than ever. It is still looking forward. Konti-Hidroplast competes in the market for polyethylene and polypropylene pipes for drinking water, gasification, atmospheric water, sewage, drop-by-drop irrigation systems, and transportation of other fluids. After being a company that sold its products only on the Macedonian market, it now has a leading position in the Bulgarian, Greek, Albanian and Kosovo markets. The company's revenue rose from 6–7 million euros in 2000 to 29 million in 2008. Due to the financial crisis, it fell to 18 million euros in 2010, but the forecast for 2011 was positive. The main reason for the decline was the fact that various governments use Konti-Hidroplast's products for infrastructure projects, and they cut investments in these projects during the crisis.

Since 2005 Konti-Hidroplast has experienced a boom in exports; now they account for 95 % of the company's total revenue. Ten years ago the company did not export anything; now it has opened its own subsidiaries in the regional markets. "But it was not an easy ride", Mr. Madzunkov says, "Sometimes people will say to me, 'Mitko, do not risk too much or you might lose all', but I was stubborn and kept going and I made this". His vision is always to follow and implement new technologies and innovations in production processes, management of resources, and the overall work of the company. Every 3–5 years Konti-Hidroplast implements new technologies. These investments enable it to support its competitiveness factors: quality, price, and speed.

Another big success for Konti-Hidroplast is the transition of the company's management from the founder and owner to his son, who is now CEO. Mr. Boris

Madzunkov is a young manager with a business background and 10 years of experience at the company. Since he stepped in as CEO, Konti-Hidroplast has experienced strong growth in exports. He has identified entrepreneurial intuition and knowledge of the market as the main strengths of the company. An entrepreneurial spirit guides Konti-hidroplast while its products continue to expand in other markets and increase its presence in existing export markets. The company derives its strength also from innovation, its image, and the motivation of its employees. At this moment the company has three patents and one pending approval. Every year approximately 10 % of the income is invested in R&D because the management believes this will create new products and an opportunity to meet the needs of customers before the competition.

A challenge for Konti-hidroplast is to minimize its dependence on large infrastructural projects financed by governments and state institutions, so that it can avoid declines in revenue as a result of crises. Another major limiting factor for global growth is the high cost of transporting products over long distances. An innovation-driven company with a strong entrepreneurial spirit, such as Konti-Hidroplast, is likely to find a solution to this issue. This might involve opening production facilities in other countries, or inventing new products that are more suitable for long-distance transportation.

HCs distinguish themselves by their evident ambition and devotion as well as the drive that they have to grow and be successful, to face challenges, and to create opportunities from them. As a HC, Konti-Hidroplast, has learned that willpower and goals come first. This philosophy is not easy to pursue but it is absolutely necessary to achieve success. Do not focus on short-term gains but invest in long-term achievements and respect your employees so that your company is successful.

Conclusion

Macedonia is a small country still trying to generate strong economic development. High unemployment and lack of exports hinder this development. It is difficult to be a champion in this environment; therefore the HCs should be viewed as examples to be followed. Through this research, the following characteristics of HCs in Macedonia were identified:

- Exports: It is hard to be a HC if you do not export. Macedonia is a small market and exporting is the only way for companies to grow and successfully compete with international companies. All the identified Macedonian HCs have had strong growth as a result of their exports. Export activities stimulate companies to be more open to innovation, better identify the needs of customers, and create solutions that add value and differentiate them in the global economy. It is very simple: if Macedonian companies do not start exporting they will have bigger problems when international companies start trading heavily in local markets.
- Niche market: Macedonian champions have discovered that they cannot compete in everything with the big companies in international markets. They can play an important role in certain segments at a regional or global level, and can successfully compete with the large companies in those

markets. This niche strategy has enabled the HCs to focus their resources and skills and create superior products recognized by the customers as a quality product with added value.

- Added value: Macedonian HCs create brands in their fields. They avoid the commodity trap and always look for ways that their products can add value so that they can be recognized on the global market. It is not easy, but all of them are strong in this aspect.
- Leadership: These companies are run by people who have the leadership skills that are needed for creating a vision and attracting people with whom they can achieve the established goals. As real leaders, they put the company's interest first. They create a pleasant environment for their employees. They invest in young managers, innovation and R&D. They create a company.

Macedonian companies share the characteristics of the original HCs proposed by Hermann Simon. Maybe the Macedonian champions are not so big and do not participate significantly in the country's export activities. Yet, they are emerging and will play important roles in Macedonia and the global economy. Thus, when we talk about Macedonian champions, we can call them emerging champions.

References

CIA. (2011). *World Fact Book - Macedonia*. Retrieved August 11, 2011, from https://www.cia.gov/library/publications/the-world-factbook/geos/mk.html

Invest in Macedonia. (2011). *Small and medium-size enterprises in Macedonia*. Retrieved August 5, 2011, from http://www.investinmacedonia.com/

NBRM. (2011). *Foreign trade*. Retrieved August 10, 2011, from http://www.nbrm.mk/?ItemID=EA9313A61C028F44B00B681EF302F59D

Schwab, K. (2010). *The Global Competitiveness Report 2010–2011*. World Economic Forum.

US Department of State. (2011). *Background note Macedonia*. Retrieved August 10, 2011, from http://www.state.gov/r/pa/ei/bgn/26759.htm

World Bank. (2011). *Macedonia country brief*. Retrieved August 11, 2011, from http://www.worldbank.org/en/country/macedonia

World Bank. (2013). *Data; countries and economies*. http://data.worldbank.org/country

Hidden Champions from Romania

Bogdan Rusu

Overview

Official name:	Romania
Type of government:	Unitary semi-presidential republic
Population in 2012:	19,043,767
Land area:	238,391 km^2

History

1914/1920	Romania enters World War I on the side of the Allied Triple Entente. The Central Powers conquer most of the country inflicting heavy losses on the Romanian army. The Entente powers give Transylvania to Romania by the Treaty of Trianon.
1940	The Soviet Union occupies northern Bukovina and Bessarabia. Hungary occupies northern Transylvania, and Bulgaria occupies southern Dobruja. After 1940, Ion Antonescu and the Iron Guard share power in Romania.
1939/1945	Romania enters World War II on the side of the Axis powers.
1944	Romania changes sides and joins the Allies
1947	The Communist government forces King Michael I to leave the country. Romania is proclaimed a republic but it remains under the control of thc USSR until the 1950s.

B. Rusu (✉)
"Gh. Asachi" Technical University of Iaşi, Engineering and Management Department, Iaşi, Romania
e-mail: bmcrusu@tuiasi.ro

P. McKiernan and D. Purg (eds.), *Hidden Champions in CEE and Turkey*, DOI 10.1007/978-3-642-40504-4_17, © Springer-Verlag Berlin Heidelberg 2013

1989	Nicolae Ceauşescu makes Romania a police state and imposes a cult of personality, which leads to the Romanian Revolution. After Ceauşescu, the National Salvation Front, led by Ion Iliescu restores order and democracy.
1990/1996	Socialist parties govern Romania.
1993	Romania applies for membership of the European Union.
2000	Social Democrats return to power with Iliescu.
2004	Traian Băsescu elected president. Romania joins NATO.
2007	(January 1st) Romania joins the European Union.

1 Introduction: Context

In 2012 there were about 19.0 million Romanians (National Institute of Statistics 2012, p.1) living in an area of 238,391 km^2. Romania borders on Hungary, Serbia, Bulgaria, Ukraine, the Republic of Moldova and the Black Sea. It is one of the poorest countries in the EU with a GDP per capita of 5,800 euros in 2010 (Eurostat 2013). Following the EU pattern, the vast majority of Romanian enterprises are SMEs, less that 1 % being large companies (National Institute of Statistics 2013). The latter are distributed across most industrial sectors, including mining, hydro-electric and nuclear energy production, aerospace, automotive, metallurgical, chemical, aluminium production, wood processing, textile and IT, to name just a few. Romania is also known in the EU for its great natural resources and a growing tourism industry, with key attractions including the Carpathian Mountains, the Danube Delta, and the resorts and beaches of the Black Sea. More information can be found in Exhibit 1.

Iacob (2002, pp. 50–52) provides an in-depth analysis of Romanian transformation. The country became independent in 1878 and completed its unity only in 1918, and therefore had to transform itself and continue to modernize so as to become competitive in Europe. The first key economic reform was the transfer of nearly 25 % of the Romania's monastery-owned land to the state in December 1863. Other measures initiated by the state include bureaucratization (such as creating modern institutions) and involvement in the economic life through the 1887 law that encouraged industry and the construction of railroads, which generated high industrial growth. These significant developments reflected in the number of mechanized enterprises (from 45 in 1862 to 16,916 in 1939), crude oil extraction (which increased 8,400 % in 1905 as compared to 1866, reaching over 8.7 million tons in 1936), railroad constructions and installed telephones.

Since 1919 there have been three major changes periods. The first was an integration process of the united provinces and economic development (1918–1928). The second was marked by the profound transformation from capitalism to socialism (1945–1962) and the last commenced in 1989: a transformation back to capitalism and modernization in terms of EU integration (Iacob 2002, p. 57).

Exhibit 1 Core economic indicators

	1999	2000	2001	2002	2003	2004	2005	2006	2007	2008	2009	2010	2011
GDP per capita (current $US)	1,583.85	1,650.97	1,815.51	2,101.74	2,736.97	3,481.20	4,572.05	5,681.09	7,856.48	9,497.95	7,650.96	7,686.92	7,539.26
GDP per capita growth (annual %)	−1.04	2.23	7.19	6.69	5.50	8.69	4.42	8.13	6.20	8.09	−6.43	−0.74	2.56
Long-term unemployment (% of total unemployment)	45.20	49.20	48.60	56.50	61.50	59.00	56.30	57.80	50.00	41.30	31.60	34.90	41.90
Foreign direct investment, net inflows (% of GDP)	2.92	2.80	2.88	2.50	3.10	8.53	6.94	9.34	6.08	6.78	3.00	1.94	1.40
GDP (current $US m)	35,592.34	37,052.64	40,180.75	45,824.53	59,507.35	75,489.44	98,913.39	122,641.51	169,282.49	204,335.23	164,345.72	164,792.25	182,610.66
Exports of goods and services (current $US m)	9,972.26	12,113.00	13,418.00	16,223.00	20,646.00	27,121.12	32,565.02	36,246.54	52,010.58	62,181.63	50,292.03	58,371.88	73,106.47
Exports of goods and services (% of GDP)	28.02	32.69	33.39	35.40	34.69	35.93	32.92	29.55	30.72	30.43	30.60	35.42	40.03
Merchandise exports (current $US m)	8,518.12	10,411.98	11,393.84	13,876.55	17,662.28	23,553.22	27,687.54	32,457.88	40,488.20	49,534.99	40,567.20	49,498.85	63,0116.64
Merchandise exports to high-income economies (% of total merchandise exports)	79.73	77.63	82.14	84.27	83.34	81.31	76.87	75.80	76.28	73.21	77.09	75.49	75.08

(continued)

Exhibit 1 (continued)

	1999	2000	2001	2002	2003	2004	2005	2006	2007	2008	2009	2010	2011
Merchandise exports to developing economies in Europe & Central Asia (% of total merchandise exports)	11.66	14.26	10.23	8.46	10.07	12.97	15.25	16.34	17.65	19.82	16.14	18.26	18.15
Ores and metals exports (% of merchandise exports)	5.27	6.92	4.89	4.24	4.15	4.68	3.93	5.25	5.22	4.75	3.61	4.24	4.14
Agricultural raw materials exports (% of merchandise exports)	4.88	4.85	3.66	3.27	3.14	2.84	2.29	2.17	2.00	1.59	1.83	2.04	2.14
Food exports (% of merchandise exports)	5.52	3.13	3.71	3.07	3.15	3.03	2.95	3.27	3.72	6.18	7.42	8.07	8.55
Fuel exports (% of merchandise exports)	4.86	7.16	6.21	7.91	6.47	6.73	10.64	9.98	7.52	9.11	5.89	5.20	5.48
Manufactures exports (% of merchandise exports)	78.47	77.28	81.04	81.05	82.53	82.31	79.54	79.25	79.77	76.53	79.00	78.54	77.79
High-technology exports (% of manufactured exports)	3.55	5.87	6.14	3.80	3.97	3.72	3.84	4.83	3.48	6.69	9.11	10.95	10.18

Source: World Bank (2013)

Verdery (1991) explains the economic development and political implications in Romania and its relations with the countries within the Eastern European Block and Union of Soviet Socialist Republics (USSR). For 2 decades after 1947, the communist regime in Romania with Soviet support embraced a forced industrialization program (p. 103). As a result, Romania exported not only agricultural products but equipment and machineries produced by the newly developed industries. Therefore, Czechoslovakia and Eastern Germany complained about this competition (p. 105) that led to a proposal of specialization of exports for the countries within the Eastern Bloc. Romania rejected its "agricultural role", which would have stopped its industrial development and refused to "subordinate national needs to a supranational planning body in which others would dictate the form of the country's economy" (p.105).

Dăianu (1999, pp. 227–244) provides an in-depth analysis of the dynamics of disequilibria affecting Romania, commencing with the communist period. The intense industrialization financed by loans led in the early 1989's to a large external debt (about 10 billion US). Ceauşescu's decision to reject economic reforms for a market economy that could increase competitiveness, and his strong desire to repay all the depth in advance, led to "shock therapy" trough severe restrictions of internal consumption and investments, including imports of industrial equipment and machineries as well as consumer goods from Western countries (p. 228). These decisions affected the population that had money; it was difficult to find goods of good quality. The Romanian population had high hopes of immediate improvement of the standard of living after the revolution of 1989 and a high level of intolerance to further austerity measures (p. 231). In a very short time, Romania experienced a unique phenomenon among Eastern European countries: after owning over 2.8 billion US dollars before December 1989, it had a deficit of over 1.5 billion a year later. There were two important consequences: First, there was no cultural understanding or acceptance of a market economy and, second, no funds were available for start-up entrepreneurs. However, those who saw opportunities set up their own businesses to satisfy identified market needs, importing Western consumer goods as a start.

The National Salvation Front (NFS), led by Ion Iliescu, started a political revolution at the end of 1989 as a rejection of socialism and Ceauşescu. It became violent because Romanians did not want simply to change the political system but wished to be free and transform the entire society (Library of Congress – Federal Research Division 2006).

Aiming to integrate into the EU, Romania had to adjust itself to function efficiently and effectively within the new structures. The key problems that had to be solved included: "a new macroeconomic equilibrium and keeping inflation under control, restructuring enterprises, [and a] new budgetary system" (Ioviţu 1999, p. 16). It also implied "a gradual transfer of a part of national sovereignty towards a common institution that thus gains a supranational character" (Maha 2002, p. 66) such as customs, free trade zones and harmonization of laws, rules, and regulations.

The constitution was revised to enable the supremacy of EU law after the accession. Albi (2005, p. 103) noted that "[Romania's] constitutional amendment procedure is the most rigid amongst all the countries".

There are several factors that contributed to the slow introduction of economic reforms: a lack of experience with economic reforms during Ceauşescu's regime, Ion Iliescu's education and beliefs, and the population's rejection of further austerity. Most of the large companies remained the property of the state and some of the small businesses were partially privatized "leaving 70 % share of the firms in state ownership" (David-Barrett 2008, p. 9).

Aiming to join the European Union, Romania commenced negotiations in February 2000, which drove the will to follow the accession process and implement the necessary reforms for convergence on economic, institutional, legislative, social and political level (Dumitru 2008, p. 15). Romania's economic growth was partly due to the high amounts of foreign direct investment that was positively influenced by the lifting of the restriction to purchase land and property by foreign companies and investors in October 2003 (David-Barrett 2008, p. 12) (see Exhibit 2).

In 2008 Romania had one of the lowest average monthly labor cost in EU "€365, compared to an average €842 in the CEE-8, and €3,431 in the EU-15" (David-Barrett 2008, p. 12). That proved attractive to important investors, such as Renault, Ford, Nokia and Mittal Steel, to name just a few. Further significant inflows of direct investment were generated by the sale of the state's 62 % stake of Banca Comercială Română to Austria's Erste Bank and the 46 % stake of Romtelecom to Greece's COSMOTE.

Romania has many Hidden Champions (HCs), but some of them became visible to big companies seeking growth in Romania and abroad; these larger companies have acquired HCs and integrated them into their group. Such examples are RADIX, which was bought by Ness Technologies (Vasile 2005). Bit Defender became a partner of Microsoft after it was nominated the world's best-buy anti-virus software; and Nestlé bought Waffles Joe.

Some of the identified and interviewed HCs from Romania are listed in alphabetic order in Exhibit 3 below. The list is short; we could not identify all Romanian HCs due to the physical distance across Romania. In addition, time constraints for the owners and managers also prevented us reaching a large number of HCs. While the number of companies interviewed is small, all of them have been able to enhance their market leadership both in their domestic market and abroad, hence we decided to treat them as regional champions, or champions that may become regional leaders.

Exhibit 2 Foreign direct investments attracted by Romania 2004–2010

FDI Value (€b)						
2004	2005	2006	2007	2008	2009	2010
5.183	5.213	9.056	7.25	9.496	3.49	2.22

Source: National Bank of Romania (2012), Balance of Payments

Exhibit 3 Romanian hidden champions

Name	Market leadership definition	Revenue 2009 (in €m)	Revenue 2000 (in €m)	Employees 2009
Gliga	Biggest provider of stringed instruments for school students, professionals, and maestros, and related high quality accessories through the internet	2.68	1.48	176
Greapfruit	Largest designer of mainly internet solutions for building up client's identity, recognition, and reputation in Romania; now spreading abroad	0.69	0.005	40
ELECTRA group	Biggest manufacturer of interphone in Romania; now spreading abroad, and also diversifying to alarm-system solutions for residential developers	3.11	0.52	140

Source: Authors of the chapter (http://www.mfinante.ro)

2 Three Case Studies

2.1 Gliga String Instruments

Overview

Address: Str. Pandurilor 120, Reghin, Mureş County, Romania
Tel: +40265511011
Email: office@gliga.ro
Web: http://www.gliga.ro

Company Information

Industry:	Manufacture of stringed musical instruments
Year of establishment:	1991
Sales revenue in 2009:	€3.8 million
Sales revenue in 2000:	€1.48 million
Average number employees in 2009:	500
Brain(s) behind the company:	Founder Vasile Gliga and CEO Elena Gliga

2.1.1 Nature of Market Leadership

There are *the* stringed instruments made by master luthiers from Italy, France, and Germany, but there is also a market for other fine instruments. Gliga is the largest producer of stringed instruments in Europe, covering all four main categories of the market: School, Student, Professional, and Maestro, from 1/32 to 4/4.

2.1.2 Nature of Competitive Advantage

Gliga's competitive advantage is twofold: the craftsmanship of its employees, and the quality of wood used in production. Employees demonstrate consistent skills and responsibility developed over time. Competitors have difficulty accessing the same high quality wood, including that which has been in storage for decades.

2.1.3 Core Lessons Learned on the Path to Business Success

1. Growing a brand takes time, perseverance, responsibility, craftsmanship, and seriousness. A certain amount of adversity and hardship constitute a positive factor as it strengthens your position and persuades you to export 98 % of your output across the world, providing you with more protection during hard economic times.
2. When constrained in terms of growth, do not give up. Think positive and innovate to open up a new niche for customized products. Skilled staff with a positive attitude who never say, "this can't be done", create value for both retailers and end users.
3. Act as a socially responsible company by providing care for the community. Your employees will be proud, and they will be envied by other community members who recognize your achievements.

2.1.4 Gliga String Instruments: Hidden Champion

The violin is one of the most virtuous instruments, providing the artist with the opportunity to fill your soul with intense emotions, but it also puts him or her through many years of disciplined practice. A musical career requires changing to a better class of instrument three or four times before reaching master level. And this is what Gliga does best: supplying stringed instruments suitable for music from early learning to peak performance.

Romania is the largest producer of musical instruments in Europe in terms of the number of units manufactured. Apart from Gliga, there are five other producers in Reghin, and a factory, Hora S.A., that has a large product portfolio.

Whilst manufacturing excellent instruments at school, student, professional and maestro levels, Gliga is competing with premium brands and great luthiers from Italy, Germany or France, not on price but on quality. The company has differentiated itself from Chinese instruments through consistent quality, personalized made-to-order maestro instruments, access to high quality aged and rare wood and their maestro class instruments are finding their way into the great orchestras of the world.

Vasile Gliga grew up in Transylvania's Gurghiului Mountains where high-quality wood is available for stringed instruments. He had an unusual start in life that drove determination and craftsmanship. At the age of 18 years, he was forced to leave high school and start working as an apprentice, sculpturing the necks of violins on the same shop floor as his wife. He had to work through university to support his family, and learned from other skilled luthiers how to make all parts and assemble violins. In 1991, the family decided to open up their own business and started a two-man company. By 2009 it was manufacturing 40,000 instruments per year. Over 98 % of the instruments comply with Stradivari vibration length standards.

There are two main factors that influence an instrument's quality: the wood and the craftsmanship. Violins are made of spruce (the top) and flamed maple (the back, the neck and the ribs). The more curly the wood grain, the higher the value of the instrument from which it is made because of its rare occurrence in the tree (maybe 1 tree in 1000 having this "defect"). It provides personality. Beyond rarity, the wood for professional instruments should be allowed to dry naturally for a minimum of 3–5 years, reaching 10–20 years for maestro class. The aging process of the wood provides a better sound. Only 10 out of the 250 employees may work on maestro-level instruments. Entry level instruments require 50 h spread over 3 months, compared to 300 h spread over a 1-year period for professional instruments.

Gliga manufactures violins, violas, cellos and double basses, but also cases and bows, in sizes from 1/32 to 4/4, and covers all four main market categories for stringed instruments: beginning (school level), intermediate, advanced (student level), professional and maestro. All are handmade and finished in oil or nitro varnish (for the beginning level) and ebony accessories (or maple accessories for special orders), with a price range from 100 to 3,000 euros.

In the very early days, production consisted of a maximum of only two master-class instruments every month. Later it increased to ten instruments per month. But there was no room for error, due to the rarity of flamed maple with its excellent qualities. With a weak brand name, Gliga had to sell up to 90 % of its output as unfinished parts and whole instruments to high-end producers. These were assembled, finished, and sold under their brand name. Now this percentage has dropped to around 20 %.

In the last decade the world market for stringed instruments has decreased. Every year there are fewer children likely to embrace classical music while computers and the Internet modify social norms and behaviours. The beginning, intermediate, or advanced-level instruments wear relatively quickly compared to professional and masters' instruments, which are manufactured to last several generations, maybe up to several hundreds of years. Employees must demonstrate the serious responsibility and skills required to deliver stringed instruments with consistently high quality.

Gliga exports 98 % of its production: over 50 % to the USA, over 25 % to Europe, 10 % to Japan, 10 % to Australia, and the remainder to a small number of customers in Thailand, Singapore, Taiwan, and Malaysia. Gliga also sells on the Internet through its virtual shop, where each instrument is depicted in ten pictures that disappear from the website after purchase. Instruments can be returned within 7 days if customers are not completely satisfied.

Exports have grown through direct contact with retailers. Since 1993, when Gliga attended the most prestigious musical exhibitions in Europe and USA, trust has gradually developed through personal relations and “gentlemen’s agreements” based on firm orders via e-mail or phone. On occasion, a small number of artists need instruments that have a particular look on stage. Gliga has the ability to fulfill any special requirements, such as extra sculpturing, paint, or varnish; or an instrument can be pyrographed to the artist’s specifications.

“For the artist, the instrument must look extraordinarily good to start with”, said Vasile Gliga, “but it must also be ready to sing perfectly from the moment he or she puts hands on it; the craftsmanship and the sound of the instrument both being very important. If the strings are a few tenths of a millimetre higher, or the distances are not perfect, then it will not fit in the artist’s hand. The set-up of the instrument [i.e., bridge, tailpiece, fingerboard, pegs, soundpost, strings] is a very important issue”.

Gliga has exhibited extraordinary social responsibility and care for the community by funding the Mirona nursery and elementary school for children of company employees, and for children throughout Romania. The school integrates “Violin Dances”, a dancesport club. It has received many prizes from various championships in the UK, USA, Germany, Singapore, Denmark and China.

While concerned about the future, Vasile Gliga is content with his competitive position and the overall development of the company, especially during hard economic times. “Honesty, altruism, perseverance, passion, and the desire to excel in work; these are the virtues most of us aim for in all stages of our lives. And they all impact on the way we do business, where striving for excellence is vital”.

There are some lessons to be learned from Gliga: When constrained in terms of growth, innovate and open up a new niche for customized products, consolidate your relationship with both retailers and end users, whether they are a school, a student, a professional or a master, and never say, “this can’t be done”. Act as a socially responsible company by providing care for the community. Last but not least, if your products compete with others at a similar price/quality ratio, bypass the wholesaler and even the retailer, and sell directly through the Internet. If you have a high-quality product, you will succeed in gaining the trust of buyers.

2.2 Grapefruit

Overview

Address: Bd. Poitiers nr.16, Iasi, Romania
Tel: +40332882993
Email: office@grapefruit.ro
Web: http://www.grapefruit.ro

Company Information

Industry:	Branding industry
Year of establishment:	1999
Sales revenues in 2009:	€0.69 million
Sales revenues in 2000:	€5,000
Average number employees in 2009:	40
Brain(s) behind the company:	CEO Marius Ursache; founded by Marius Ursache, Stefan Liute and Laurian Gridinoc

2.2.1 Nature of Market Leadership

Grapefruit is a leading consultant in marketing, advertising, and image design for clients (usually big domestic and foreign companies). This market is vulnerable to economic recessions; however, Grapefruit has managed to provide unprecedented quality of service, resulting in its leading position in terms of turnover.

2.2.2 Nature of Competitive Advantage

The core of the company's competitive advantage resides in designing solutions that not only enhance company image but also provide an extended user experience based on three key principles applied to everything that the company does: (1) Identifying what is relevant to the end-user as this shows knowledge of the client's needs, (2) building trust and credibility through actions, and (3), design, which involves solving real end-user problems until someone who is online gets to the flow state when using that application.

2.2.3 Core Lessons Learned on the Path to Business Success

1. Find what is relevant to the end-users by using research that provides a deep understanding of their behaviour, needs and desires. Apply this research as the only way to design the right features for the product.
2. Focus on passionate and loyal customers in designing product features, and not on those who use the product or application only occasionally.
3. Master your business perspective in three categories: As a *designer and strategist* who gets his hands "dirty" well above the elbows; as *manager* who must organize and keep people happy, and keep budgets under control; and an *entrepreneur* who must move away from the previous two to find a vision and gather appropriate resources to generate value.

2.2.4 Grapefruit: Hidden Champion

Every time you see a well-made company logo, it evokes an image of professionalism and quality. If you recognize it, you may be persuaded to use the company's products and feel associated with that particular brand, or at least talk and dream about it. If you wish to develop such a brand for your company, Grapefruit is a business structured to solve the issue. Grapefruit, being a service company, is not a typical HC but does show some HC characteristics; it creates the majority of its revenue abroad while providing a service to foreign MNCs.

The company was set up by Marius Ursache, an MD by training, with a real talent for drawing and a passion for details. He started working part time as a graphic artist at age 14, and later on at 17 he landed a full-time job as a cartoonist and graphic artist with a media company in Iasi. After 5-years in this field, his talent enabled him to enhance his skills through a summer holiday job in the UK in 1998, and also through a 4-month contract with a design agency in the USA the following year. It was there that he realized he wanted to return to Romania and open up his own company—Grapefruit Design (later shortened to 'Grapefruit')—with two other good friends; an IT specialist and software developer, and a very bright strategist and communicator.

Mr. Ursache defines Grapefruit's industry category as "professional services" (branding), which includes marketing consultancy, advertising, and design. Based on turnover figures from the Ministry of Finance website, Grapefruit was the largest branding company in Romania in 2009. Branding is not a clear-cut niche. There are some specialized companies such as Brand Taylors, Brandient, BrandFusion, and Grapefruit, in a market that is estimated to be worth 3–4 million euros in Romania. However, advertising agencies also offer branding services that not only include brand strategies, visual identity and package design, but also communication strategies and digital branding in online and mobile environments; indeed, anything that has an impact in brand creation and development. This extended market is estimated to be worth 20 million euros per year; not big, yet quite lucrative since it does not bear much of the input costs. It is only labour intensive, and labour in Romania is internationally competitive both in terms of price and quality.

Back in 2000, the three friends did not imagine the growth that was to come in the next decade. They were honest and passionate, and they benefited from what Marius had brought back from the USA: managerial expertise, exquisite client service, and honesty, as fundamental values with which to run the company. At the time, Romanian firms were not ready for Grapefruit's services. For the first couple of years they found customers from abroad through the Internet, or through recommendations. But wherever excellence occurs, reputation follows. The first major Romanian customer was Connex, one of the largest mobile phone operators (later bought by Vodafone), following an article about Grapefruit in Biz Magazine. Working with Connex brought higher visibility on the Romanian market, which further opened them to new Romanian clients. Such achievement deserves even higher merit considering that Grapefruit was not based in Bucharest but in Iasi. They opened the Bucharest office only in 2006, after 6 years.

By that time, Marius had recognized a problem: the more choices an end user or customer is willing to consider, the less loyal he becomes, regardless of the level of advertising. Therefore, the way to maintain market share is not necessarily to expand the client's advertising and promotion budgets on discounted products, but to redesign the company product as a core component of the brand. He looked at iPhone's growth since 2007 in a market previously dominated by Nokia,

Blackberry and other players; a growth based not primarily on technology (such as processor speed, screen resolution and internal memory) but on the context and content people use the phones for, which is normally business or personal. In a similar way, Grapefruit started developing user-friendly, customized applications that effectively deal with different user problems.

By designing solutions for the end-user's problems that were better than those of the competition, while at the same time satisfying client's needs, Grapefruit soon had a competitive edge and seized the leading position. "We do a lot of research at the beginning of each project", said Mr. Ursache. "We analyse what is happening and which brands and products our client is competing with. We do a benchmarking analysis, find out who are the end users, and interview them and identify specific behaviours for each meaningful group. In order to solve the problems efficiently and effectively and satisfy specific needs, we segment customers into very narrow groups. We focus on the behaviour of each group and pay special attention to those who are the most passionate and loyal to our client's brand. They are the ones who provide the most meaningful feedback, spread the 'good word', and enhance product reputation. They are prophets; chief messengers who can help build brand recognition effectively. We work with them".

This approach proved to increase the effectiveness of branding, so the company soon attracted bigger business, including ING Romania, Dacia (part of the Renault Group), E.ON Energie, and Phillip Morris. For example, Grapefruit has optimized ING's Internet Banking application, Home'Bank, and they have transformed the brand of Dacia by designing the country's website, Bautozar.ro, for used cars. The design considerably improved Dacia's advantage over their competitors, whose websites were not as user-friendly. In particular, Grapefruit's contribution lies in defining search criteria which better match the needs and aspirations of the buyer in an online environment. A specific problem for competing websites is that in many cases they list cars that have been already sold. Grapefruit's design has resolved this issue; all listings automatically expire after 2 weeks, but there is a simplified process for reregistering cars not sold in that period.

Overall, Grapefruit's key competitive advantage lies in designing solutions that not only enhance an image "as packaging" but provide key improvements to the customer experience through the initial research and analysis phase to an appropriate strategy, solutions that range from visual identities to package designs, communication plans and materials, and digital and mobile presentations and tools.

Over the last decade, Grapefruit's market has evolved through consumer education. Shaping the customer through education has proven to work in the company's favour, in spite of increasing competition. However, the Grapefruit team, with its passion for things well done, has also needed to transform its own mentality on occasions. "I have to constantly change my perspective over this business; as it were, to wear alternately one of three hats: The *design consultant*, who gets his hands "dirty" well above the elbow; the *manager*, who must organize and keep the team and clients happy, keep budgets under control, and keep projects running; and the *entrepreneur*, who must move away from the previous two to find a vision for the future and gather appropriate resources to generate value. It took us about 6 years to evolve from the stage where if one of us was missing then the organization would stagger to a more stable business", Marius Ursache emphasized.

Despite the successes of the past, Grapefruit is not yet pleased with its market leader position. It is looking to continue its adaptation process and expand its business over the border. "The passion for novel successes is all but death".

What specific lessons does Grapefruit teach us? Find what is relevant to the end user, focus on the most passionate and loyal customers when designing product features, and do not view your own business statically—your identity should not be fixed. Hence, the CEO should regularly shift perspectives when thinking about the business: How would you act as a consultant to the business? How would you act as a manager, and how would you act as an entrepreneur? Merge the three perspectives whenever you can.

2.3 ELECTRA

Overview

Address:	Bd. Chimiei nr.8, Iasi, Romania
Tel:	+40232214370
Email:	office@electra.ro
Web:	http://www.electra.ro

Company Information

Industry:	Manufacture of consumer electronic products. Electric and electronic industry, Manufacturing of machines and electronic equipment, printed circuits and electronic assemblies
Year of establishment:	1991
Sales revenues in 2009 (for the Group):	€3.11 million
Sales revenues in 2000:	€0.52 million
Average number employees in 2009:	140
Brain(s) behind the company:	CEO and founder Marian Berdan

2.3.1 Nature of Market Leadership

ELECTRA manufactures high-quality interphones and other related security system solutions for a wide range of buildings, ranging from single villas to large residential compounds. The company currently covers nearly 70 % of the Romanian market. Recently, since the domestic market could not provide enough of growth opportunities, the company has started to grow internationally.

2.3.2 Nature of Competitive Advantage

The core of ELECTRA's competitive advantage is based on three interlinked factors: innovation, quality, and Romania-based manufacturing. Innovations go beyond aesthetic and functional features and include vertical integration to a better product and market control. In particular, vertical integration and strong R&D are implemented through strategic partnerships with German and US companies. Next, the company stopped its reliance on Chinese imports. Third, in cooperation with strategic partners it developed its own radio frequency identification technology and thus opened up the market for apartment alarm systems with a programmable card tag. All these activities are in preparation for the company to find a way into the EU interphones market.

2.3.3 Core Lessons Learned on the Path to Business Success

1. Make consistent efforts to outgrow competitors when the market expands, through provision of better value to end users for both product and associated service. It may prove difficult to do so because you may not see the reason to work hard while the market expands by itself during economic growth.
2. Opportunities cannot grow if you do not prepare for them. Investment in R&D opens doors to strategic alliances and partners that have a mutual interest in your development in both internal and international markets.
3. Take care of people. Loyal, dedicated and skilful workers, who enthusiastically put their minds and souls into the company, help it to sail through the rough waters of an economic crisis and on to new opportunities.

2.3.4 ELECTRA: Hidden Champion

Whether you live in a house or a block of flats, you probably use an interphone when someone comes to visit, providing you with the comfort of hearing and even seeing your guest. And that is what ELECTRA does best: constructing the interphones. In short, it solves security needs for apartment owners. Its products are used by nearly 70 % of Romanians already; and now the company is step by step expanding into Europe. Customers purchase ELECTRA's devices through independent local companies who install and service them. The Romanian market of nearly 3.5 million apartments grew rapidly up until 2006, enabling the company to manufacture and sell up to 25,000 units per month at that time. ELECTRA found enough growth opportunities at home, so there was no immediate need to expand abroad.

Compared to the products of their competition, ELECTRA's interphones were considered good value for money: robust devices with good performance and fast service, all at a reasonable price, which convinced customers to purchase them. But then, aesthetic appearance became a factor also. While their interphones had excellent functional design and reliability, they were not aesthetically appealing. So, in 2009, Marian Berdan added a new requirement—the product should look good. Consequently, the R&D team stopped a product, just before its launch, to add an aesthetic dimension to it. They designed a minimalist and futuristic touch monitor with a flat panel. This new product used US and German technology; however it was only one tenth of the cost of similar products from the West.

The company stimulated growth through expanding the technological and aesthetic variability of its products, with both analogic and digital solutions. While analog systems are solely based on audio, and can be used only in individual houses or apartments, digital technology enables the flexibility and interconnectivity required for both individual units *and* residential compounds consisting of several blocks of flats. Digital interphones, though more expensive, can cover up to 1,000 apartments and hence create lower costs per apartment. However, the sale of higher-priced multi-apartment digital and lower-priced single-apartment analog interphones is not straightforward. "When selling a product, you must know the individual and the address, enabling effective segmentation of appropriate product features. However, in the same apartment block there may be a retired person with a limited budget, someone with small children, and businesspersons. If we want to address these diverse individuals, we need to design a system, either digital or analogical, that serves all the needs well, even if in one product".

In order to enhance quality, ELECTRA invested in better machinery that provided both higher quality and higher production speed, which led to increased capacity and less waste. And in 2008, for technical and strategic reasons, the company split into three entities: ELECTRA, Printed Circuit Boards (PCB ELECTRA), and Electronic Manufacturing Services (EMS ELECTRA), thus enhancing the group's competitive position. PCB and EMS started to generate a larger turnover from external customers—some from the EU—compared to internal orders.

On the technical side, PCB specializes in chemical processes for circuit boards, mostly developed for specific suppliers and customers. EMS specializes in electronic, electromechanical, and metallurgical processes in components and parts-soldering, which is very different from the interphone business. In general, both businesses are pretty much independent of each other. On the strategic side, splitting the business enabled better control of critical operations and greater flexibility. Such flexibility was required for better management of strategic partnerships, two with German companies and one from the USA. One of the German partners bought 15 % of EMS, and, with the other ELECTRA, developed its radio frequency identification technology. Now the group has about 140 employees, half in ELECTRA, and about 35 at both PCB ELECTRA and EMS ELECTRA. The development of radio frequency identification technology also opened up the market for apartment alarm systems and the challenge to connect the video-door phone to the internet, provide security and control access. The ability to offer alarm systems, along with a radical leap in the aesthetics of digital interphones, made ELECTRA much more interesting to residential developers.

ELECTRA is by no means the cheapest interphone company, but rather the one that has the vision to build its business further through R&D strategic partnerships with the West. This vision has elevated ELECTRA's business to a new level by offering an integrated system solution (interphones + alarm system) to the construction industry. However, construction and residential development is perhaps still in a neutral stage, and the company has also been subject to the financial crisis. "However", said Mr. Berdan, "I am doing very well considering the crisis. I believe that in the future it may be even a little bit easier, especially if we find a way into the German market. We are a company that learns and innovates continuously".

To sum up: ELECTRA, with Marian Berdan as its captain, has the ability to take advantage of positive as well as negative trends in the environment. The company outgrew its competitors by offering superior value for money as well as offering more aesthetically appealing products when the market expanded. However, even when the crisis loomed, ELECTRA continued to invest nearly 15 % of its turnover in R&D and set up strategic partnerships to expand its business. Nowadays, the company not only has state-of-the-art generations of interphones but also offers alarm systems, and residential developers can see even more value in doing business with them.

Conclusion

The Romanian economy is dissimilar to the Western (German) economy; hence our HCs do not resemble much those discussed by Simon. Though different, the companies presented here are among the most successful companies in Romania, able to carve their niche markets and establish leadership in them. Till 2008, the growth of the Romanian economy was sufficient to offer these companies enough growth opportunities at home; therefore their international endeavors started to mostly after 2008. From this perspective, their relatively weak international market position is understandable. But in future, we can expect that their portion of the international business pie will be considerably larger. Why?

Firstly, they are set up and run by passionate, strong, committed leaders, who set their goals and business priorities very high. All of them state great goals for the future, and their past leadership behaviour shows that they are willing to go a long way to meet these goals.

Next, though on average they do not invest so much in R&D (except ELECTRA) they are by all standards very inventive, especially in sales and marketing activities. They have sufficient entrepreneurial ability to try out risky sales approaches; for example, the sale of violins through the internet, which has paid off well for Gliga. Bearing in mind that the majority of markets today are saturated with consumer goods and supply considerably exceeds demand, the ability to market, sell and distribute your products and services seems to be the most important factor, and all three companies presented here are very good at that. Indeed, Grapefruit is to some extent in the business of advising companies on the skill of promoting and selling their products, particularly through virtual platforms.

In terms of product characteristics, all of these companies started with superior price/performance ratios partly because they were leveraging with lower labour costs. In consequent stages they added more and more value to their products and services by focusing also on aesthetic dimensions and offering more holistic products and service solutions.

Perhaps the most important lesson that can be grasped from our Romanian Hidden Champions is their capacity to learn. The most amazing thing is how well they are able to scan the market and adjust to it quickly. If they fail, they fail for a lack of learning. And out of all the capabilities they have, this learning ability is the best predictor of their future success.

References

Albi, A. (2005). *EU enlargement and the constitutions of Central and Eastern Europe*. Cambridge: Cambridge University Press.

Dăianu, D. (1999). *Transformarea ca proces real* (2nd ed.). Bucureşti: Institutul Român pentru Libera Întreprindere (IRLI).

David-Barrett, L. (2008). Economic background. In A. Jolly & A. Henson (Eds.), *Romania's business environment: Global market briefings* (pp. 9–14). London: GMB Publishing.

Dumitru, I. (2008). Macroeconomic outlook. In A. Jolly & A. Henson (Eds.), *Romania's business environment: Global market briefings* (pp. 15–22). London: GMB Publishing.

Eurostat. (2013). *Regional GDP per capita in the EU in 2010: Eight capital regions in the ten first places*. Retrieved May 15, 2013, from http://europa.eu/rapid/press-release_STAT-13-46_en.htm

Iacob, G. (2002). Noi şi Europa – O perspectivă istorică. In A. Neculau (Ed.), *Noi şi Europa* (pp. 45–60). Iaşi: Editura Polirom.

Iovitu, M. (1999). *Tranziţia la economia de piaţă: Confruntări de idei contemporarne*. Bucureşti: Editura Economică.

Library of Congress – Federal Research Division. (2006). *Country profile: Romania*. Retrieved May 15, 2013, from http://lcweb2.loc.gov/frd/cs/profiles/Romania.pdf

Maha, L. (2002). România şi integrarea în Uniunea Europeană; perspectivă economică. In A. Neculau (Ed.), *Noi şi Europa* (pp. 65–77). Iaşi: Editura Polirom.

National Bank of Romania. (2012). *Investiţiile străine directe în România în anul 2012 – Raport anual 2013* (p. 19, ISSN 2247-5095, versiune online). Retrieved May 15, 2013, from http://www.bnr.ro/SearchResult.aspx

National Institute of Statistics. (2012). *Comunicat de presă 24 august 2012 privind rezultatele provizorii ale Recensământului Populaţiei şi Locuinţelor - 2011*, Retrieved May 15, 2013, from http://www.insse.ro/cms/files%5Cstatistici%5Ccomunicate%5Calte%5C2012%5CRPL_rezultate%20preliminare.pdf

National Institute of Statistics. (2013). *Statistical Yarbook 2011, "Enterprise Activity – Chapter 15.1 - Active economic and social operators of national economy, by size class"*, Retrieved May 15, 2013, from http://www.insse.ro/cms/files/Anuar%20statistic/15/15%20Activitatea%20intreprinderii_en.pdf

Vasile, L. (2005). *Radix a fost preluata de Ness Technologies. Ziarul de Iasi*. Retrieved March 29, 2011, from http://www.ziaruldeiasi.ro/economic/radix-a-fost-preluata-de-ness-technologies~ni3m6i

Verdery, K. (1991). *National ideology under communism: Identity and cultural politics in Ceauşescu's Romania*. Berkeley, CA: University of California Press.

World Bank. (2013). *Data; countries and economies*. http://data.worldbank.org/country

Hidden Champions of Russia

Irina I. Skorobogatykh, Olga V. Saginova, and Zhanna B. Musatova

Overview

Official name:	Russian Federation
Type of government:	Federation
Population in 2011:	142,960,000
Land area:	16,376,870 km^2

History

1917/1922	The Soviets seize control of the government in the October Revolution in 1917 Nationalization of land and all businesses.
1922	(December) The Union of the Soviet Socialist Republics (USSR) is set up by the Russian Communist Party.
1929/1939	A period of massive industrialization. Joseph Stalin assumes full-control over Russian society.
1941/1945	World War II, in which the Soviet Union loses around 27 million people.
1945/1989	Cold War period, in which the Soviet Union dominates the Warsaw Pact and faces off the United States in a number of conflicts, including the Korean War and the Vietnam War.

I.I. Skorobogatykh (✉)
Marketing Department, Plekhanov Russian University of Economics, Moscow, Russia
e-mail: skorobogatykh.II@rea.ru

O.V. Saginova
Comparative Economics and Entrepreneurship Department, Plekhanov Russian University of Economics, Moscow, Russia

Z.B. Musatova
School of Business, Plekhanov Russian University of Economics, Moscow, Russia

P. McKiernan and D. Purg (eds.), *Hidden Champions in CEE and Turkey*,
DOI 10.1007/978-3-642-40504-4_18,

1989/1991	The breakup of the Soviet Union leads to the restoration of the Baltic republics. The Georgian SSR and the Moldavian SSR start seeking greater autonomy. End of the USSR and formation of the Russian Federation in December 1991.
1993	(Autumn) Yeltsin's dispute with parliament resolved by bringing tanks to the Russian White House. Subsequently, Yeltsin imposes the current Russian constitution with strong presidential powers.
1994/1998	Economic reforms consolidate a semi-criminal oligarchy and result in a deep depression and financial crash in 1998.
2000/2008	Vladimir Putin appointed Prime Minister. Under his governance Russia's economic development surpasses that of most other resource-rich countries.

1 Introduction: Context

The Russian Federation is the largest country by territory. It is located in Europe and Asia and covers eight time zones. The Urals—the oldest mountains in the world—are situated on Russia's territory. They are rich in natural resources—especially copper, iron ore, titanium, and semiprecious stones. The Ural Mountains divide Russia into its European and Asian parts.

Russia also has Lake Baikal, located in the south part of Siberia. It is the largest freshwater reservoir and the deepest lake in the world. Russia has access to different seas and oceans: the Baltic Sea, the Black Sea, the Arctic Ocean, and the Pacific Ocean.

This geographical position has provided Russia a wide variety of natural resources: gas, oil, strategic minerals, timber, fish, sea-food, and more. These resources give Russia's economy an important competitive advantage in the global economic system.

The different climate zones facilitate the development of agriculture. Russia is one of the world's largest exporters of grain, sugar beets, sunflower seeds, meat, and dairy products.

Russia has developed different industry sectors, such as automobiles and truck production, agricultural equipment, advanced aircraft and helicopter production, aerospace, mining and extractive industry, pharmaceutical production, medical and scientific instruments production, construction materials, and more.

Russia has a population around 143 million (World Bank, April 2011), represented by different nationalities and cultures. Most Russians live in over 1,000 major cities, 16 of which have a metropolitan population of more than one million. The most developed economic regions of Russia are located in the centre of the country (Moscow and the Moscow region), Saint-Petersburg, and the Ural Mountains (Yekaterinburg, Perm, Cheliabinsk). The location of oil and gas production is concentrated in Eastern Siberia, Tatarstan, Sakhalin Iceland (Far East), and the Pacific Ocean. Other economically developed regions are located in the

Volga river region (Samara, Saratov), and in the south of Russia (Rostov on Don, Krasnodar).

Before the communist revolution in 1917, Russia was one of the largest economies in the world. It had passed through an industrial revolution, including the development of new plants and factories for the extraction of metal and other natural resources, textile, and heavy industry. The Revolution of 1917, the First World War and the Civil War, had a negative impact on the economic development of the country. After the revolution, the Russian government and the Communist Party encouraged the development of heavy industries, transport, machinery, aviation, and airspace travel, rather than the production of consumer products. The Soviet period played an important role in the development of the education system in the Soviet Union and Russia. The government was primarily interested in providing fundamental education in physics, mathematics, chemistry, biology, and foreign languages and economics, and it created a very good system to educate engineers, mathematicians, and other science specialists.[1]

During Soviet times, the state was the major stakeholder of companies. It set the goals and centrally distributed its resources to reach those goals. With no market competition, all the evaluation criteria, such as effectiveness and efficiency, were narrowly used only as a tool of control for the implementation of centralized plans. Being separated from the rest of the world, companies were limited in their development by the market of the Soviet bloc countries, which had an insignificant and controlled access to other markets. This resulted in lack of innovation except in a few typically non-commercial entities that were strategic for the state-based industries (e.g. military, aerospace, etc.) and if any innovations occurred in other areas, conditions for their successful commercialization were often missing.

Since 1990 Russia has passed from a centrally-planned and isolated economic structure to a market-oriented economy. These changes were quite dramatic for the country and its economic system. Their effect was exacerbated by the collapse of the Soviet Union and the disintegration of economic and business relationships with former socialists republics, which became independent states at the same time.

The peaceful downfall of the USSR and the collapse of the Soviet state-planned economy during the perestroika period[2] ushered in a decade of deindustrialization and sharp economic decline, followed by 2 decades of privatization and consolidation of property. At the very start of the transition period, the market value of assets could not be reasonably determined and it has taken about 20 years for major companies to reach current market value levels. Thus, the strategies of these companies included acquisitions and enlargement of market share but not competiveness. Efficiency, innovation, and long-term development were not

[1] This fact is important for our project because the majority of leaders of Hidden Champions in Russia were educated at leading Russian universities with long histories of educational programmes.

[2] *Perestroika* is the period from 1986 to 1991, initiated by Mikhail Gorbachev, leader of Soviet Union Communist Party. Its main aim was to renovate and rebuild the economic, political, and social mechanism of the Soviet Union.

priorities. Smaller companies were experiencing other challenges. Survival issues were of great importance in the first stage, followed by profit maximization later on, but again there was a lack of a long-term strategic perspective.

The insecure environment of the transition period was characterized by continuously changing legislation, a lack of an appropriate taxation system, the dominating role of state regulators, as well as high criminalization of the economy. To a great extent this led to an overall lack of transparency at all levels, involving very modest financial disclosures and corporate governance, if any, and an unwillingness to engage in PR or share any company information with society. This was done in order to reduce the risks of unfriendly actions by different economic and political subjects.

Since the 1990s, the new market orientation and reform of the Russian economy has led to the privatization of different production plants. This period gave the Russian economy an opportunity to compete globally in the commodity sector: oil and gas, timber, energy, aluminium, titanium and electric energy.[3]

Luckily, the economy bounced back quickly from the 1998 crisis and enjoyed a decade of sustained growth, averaging 7 % annually. The economy prospered due to several factors: a devalued ruble, stabilization of the institutional environment (achieved through a set of economic reforms covering taxation, the banking sector, the labour market, and real estate), tight fiscal policy, and favourable commodity prices. Household consumption and fixed capital investments grew by 10 % annually and thus fuelled the growth of the economy. Last but not least, inflation and exchange rates stabilized.

The 2008–2009 global economic crises opened a new period of economic development in Russia. The Central Bank of the Russian Federation holds 200 billion US dollars to protect the liquidity and financial system of the country. This helped the Russian economy return to growth at the beginning of 2010.

In 2010, The Russian Federation was ranked 123th out of 183 economies according to the World Bank project *Doing Business*. At present Russia is among the largest developing emerging economies in the world with its GDP per capita at PPP reaching 15,900 US dollars in 2010. The average growth rate for the last 10 years has been around 6 %. In 2010, Russia exported products worth a total of 376.7 billion US dollars,[4] including natural resources such as oil and petroleum products, natural gas, timber and timber products, metals, and chemicals. Most Russian foreign trade is done with Europe, the CIS, China, and Japan. To sum up: in the global division of labour Russia has a clear profile—it specializes and competes in the export of natural resources (Exhibit 1).

The potential of Russia's hidden champions (HCs) is determined by three main factors: (1) a long period of planned Soviet economy, resulting in a lack of involvement in the world market, absence of competition, and no efficiency criteria;

[3] Facts and figures about the Russian economy from the official site of Ministry of Economic Development http://www.economy.gov.ru

[4] Data from http://www.vniki.ru/site

Exhibit 1 Core economic indicators for Russia

	1999	2000	2001	2002	2003	2004	2005	2006	2007	2008	2009	2010	2011
GDP per capita (current $US)	1,338.99	1,775.14	2,100.74	2,375.16	2,976.14	4,108.57	5,337.07	6,946.88	9,146.42	11,700.22	8,615.66	10,481.37	13,089.34
GDP per capita growth (annual %)	6.83	10.00	5.35	5.21	7.82	7.73	6.90	8.65	8.84	5.36	−7.79	4.33	4.33
Long-term unemployment (% of total unemployment	47.00	46.20	39.20	38.80	37.20	38.50	38.50	41.70	40.60	35.20			
Foreign direct investment, net inflows (% of GDP)	1.69	1.05	0.90	1.00	1.85	2.61	1.69	3.00	4.24	4.52	2.99	2.91	2.85
GDP (current $US m)	195,905.77	259,708.50	306,602.67	345,110.44	430,347.77	591,016.69	764,000.90	989,930.54	1,299,705.76	1,660,846.39	1,222,648.13	1,487,515.61	1,857,769.68
Exports of goods and services (current $US m)	84,671.00	114,429.43	113,116.22	121,649.12	151,697.51	203,415.48	268,951.74	333,908.28	392,044.03	520,003.70	341,584.67	445,512.96	576,863.49
Exports of goods and services (% of GDP)	43.22	44.06	36.89	35.25	35.25	34.42	35.20	33.73	30.16	31.31	27.94	29.95	31.05
Merchandise exports (current $US m)	75,665.00	105,565.00	101,884.00	107,301.00	135,929.00	183,207.00	243,798.00	303,551.00	354,403.00	471,606.00	303,388.00	400,419.00	521,968.00

(continued)

Exhibit 1 (continued)

	1999	2000	2001	2002	2003	2004	2005	2006	2007	2008	2009	2010	2011
Merchandise exports to high-income economies (% of total merchandise exports)	65.93	68.14	70.20	64.27	63.80	67.49	66.75	68.40	64.28	64.31	54.58	60.32	n/a
Merchandise exports to developing economies in Europe & Central Asia (% of total merchandise exports)	21.15	21.56	18.58	21.34	23.04	19.46	21.61	20.47	24.46	24.81	15.79	14.13	
Ores and metals exports (% of merchandise exports)	11.71	9.29	7.97	7.39	6.92	7.67	6.66	8.20	8.33	5.57	5.73	5.58	5.28
Agricultural raw materials exports (% of merchandise exports)	3.58	3.09	3.12	3.38	3.23	3.01	2.79	2.62	2.85	2.07	2.30	2.07	2.08
Food exports (% of merchandise exports)	1.01	1.25	1.44	2.03	2.00	1.35	1.60	1.60	2.33	1.78	3.24	2.00	2.35

Fuel exports (% of merchandise exports)	41.76	50.58	51.80	52.47	54.49	54.69	61.77	48.72	61.45	65.66	66.69	64.36	59.03
Manufactures exports (% of merchandise exports)	24.72	23.59	23.18	22.82	21.69	22.39	18.75	16.50	16.96	16.74	17.21	14.67	14.29
High-technology exports (% of manufactured exports)	12.34	16.07	14.04	19.16	18.98	12.92	8.44	7.78	6.88	6.47	9.23	8.85	

Source: World Bank (2013)

(2) a specific transition period from the early 1990s to the present, involving a dramatic shift to an oligarchic economy with a significant role of the state, high barriers to setting up a company, and high risks to small-to-medium enterprises (SMEs), such as bureaucracy, corruption, a complicated taxation system, and a lack of transparency; and (3) a national economy based to a very large extent on natural resources, with a relatively small number of companies accounting for a large portion of the total market capitalization. As a consequence, large corporations tightly connected to the state (through ownership stakes as well as other power structures, such as politics) dominate key Russian export sectors. The majority of these enterprises operate in national strategic industries: energy and natural resources; defence, and aviation. Public giants, such as Gazprom, Rosneft, TNK-BP, Nornikel, NLMK, Transneft and Rusal, are largely state-controlled corporations. Despite its significant exports of military equipment and nuclear power plants Russia remains primarily an exporter of commodities.

Another key factor in the Russian economy is the growing domestic consumption resulting in growth in construction, retail, telecommunications, HORECA, and transport.[5] In general, global producers have proved more competitive in consumer markets than Russian firms, but Russian companies have done better in construction, retail, and services.

Russia has 40 million regular Internet users and the Internet is the fastest growing sales channel. The decade-long consumption boom also boosted medium-sized and large importers of electronics, home appliances, cosmetics, and clothes, and attracted most of the world's largest corporations in these sectors. The world's leading car-makers, and Russia's automotive industry in general, also benefited from the growth of the Russian middle class (Skorobogatykh 2011).

To sum up: the overall structure of the Russian economy is defined by large corporations exporting raw materials and metals, as well as importers of consumer goods and global companies in the fast-moving consumer goods sector. Large and middle-sized national companies have grown in the construction and retail sectors. Several infrastructural quasi-monopolies are maintained in railway transport, post, and banking. By contrast, the share of SMEs is by all estimates very low, accounting for 15 % of GDP and employing only 20 % of the total workforce.

For this research project, 29 Russian companies were identified and interviewed. The majority of production, manufacturing, and scientific companies are located in the central metropolitan cities—Moscow and Saint Petersburg. This situation was inherited from the Soviet period, or even before, when most of the plants and factories were located closer to the human resources and higher education institutions. Of the 29 HCs, five were selected as case studies because of the originality of their products, successful market strategies, strong presence on

[5] Domestic consumption steadily grew in the 2000s as the average disposable income doubled during the last decade. However, disposable income grew faster than productivity and pensions and salaries in the civil service were significantly increased, which hit the economy like a boomerang in the following years.

national and international markets, innovative approach to R&D and production, ecology protection, sustainable development, and development of talent. These are summarized in Exhibit 2. Numbers related to revenues and employees were difficult to get because of the prevalence of a business culture of low transparency in Russia. Still, the five cases described in greater detail in the next section allow the reader to get a good understanding of the organizational behaviour of Russian HCs. All of them are strong champions with market leadership, at least at the continental level.

2 Five Case Studies[6]

2.1 Luxoft[7]

Overview

Address:	10–3, 1-Volokolamsky proezd, 123060 Moscow, Russia
Tel:	+74959678030
Fax:	+74959678032
Email:	russia@luxoft.com
Skype:	reception.luxoft

Company Information

Industry:	Production and sale of unique IT and software solutions for banking services and automotive manufacturers
Year of establishment:	1995
Sales revenue in 2010:	€143 million
Sales revenue in 2000:	n/a
Average number employees in 2010:	4,300
Brain(s) behind the company:	Dmitry Loschinin

[6] The authors would like to thank for their contribution and help: Ekaterina Okhmatovskaya—student at Plekhanov Graduate School (International Marketing Management program), and Daria Barillo—4th year student (Bachelor level) at the Marketing Department of Plekhanov Russian University of Economics. They collected secondary data about HCs in Russia, organized interviews with Russian companies identified as HCs, and participated in some interviews. We also would like to thank Pavel Lebedev (MBA, consultant, Academy of National Economy, Moscow, Russia), and Timur Atnashev (Academy of National Economy, coordinator of IMTA alumni in Russia) who helped build Russia's HC database and collect some facts about the development of Russia's economy at the very beginning of the project.

[7] http://www.luxoft.ru/

Exhibit 2 Russian hidden champions

Name	Market leadership definition	Revenues 2010 (in M €)
ABBY	One of the leaders in linguistic and translation software in the world	36
Acron	Leading manufacturer of mineral fertilizers, organic, and inorganic chemistry on CIS markets, China, India	
Bask	Production of innovative sports and casual clothes. Company has leading position in Russia, CIS, and North European markets before economic recession in 2008. Now they are trying to come back to position	11.5
Grishko Ltd	Leading producer of ballet and dance shoes with over 30 % of global market share	
Isotope[a]	Product for reducing of radiological threats	
IstraSoft	Leader in computer technology and programs for education in Russia, in CIS, In Europe	74
JSC Chelyabinsk Zinc Plant	2 % of global market share in Zink production (plus leading position in implementing new system for ecology protection and sustainable development)	
Kaspersky Lab	Among the top four producers of anti-virus software in the world	282
Luxoft	Main supplier of IT solutions and services for banking industry, and automotive industry (production of infotainment software for drivers) with 24.5 % of world market	204
Materia Medica Holding	Sixth place in sales volumes in production of medicine for prevention of flu in CIS countries (Russia, Kazakhstan, Ukraine, Belorussia)	
Moscow ship-building and ship-repair factory	In 2009 produced 5 snow-white yachts of ice class for Moscow-river cruise of premium class (Radisson Yachts cruise). Leading position in Russia and CIS in motor yachts for cruise and for private use	
Nanotechnology MDT	European leadership in production of Zond Microscopes with 16 % of the global market share	
Novikov Group	Market leadership in hospitality business in Russia	80.5
NTO IRE-Polus (Photonics)[b]	Leading producer of fibre lasers in the world (80 % of global market share)	
Parallels, Inc	Leader in virtualization and automation software (cloud software) and calculus in the world	74
Petrovaksfarm	Leading position in Russia and CIS in immune-modulators medicine	
Pharmstandard	One of the leading producers of original medicals in Russian, and CIS markets	
Rosatom	Uranium production	

(continued)

Exhibit 2 (continued)

Name	Market leadership definition	Revenues 2010 (in M €)
Roshimzaschita	Leading manufacturer of protection frames for protection of the persons working in harmful and life-threatening conditions (e.g., technological accidents, terrorist attracts. . .) in Russia, CIS, Europe	
Russian Helikopters	One of leading manufacturers of helicopters in the world with 13.5 % of global market share	18.45
Saranskkabel	Leading producer of optical and other cables in Russian and CIS markets	
Sitronics	IT, telecom solutions, microelectronics	
SKIF-M	Leading producer of modern mills for aerospace industry in the world	
Technonikol	The first in Europe in production of roofing membranes	
Transas	20 % of world market of system for safety navigation in aviation	250
Tyumen Accumulator Plant Ltd	Leading manufacturer of lead-acid starter, rechargeable batteries for diesel locomotives, traction batteries, lead stationary batteries in Russia, CIS, Mongolia, North China	
"VEMZ" Vladimirskiy Electromotive Plant	Leading position in Russia and CIS in manufacturing of induction (asynchronous) motors	
VSMPO-AVISMA Corporation	World # 1 titanium producer, supplier # 1 for Boeing and Airbus Corporations	
Yandex	Leader in search engine and internet portal for Russian speaking countries	206

[a]Isotope was presented with a Russian State Award (on 12-th of June 2010), and an award was given to the company director by President Dmitry Medvedev in Kremlin Palace
[b]CEO and President of this company professor Valentine Gapontsev came into business when he was over 50 y.o. and in 2011 he was ranked among 200 Russian billionaires in Forbes Journal, and in June 2011 he was appointed the Russian State Award, which was given to him by President D. Medvedev in Kremlin
Source: Authors of the chapter

2.1.1 Nature of Market Leadership

Luxoft is a world leader in the production of customized software for banking services, automobile infotainment and other purposes.

2.1.2 Nature of Competitive Advantage

Luxoft provides superior ICT software and services solutions and is continuously improving through state-of-the-art technological projects for the most demanding and technically advanced sectors of the economy, most commonly for multinationals with a significant business presence in Russia. Its key clients are from the automotive sector, for which Luxoft is producing software solutions related to communications, infotainment, in-car access to online services, messaging, social networking, and multimedia. An even greater strategic role for Luxoft's long-term development is driven by the aerospace industry. The company is developing a whole range of services ranging from customer support and supply chain management to service, engineering and manufacturing data distribution.

2.1.3 Core Lessons Learned on the Path to Business Success

1. Gain access to technological frontiers by operating in the most technologically advanced industries, such as the aero- and airspace industry. By spreading these technologies to other industries, create value for society and yourself.
2. Build your global expansion strategy on professional networks and communities of practice. Try to position yourself centrally; such networks can serve as a door to new strategic partners as well as help leverage your brand and reputation globally. Last but not least, this will help you gain access to information and knowledge relevant to your market and business in the future.
3. Invest in talent development and the promotion of well-educated employees. Build close ties with the best universities, which will channel potential to you. This is especially important in the ICT sector, where development of programming knowledge is an ever-lasting process.

2.1.4 Luxoft: Hidden Champion

Luxoft was established in 1995 as an organizational department responsible for the development of novel ICT solutions for Information Business Systems (IBS), the largest Russian IT company. To focus on the growing market for offshore software services in the US and Europe, a development centre was incorporated and named Luxoft in April 2000.

Company founder Dmitry Loschinin, started work as a software engineer in the late 1980s after he graduated from the Moscow State University with a diploma in mathematics and cybernetics. His background in programming and mathematics was later upgraded in an executive programme at the Wharton Business School, University of Pennsylvania. Before Luxoft, Dmitry acquired managerial experience at leading multinationals such as KED GmbH, MCP GmbH and IBM. With his business experience and mathematical knowledge, he soon successfully set up the business model of the innovative ICT Company.

At first, the company focused on ICT software and services solutions for the most demanding and technically advanced sectors of the economy. To satisfy the clients' demands, Luxoft's ICT products offered state-of-the-art software platforms, customized solutions, and professional services. Initially Dmitry based the company in Moscow, from where he supplied global industry leaders. After the relationships with them had developed sufficiently, he embarked on an international expansion, opening developing centres and representative offices in other countries. Luxoft has international offices and development centres in Russia, Vietnam, Poland, Germany, North America, the UK, Ukraine, and Romania.

Dmitry is a world-class expert in outsourcing; he is certified as an outsourcing professional and is a member of the Outsourcing Hall of Fame. He also plays an impactful role in the International Association of Outsourcing Professionals (IAOP). This network helped Dmitry strengthen the global reach of his company. Luxoft is nowadays ranked as number one in Central and Eastern Europe in the area of high technology software production and offshore software services,[8] especially in the domain of IT-services in outsourcing.[9] The company makes good use of co-operation by being a partner to many global and national leaders in the ICT industry.

Luxoft's key clients are Russian companies and multinationals with a significant business presence in Russia. Especially important are clients from the automotive sector. For this industry Luxoft is producing software intensive technologies, including communications, infotainment, in-car access to online services, messaging and social networking, wireless communications and multimedia. Clients from the aerospace industry play an even greater role, especially for new product development. To further transform its own technological capabilities, Luxoft offers aviation companies a whole range of services, including customer support, supply chain management, service, engineering, and manufacturing data distribution. Luxoft delves into the problems and challenges of its clients so as to create the solution of tomorrow.

Customer diversification and close customer relationships have been the basis of company growth since the beginning. Customer partnership is based on a culture of engineering excellence, innovation, and deep domain expertise. Over the years, the company developed close partnerships with firms in a diverse set of industries: banking and finance, telecommunications, automotive, manufacturing, aerospace, energy and utilities, computer software, and media. Luxoft has worked with Deutsche Bank, UBS, the New York Media Group, Vympelcom, Porsche, BMW, Mercedes, Boeing, IBM, Harman, Avaya, Alstom, and Sabre. A very important contribution to its customers is Luxoft's experience with many industries. Basically, Luxoft is a repository of all possible ICT solutions. It can extract the best of them for the client's problem at any moment.

The core of the company's success so far has been its commitment to ICT talents. To secure an inflow of the best talent, Luxoft has built strong ties with leading local colleges and universities in Eastern Europe and South East Asia. By providing a range of scholarships and internships, Luxoft has created opportunities for gifted IT students to launch their careers at that company. At the same time, this gives Luxoft an opportunity to assess their capabilities before employing them. Among the 4,500 employees, more than 80 % have a master- level education, and the majority have years of experience in ICT and computer engineering.

[8] An offshore software service is provision of software development services by an external supplier positioned in a country that is geographically remote from the client enterprise; a type of offshore outsourcing (http://en.wikipedia.org/wiki/Offshore_software).

[9] "IT outsourcing" is a phrase used to describe the practice of seeking resources—or subcontracting—outside of an organizational structure for all or part of an IT (Information Technology) function (http://www.webopedia.com/TERM/I/IT_outsourcing.html).

Three main lessons can be learned from Luxoft's success story: (1) Gain access to technological frontiers by positioning yourself in a technologically advanced sector such as aero- and airspace industries; then by spreading these technologies to other industries create value for society and yourself. (2) Build your global expansion strategy on professional networks and communities, and position your core leaders centrally in them. Such networks can serve as doors to novel strategic partners and as leverage for brand and reputation development. Through professional networks you can gain access to information and knowledge relevant to your market and business intuition of what is coming next. (3) Invest in talent development and the promotion of well-trained employees to different positions. In the ICT sector, where programming knowledge never stops developing, such investment is crucial.

2.2 Grishko[10]

Overview

Address: Proezd Zavoda Serp i Molot, Moscow, Russia

Company Information

Industry:	Production of ballet shoes, dance shoes, and dance costumes
Year of establishment:	1989
Sales revenue in 2010:	n.a.
Sales revenue in 2000:	n.a.
Average number employees in 2010:	500
Brain(s) behind the company:	Nikolai Grishko

2.2.1 Nature of Market Leadership

Grishko is the world's third largest producer of pointe shoes for ballet and a leader in the production of ballet and dance shoes and costumes for training and performance.

2.2.2 Nature of Competitive Advantage

Grishko possesses secrets in the complex fine art of pointe making, and has a reasonable price-performance ratio relative to its closest competitors. The company produces pointe shoes exclusively for the most prominent ballet dancers in the

[10] http://www.grishko.com/pointe.cfm

world, catering to the specific needs of individuals, as well as different national ballet schools. The demand for Grishko shoes exceeds supply. This is so because Grishko's design is known to minimize foot deformation. The company has also managed to design an efficient business model.

2.2.3 Core Lessons Learned on the Path to Business Success

1. Mind the price differences between domestic and foreign products. Focus on products of superior quality and offer them at much lower prices. If you can manage to do that, a lucrative business may eventually evolve.
2. Superior products usually involve some secrets. Find a way into the trade and its craftwork knowledge. For example, Mr. Grishko cooperated with a colleague who did his PhD on pointes craftwork secrets.
3. Having a good product is necessary but not sufficient for long-term business success. One also needs a good business model. Hence, before going into large-scale business, do some in-depth research on the industry value chain, potential suppliers, distribution system opportunities, and production facilities.
4. Convince the most demanding clients that you have a good product. For example, Russian theatres had their own workshops producing ballet shoes and costumes, so Grishko had to struggle to convince dancers to try out his pointes. Once they were convinced, the business flourished.

2.2.4 Grishko: Hidden Champion

Russia has always been a country of ballet. In the nineteenth century, special theatre workshops, organized as guilds, designed custom-made shoes, so-called "pointes", for famous Russian ballerinas. The secret of pointe making was passed on by word of mouth. It was an industrial secret transmitted from generation to generation and each master added something new to the stock of knowledge. This is why pointes made by Russian masters have been famous globally, as famous as the Russian ballet. However, these theatre workshops were closed in 1917. Nevertheless, the secrets of this complex fine art were preserved, and after many years they were re-established by the Grishko company masters. Now Grishko's pointes are as popular all over the world as were those produced by the guilds.

The company started production in 1989. The idea to manufacture pointe shoes came when Nikolai Grishko saw that foreign dancers visiting Moscow were buying very cheap Russian shoes to take home, where they cost at least 50 US dollars. The significant price difference made Nikolai wonder how to grasp that business opportunity. After graduating from the Moscow Institute of Foreign Affairs in 1975, Nikolai started his professional career as a diplomat, and then became an associate professor at the Plekhanov Institute of National Economy.[11] He incidentally met a PhD student working on a dissertation on the design of ballet shoes. This is still the only dissertation in the world on that topic. Together they worked out the idea of ballet shoe production, which they successfully put into practice in 1989.

[11] The formal name of the Plekhanov Russian University of Economics.

They set up a cooperative, the only private business model allowed in the Soviet Union during the perestroika. Over the next 2 years, they did no business, only in-depth research on the industry value chain. They studied supplier options, distribution system opportunities and production facilities. The first revenues were created in 1991. The first products were not sold in Russia but in the USA, where a committed distributor was found. In the early 1990s the company produced 500 pairs of shoes per month. Only after its success abroad, in the late 1990s, did the company win over Russian ballet dancers as well, first from the Mariinsky Theatre in St Petersburg, then (by offering a 30 % discount) from the Bolshoi Theatre in Moscow. These theatres had their own workshops producing ballet shoes and costumes; therefore Grishko had to convince the dancers that his products were much better. Since then the demand for high-quality pointes from Russia has been growing. At present, Grishko is making 1,400 pairs per day or more than 350,000 pairs per year. Some shoes are produced exclusively for the most prominent ballet dancers in the world, catering for specific needs of individuals as well as different national ballet schools.

The production of pointe shoes is a very complex process, resembling craftwork. Shoemaking involves 40 different details and about 50 operations, most of which are done by hand. In general, it takes 3 months of theory study and a year of shop-floor experience for someone to start mastering pointe shoe production. The company realized that disabled people could meet the demands of the work. It employs around 76 people with hearing disabilities and participates in two Moscow programs to develop and modernize jobs for disabled people. Employees feel that they are a valuable part of the company and society. In this way the company business model is adding value to a wide range of stakeholders.

The leadership position of Grishko has created several challenges; the most arduous one is increasing production capacity to meet increasing demand. Nowadays, the company faces a gap of 3 months before its supply meets the demand for its shoes. Hence, training and personnel development is of utmost importance. Despite the waiting line, there is no shortage of clients because of the supreme quality of Grishko's pointes. This is so because Grishko's superior design minimizes feet deformation, which is a major problem for professional ballerinas.

The Grishko brand is very popular in more than 70 countries around the world. Its products are sold in six specialized and nine mono-brand stores. Its global market share is estimated at 30 % and is growing. All of the competitors are companies with centuries of tradition. Among Grishko's most prominent competitors are world-known brands such as Bloch, an Australian company set up by Jacob Bloch who moved from Europe to Australia in 1931, during the Great Depression. Another brand worth mentioning is Capezio. It is produced by a company founded by Salvatore Capezio who opened his first store in New York in 1887. As for Gaynor Minden's pointe shoes, they are considered controversial by many ballet dancers, as much of their construction involves synthetic materials—a major change in ballet. In general, professional ballet dancers never use pointes produced with artificial materials, as this damages their feet.

Grishko's pricing is different in Russia and abroad. Outside Russia, pointe shoes usually cost more than 40 US dollars, while in Russia the company sells them for no more than 25 dollars. Grishko sees this as a social project. By reducing prices Grishko makes ballet dancing more accessible to young Russian talents. Besides, Grishko provides 30 scholarships to the most talented students of the Russian ballet schools. Young Russian ballet dancers start using Grishko shoes when they are still in ballet schools. Having grown in Grishko pointes, they stay loyal to the brand throughout their professional careers.

After winning the Russian market for pointe shoes, the company started to diversify and produce a range of shoes for diverse dances: classical, jazz, sport, step, folk, flamenco, and rehearsal. Numerous dance and sport groups, studios, theatres, folk-dance ensembles, as well as dance and gymnastics schools, use Grishko shoes and dancewear. These dance accessories are manufactured from top quality ecologically pure materials. Some products are unique and have a licence. Ecological and natural materials are very important for high-quality dance shoes.

Grishko believes that the core of his company's success is the profound belief and commitment to be the best in both price and quality. The company sees itself as an ambassador of Russia: "We put 'Made in Russia' on our pointe shoes. This creates a different image for our country—without weapons—and we are proud of this."

Grishko has received several state and private awards for his business and social activities. In 2008, he received a special award, "The leader of Russian Economy". This prestigious award is largely a recognition of the company's ability to come up with a unique business model to create growth and reduce the 3-month gap between receiving and meeting orders. Grishko achieved this despite being in a mature industry with established competitors in the business for more than a century. Behind the successful business model is a trade secret for producing high-quality, hand-made products. This secret is internalized and continuously updated by special training of workers. Grishko successfully merges traditional and social marketing.

2.3 Russian Helicopters[12]

Overview

Tel: +7495981–6373
Fax: +7495981–6395
Email: info@rus-helicopters.com

[12] http://rus-helicopters.ru/

Company Information

Industry:	Production and sale of helicopters
Year of establishment:	2003
Sales revenue in 2010:	n/a
Sales revenue in 2000:	n/a
Average number employees in 2010:	500
Brain(s) behind the company:	The management team

2.3.1 Nature of Market Leadership

Russian Helicopters is the world's and Europe's fourth largest producer of high-weight efficient helicopters. The company is a market leader in the emerging economies (CIS, Asia, Africa, and Latin America). In the CIS region, the company holds 85 % of the market.

2.3.2 Nature of Competitive Advantage

Russian Helicopters is one of the leading players in the global helicopter industry. It was founded in 2007 as a joint stock holding company. The holding coordinates the activities of the five assembly plants, two design bureaus, two component production plants, and one overhaul plant, all of which were previously autonomous. Through this centralized coordination from the holding's headquarters, the company strives for global leadership by centralizing R&D activities, elimination of duplication of activities and other production inefficiencies, and highly unified global marketing sales efforts. Initially, most sales were in emerging economies: CIS, Asia, Africa, and Latin America.

2.3.3 Core Lessons Learned on the Path to Business Success

1. If you have a high-quality, technologically complex product manufactured by separate production plants, their merger under a common governance scheme may reduce inefficiencies, improve R&D, and increase market power.
2. Unify your sales and marketing efforts and focus on emerging economies.
3. It is not enough to have a superior product. Make sure that the whole business model design, and especially the design of after-sales activities, supports your long-term business success.

2.3.4 Rusian Helicopters: Hidden Champion

Russian Helicopters is one of the leading companies in the global helicopter industry. It is the sole Russian designer and manufacturer of helicopters, and one of the few companies worldwide with the capability to design, manufacture, service and test modern civilian and military helicopters. This company, headquartered in Moscow, was founded in 2007 as a joint stock company organized as a holding; however, some of the enterprises of the holding have existed for more than 60 years. The holding coordinates the activities of five assembly plants located in different regions of the Russian Federation, two design bureaus, two component production plants, one overhaul plant, and one helicopter service company providing aftermarket services in Russia and abroad.

The company tries to satisfy the needs of multiple stakeholders, the most prominent one being Russia itself. The main reason for setting up the holding was the need to preserve the production of helicopters in the homeland, as well as to strengthen Russia's presence in the helicopter industry globally.

The holding is composed of a set of companies with a long experience in helicopter design. It can successfully challenge the global competition with its consolidated R&D activities under one roof, and elimination of duplication and other production inefficiencies, as well as its focused and highly-unified global marketing sales efforts.

By focusing sales and after-sales activities on emerging economies (CIS, Asia, Africa and Latin America), the company has established a leading position in some segments of the helicopter industry globally. In particular, the company is number one in the world in the production of medium and ultra-heavy machines[13] for civil purposes, as well as in the manufacturing of attack helicopters. Overall, Russian Helicopters is the third largest helicopter producer in the world, holding around 13 % of the global market. The company sells predominantly in Russia and the CIS region, where it is a market leader with an 85 % market share. According to company statistics, in 2011 there were over 8,500 Russian helicopters registered in more than 100 countries around the world. The company's global market share in 2011 was expected to increase to 15 %. The company is now considering new regions: India, China, Latin America, the Middle East, and Africa.

Russian Helicopters' main competitors include Bell Helicopter, Sikorsky, Eurocopter, Boeing, and Agusta Westland. At the state level, where the deals are normally made, the competition is largely between monopolies.

The data in Exhibit 3 show that Russian Helicopters almost tripled its revenues over a 3-year period, with the number of units sold increasing only slightly. The extra value was created by a more holistic approach to clients, offering them a full range of services and consultancy.

At present, the company employs 35,000 workers, engineers and management staff. According to CEO Dmitry Petrov, and Director of Strategic Planning Vladimir Makareikin, one of the main strategic challenges is talent management. They aim to improve the capabilities of the existing workforce as well as to assure continuous inflow of top talents into the company. Hence they have established close ties with Russian schools and universities of technology, engineering, economics and management.

From a technological perspective, the company works heavily on advanced technologies for helicopters for different purposes,[14] including transportation of freight and people, and work in extreme geographical regions and conditions, for instance for oil and gas extraction. Therefore, Russian Helicopters has to be

[13] Maximum Take Off Weight (MTOW) of more than 20 tonnes.

[14] Effective helicopters means good value for money.

Exhibit 3 Major economic figures for Russian helicopters

Year	Production (units)	Revenues
2007	102	
2008	169	362.2 mln RUR ($ 90 M)
2009	183	757.7 mln RUR ($ 195 M)
2010	214	813 mln RUR ($270 M)

Source: Russian Helicopters' Annual reports

exceptionally strong in R&D. Its Mil and Kamov design bureaus are ranked amongst the largest and most respected helicopter design facilities in the world. The history of the two bureaus is closely intertwined with the lives of the two men after whom they were named, Nikolai Ilich Kamov and Mikhail Leontyevich Mil, generally considered the fathers of the Russian helicopter industry. Nikolai Kamov, credited with the coining of the Russian word for helicopter, "vertolyot", was heavily involved in the theoretical research and production of the autogyro, a predecessor of the helicopter, as early as the 1920s.

Apart from the technological improvement of its core product, the company also innovates in pre-sales and after-sales activities. In fact, the forthcoming major revenue streams are expected to be generated from aftermarket services and maintenance of products through a network of globally distributed third-party service centres. The support business of the Helicopter Service Company and the Novosibirsk Aircraft Repairing Plant plays a crucial role in creating that revenue stream. It supplies component parts and materials as well as educational services to an already established third party network of 37 Russian and 46 international service centres. In addition, it is now setting up pivot service centres in key growth markets: India, China, and Latin America.

To sum up, the precondition for the global market leadership of Russian Helicopters was its state-of-the-art products: helicopters, ranging from very light to heavy, with options for fire-fighting equipment. The product diversity was sufficient to meet the needs of each specific customer. However, these products needed to be launched on the global market through a well-designed business model based on close partnerships with national and international leaders in the helicopter industry, and close ties with research and education institutions in Russia.

2.4 YANDEX[15]

Overview

Address: 16, Lev Tolstoy St., Moscow 119021, Russia
Tel: +7495739-70-00
Fax: +7495739-70-70
Email: pr@yandex-team.ru

[15] http://www.yandex.ru

Company Information

Industry:	Computer programming, consultancy, and related activities
Year of establishment:	1997
Sales revenue in 2010:	n.a.
Sales revenue in 2000:	n.a.
Average number employees in 2010:	800
Brain(s) behind the company:	Chief Technology Officer Ilya Segalovich; CEO Arkady Volozh

2.4.1 Nature of Market Leadership

Yandex is the leading Internetcompany in Russia with a mission to provide an answer to any question Internet users may have. Yandex is recognized as the most popular search engine in Russian-speaking countries.

2.4.2 Nature of Competitive Advantage

Yandex is an abbreviation that expands into "Yet Another Index". The company holds a global leadership position because of its superior capability in three areas of innovation: product, process, and business model. Yandex was launched in 1997 as a search engine that took into account Russian language morphology. In 1998 the company made a second innovation leap by becoming a world leader in contextual advertising, which soon turned into its main revenue stream.

In 2001 Yandex launched Yandex.Direct: a tool that anyone could use directly, without any intermediary, to place his advertisement on a Yandex website. During the first year, more than 2,500 advertisers used this opportunity to place ads. In 2009, the company's innovative approach was manifested in a new method of machine-learning, MatrixNet, which represented a significant leap in comparison to foreign search engines like Google and Yahoo. In May 2011, Yandex raised 1.3 billion US dollars in an initial public offering on NASDAQ, which was the biggest such offering for a dotcom since Google Inc. went public in 2004. The company's capitalization has reached 8 billion US dollars.

2.4.3 Core Lessons Learned on the Path to Business Success

1. If technological innovation is the core of your business leadership, set up your own school through which you can successfully create and maintain a scientific environment favourable to the development of new technologies, and the recruitment of new talent.
2. If you are in a business where some competitors are globally stronger because of network effects (The more connected you are, the more attractive you are to newcomers), focus on language and region specifics, and design your products to better cover them.
3. Always try to meet the diverse interests of multiple stakeholders.

2.4.4 Yandex: Hidden Champion

Yandex is the leading Internet company in Russia with a mission to provide an answer to any question that Internet users may have. This explains why Yandex is recognized as the most popular search engine in Russian speaking countries. Yandex owns many popular websites, including narod.ru that creates small and simple websites free of charge.

The word "Yandex" was invented by the company's two principal founders, Chief Technology Officer Ilya Segalovich (currently the owner of 4.15 % of the company), and CEO Arkady Volozh (currently the owner of 19.77 % of the company). At the time, Ilya was experimenting with different derivatives of words that described the essence of the technology. As a result, the team came up with "Yandex".

Arkady Volozh and Ilya Segalovich were schoolmates and friends; Volozh graduated from the Gubkin Russian State University of Oil and Gas, and Segalovich from the Russian State University of Geological Prospecting in 1986. They shared a passion for programming and computer sciences, which resulted in the establishment of Yandex.

The official launch date of the Yandex.ru search engine was September 23, 1997. The Yandex search engine of 1997 took into account Russian language morphology and distance between words, and computed the relevance of a document using a complex algorithm. Thanks to the rising popularity of the Internet among Russians, and the strategic acquisition of competitive search engines like Aport and Rambler, Yandex took over the whole Russian market in 3 years. In 2000, at the time of the Internet boom, the capitalization of Yandex was estimated as 15 million US dollars.

In 1998, Yandex was among the first global companies to start contextual advertising, which provided an additional answer to users' queries. This type of advertising displays directly to its target audience, presenting the company with an additional revenue stream. This set the basis of Yandex's business model. In 2001, Yandex launched Yandex.Direct which enabled anybody to place ads on Yandex's websites without an intermediary. During the first year of the system's operation, more than 2,500 advertisers placed their ads on Yandex. This business approach proved to be very successful, particularly due to changes in the Internet advertising market in Russia, which after 2006 became bigger than traditional media advertising. In 2010 Russia's contextual advertising market was worth about 300 million euros and Yandex.Direct was able to grab more than 60 % of the Internet advertising pie. The estimated number of advertisers was around 120,000.

After 2005, the company expanded outside of Russia by opening representative offices in Ukraine, Kazakhstan, and Belarus. In 2006, Yandex began opening development offices outside Moscow—in St. Petersburg, and in Simferopol Ukraine. In 2009 the company opened an office also in the Silicon Valley in the USA.

Yandex's innovative approach led to a new method of machine learning, MatrixNet, launched in 2009. This breakthrough technology, which takes into account thousands of search factors and their combinations, has enabled Yandex to make more precise searches as well as refine the quality of search results considerably. Thanks to MatrixNet, Yandex has made a significant leap compared to Google and Yahoo.

Software development and data analysis are the company's core capabilities, and talent development is its core policy. Hence, in 2008 Yandex opened the School of Data Analysis—a 2-year Master's Programme—to educate home-grown specialists in data analysis and information retrieval free of charge. Through this institution Yandex aims to create and maintain a scientific environment that is favourable for developing new technologies, recruiting new talent, and ensuring that Yandex remains at the forefront of innovation. In line with this strategy, in 2010 Yandex launched its investment programmes, Yandex.Start and Yandex.Factory, aimed at supporting young talented teams, stimulating the emergence of start-ups, and developing the industry as a whole.

Yandex is the largest Russian Internet company developing world-class proprietary technologies. In 2011, Yandex's average search share per quarter in Russia was 64.6 %, while Google held only 22.5 %. Yandex's share was 30 % in Ukraine, 39 % in Belarus and 25 % in Kazakhstan. According to Alexa.com, Yandex.ru is in 22nd position among the "Top 500" global websites.

These figures confirm that Yandex is considered one of the most successful dotcom in the world. Its success is built on innovative, continuous technological development of a range of information services on the Internet, and a distinctive business model that satisfies diverse interests of multiple stakeholders. It is well adjusted to the context of the CIS market. Hence, through its orientation to small and medium businesses (contextual advertising), individual Internet users (information services), and corporate business (media advertising), the company has managed to achieve sustainable development.

2.5 JCG Nanotechnology NT-MDT[16]

Company Information

Industry:	Production and sale of nanotechnology instrumentation
Year of establishment:	1990
Sales revenue in 2010:	n/a
Sales revenue in 2000:	n/a
Average number employees in 2010:	300
Brain(s) behind the company:	Viktor Bykov

[16] http://www.ntmdt.com/

2.5.1 Nature of Market Leadership

Nanotechnology MTD is the world's third largest producer of zoned microscopes. Its share of the global market in 2010 was 16 %, while its closest competitor had only 8 %. This type of microscope is increasingly important in research and development in a range of industries, from semiconductors to life sciences.

2.5.2 Nature of Competitive Advantage

Nanotechnology MTD was started as a research project in 1990 by a group of scientists led by Viktor Bykov, working at the Moscow Institute of Physics and Technology. The project resulted in the first scanning tunnel microscope (STM). Unlike most researchers at that time, Viktor Bykov decided to commercialize a device called NT-MDT, an electronic scanning probe microscope. His passionate efforts and firm belief in the product soon brought in the first clients, mainly research institutes. At present, the company serves many clients from diverse high-end technological sectors, including aerospace, biomedical and life sciences, electronics, nanotechnology, semiconductors, electronics, telecommunications, and research centres and universities. MTD's competitive advantage is its customized production of complex nano-scanning solutions that operate under a variety of conditions—in a vacuum, at extra-high or super-low temperatures, in liquids, and so forth.

2.5.3 Core Lessons Learned on the Path to Business Success

1. If you are a scientist with a useful invention in applied sciences, this discovery should not be an end in itself. Try to commercialize the idea with all the passion and vigour that you possess. A combination of passion and reason will create the necessary energy to start the business ball rolling.
2. When trying to commercialize a new discovery, focus first on research institutes with fellow scientists who speak the same language as yourself, and gain a deep understanding of the value of your discovery.
3. To boost your growth, penetrate universities and encourage students to use your products in their research projects. Design your product as an educational system. These students may one day become decision-makers at research centres, and they are loyal clients already!

2.5.4 NT-MDT: Hidden Champion

JCG Nanotechnology NT-MDT is representative of the research intensive, high-tech, Russian HCs. It started as a research project in 1990 by a group of scientists lead by Viktor Bykov, a graduate of Moscow Institute of Physics and Technology, a leading Russian technical university. Their research project succeeded in designing the first scanning tunnel microscope (STM). The basic principles of STM devices were first developed in 1981 by Gerd Binning and Heinrich Rohrer, who then received the Nobel Prize in Physics[17] in 1986 for their discoveries in the area of

[17] They shared the Nobel Prize with Ernst Ruska who first designed an electron microscope.

electronic microscopes. Since then two types of microscopes—scanning tunnel microscope (STM) and scanning probe microscopes (SPM)—have been developed and used for specific research and engineering purposes.

It was because of Bykov's passion for research, his entrepreneurial talent and his strategic foresight, that the research team sustained its commitment to basic science, and did not abandon it as many other researchers in Russia had done after government financing ceased in the early 1990s, causing severe cuts in researchers' salaries. In subsequent joint efforts, Bykov's research team did what many talented researchers failed to do—commercialize their research results. In particular, they developed and commercialized a device called NT-MDT, an electronic scanning probe form of microscopy. This type of microscopy has become increasingly important in materials research and development, across a range of industries from semiconductors to life sciences. It probably would not be right to say that Bykov, from the very start, visualized his business as it is today. But market reforms launched in Russia in the early 1990s, combined with his entrepreneurial and leadership skills, made it possible to produce and successfully install more than 2,000 devices at major scientific research and production centres in Europe, Asia, and North America.

Today, NT-MDT is a leader in the Russian STM market, and has a great reputation around the world. Company growth compared to that of its competitors shows its impact on market trends in the STM segment. There are four or five other Russian companies in this market segment, but all of them are much smaller in size, sales volume, and product portfolio.

The microscopes market, in a wider sense, is dominated by global companies offering a wide range of products across a variety of platforms, including FEI Company, Hitachi High-Technologies, JEOL, Carl Zeiss, and Oxford Instruments Plasma Technology Ltd. STM represents an important market segment, mainly populated by medium-sized and small private companies.

The world market of SPMs is mainly concentrated in the developed countries, which invest a lot in basic science and future technologies. The main consumers of SPM products are major nano-technological research centres. Each research project is best performed with customized nano-technological instrumentation. Customization is carried out for clients according to specific needs, functionality, and ergonomic design. These innovative technologies meet the many needs of students, cutting edge researchers, and industrial users at R&D centres. Key end-users of the company's products are firms in the field of aerospace, biomedical and life sciences, electronics, nanotechnology and nano-materials production, telecommunications, and semiconductors and electronics, as well as research centers and universities. They mainly seek technologically superior products:, superior performance characteristics, superior resolution, superior complexity, and shrinking geometries in materials research.

Accordingly, the most attractive markets for NT-MTD are located in the USA, Europe, and the Asia-Pacific region. NT-MDT's market share in the EU is 35 % and the sales volume there has been increasing steadily from year to year, even through the financial recession. The Asia-Pacific region (Japan, South Korea and India) is the fastest-growing region, and NT-MDT has shown significant progress in sales revenues there. Recently, the company has established distributors in Beijing and Shanghai and both have shown good results. But the biggest market breakthrough that the company has achieved is in the USA. The sales figures there tripled from 2009 to 2010. NT-MDT intends to extend its presence in the market and attain 30 % of market share.

NT-MTD believes that a good method for boosting sales is to penetrate university classrooms. If you provide students with an opportunity to use company products in their research projects, they may be loyal clients when they become research centre decision-makers. That is why a popular product line of NT-MDT is its educational devices, NANOEDUCATOR. Devices are designed for a wide range of uses and are appropriate for first-time microscope users. Recently, *R&D Magazine* has ranked the NANOEDUCATOR training laboratory among the −100 most technologically significant products introduced into the marketplace. Mr. Bykov demonstrated this product to Russian President D. Medvedev during a hi-tech exhibition in 2008. The company is always working to improve this product category and has adjusted its use for both Windows XP and Mac OS operating systems. Data sharing via iPhone TM and iPad TM is also possible.

To summarize: the success story of NT-MTD is to a large extent based on Mr. Bykov's use of initiative and creativity, and his recognition of young talent as the main innovator. Much work is done in teams. Investment into R&D is a core part of the company business model. Growth is realized through global expansion and a high level of entrepreneurial skills. Last but not least, Mr. Bykov is also an inspirational lecturer and chair at Moscow Institute of Physics and Technology, viewing his teaching as a way to inspire young talent in science, technology and business. He is constantly searching for the best talent: "Graduates with degrees in physics or other technical sciences can always learn marketing and strategy if they understand the principles of our products; without this understanding they are useless to our business".

Conclusion

The founders and owners of most Russian HCs, not only the five companies presented here, are strong leaders, all endowed with strong personalities, daring to challenge conventional wisdom. They have good market-trend intuition and state-of-the-art scientific knowledge in mathematics, physics, or other sciences. Many also hold MBA degrees. They carry years of experience and deep knowledge of their specific business segment, and have the ability to inspire young talent to join their enterprises, as well as the ability to persuade other external stakeholders such as government and big business to take advantage of the benefits that they offer to them.

However, the great majority of Russian HCs succeeded in a time of favourable market trends. Raising market demand was prevalent in the IT and software sector, research instruments, and helicopters. An attractive price/quality ratio was another contributing factor. Last but not least, many of the Russian HCs created value for a wide range of stakeholders, i.e., higher education institutions, governments, and research institutes, among others.

Most of the companies have a strong presence in the national economy, and now they are growing abroad; usually first conquering the CIS region, and then gradually getting into other emerging economies. The main markets for Russian HCs are China, Latin America, India, Africa, and the CIS. They monitor competition closely and know all the major competitors personally.

Most companies (16 out of 29 investigated) were established at the beginning of perestroika; some even before the 1930s. These senior HCs are mainly involved in heavy industry and metallurgy; some of them are closely tied to nuclear research and development. Companies from the IT sector were mainly founded at the beginning of 1990, when ICT industry developments became less ambiguous and uncertain.

The interviewed HCs are real innovators; in fact they have come up with technological solutions that have shaped their industry technological frontiers. In general, innovations can be grouped into four main types: technological, processing, organizational, and marketing. Most of these companies are technological innovators—they carry out their intensive research activities and commercialize their innovations. Some of them are also processing innovators, improving their production processes and benefiting from them. Several of them are marketing innovators—they are introducing new forms and instruments of marketing and promotions. A few of them are also organizational innovators; that is, innovating their whole business model and revenue streams.

However, all of them can be considered guiding stars leading the way along a path that other Russian companies should follow.

References

Skorobogatykh, I. (2011). *Relationship marketing for networking of actors in the luxury industry* (Summary of Doctoral Thesis, Plekhanov Russian University of Economics. Moscow, Russia).

World Bank. (2013). *Data; countries and economies.* http://data.worldbank.org/country

Hidden Champions of Serbia

Vesna Rašković Depalov, Marija Todorović, and Sanja Marinković

Overview

Official name:	Republic of Serbia
Type of government:	Republic
Population in 2011:	7,258,745
Land area:	88,460 km^2

History

1918/1929	Unification of the former Austro-Hungarian Southern Slavs with Serbia in the Kingdom of Serbs, Croats and Slovenes.
1929	The kingdom becomes known as Yugoslavia.
1941/1945	Germany attacks Yugoslavia; Belgrade and other cities are bombed. The occupation has divided the country. Tito's government abolishes the monarchy and in 1946 declares a People's Republic of Yugoslavia with six states.
1948	Tito separates Yugoslavia from the Soviet Bloc and seeks economic assistance from the United States and Western Europe.
1989	Slobodan Milosević becomes president of Serbia.
1991/1992	Slovenia, Croatia, and then Macedonia declare independence.
1992	Bosnia and Herzegovina declares independence and a civil war starts. Formation of a new Federal Republic of Yugoslavia consisting of Serbia (with Kosovo and Vojvodina) and Montenegro.

V.R. Depalov (✉)
Faculty of Engineering, University of Novi Sad, Novi Sad, Serbia
e-mail: raskovicv@uns.ac.rs

M. Todorović • S. Marinković
Faculty of Organizational Sciences, University of Belgrade, Belgrade, Serbia

P. McKiernan and D. Purg (eds.), *Hidden Champions in CEE and Turkey*, 307
DOI 10.1007/978-3-642-40504-4_19, © Springer-Verlag Berlin Heidelberg 2013

1995	Serbia accepts about 620,000 refugees (Serbs expelled from Croatia and other states).
1995	Dayton Peace Agreement.
1999	NATO bombing of Yugoslavia.
2000	The opposition beats Milosević in the elections.
2003	New official name of the country: State Union of Serbia and Montenegro. Prime Minister Zoran Djindjić is assassinated.
2006	Montenegro declares independence and Serbia is constituted as an independent state.
2008	The Stabilization and Association Agreement (SAA) is signed.
2009	Serbia applies for EU membership; EU unfreezes the trade agreement with Serbia and drops the visa requirement for Serbian citizens.
2010/2011	The European Parliament and many other countries ratify Serbia's SAA.

1 Introduction: Context

Serbia is located at the crossroads of Central and Southeastern Europe. This is considered a good position to develop as a transportation hub. Roads in Serbia provide the shortest link between Western and Central Europe on the one side, and the Middle East, Asia, and Africa, on the other. The country has a population of around 7.3 million. The Republic of Serbia has good potential for economic development, as the country is fortunate to have many natural resources and a lot of arable agricultural land. Belgrade, with a population of 1.6 million, is the capital city and Serbia's administrative, economic, and cultural centre.

In the former Yugoslavia, Serbia had the most developed automobile industry among all the countries of Central and Eastern Europe (CEE). Its annual production exceeded 100,000 vehicles. These were exported to the United States (as the "Yugo" brand) and many other countries around the world. Since the turbulent 1990s, Serbia's economy has been going through a transition towards a well-functioning market economy. A program of democratic and economic reforms has provided the basis for economic growth. In the period from 2001 to 2008, significant economic growth was achieved, (average annual economic growth was 5.24 %), together with reduced inflation, increased foreign exchange reserves, and exchange rate stability (Bosnjak 2011; World Bank 2013). GDP per capita shrunk by 3.1 % in 2009. Some data on economic growth are shown in Exhibit 1 below.

The main generators of growth were the service industries: trade, transport, storage and communications, financial intermediation, postal services, and telecommunications. Agriculture and manufacturing also contributed to economic growth to a certain extent. Rising living standards followed the growth of economic activity; GDP per capita in 2009 was almost four times higher than in 2001 (Serbian Chamber of Commerce 2011). The business community of entrepreneurs and SMEs in Serbia makes up 99 % of all enterprises. This sector employs two thirds of the total number of workers, and creates around 60 % of GDP. A comparative analysis of the

Exhibit 1 Core economic indicators for Serbia

	1999	2000	2001	2002	2003	2004	2005	2006	2007	2008	2009	2010	2011
GDP per capita (current $US)	2,338.43	809.28	1,518.03	2,013.67	2,613.53	3,168.88	3,391.37	3,942.63	5,276.93	6,497.84	5,484.05	5,269.64	6,310.37
GDP per capita growth (annual %)	−10.88	5.68	5.48	4.17	2.94	9.56	5.72	4.01	5.83	4.24	−3.11	1.36	2.43
Long-term unemployment (% of total unemployment)	n/a	n/a	n/a	n/a	n/a	n/a	n/a	n/a	n/a	71.13	n/a	n/a	n/a
Foreign direct investment, net inflows (% of GDP)	0.64	0.85	1.56	3.76	7.19	4.35			8.81	6.27	4.82	3.49	5.89
GDP (current $US m)	17,632.71	6,082.79	11,390.47	15,102.57	19,550.78	23,649.85	25,234.41	29,221.08	38,952.09	47,760.58	40,147.70	38,423.27	45,819.56
Exports of goods and services (current $US m)	3,086.44	1,451.06	2,425.99	2,962.73	4,359.10	5,556.70	6,606.11	8,729.78	11,884.36	14,842.27	11,800.40	13,406.75	16,531.73
Exports of goods and services (% of GDP)	17.50	23.86	21.30	19.62	22.30	23.50	26.18	29.87	30.51	31.08	29.39	34.89	36.08
Merchandise exports (current $US m)	n/a	n/a	n/a	n/a	n/a	3,523.36	4,482.00	6,428.00	8,824.70	10,972.08	8,345.08	9,795.10	11,776.70

(continued)

Exhibit 1 (continued)

	1999	2000	2001	2002	2003	2004	2005	2006	2007	2008	2009	2010	2011
Merchandise exports to high-income economies (% of total merchandise exports)	n/a	n/a	n/a	n/a	n/a	0.00	99.82	59.37	58.45	59.28	58.11	56.50	n/a
Merchandise exports to developing economies in Europe & Central Asia (% of total merchandise exports)	n/a	n/a	n/a	n/a	n/a	100.00	0.18	31.20	32.19	31.57	31.35	32.48	n/a
Ores and metals exports (% of merchandise exports)	12.61	15.59	14.15	12.15	n/a	10.90	9.20	11.29	10.29	n/a	n/a	n/a	n/a
Agricultural raw materials exports (% of merchandise exports)	4.58	5.74	4.06	4.00	n/a	3.98	2.97	2.31	2.04	n/a	n/a	n/a	n/a
Food exports (% of merchandise exports)	21.62	16.97	16.42	23.14	n/a	20.62	19.75	19.04	18.61	n/a	n/a	n/a	n/a

Fuel exports (% of merchandise exports)	2.38	0.26	2.64	3.41	n/a	2.40	3.66	3.51	2.62	n/a	n/a	n/a	n/a
Manufactures exports (% of merchandise exports)	58.80	61.42	62.73	57.30	n/a	61.71	64.15	63.68	65.93	n/a	n/a	n/a	n/a
High-technology exports (% of manufactured exports)	n/a	n/a	n/a	n/a	n/a	n/a	n/a	n/a	n/a	n/a	n/a	n/a	n/a

Source: World Bank (2013)

Exhibit 2 Serbian exports

Iron and steel	9.6 %
Non-ferrous metals	7.0 %
Cereal and products	5.8 %
Vegetables and fruits	5.4 %
Miscellaneous manufactured articles, dominated by weapons and various products	4.9 %
Clothing	4.2 %
Footwear	2.1 %

Serbian SME sector and that of the EU has shown that Serbia is similar to the EU in terms of average number of enterprises, SME employment, turnover, and contribution to GDP. It is below the EU average in terms of turnover per employee, added value per employee, and profit per employee (Hadzic 2011; Szabó et al. 2010).

One of the main characteristics of Serbian foreign trade in 2010 was an export value growth of 25.1 %; Exports of goods amounted to 7,446.9 million euros. This growth stemmed mostly from higher exports of ferrous and non-ferrous metals, as well as agricultural products (see Exhibit 2). Serbia's most important trade partners are the EU countries, accounting for 4,272 million euros of exports or 57.4 % of the total. The country's second most important group of trading partners are the CEFTA countries, with whom Serbia had a 1,090.6 million euro trade surplus in 2010.

The ICT industry in Serbia is small, but with great potential. About 250 new ICT companies are set up every year, and more than half of that number are engaged in providing computer-programming services. The number of ICT companies increases by 20 % each year. There are many leading global ICT firms that have already made a decision to set up their businesses in Serbia, namely Cisco Systems, Ericsson, IBM, INTEL, Microsoft, Motorola, Oracle, Redhat, Siemens, and T-Mobile (SIEPA 2011). Microsoft opened its fourth R&D centre in Belgrade; the other three are in the US, China and India. Serbia is becoming one of Europe's most attractive ICT hot spots with a growth rate in the ICT sector of 18.9 % in 2008 (Serbian Chamber of Commerce 2011). Over the past few years, the development and promotion of ICT services, such as mobile telecommunications, Internet technologies, and data transfers, have increased significantly. The number of economic entities using and dealing with ICTs in Serbia is also growing, and currently there are around 2,700 ICT companies (SIEPA 2011).

Three groups of companies have been identified in Serbia: strong Hidden Champions (HCs), prospective HCs, and start-ups with emerging competitive advantages. The first group includes companies such as RT-RK CBS and EXECOM. The second group includes Novkabel, Duochem, PrviPartizan, and Copper Mill Sevojno. Serbia's start-up companies with an emerging competitive advantage, one of which is PlusPlus New Technologies, do not appear to have an analogue among Simon's HCs.

All strong HCs in Serbia are computing and telecommunication technology-based companies, established by professors and engineers from the Faculty of Engineering at Serbia's University of Novi Sad (See Exhibit 3). These companies

Exhibit 3 Serbian hidden champions

Name	Market leadership definition	Revenue 2010 (in €m)	Revenue 2000 (in €m)	Employees 2010
RT-RK	For the last 4 years a leader in EU, USA, Turkish, Israeli, and Russian markets in providing cost efficient software and hardware solutions for automating functional testing of multimedia devices, especially set-top boxes and TV sets	8	0.5	250
EXECOM	A leader in the Custom Software Solutions Market in Western Europe for the past couple of years	1.7	0.043	55
Novkabel	A leading cable producer, mostly for the electronic and telecommunications industries in former Yugoslav republic. From 2010, a leader in the CEFTA countries	2.5	25.5	600
DUOCHEM	A leader in biocides, rodenticides and insecticides in Serbia, with a 60 % share of the market	0.9	n/a	12
Prvi Partizan	Number one in Serbia in producing ammunition for the military, sport shooting, and hunting. In the top 5 in the North American and Western European market with its main products, ammunition up to 12.7 mm	45	12	708
Copper Mill Sevojno	First in Ex-Yugoslav republic region, and in the top 3 in Italy and Austria, in the production of construction sheets and industrial strips, made of copper and copper alloys	260	68	1,000
PlusPlus New Technologies	Leader in ex-YU countries as teletext system producer. Their teletext covers 100 % of the Serbian market and is present in all ex-YU countries (Montenegro 100 %, Macedonia 100 %, Bosnia 70 %, Croatia, and Slovenia). The market has expanded to Cyprus	0.1	n/a	6

Source: Authors of the chapter

were established during the turbulent times of the 1990s, characterized by embargoes and hyperinflation, or soon after that. To be profitable in those times, they turned to the ICT sector since it requires low investments, returns income from day 1, and in the long run yields scalable products.

2 Seven Case Studies

2.1 RT-RK Computer Based Systems LLC (RT-RK CBS)[1]

Overview

Address:	Fruškogorska 11, 21000 Novi Sad, Serbia
Tel:	+381 214801100
Email:	info@rt-rk.com
Web:	http://www.rt-rk.com

Company Information

Industry:	Computer programming, consultancy and related activities and partly research and experimental development in natural sciences and engineering
Year of establishment:	2005
Sales revenue in 2010:	€8 million
Sales revenue in 2000:	€500,000
Average number of employees in 2010:	250
Brain(s) behind the company:	CEO Prof. Vladimir Kovačević

2.1.1 Nature of Market Leadership

RT-RK for the last 4 years has been a leader in the EU, USA, Turkish, Israeli and Russian markets, providing cost-efficient software and hardware solutions for functional testing of multimedia devices, especially set-top boxes and TV sets.

2.1.2 Nature of Competitive Advantage

The company's competitive advantage is its capability for design of both hardware and software solutions while competitors are focused on either of the two. This capability has been established through a strategic partnership and close ties with the University of Novi Sad. It has a twofold value: a strong advantage regarding price, and educating students in specific expertise needed by the company.

[1] http://www.rt-rk.com

2.1.3 Core Lessons Learned on the Path to Business Success

1. Establish strong discipline and a professional approach among employees. RT-RK has employed over 250 engineers capable of handling projects of different complexity and magnitude.
2. Invest in innovation and close cooperation with universities. This ensures availability of experts and expertise.
3. Create a total product, integrating software and hardware.

2.1.4 RT-RK: Strong Hidden Champion

Until now there has been no standardization or single application capable of supporting all verification and testing processes in TV and set-top box production. Currently available solutions mainly take care of either the hardware or software part of the system and test management.

RT-RK CBS software engineers possess full-system knowledge of those devices, which is rarely the case, and are thus capable of providing full-device testing solutions. The advantages of its BLACK BOX TESTING[2] over other testing frameworks include reusability of existing infrastructure with different software IP blocks and hardware solutions. This provides significant cost and time savings.

RT-RK CBS's management team recognized a dramatic change on the market. The switch from analogue to digital transmission opened up many new opportunities but also changed and affected some of RT-RK CBS traditional customers, as today there are basically no TV manufacturers left in Europe.

"Having this in mind", said Nikola Teslić, CTO of the company and the mastermind behind its success, "our goals have been to develop different technologies that would address different markets, thus eliminating the single market threat. For example, in 2010 we brought our DLNA testing suite to the market, and the plan for 2011 is to have one of the first test suites for HbbTV, the new European standard for interactive services over the Internet. Externally, new-niche, highly specialized production facilities intended to serve solely EU markets, could be a great chance for us. If this trend continues, we will have greater opportunities, as the customer base will broaden to the 'neighbourhood'. Last but not least, our goal is to deepen cooperation with our biggest clients, ensuring stability of the core business".

From the beginning, RT-RK CBS has been an R&D company for product development in consumer electronics, communications, and multimedia. The focus is on excellent customer support during the project and product lifecycle, as well as close joint work on customers' products, sharing of successes and risks on the market, and providing attractive prices for different business models. To a large extent, RT-RK CBS is an ODM for big clients.

RT-RK CBS was officially founded in 2005 as a daughter company of a University spin-off named FTN-IRAM-RT, incorporated in 1991. In 2009 RT-RK CBS acquired a major ownership stake in MicronasNIT, a company owned by

[2] http://www.bbt.rs

Germany's Micronas GmbH, in order to consolidate its own operations and leverage sales in foreign markets.

"We have been able to increase exports using our relationship with Micronas GmbH. This joint venture has opened new markets and business opportunities through Micronas GmbH and their worldwide subsidiaries and business partners around the globe", Nikola Teslić said.

For the last several years, RT-RK CBS has been one of the leaders in providing cost-efficient software and hardware solutions for automating functional testing of multimedia devices, especially set top-boxes and TV sets, and has been actively serving markets in the EU, USA, Turkey, Israel, and Russia.

The main customers are the Tier-1 companies in the ICT industry, namely silicon vendors and OEM/ODM companies such as Micronas (15 years), Cirrus Logic (6 years), Vestel (5 years), Zoran (3 years), and others. Using a main transition wave,[3] RT-RK CBS has positioned BLACK BOX TESTING as reliable software of so-called military quality.

Next, the short transition wave technology offers value for the clients by shortening time to market to only 3 to 4 months, and offering higher value for less money. Last but not least, this technology requires less severe investments into clients' fixed assets.

"In pursuit of a price-optimized testing solution, we developed two pricing models. Customers with well-defined requirements and project schedules are best satisfied with a 'fixed-price' business model. Why? Because in using this option, the customer pays a pre-negotiated fixed price for the turnkey project, with pre-set project deliverables. The second version is the 'time and material' pricing model, developed for long-term projects where the total effort cannot be estimated reliably in advance, and the scope of work varies considerably during the implementation", said Milenko Berić, CFO of the company.

To sum up: The company has fine-tuned the pricing models for big clients in such a way as to best meet their needs and create the most value with the smallest amount of resources. Such congruence can be reached only if all internal operations and employees' capabilities are matched to the requirements of the pricing models. First, all RT-RK CBS employees are strongly self-disciplined and highly educated; they have all the necessary expertise. In particular, the company employs 250 committed engineers capable of handling a variety of projects of different complexity and magnitude. Next, investment in innovation is a core driver behind the company's overall business model. In particular, more than 15 % of income is reinvested back into R&D. The company owns 30 patents and, remarkably, has created an average ROI of more than 80 % over the past 10 years. Last but not least, such a burst of innovation and creation was possible only because of a close partnership with Serbia's University of Novi Sad, which creates the latest ICT knowledge and supplies well-educated IT experts.

[3] From CRT's to flat panel TVs, which meant a big change in the architecture of chips for flat panel TVs.

2.2 EXECOM[4]

Overview

Address:	Bulevar Kralja Petra I 89, 21000 Novi Sad, Serbia
Tel:	+381 214770500
Email:	info@execom.eu
Web:	http://www.execom.eu

Company Information

Industry:	Computer programming, consultancy and related activities
Year of establishment:	1995
Sales revenue in 2010:	€1.7 million
Sales revenue in 2000:	€43,236 million
Average number of employees in 2010:	55
Brain(s) behind the company:	Managing partners Petar Ulić and Branko Milikić

2.2.1 Nature of Market Leadership

A leader in designing custom-made software solutions in Western Europe for the last few years.

2.2.2 Nature of Competitive Advantage

EXECOM builds its competitive advantage on standardized processes, investment in young people, building dedicated cells around clients, and keeping communication channels open and transparent inside and outside the company. The company is committed to satisfying the most demanding client requirements regarding ICT issues.

2.2.3 Core Lessons Learned on the Path to Business Success

1. Enter a niche market with solid domain knowledge. This will equip you with the capability to pursue more demanding, and hence more profitable, business opportunities.
2. Always stand out with the quality of your services and your expertise.

[4] http://www.execom.eu

3. To stay competitive, work with verified technologies. This will improve the software development process.
4. When working closely with clients, the need for innovation is driven by both parties. This mutual drive process creates an innovative approach resulting in efficient and reliable solutions.

2.2.4 EXECOM: Strong Hidden Champion

Deloitte ranked EXECOM in 2009 as the 10th fastest growing technology company in Central Europe, based on the percentage of revenue over a 5-year period. This growth has been generated through three main categories of software solutions: (1) for technical automation, (2) for telecommunications, and (3) for various data analyses, and processing and visualization. In general, the growth has been achieved because the company manages to come up with novel or improved ICT solutions in each of the three areas. One can say the growth was fuelled by continuous creation of innovative ICT solutions.

In the area of technical automation in particular, the company has developed a novel software platform for clinical and chemical analysts that can shorten the work time of operators by more than 25 %. Being a platform solution, its applicability extends to a wide range of analysts for different industry sectors.

In the telecommunications market, EXECOM created a novel back office solution for Telecoms, which enables faster and more efficient files exchange between operators, a clearinghouse, and inner partners. Next, it supports call event processing rules, and increases the efficiency of fraud management systems. Last but not least, the company has created a set of solutions that manage satellite communications, enabling efficient Internet and telephone access to vessels. This technology allows prepaid phone cards to be sold online aboard clients' vessels, and is instrumental in solutions for remote assistance to companies and other users of web platforms.

This wide range of innovative ICT products, and the growth of the company over the last 5 years, is to some extent a reflection of market dynamics. Over the last decade, the market for custom software solutions has been growing significantly, both in turnover and in prices. This trend has been most apparent in Western Europe, the core market region for EXECOM. Put differently, EXECOM's business system is well designed to satisfy ICT system requirements for any company, however unique in its demands.

Mr. Petar Ulić, a EXECOM managing partner, emphasized the importance of relationships with clients: "Our business logic is fairly simple: we build unique relationships with our clients, which results in a growing network of partners. To implement this business logic successfully, we invest a lot in our young experts. We train them and expose them to a wide range of challenging projects, where they can gather experience in ICT knowledge frontiers. Dealing with state-of-the art technologies is a powerful motivation; therefore, we practically have no brain-drain, though our people are trained professionals and employable all over the world".

EXECOM embarked on international expansion in 1999. Consequently, big clients were found in the Netherlands, Germany, Sweden, the UK, France, Switzerland, Austria, the Czech Republic, Italy and Russia. Each regional customer created a new set of business opportunities through word-of-mouth recommendations. In parallel with its internationalization, the company established offices in the Czech Republic in 2001 and the Netherlands in 2006.

EXECOM is striving to make the right strategy decisions. Ms Aleksandra Popara, the Marketing and Communications Manager, says: "We thoughtfully consider competitors, as well as present and potential barriers to entry, before committing ourselves to entering a specific niche. In general, the less competition, the better. Next, the closer the niche to our knowledge domain, the better". In that way, despite continuous expansion to novel niches, the company manages its risks. EXECOM enters only low-competition niches for which it has the required knowledge.

EXECOM teaches us that innovation, expert knowledge, flexibility in handling a diverse customer base, integration into customers' business systems, and expansion into new low-competition niches, where the required knowledge corresponds to the company's expertise and the existing competition is weak, appears to be a winning formula in the ICT business. Many of the elements of this formula may work effectively in other industry settings as well.

2.3 Novkabel[5]

Overview

Address:	Industrijska bb, 21000 Novi Sad, Serbia
Tel:	+381 21442852
Email:	info@novkabel.com
Web:	http://www.novkabel.com

Company Information

Industry:	Electrical machinery and optical equipment
Year of establishment:	1921
Sales revenue in 2010:	€2.5 million
Sales revenue in 2000:	€25.5 million
Average number of employees in 2010:	600
Brain(s) behind the company:	CEO, Dragan Cvetković

[5] http://www.novkabel.com

2.3.1 Nature of Market Leadership

A leader in the production of cables, mostly for the electronic and telecommunication industry in the Western Balkan region. Since 2010, the company's market leadership has expanded to CEFTA countries. The business has also expanded to Russia by developing a new type of cable, customized to suit customer needs.

2.3.2 Nature of Competitive Advantage

The company is concentrating on contract manufacturing and focusing on specific types of cables and sub-specialization. After signing a preliminary agreement, development of a particular type of the cable is carried out together with the client. Novkabel's flexibility and expertise in manufacturing, along with entrepreneurial business skills, are its key business competence.

2.3.3 Core Lessons Learned on the Path to Business Success

Novkabel is a company whose products are input components for other manufacturers. It operates mostly in markets where there are a small number of large customers. To succeed in this environment, try to:

1. Increase market share through a proactive approach and strong leadership. Persistency and belief in success are important.
2. If doing business with big powerful clients, customize your products to meet their needs completely; and above all, exceed their expectations, meet deadlines, and provide quality superior to that of your competitors.
3. Nourish strategic business relationships with core customers as you would with your own children.

2.3.4 Novkabel: Prospective Hidden Champion

Founded in 1921, Novkabel is the oldest cable producer in the Balkans. Being one of many companies that produce components for everyday products, it can be said to be in the commodity business. Its products are used in a wide range of industries: construction, power distribution, telecommunication, oil industry, mining, automobile, railways, shipbuilding, and aeronautics. Exports go mainly to industries located in CEE, where transportation costs do not exceed the benefits created by a favourable cost/price ratio. However, Novkabel is an absolute leader in terms of market share in the ex-Yugoslav Republic, especially in supplying cables for the electronics and telecommunication industries.

In the beginning, when Tayloristic scientific management was still in its infancy, production was mostly artisan; only 14 workers produced simple cables. The company continued to develop its management expertise and cable technology, and in the 1960s it built new facilities. During the 1980s the factory went through a second phase of development and expansion, which included a longer list of products, and thus created considerable growth in sales. In parallel with the transition of the political regime, the ownership of Novcabel changed in the 1990s. In 1998, the company was transformed from a collectively-owned business entity to a joint-stock company. During the last decade it went through another major business transition and survived the turmoil. In particular, the transition period until 2009 had led to falling levels of production and loss of markets. In 2009, restructuring and new investments brought about a successful return to a competitive position in CEE.

So, what was the entrepreneurial spirit that created such a comeback for Novkabel? First and foremost, the company leveraged the advantage of its inherent knowledge and years of experience in the cable business, and added these to novel marketing approaches. Most importantly, Novkabel created a passion for growth and development among its employees.

To some extent a tipping point was reached when the company's management made the decision to serve as an ODM for big customers; that is, to design new cable solutions when large quantities of specific products are requested. The company has also extended into contract manufacturing, creating some novel technological solutions along the way.

To sum up: company's flexibility and expertise in manufacturing are its key business competencies. Novkabel has the capacity to satisfy the cable requirements of a diverse range of customers. Now, the main strategic direction is to build up close, trust-based strategic partnerships with customers, so as to share the risks and be successful in an unpredictable future.

2.4 DUOCHEM[6]

Overview

Address:	Ruzveltova 38, 11120 Beograd, Serbia
Tel:	+381 113440493
Email:	office@duochem.rs
Web:	http://www.duochem.rs

Company Information

Industry:	Manufacture of pesticides and other agrochemical products
Year of establishment:	2000
Sales revenue in 2010:	€900,000
Sales revenue in 2000:	n/a
Average number of employees in 2010:	12
Brain(s) behind the company:	CEO and founder, Suren Husinec

[6] http://www.duochem.rs

2.4.1 Nature of Market Leadership

A leader in the marketing of biocides, rodenticides and insecticides in Serbia, with 60 % of market share.

2.4.2 Nature of Competitive Advantage

DUOCHEM's advantage is its in-house production of basic raw materials, which gives the final products an advantage over those of competitors in terms of quality and price. In addition, the company's manufacturing process complies with highest environmental standards, which places DUOCHEM miles ahead of its local competition. Furthermore, the company has developed partnerships with other providers so that customers can buy whatever chemical product they need at one outlet.

2.4.3 Core Lessons Learned on the Path to Business Success

1. Build up knowledge, experience, and professional networks in top academic and industrial labs all over the world (Serbia, Scotland, USA, France and Armenia).
2. Leverage a strong scientific background in business by promoting your scientific innovation in professional circles that can provide you with good business opportunities. Then, pursue these opportunities.
3. Be demanding but fair; be modest, motivated, and persistent. Be willing to implement the highest standards whether manufacturing products for global or niche markets.

2.4.4 DUOCHEM: Prospective Hidden Champion

Only a few companies in the world, including DUOCHEM, synthesize generic active ingredients[7] for producing rodenticides; most are just formulators that buy active ingredients to manufacture, and then sell, final products.

"It may not be prestigious to be in the business of producing rodenticides and insecticides; hence the majority of companies in our business only carry rodenticides and insecticides as part of their product list. I spotted this low attractiveness of rodenticides and insecticides, and see it as an opportunity to use my expert knowledge in chemistry and turn it into something profitable", said CEO and founder of DUOCHEM, Mr. Suren Husinec.

As a scientist and chemist with an international reputation, Mr. Husinec has implemented a scientific approach acquired through years of experience in the world's best laboratories. While working as a scientific advisor at the University of Belgrade, he came up with an innovative technological process for producing basic raw materials, active ingredients, and finished products. The idea of applying this process to an unattractive product—where the competition is scarce—might be a formula for success, and so he founded DUOCHEM in 2000 as a spin-off company of the university's Institute of Chemistry, Technology and Metallurgy.

[7] Coumatetralyl, Bromadiolone and Brodifacoum.

Rodenticides, a niche-market product, were introduced to markets outside Serbia through personal, academic contacts who recommended the company to major distributors all over Europe. These distributors are powerful companies, covering multi-billion dollar markets not only in Europe but also abroad.

Nowadays, DUOCHEM's market share in Serbia is 60 %, while the strongest local competitor has 20 %. DUOCHEM's share in CEE, Western Europe, and other parts of the world is still very small; however, the company's reputation is spreading rapidly and it is only a question of time, and maybe some luck, when this reputation will be transformed into market share. The problem of low market share is partly due to country-specific regulations.

As Mr. Husinec emphasized, "Such products are subject to local country registration procedure and hence regulation. This is a time-consuming process that requires heavy investment, sometimes not feasible for smaller companies. However, we have filed for a set of country registrations; so in 2012 we expect our exports to rise sharply".

In addition, the market of biocides, rodenticides and insecticides has changed over the last decade in terms of size, volume and prices, particularly in Europe. Newly introduced legislation in the EU, based on the safety of products and environmental protection standards for manufacturers, has resulted in a big clean-up of products and processes. Those products and manufacturers not complying with new safety and environmental standards will soon be forced out of this competitive game. Expectations are that prices will go up because of the heavy investment needed to meet new standards. However, DUOCHEM has an advantage over many of its competitors, being a relatively new and flexible company without the need for specialized investments. Its upfront design production capacity to deal with new environmental protection standards has created a cost advantage and competitive pricing.

Last but not least, though specializing in rodenticides and insecticides, DUOCHEM wanted to create a one-stop shop; hence it concluded a set of cooperative agreements with several well-known manufacturers across the EU. Nowadays, DUOCHEM can satisfy a range of customer demands in one place.

DUOCHEM's success story is different from that of the previously discussed HCs. It involves a set of strategic decisions that can be summarized as: (1) Innovating the process for manufacturing established product categories, (2) specializing in product categories that appear to be unattractive to the competition, (3) making investments that take into account future regulatory requirements, and (4) creating partnerships to build up customer satisfaction in the "one-stop" environment.

2.5 Prvi Partizan[8]

Overview

Address:	Milosa Obrenovica 2, 31000 Uzice, Serbia
Tel:	+381 31563442
Email:	office@prvipartizan.com
Web:	http://www.prvipartizan.com

Company Information

Industry:	Machinery and equipment production
Year of establishment:	1928
Sales revenue in 2010:	€45 million
Sales revenue in 2000:	€12 million
Average number of employees in 2010:	707
Brain(s) behind the company:	Dobrosav Andrić

2.5.1 Nature of Market Leadership

Prvi Partizan is number one in Serbia in the production of ammunition for the military, sports shooting, and hunting. Its main product—ammunition for guns below 12.7 mm caliber—places it among the top-five companies in its sector in the North American and Western European markets.

2.5.2 Nature of Competitive Advantage

The company has experienced, highly-educated and professional personnel who provide customer satisfaction in terms of quality, quantity, and conditions of production, as well as the ability to transfer knowledge, technology and equipment to a "turnkey" project.

2.5.3 Core Lessons Learned on the Path to Business Success

1. Exceed professional standards set by international regulatory bodies.
2. Invest in the development of a global network of customers. This network will attract new customers.
3. Relate brand visibility with the functionality and reliability of your products, and with competitive prices.

[8] http://www.prvipartizan.com

4. Trace market trends and standards, especially in the area of environmental protection, and invest in them proactively, for example in research and development of so-called ecological ammunition.
5. Build up turnkey services. These have placed Prvi Partizan among the most important producers of ammunition in the world.

2.5.4 Prvi Partizan: Prospective Hidden Champion

Prvi Partizan has been a leading producer of ammunition for military, sports shooting, and hunting in Serbia for more than 80 years. Its strongest market position is in ammunition for guns below 12.7 mm caliber, where Prvi Partizan is among the top five companies in North America and Western Europe. However, this market leadership position was achieved only after the company gained the trust, and developed a global network, of customers and dealers. Potential clients were approached mostly at fairs. The company nowadays receives 97 % of its total sales revenue through exports, while 10 years ago this figure was only 30 %.

Overall, Prvi Partizan's ammunition is highly valued because of its quality, reliability, and safety in accordance with NATO standards. The company has built a state-of-the-art factory where, apart from ammunition, the production programme includes a wide range of commercial and military firearms, including pistols.

However, customers in core markets have recently become very choosy because of a decline in their purchasing power, especially for commercial ammunition. A core objective of the company is therefore to reduce operating costs and increase operation efficiency. Part of the innovation process involves the development of new, so-called ecological ammunition, done in collaboration with partners.

Prvi Partizan is one of the senior companies to have the potential to skyrocket among the real HCs, especially if it succeeds in its product innovations and experiences some luck.

2.6 Copper Mill Sevojno[9]

Address:	Prvomajska bb, 31205 Sevojno, Serbia
Tel:	+381 31594–340
Web:	http://www.coppersev.com

[9] http://www.coppersev.com

Company Information

Industry:	Manufacture of basic precious and other non-ferrous metals
Year of establishment:	1952
Sales revenue in 2010:	€260 million
Sales revenue in 2000:	€68 million
Average number of employees in 2010:	1,000
Brain(s) behind the company:	CEO Marko Mitrović

2.6.1 Nature of Market Leadership

First in the Western Balkan region and in the top three in Italy and Austria in the production of construction sheets and industrial strips from copper and copper alloys.

2.6.2 Nature of Competitive Advantage

The company has vast experience in copper fabrication. Because of the important role of its products for customers' businesses—usually they create the A type of costs—maintaining and improving product quality are critical competencies and key to the company's success.

2.6.3 Core Lessons Learned on the Path to Business Success

1. If you are in a business where your raw material prices are determined by the economic situation of the region, and these prices can make the difference between success and failure, then develop close ties with your customers.
2. When external changes, such as drastic increases in the price of raw material or the actions of your competition, destabilize your business system, focus all your attention on maintaining system stability, both in terms of production and finances.
3. If you are in the commodity business, it is not enough to stay competitive only on price; make sure you are also superior in product quality, delivery, and payment terms.

2.6.4 Copper Mill Sevojno: Prospective Hidden Champion

Copper Mill Sevojno, as the name suggests, is in the business of manufacturing products from copper and copper alloys, including industrial sheets, strips, tubes, rods, and bars. These products are indispensable to a range of industries from engineering to electro-technics and electronics.

Copper Mill Sevojno is also one of the oldest ex-Yugoslav companies, set up in 1952 to support the industrialization of the country. Initial production capacity was around 25,000 t/year, delivered by 5,000 employees. This low productivity was subsequently improved over the years by expansion of capacities and technological improvements towards total automation of the production. In 2000, the company created 68 million euros in revenue with 1,000 employees and more than 60 % of its sales were achieved abroad. In 2010 the company's revenue was approximately 260 million euros and exports had increased to 90 % of sales. This made Copper Mill Sevojno the largest copper and copper alloys manufacturer in the region, and one of larger factories of this type in Europe.

What drove such fast growth? The success was an outcome of years of experience in the copper business, technological improvements in the production process, increased market orientation, and flexibility in pursuing business opportunities. Recently, an increase in raw material prices and increased competition—partly induced by large fixed costs—refocused the company's attention on cost control and operational efficiency. As a consequence, the workforce was downsized and existing capacities were improved through reorganization. Altogether, these strategic decisions resulted in good business results for the company, including strengthening of relationships with customers.

Again, the case of Copper Mill Sevojno is one of those HC stories that teach us how to come out of a recession as a winner, and how to balance conflicting investment demands between customers and innovation with cost efficiency and control.

2.7 Plusplus New Technologies

Overview

Address:	38 Takovska St., Beograd 11120, Serbia
Tel:	+ 381 113294945
Email:	kontakt@plusplusnt.rs
Web:	http://www.plusplusnt.rs

Company Information

Industry:	Computer programming, consultancy and related activities
Year of establishment:	2002
Sales revenue in 2010:	€100,000
Sales revenue in 2000:	n/a
Average number of employees in 2010:	6
Brain(s) behind the company:	Gvozden Marinković

2.7.1 Nature of Market Leadership

PlusPlus NT was the first local teletext system producer in the Western Balkan market. It is a leader in the region, with its teletext covering 100 % of the Serbian and Macedonian markets and much of Croatia, and Slovenia. PlusPlus NT is now expanding into Cyprus and other countries in the region.

2.7.2 Nature of Competitive Advantage

PlusPlus NT is a small company experiencing stable development in a very competitive and dynamic ICT market. The most important competence of PlusPlus NT today is its ability to combine experience in different areas of ICT and design of teletext systems. Hence, the company's products and services are characterized by a good price-quality ratio.

2.7.3 Core Lessons Learned on the Path to Business Success

1. If you are a young and small company, be patient and persistently build up your experience, range of products, and service offerings. If you survive long enough, success will follow.
2. When trying to work out long-term partnerships, you need to meet all deadlines and quality requirements before the first transaction.
3. Successful cooperative development efforts are the best marketing tool to win more business.

2.7.4 PlusPlus NT: Start-Up Hidden Champion

When using teletext, one rarely reflects on how it is created, but people from PlusPlus NT know a great deal about its production. In fact, most customers from ex-Yugoslavia countries use teletext created by this small company from Serbia.

The company's origins go back to PlusPlus, founded in 2002 as a computer engineering company. It was a business incubator for PlusPlus NT. In the early 2000's, teletext services were relatively new on the Serbian market, and only a few imported expensive systems existed. In cooperation with a smaller hardware company, PlusPlus developed a user-friendly teletext solution based on open source technologies. In 2009, the company was incorporated and introduced these teletext systems and a wide range of other ICT products, including systems for live betting and Internet betting, software for traffic cadastres, portals for tourist agencies, systems for mobile marketing via Bluetooth technology, and systems for call centres. Employees were mainly young enthusiastic experts specializing in different ICT areas. They worked closely with engineers from the School of Electrical Engineering at the University of Belgrade.

This new teletext system has captured 100 % of the market share in Serbia, Macedonia, and Montenegro, as well as 70 % of the market in Bosnia. Furthermore, PlusPlus has the potential to take over market leadership in Croatia and Slovenia. The main buyers are TV stations that prefer the teletext system on a turnkey basis. Betting companies are also important buyers.

About 5 % of the company's average income is invested in R&D. However, PlusPlus NT does not have patents, as intellectual property rights are difficult to protect in the IT sector. Product development is often based on open-source technologies. The main drivers of innovation are the technological competencies of the company that it uses in its attempts to address under-satisfied customers. Apart from employees and their associates from the University, stakeholders are also often involved in the innovation process. Very often, clients finance the innovation process themselves, so that they are also heavily involved in generating ideas and requirements.

Cooperative, innovative networks between employees, external associates, customers and stakeholders appears to be the most important driver of success for many ICT start-up champions, not just PlusPlus NT. Together they create the product that they aspire to see.

Conclusion

Although there have been many historical turbulences in the region, we can conclude that Serbia has companies that can be globally competitive. It is difficult to come up with numbers and general conclusions when there are only two real HCs (RT-RK CBS and EXECOM) in our sample. Still, some interesting features worth mentioning.

In terms of growth and market leadership, Serbia's HCs have the same characteristics as Simon's (Simon 2009). The goals of Serbia's HCs are based on great visions, established very early on and maintained over the long term. Their flexibility is not sacrificed for efficiency. Their market leadership is based on superior performances, not aggressive pricing. Their revenues have increased consistently over their lifetime.

Serbian HCs operate in narrowly defined niches in which they invest all their knowledge, resources, and professional networks. The choice of market niches is based on professional knowledge, in-depth-understanding of the industry, and a passion to create novel products. Many HCs manufacture products that serve a wide range of industries.

Serbian HCs pursue globalization early on in their lifetime. They focus predominantly on Western European and CEE markets. They enter foreign markets either through their own subsidiaries or joint ventures. The latter strategy is preferred over the former when the partnership creates synergies in distribution or reduces the risks typical of new ventures.

Long and close relationships with customers are also an important driver of success. Customer requirements are usually both performance and price-oriented; hence Serbian HCs compete well in both fields. In general, dependence on core customers is high, since on average more than 50 % of the HCs' revenues are created by their top three to five customers.

Serbian HCs gain their market leading positions predominately through innovations. These are equally technology and market-driven. The two strong Serbian HCs, RT-RK CBS and EXECOM, invest 15–37 % of their revenues in R&D and have an average ROI of 56–80 %.

Serbian HCs are well-informed about their competitors in world markets. The ties that they have with the University and its student scholarship programs create excellent competitive advantages by educating and developing highly specific experts.

Serbian HCs are completely convinced that their companies are very attractive to highly skilled workers. CEOs have been staying at the helm for a long time. Their personalities, vision, and commitment are very strong drivers of success.

As for the group of potential HCs (Novekabel, DUOCHEM, Prvi Partizan and Copper Mill Sevojno), three of them have been producing for their markets for 60–80 years. They have been through rough times and are now each finding a way to regain a market leadership position. They have sustainable business practices and growth because they pay attention to market trends, implement a marketing approach, make internal changes, find niche market products, and customize them to customer needs. Finally, they are all characterized by strong leadership or entrepreneurship.

References

Bosnjak, M. (2011). *Rezultati i izazovi ekonomskih reformi u Srbiji u tranzicionom periodu 2001–2008. godina*. Retrieved April 20, 2011, from http://www.mfin.gov.rs/userfiles/file/dokumenti/rezultati%20i%20izazovi%20ek%20reformi%2011%2011%202010%20.pdf

Hadzic, M., & Pavlovic, P. (2011). How to overcome (SME) crisis: Serbian case. *Acta Polytechnica Hungarica, 8*(1), 61–80.

Serbian Chamber of Commerce. (2011). *Economy of Serbia*. Retrieved April 10, 2011 from http://www.pks.rs/PrivredauSrbiji/tabid/1788/language/sr-Latn-CS/Default.aspx

SIEPA - Serbia Investment and Export Promotion Agency. (2011). *ICT industry in Serbia*. Retrieved April 10, 2011 from http://www.siepa.gov.rs/site/en/home/1/key_industries/it_industry/

Simon, H. (2009). *Hidden champions of the twenty-first century*. Berlin: Springer.

Szabó, A., Yordanova, D., Kristi, D., Erić, D., Szabó, Z., Gál, M., et al. (2010). The impact of the economic crises on SMEs in selected CEE countries". *ERENET Profile, 5*(3), 6–29.

World Bank (2013). *Data; countries and economies*. http://data.worldbank.org/country

Hidden Champions of Slovakia

Janka Táborecká-Petrovičová, Jaroslav Ďaďo, and Tamara Bobáková

Overview

Official name:	Slovak Republic
Type of government:	Republic, with parliamentary democracy
Population in 2011:	5,398,384
Land area:	48,088 km^2

History

	Up until 1918 Slovakia was part of Austria-Hungary.
1918	(October) After the end of World War I and the dissolution of the Austro-Hungarian Empire, Slovaks and Czechs form an independent state: the Czechoslovak Republic (ČSR).
1939/1945	The Slovak Republic becomes an independent state in Central Europe under Nazi German control.
1945	After World War II, the victorious powers restore Czechoslovakia. Elections are held in 1946. The Czechoslovak Communist Party, winning 38 % of the total vote, seizes power in February 1948. Strict communist control characterizes the next 4 decades.
1968	(January-August) Communist control is interrupted only briefly in the so-called Prague Spring of 1968, followed by the invasion and

J. Táborecká-Petrovičová (✉) • J. Ďaďo
Department of Corporate Economics and Management, Faculty of Economics Matej Bel University, Banská Bystrica, Slovakia
e-mail: Janka.Taborecka@umb.sk

T. Bobáková
Simon-Kucher & Partners, Luxembourg, Luxembourg

P. McKiernan and D. Purg (eds.), *Hidden Champions in CEE and Turkey*,
DOI 10.1007/978-3-642-40504-4_20, © Springer-Verlag Berlin Heidelberg 2013

	occupation of the country by the armies of four Soviet bloc countries. In November 1989, the Velvet Revolution brings democracy and the downfall of Communist rule in Czechoslovakia. The first free elections in Czechoslovakia since 1948 take place in June 1990.
1993	(January) A peaceful declaration of the Slovak Republic's independence from the Czech Republic. Both states obtain immediate recognition from the USA and their European neighbours and are admitted to the IMF (The former Czechoslovak Republic was one of the founding members of the IMF.)
2000	Slovakia is invited to join the OECD, and begins its European Union accession process.
2004	(March) Slovakia admitted into NATO.
2004	(May) Slovakia joins the EU.
2009	(January) Slovakia adopts the single European currency, the euro.

1 Introduction: Context

Slovakia has come a long way in the last 2 decades. A peaceful end to Communist rule, separation from the Czechs, and extensive reforms in areas such as taxation, social welfare, and pensions, have all helped turn the country into a small but thriving open economy. Its per-capita annual GDP in 2010 of $US 16,036 ranks Slovakia 58th in the world, but its GDP growth (4 % in 2010) puts it at an advantage compared to many older, more established economies. The negative consequences of the world economic crisis were also felt by Slovakia. In particular, they caused higher unemployment but by now the economy seems to be headed towards recovery. This five-and-a-half-million strong country has produced a number of innovative Hidden Champions (HCs).

The "young" and "old" can be found together in Slovakia, a "little-big country" located in the central part of Europe, sharing borders with Austria, the Czech Republic, Poland, Hungary and Ukraine. After the constitution of the Slovak Republic, the government restructured enterprises and banks, and initiated large-scale privatizations, opening them for foreign investment. Between 1993 and 1994, GDP grew by 6.2 %, inflation fell to about 13 %, and the budget deficit was brought under control. The process of privatization also created an opportunity for establishing new small businesses. Almost immediately after the right-wing government had won a second term, it introduced wide-ranging reforms including a flat income tax, a mandatory pension pillar, and better-targeted social benefits. These reforms increased incentives to work, create jobs, and invest, thus fostering growth and economic catching-up. After Slovakia became a member of the EU in 2004, the former coalition government successfully prepared the country for adoption of the euro in 2009, substituting the Slovak crown (Národná Banka Slovenska 2010).

Slovakia is a landlocked country of rugged mountains, vast forests and open fields. It has its own official Slovak language. The capital city, Bratislava, is only

60 km from Vienna. Knowing Slovak history and understanding the mentality of its people is the key to doing business successfully with Slovaks. Slovak people are proud of their country and their rich cultural heritage, and they value their national identity. It is important for foreigners not to confuse Slovakia with Slovenia, the former Yugoslav country.

Everyday life in Slovakia is influenced by traditional values. Established gender roles, an emphasis on Catholicism, class differences, hierarchy, and respect for elders, are all still prevalent to some extent. As the country becomes more modernized and Westernized, Slovak culture is gradually changing but it still maintains a high level of tradition. Industrial action is a very unusual form of protest. The labour force has traditionally been skilled and educated, as evidenced for example by its high productivity in the weapons industry in the 1970s and 1980s (Uramová and Kožiak 2008).

The most important reforms affecting the business environment were started in 2004 with the introduction of a new tax system, the streamlining of administrative procedures for starting a business, a change of the existing social safety system to a social security system, streamlining of communications with tax authorities, and the adoption of legislation for a more flexible bankruptcy process. A new income tax law came into effect on January 1, 2004, introducing a so-called flat tax of 19 % for all types of corporate entities and individuals, and eliminated a large range of exemptions (Daborowski 2011). The taxation of dividends was abolished. The VAT law changed and the rate was increased to 20 % in 2011.

In 2007, economic growth stood at 10.4 %. This growth stemmed from Slovakia's low cost base, flat tax rate, high productivity growth, strong private consumption, and strong external demand. The automotive sector has been the largest driver of growth in recent years as many car manufacturers (Volkswagen, Kia and Peugeot) built plants in Slovakia. The automotive sector accounts for nearly half of Slovakia's exports. Samsung Electronics has been tipped to become Slovakia's largest exporter, as the economy shifts towards high-tech industries.

The economic structure of Slovakia in 2010 is similar to that of other developed countries, with its service sector at 61 % of GDP, industry at 35 %, and agriculture 3.9 %. An average monthly salary of less than 800 euros is a strong motive for foreign direct investment. In 2004 the Slovak Republic was accepted as a member of the EU, and now Slovak businesses compete with other EU companies in a single market and under the same conditions. A policy of support was directed towards Slovak SMEs to help them adapt as much as possible to the competitive business environment of the EU. The share of SMEs in the Slovak economy is now comparable to that in developed countries; they make up 88 % of the total number of all enterprises. In 2009, they created more than 54 % of GDP, and of the total number employed (excluding self-employment) in 2009, 56.81 % worked for SMEs. In the first three quarters of 2010, this percentage was 57.89 %. SMEs are therefore an essential part of the Slovak economy; they promote growth and development.

But Slovak SMEs are in a less than ideal situation. A survey of SMEs by the National Agency for Development shows that some companies have not made significant changes despite the country's membership of the EU. This means that they are not taking full advantage of the opportunities that a single market allows. Instead of seeking new outlets for their production, they continue to focus on domestic markets that are characterized by increasing competition. The advantages that stem from low labour costs will gradually wither away; therefore it is necessary to build a long-term competitive advantage while eliminating existing shortcomings.

Support for SMEs in Slovakia takes different forms. When financial and material resources are limited, SMEs are oriented towards activities that do not require a lot of fixed assets. They focus on sophisticated activities, based on know-how and intellectual property. The trade-off, however, is that their intellectual property is not given the same legal protection.

One of the most important sources of support for SMEs was the 2003/4 Slovak-Dutch project "Improving the Business Environment of Slovakia". It was funded by the Dutch government and aimed at increasing the business administration capacity of Slovak institutions. The main partners in the project included NADSME, Slovakia's Ministry of Economy, and the Dutch research and consulting institution ECORYS.

Foreign trade is important to Slovakia's economy as we see from the core foreign trade indicators presented in Exhibit 1. In 1994 imports and exports each totaled more than 6 billion US dollars. Crude oil, natural gas, machinery, and transportation equipment are Slovakia's main imports, while exports include machinery, chemicals, fuels, steel, and weapons. The Czech Republic, Slovakia's main trading partner, supplies about 9 % of Slovakia's imports and purchases approximately 10 % of its exports. Germany, which buys 15.3 % of Slovak exports, Poland, France, Hungary, and Russia are Slovakia's other leading foreign trade partners. In 2010, Slovakia almost balanced its foreign trade; total exports were valued at US 70,748. Imports from China and South Korea are also important to Slovakia (Exhibit 2).

2 Six Case Studies

2.1 ESET

Overview

Address: Aupark Tower, Einsteinova 24, 85101 Bratislava, Slovakia
Tel: +421232244111
Email: marketing@eset.sk
Web: http://www.eset.sk

Exhibit 1 Core economic indicators in Slovakia

	1999	2000	2001	2002	2003	2004	2005	2006	2007	2008	2009	2010	2011
GDP per capita (current US$)	5,550.00	5,330.40	5,636.64	6,439.48	8,520.59	10,417.81	11,384.53	12,798.53	15,583.40	18,109.06	16,100.08	16,036.07	17,782.02
GDP growth (annual %)	−0.06	1.51	3.67	4.58	4.76	5.00	6.56	8.26	10.37	5.57	−5.14	3.96	3.96
Long-term unemployment (% of total unemployment)	46.90	53.90	53.70	59.80	61.20	60.60	68.10	73.10	70.80	66.00	50.90	59.30	63.90
Foreign direct investment, net inflows (% of GDP)	1.18	7.15		11.85	1.22	5.42	4.89	5.90	4.63	4.16	1.84	0.76	3.81
GDP (current US$ m)	29,947.93	28,724.04	30,318.73	34,638.31	45,837.42	56,073.23	61,328.47	69,002.10	84,108.56	97,908.89	87,239.75	87,077.44	95,994.15
Exports of goods and services (current US$ m)	18,317.13	20,235.66	22,045.54	24,634.25	34,765.50	41,799.44	46,764.13	58,299.66	73,053.34	81,724.62	61,833.16	70,748.19	85,487.91
Exports of goods and services (% of GDP)	61.16	70.45	72.71	71.12	75.85	74.54	76.25	84.49	86.86	83.47	70.88	81.25	89.06
Merchandise exports (current US$ m)	10,211.29	11,831.88	12,594.76	14,405.37	21,837.27	27,744.73	31,889.28	41,861.51	58,515.54	71,142.12	56,081.71	64,663.54	79,308.12

(continued)

Exhibit 1 (continued)

	1999	2000	2001	2002	2003	2004	2005	2006	2007	2008	2009	2010	2011
Merchandise exports to high-income economies (% of total merchandise exports)	92.95	93.20	93.20	93.02	92.85	92.10	90.96	90.83	89.12	86.84	87.08	88.90	89.72
Merchandise exports to developing economies in Europe & Central Asia (% of total merchandise exports)	4.58	4.62	5.01	5.51	5.79	6.24	7.12	7.20	8.68	10.67	10.02	9.22	8.88
Ores and metals exports (% of merchandise exports)	3.46	3.43	3.46	3.09	2.43	2.87	2.55	3.63	2.78	2.45	2.36	3.03	3.00
Agricultural raw materials exports (% of merchandise exports)	2.48	2.18	2.07	1.90	1.56	1.52	1.74	1.29	1.06	0.94	1.23	1.22	1.02
Food exports (% of merchandise exports)	3.95	3.19	3.56	3.57	3.06	3.73	4.57	4.17	3.86	3.63	4.67	4.29	4.84

Fuel exports (% of merchandise exports)	4.71	6.96	6.54	5.98	5.07	6.30	5.81	5.45	4.47	4.98	4.52	4.77	6.32
Manufactures exports (% of merchandise exports)	84.94	83.71	83.84	85.28	87.73	85.36	83.34	82.59	85.81	85.79	86.98	86.51	84.70
High-technology exports (% of manufactured exports)	4.28	3.63	3.86	3.21	3.80	5.48	7.44	6.72	5.35	5.26	5.70	6.77	7.10

Source: World Bank (2013)

Exhibit 2 Hidden champions from Slovakia

Name	Short market leadership description	Revenue 2010 (€m)	Revenue 2000 (€m)	Employees 2010
Eset	Internet security. First in the world to introduce proactive security, clever programming and ongoing innovation, leader in CEE countries, more than 100 mil. users globally	137	0.55	340 (in Slovakia)
ACE enterprise	Integration and optimization of information systems (e.g. SAP). Highly customizable technology, quick delivery (in hours), low costs	1.0	n/a	30
Sygic	GPS navigation software for mobile devices. Flexible organizational structure, fast decisions, quick innovations ahead of competition. Versatile software for many platforms. No. 2 in CEE, more than 1 mil. Users	6.2	n/a	70
Media Control	Electrical, plumbing, and other construction installation activities. Specialized design activities. Manufacturer of consumer electronics	2.0	n/a	8 (2 ext)
Grand power	Pistols. High-quality weapons exported to e.g. USA, Russia, EU. International patents, innovations—barrel-locking mechanism and significantly diminished recoil	2.9	n/a	47
Kvety.sk	Flowers—internet sale and delivery. High-end offerings, exclusivity, customizable requirements. Keeps costs down by renting plantations. High level of trust. Started to expand abroad only recently	1.3	n/a	25

Source: Authors of the chapter

Company Information

Industry:	Computer programming, consultancy and related activities
Year of establishment:	1992
Sales revenues in 2010:	€137 million
Sales revenues in 2000:	€550,000
Average number of employees in 2010:	340
Brain(s) behind the company:	CEO and founder Miroslav Trnka

2.1.1 Nature of Market Leadership

The company is an industry leader in proactive malware detection, offering the fastest and most effective antivirus program worldwide. It protects over 100 million users worldwide. The company has grown 524 % over the past 5 years, and was included in Gartner's 2009 Magic Quadrant for Endpoint Protection Platforms.

2.1.2 Nature of Competitive Advantage

The antivirus program ESET NOD32 is considered one of the fastest and most effective in the world. It holds the world record for the number of Virus Bulletin "VB100 Awards", given by a UK independent antivirus testing authority, and has never missed a single in-the-wild worm or virus since the testing began in 1998. Hence, the competitive advantage of this ICT company, as is typical in the ICT business, lies in its distinctive product; it is much more holistic than those of the competitors.

2.1.3 Core Lessons Learned on the Path to Business Success

1. Establish an open and inspiring culture in the company and use the creativity of enthusiastic people to discover new opportunities and ideas. In the case of ESET, what started as the brainchild of a few friends has evolved into an antivirus program considered one of the fastest and most effective in the world.
2. Be a strong and visionary leader, rely on your intuition and do not underestimate the continuity of leadership. *CRN*, a leading international IT trade magazine, has recognized ESET's CEO, Miroslav Trnka, as one of the most innovative managers in the field of information technology.
3. If you take the same path as everybody, you will not be different. It is better to find your own solutions that distinguish you from competitors—such as progressive technology or increased service quality.

2.1.4 ESET: Hidden Champion

Nowadays we would find it difficult to imagine our lives without the Internet, which has simplified communication enormously for both companies and individuals. For secure use of this popular medium, it is necessary to have our data and communication protected from viruses, spyware and other threats that rapidly propagate on the web. Perhaps you have noticed the eye-like NOD32 icon in your computer. This is the antivirus program developed by ESET.

Founded in 1992, ESET, is a leading Internet security provider for companies of all sizes, home users, and mobile phone users. With its global headquarters in Bratislava, and two research and development centers—in Bratislava and Krakow—ESET pioneered and continues to lead the industry in proactive threat detection.

Developing its activities through sales and distribution centres in Bratislava (EMEA), San Diego (North America), Buenos Aires (Latin America), and Singapore (APAC), the company has a presence in more than 180 countries and employs over 700 people worldwide.

ESET's leadership is evidenced by the fact that the company's flagship software protects over 100 million users worldwide. This translates into a growth of 524 % over the past 5 years. The consultancy firm Gartner's awarded the "2009 Magic Quadrant for Endpoint Protection Platforms" to ESET. In addition, this HC bears other distinctions, such as the greatest number of Virus Bulletin 100 awards since May 1998—the highest number of "Advanced+" ratings in retrospective testing.

ESET was nominated for Deloitte's Technology Fast 500 as one of the fastest-growing technology companies in the EMEA region.

The beginnings of ESET date back to 1987 when two young programming enthusiasts, Peter Paško and Miroslav Trnka, became aware of one of the world's first computer viruses. They dubbed it "Vienna" and wrote a program for its detection. Many other virus discoveries quickly followed, which sparked the idea to devise a universal software solution to counter what was then a relatively unknown computer threat. In 1992, together with their common friend Rudolf Hrubý, they formally established ESET as a privately owned limited liability company.

Their real success began some 10 years ago when they introduced an innovative technology called "proactive security". In lay terms, this technology enables swifter detection of the threat, which in turn significantly increases user protection. This is what has ensured ESET's leading position. From the user's point of view, this is an easy-to-use product that does not slow down the operating system, thanks to efficient programming.

ESET was the first company in the world to introduce this technology, and in 1997, with only 12 employees, it obtained its first award. Engineered for speed and stability, it fulfills the founders' vision to put advanced technology at the fingertips of the average PC user.

Throughout the company's expansion, the founders made it their mission to stay true to the principles underpinning the company's philosophy—responsibility, reliability and honesty. These, coupled with innovation, continue to be the driving force behind the company's success and growth.

ESET's market could be defined as "consumer endpoint security software", with households and small companies as the primary consumers. More than 100 million users worldwide, defined as the number of installations on hardware, along with product diffusiveness, makes the company a leader. ESET exports primarily to Bulgaria, Romania, Ukraine, Russia, Hungary, Slovenia, the Czech Republic, and Poland. In all these countries the company holds a leading market position. Its revenue in 2010 reached about 137 million euros.

From the beginning, the company has focused on foreign markets as exports were relatively easy because of the specific character of the service. Currently, exports represent about 97 % of total sales. However, the ownership structure of ESET is completely different to that of their competitors. Its owners are six or seven physical entities, whereas most other Internet security companies are backed by foreign capital. In ESET's own words, it is probably the smallest company in the pack, with 700 employees, including those at the US subsidiary.

ESET's competitive advantage lies in the innovative technology of proactive security and its light footprint on the system. In an effort to maintain the rate of innovation, the company updates its products in 2-year cycles.

The company invests approximately 20 % of its average income in research and development. As in any fast-moving industry, market trends and changes (e.g. the shift from desktop computers towards tablets and secondary devices) need to be seen not as disruptive, but as the main drivers of innovation. However, the nature of the product enables ESET to innovate and keep its strong position without huge financial investments. Thanks to a sustained generation of new ideas, a motivated and highly qualified workforce, visionary leaders with intuition, and a sense of continuity, ESET can continue holding its position of a HC despite new challenges in the market.

2.2 ACE Enterprise Slovakia

Overview

Address:	Antolská 4, 85107 Bratislava, Slovakia
Tel:	+421269201111; +421902373220
Email:	alexc@ace-eprise.com
Web:	http://www.ace-eprise.com

Company Information

Industry:	Computer programming, consultancy and related activities
Year of establishment:	2004
Sales revenues in 2010:	€1 million
Sales revenues in 2000:	€200,000
Average number of employees in 2010:	30
Brain(s) behind the company:	CEO and founder Alex Cimbaľák

2.2.1 Nature of Market Leadership

ACE Enterprise Slovakia is a market leader in modern integration of information systems for utilities, in modern intelligent metering solutions and PDA applications for inspections and maintenance of utility networks, as well as worldwide professional consulting in this area. This is a unique technology for quick modeling of central integration hubs and generating complete professional applications for metering and maintenance support over existing systems, mainly SAP.

2.2.2 Nature of Competitive Advantage

The success of ACE Enterprise is based on the fact that it simplifies and integrates control of various complex systems without the need for special knowledge; clients can use them without the expertise of dedicated consultancies. This innovative approach has earned ACE Enterprise several awards worldwide.

2.2.3 Core Lessons Learned on the Path to Business Success

1. While a lot of businesses struggle under the impact of the economic crisis, some are able to grow despite what others perceive as a threat. In times of crisis, companies start to assess their situation more carefully, trying to find more effective solutions. ACE Enterprise can supply those solutions with efficiency. Think outside your industry's traditional borders, and when the market is saturated, develop your own niche by creatively resolving customer problems.
2. Use the know-how of your people, motivate them, involve them in the processes, give them responsibilities and trust, and let them participate. Reduce the distance between managers and employees. Build the company as a hobby for your employees and as their mission. Appreciate the creative contribution of the employees, not their ranking in the organization hierarchy.
3. Listen to your customers—what they do and what their current problems are—and then try to resolve their problems as part of their daily routine. Speak simply with clients about sophisticated issues. In this way, you will become a natural partner to the customer and make management decisions simpler. ACE tries to offer not only solutions that are suitable for today's problems but also the technology to enable resolution of future challenges. Do not be afraid to be different and a little bit controversial while presenting your product.

2.2.4 ACE Enterprise Slovakia: Hidden Champion

ACE Enterprise Slovakia is a market leader in modern integration of information systems for utility companies, modern solutions of intelligent metering and PDA applications for inspection and maintenance of utility networks, as well as worldwide professional consulting in this area. It has developed a unique technology for quick modeling of central integration hubs and generating complete professional applications for metering and maintenance support over existing systems, mainly SAP. For this purpose, ACE has created a group of software products that are used by a large number of utility companies. There are some 11,500 information systems in existence, and ACE Enterprise is able to interconnect all of them by using SAP. This innovative approach provided the company with a rapidly growing customer base as well as a number of international awards.

ACE Enterprise Slovakia is one of the younger HCs. It was established in 2004 and currently employs a team of only 30 people. However, since the very beginning the company has been showing great progress, and now has customers from 4 continents and 50 countries worldwide. At present, the company's annual sales are approaching 1.0 million euros.

When asked about the secret to the rapid growth of his business, owner Alex Cimbaľák gives a surprising answer: "The crisis!" While other companies have been dealing with the impact of the financial downturn, ACE Enterprise was able to expand in the unfavorable market. Before the crunch, corporations generally possessed enough financial resources, which meant that they had no incentive to seek effective solutions, cost saving, or fast implementation. But when trying to deal with the fallout of the crisis, many of these firms started paying more attention to efficiency and speed. Foreseeing this trend, ACE Enterprise has been able to meet their needs very effectively.

Since this HC is operating in a specific niche, while disregarding traditional IT industry borders, it is quite difficult to pinpoint its direct competitors; in each industry sector it faces someone else. ACE Enterprise has been able to carve out a part of the market under-served by established giants, such as SAP or Accenture. This company has never sold any licencee other than for its own products. It exports Slovak know-how.

Interestingly, from its beginning to 2007, the company served only foreign customers. The share of domestic clients has now grown, but exports still represent 70–75 % of total sales, of which 50 % is destined for Western Europe, especially for German clients. As evidence that a small company can win big customers, ACE counts firms such as Bentley, EON, Cotemar, Kelag, Philips, VW, Anglian Water, Hexal, enviaM, Siemens Drives, Bewag, and Baumit among its clients.

The value offered by ACE Enterprise is based on a user-friendly and highly customizable technology: ACE can provide 300 types of solutions on the same base throughout all customer branches. It can deliver within hours, as opposed to the weeks that its competitors need. Part of the secret is that the company incurs lower costs than its competition, while being able to deliver more speedily. The company invests a large proportion of its income in research and development, preferring investment in further growth to shares.

The energetic founder and owner, Alex Cimbaľák, is the engine of the company. He strongly believes in innovations and the need to detect market trends early on. He places customer requirements above everything else. In addition, he is a believer in people's abilities, and, strives to enable others to participate in decision-making. Moreover, he works together with universities, trying to inspire and interest young people in entrepreneurship by sharing his experiences and supporting students from abroad, which is not yet very common at Slovak companies.

In its 7-year existence, ACE Enterprise has been the most frequently internationally awarded company in Slovakia.[1] In 2011, it was awarded "Best IT project in Europe", and also won "Executive of the Year—Computer Software" in the International Business Awards. The company's ambition for continuous improvement makes it well-positioned for further growth.

[1] ACE is the winner of the International Quality Summit Award (IQS), New York, 2011: "BID considers ACE Enterprise Slovakia to be a model of excellence as a leading company in quality achievement; the company's orientation towards constant innovation, its customer-focused strategies and the ambition for continuous improvement through TQM have led to outstanding expansion. In this way, it has established itself as a prevailing enterprise, obtaining a highly-esteemed position in its field".

2.3 Sygic

Overview

Address:	Námestie 1. Mája 18, 811 06 Bratislava, Slovakia
Tel:	+421905489476
Email:	info@sygic.com
Web:	http://www.sygic.com

Company Information

Industry:	Manufacturer of computer, electronic, and optical products
Year of establishment:	2004
Sales revenue in 2010:	€6.2 million
Sales revenue in 2000:	n/a
Average number of employees in 2010:	70
Brain(s) behind the company:	CEO and founder Michal Štencl

2.3.1 Nature of Market Leadership

Sygic is a global leader in providing navigation systems for a wide range of mobile operating platforms. The company is set up to support virtually any upcoming operating system. Sygic is the only company in the world to supply a software development kit for the Android platform. The company holds its strongest positions in Australia and Southeast Asia, and is reaching markets in Brazil and India. In CEE, Sygic is number two. Sygic has been awarded the title of fastest growing young IT company in Slovakia. It was the first company to release turn-by-turn navigation for iPhone in 2008, Android (2008), Nokia (2009), and Bada phones (2010).

2.3.2 Nature of Competitive Advantage

The company holds a distinctive innovative capability in the area of navigation software. This capability has resulted in Sygic becoming the first company to combine car navigation, pedestrian navigation, and social network all in one application. It is also among the first to be able to integrate a navigation plug-in into its mobile IT solutions.

2.3.3 Core Lessons Learned on the Path to Business Success

1. You must monitor customer feedback and reflect demand. Sygic listens to the voices of its customers through several channels, such as Facebook and Twitter. And you must fulfill the market needs that you discover: Sygic has implemented real-time traffic service, pedestrian navigation, wiki city guides, and further

features based on market needs. According to the founder, if you create something so sophisticated, there is a probability that the competition will not follow you.
2. The success of the company is often based on the abilities of the founder. At Sygic, the founders have had a passion for programming since childhood—one of them wrote his first code at age 6. The CEO, Michal Štencl, strongly believes in his team. This, as well as his open-mindedness for new projects and ideas, strong and charismatic knowledge of the market, and unique networking abilities, have helped him build this successful HC.
3. If there is a threat of crisis, you should be able to revise your current business model. Sygic changed the model of delivering software to partners and added a new one—sale to final customers through the web portals and online marketplaces of Apple (AppStore) or Microsoft (Windows Market Place), utilizing the advantages of both.

2.3.4 Sygic: Hidden Champion

It is perhaps no surprise that most of the home-grown innovators in Slovakia compete in industries that require little up-front investment in infrastructure. As most of the established companies are backed by foreign capital, and initial financing of production and distribution infrastructure is not easy to come by, the majority of HCs in Slovakia are likely to operate in industries that do not require large quantities of capital to set up operations. As with the two previous champions, this also holds true for Sygic.

Sygic's major competitive advantages are based on flexibility and navigation expertise: intuitive user interface, fast rendering and route calculation, low demand on processors and memory, automatic adaptation to the screen, and—above all—a multiplatform engine. The application is thus meant to start quickly and run smoothly on any device. Sygic delivers its GPS software worldwide in more than 30 languages, working together with local map providers to support maps for all regions.

The company was founded in 2004 and currently employs 70 people, but its products already have over a million users worldwide. Within 3 years, Sygic earned the title of fastest growing young IT company in Slovakia, while it ranked among the top-two or top-six IT companies in CEE according to a study by Deloitte Fast 50.

While Sygic is a technologically advanced and innovative company with a strong brand presence on the market, it does not compete with the big multinationals in turnover or sales volume; the company's total turnover was 6.2 million euros in 2010. In CEE Sygic is the second largest local supplier, while the market is dominated by suppliers from the Netherlands, Germany and the United States. The only larger local company in this market is NavNGo, based in Hungary.

However, Sygic brings new features ahead of competitors because its organizational structure allows for flexibility, fast decisions, and implementation of ideas. Sygic navigation applications are sold on the mass market for mobile phones. The company also has a dedicated section to take care of business customers who can integrate navigation into their IT solutions.

Sygic has contributed to market change in a number of areas. It has the largest platform compatibility on the market. The software can run on mobile devices with less powerful processors, which makes it available for a wide range of handsets.

Sygic started exporting within 2 years of the company's incorporation. Current exports represent approximately 99 % of total sales. Of course, it is not straightforward to define a geographical export region since the products compete globally—through app stores, on-line distribution, as well as manufacturers and distributors of mobile hardware. Approximately 40 % of average income is re-invested in research and development.

In 2010, Ernst & Young awarded the title of "Entrepreneur of the Year in Slovakia" to CEO Michal Štencl. A background in economics and a strong networking ability has made him very knowledgeable about the market that he is active in.

Mr. Štencl founded the company together with another IT and mobile technology enthusiast, Viliam Sameliak. The former was developing a new operating system; the latter was the owner of a company that developed mobile devices. They decided to merge their interests, and while trying to integrate the new OS with a mobile device, they had the idea to create a platform-independent navigation system.

However, the road to the Sygic brand was not straightforward. Having established a direction, they had to pick a name that would fit, be instantly recognizable, look good in writing, and sound good in any language. In addition, the new name should not generate irrelevant Google hits—this would ensure that potential customers do not associate the name with any other brand. This shows that Sygic realized the need for international growth and expansion from the start. In other words, this is no accidental HC.

Mr. Štencl suggests that one of the strong competitive advantages that the company has is paying close attention to customer feedback. Sygic makes it easy for its customers to communicate with it via its website (Facebook, Twitter, or email). This in turns allows it to meet market needs more quickly and precisely, and fulfill its vision of bringing high-quality navigation software to every user, no matter what the platform.

2.4 Media Control

Overview

Address:	Stará Vajnorská 37/C, 83104 Bratislava, Slovakia
Tel:	+421220862104
Email:	mediacontrol@mediacontrol.sk
Web:	http://www.mediacontrol.sk

Company Information

Industry:	Electrical, plumbing, and other construction installation activities; specialized design activities; manufacture of consumer electronics
Year of establishment:	2004
Sales revenue in 2010:	€2 million
Sales revenue in 2000:	n/a
Average number of employees in 2010:	8 own, and 2 external
Brain(s) behind the company:	CEO and founder Mário Lelovský

2.4.1 Nature of Market Leadership

Media Control is one of the leading providers of products for integrating all ICT systems in the household into one holistic system. The company has won several awards including "Demonstrating Intelligent Low-Energy House—iDOM" in the InAVation Awards for the EMEA region (Europe, Middle East, and Africa) in the category of Best Project in Small and Medium Residential Objects, as well as an award for Best Energy Project in 2007.

2.4.2 Nature of Competitive Advantage

In the business of "intelligent buildings" one can usually find two areas of competing technology. The first provides heating, cooling, ventilation, and lights. These are usually business-to-business deals, like those of Siemens and ABB. The second type of technology is for audio-visual entertainment, usually for individual consumers. Media Control was the first company to integrate both systems into one product.

2.4.3 Core Lessons Learned on the Path to Business Success

1. Make life simpler for customers. Media Control does not deliver technical devices but comprehensive, intelligent solutions for households, enabling customers to use just one central control unit for everything—control of lights, heat, sound, screen, security, and so forth.
2. Enable customers to experience products in an extraordinary way. Media Control's sales premises consist of a living room with a comfortable sofa and hot coffee, where the whole family can fully immerse itself into a futuristic audio and video experience. Be available and in close touch with your customers while trying to identify and fulfill their requirements, and deliver the products that meet these requirements.
3. Continuously develop new innovative products. What sounds like science fiction today could possibly be commonplace in the household in the next few years. Focus on alternative resources, and be environmentally friendly and responsible. Media Control won a special prize for its innovative approach to solutions for

high-standard households aiming to exploit renewable energy sources. An intelligent house (iDOM) is heated and cooled exclusively from renewable resources, and is effective because it also adapts to external conditions.

2.4.4 Media Control: Hidden Champion

Imagine that you are away from home, with just one device in your hand, such as your cell phone, but you would like your bath or sauna to be warmed up before you return. Maybe you forgot the lights on, or the iron is still plugged in. Or imagine your house adapting to external conditions by itself: when the sun is too strong, the house lowers its blinds. And when the system calculates that it is more effective for the sunlight to heat the house, it repositions the blinds to let more light in. If you live in an intelligent house, this is not a dream.

The term "intelligent house" has been used for decades to describe a dwelling with a system that integrates and manages all cooperating technologies in a residential unit. It means just one control system, not only for basic services—heating, cooling, lights, ventilation, electrical wiring, and gas mains—but also for other household devices and services, such as kitchen and entertainment appliances, telecommunications, security devices (cameras and automatic door openers) and sprinklers. Instead of many remote controls—one for the TV, one for the DVD player, and another for the window shades—you have just one for everything. Intelligent buildings integrate all systems to provide better comfort and security for their occupants. Currently, energy optimization and exploitation of alternative energy sources represents a unique approach in systems integration. In 2006, Mário Lelovský, co-owner of Media Control, built an intelligent house in Bratislava to live in and demonstrate what it could do.

There are not enough data to estimate the size of the market of integrated control systems. In this field you can usually find two kinds of competitors. The first focus on the technological aspects of building maintenance—heating, cooling, ventilation systems, and lights. The second kind is more oriented towards private customers and offers audio-visual entertainment solutions, media centres, integrated music, video systems, and so forth. The specific competitive advantage of Media Control is that this company provides integration of yet un-integrated parts: the utility and the fun element. As the competition usually focuses exclusively on either the first or second element, it cannot normally connect them.

The first company to achieve that connection was Media Control. It "integrated-the-integration" into one product around four main axes: low energy consumption, fun, ecology and security. Also, as there is a general preference for local suppliers, it is one of only few companies active globally in this sector. The preference for local providers comes from the language barriers and customers' desire to have a completely customized product.

In addition to their usual unwillingness to waste time or money, Media Control's customers are increasingly interested in benefiting fully from their free time. Media Control makes life simpler for the client by integrating everything within one platform. Hence, it has made manipulation of all attributes so much simpler for the user. Media Control does not deliver just technical devices, but rather complete intelligent solutions to enable customers to conduct routine operations, such as controlling lights, heat, sound, screen, or security, from one central unit. With full integration, the costs of operating an intelligent house are significantly lower. Many of Media Control's intelligent houses are based exclusively on renewable resources. Although this represents a capital outlay, a return on investment is achieved within 10 years.

In 2007, Media Control won an InAVation Award for the EMEA region in the category of "Best Project in Small and Medium Residential Objects" out of 100 entries. This was a significant turning point not just in the history of the company, but also because it was the first time a firm from the former Communist Bloc had outshined traditional competitors from Germany and the United Kingdom.

Media Control was founded in 2004 and despite its relatively short history it has shown very interesting results. The story began when Mario Lelovský, co-owner of an AV distribution company, along with programmer Zoran Lazik, decided to sell high-tech residential technology and home automation on the Slovak market. Media Control was formed and dedicated to developing and offering complete solutions for the affluent. Like some other HCs mentioned previously, this is a small company with eight internal and two external employees. In comparison, a British competitor employs over 100 people. The company's total turnover was 1.112 million euros in 2009 and 775,000 euros in 2010. Approximately 20 % of the income is invested in research and development.

Selling this product requires the establishment of long and close relationships with customers. Because a purchase of this product is an important decision, clients need to have confidence in it and the provider. When making a decision, customers need a lot of information about the product, and every client requires unique and precise customization. Because systems are personalized for each particular customer, the experience of the team and their ability to respond to individual requirements are very important.

The leaders of the company motivate their colleagues with a friendly, humane approach, but also by finding new challenges and dealing with them. The company's mission is to enlarge its existing range of services and seek new solutions. It takes an environmentally friendly approach, and the leaders are responsible and visionary. Excited by new ideas, such as adaptive or self-learning systems and artificial intelligence, this is a company that employs cutting-edge technological solutions for the sake of their clients and the environment.

2.5 Grand Power

Overview

Address:	Poľovnícka 29, Šalková 974 01 Banská Bystrica, Slovakia
Tel:	+421484148753
Email:	jaroslav.kuracina@grandpower.eu
Web:	http://www.grandpower.eu

Company Information

Industry:	Manufacture of weapons and ammunition
Year of establishment:	2000
Sales revenue in 2010:	€2.9 million
Sales revenue in 2000:	n/a
Average number of employees in 2010:	47
Brain(s) behind the company:	CEO and founder Jaroslav Kuracina

2.5.1 Nature of Market Leadership

Grand Power designs and produces novel firearms and solutions related to firearms, and holds a significant market share in Russia, the EU, and the US, where it has international patents.

2.5.2 Nature of Competitive Advantage

The company produces high-quality gun products. Its competitive advantage lies in the ability to continuously come up with novel ideas and solutions. For example, its K100 gun has a unique, patent-protected locking system based on a locked rotating barrel. This type of locking mechanism ensures more comfortable shooting. The kick towards the shooter's arm after firing is considerably reduced in comparison to other guns of a similar calibre.

2.5.3 Core Lessons Learned on the Path to Business Success

1. To achieve success you must be a somewhat cheeky and stubborn person. At the beginning, Jaroslav Kuracina, the founder and owner of the company had a hard time with banks. They said that an idea and a patent were not enough. When he submitted his first patent, he was "considered a fool". But some 12 years later, he is the one who has reason to laugh, since even the FBI uses his K100 and his business has grown despite the crisis.
2. You should have passion for what you are doing, and have a vision. "Pistols are not only guns, they are toys for big children", Jaroslav Kuracina claims. He inherited his passion for guns from his grandfather, who was a guerilla in World War II. Mr. Kuracina drew a picture of his first gun while still in his teens. He kept on drawing during his university studies and continued towards his dream until success came.
3. Expansion of technology comes hand in hand with investments in employee training and education. Apart from the high level of technical expertise, which allows one to offer products of the highest quality, you must offer reliability and meet all requirements regarding the industrial security and codification of your products. Grand Power holds the Contractor Industrial Security Certificate (the confidentiality level of inside information), issued by the National Security Office. Protect your products by patents, utility models, and trademarks.

2.5.4 Grand Power: Hidden Champion

If you visit the premises of Grand Power you will see a modern, flourishing company, employing 47 people. The most popular models, produced in more than 2,000 pieces a month, are T10, STI GP6, K100, MK6, and GP 6C. The leadership of Grand Power, the only company in Slovakia designing and producing guns, is based not only on market figures but also on high quality, continuously reflected in the company's newly-developed and patented products. These weapons are exported mostly to Russia, the USA, and the EU. This is quite unique in Slovakia where the overall number of patents is very low.

The company was founded in 2000 as a corporation, and by 2010 had achieved revenues of around 2.9 million euros. The technological development and capital intensity of the manufacturing process are very high, and the company invests around 10 % of average income in research and development. As the Slovak market is very small, the company started developing its exporting activities from the very beginning of its existence. Current exports represent approximately 89 % of total sales. As in the case of other HCs, Grand Power considers close relationships with its customers as crucial. While price may not play a very important role in the decision-making process for customers, the quality of the product is extremely important.

To guarantee the reliability of its products, Grand Power adheres to all the requirements regarding industrial security and codification. The company holds the Contractor Industrial Security Certificate, issued by the National Security Office. The company can therefore provide technical services to customers who require a high level of confidentiality. Grand Power has also been granted a NATO Commercial and Governmental Entity Code (NCAGE) given to producers, suppliers and organizations. This system codifies products to achieve maximum effectiveness of national and international logistical support, and help to manage information regarding supplies.

Building new production facilities and a shooting range are priorities for the future. The company's technology comes hand in hand with that, as well as investment in employee training and education. Despite the recession, Grand Power has been flourishing. "The demand, especially from the USA and Russia, has risen significantly since the recession started", Mr. Kuracina says. He adds that this trend is likely to persist and he is hoping to continue raising output.

2.6 Kvety.sk

Overview

Address: Kriváň 351, 962 04 Kriváň, Slovakia
Tel: +421455249236
Email: ocenas@kvety.sk
Web: http://www.kvety.sk

Company Information

Industry:	Retail sale of flowers via mail-order houses or Internet.
Year of establishment:	1999
Sales revenue in 2010:	€1.3 million
Sales revenue in 2000:	€0.2 million
Average number of employees in 2010:	25
Brain(s) behind the company:	CEO and founder Miroslav Očenáš

2.6.1 Nature of Market Leadership

The company operates in a very specific industry—delivery of flowers ordered over the Internet. This market is mainly created by customers from other countries (110 countries), usually emigrants, and people with some connection with Slovakia. It can be defined as a premium market with exclusive products in the area of flower delivery and gifts. While it is difficult to measure some of the company's markets globally, it holds 60 % of the Slovak market whereas its closest competitor has a 10 % market share.

2.6.2 Nature of Competitive Advantage

The company provides specific advantages to its customers, including a guarantee that what they see advertized is what they get. Through customization, the company is able to fulfill the customers' whims and provide an exclusive high-level service in comparison with its competitors. Kvety.sk's main innovations include a trend-setting concept, economies of scale, and application of constraint theory. However, at a deeper level, the core advantage lies in the design of an effective distribution system. The company bypasses many of the mediators involved in the industry value chain, who all try to appropriate some of the pie. Furthermore, the company does not bear the fixed costs related to retail shops.

2.6.3 Core Lessons Learned on the Path to Business Success

1. Design an effective and simple distribution system. This company operates from a small village under the Slovak mountains and has a system of owner-operated couriers for deliveries. Kvety.sk leases plantations in developing countries and flowers are flown in fresh by airfreight, not sourced from local flower suppliers as competing companies usually do.
2. A close and trusting relationship between customer and company is crucial because 80 % of payments are via credit card, with all service guarantees. If the company fails to satisfy the customer, there is no second chance.
3. To grow further, invest in customer analysis. The company has developed its own system for monitoring the efficiency of access and purchases. It collects all statistics including the Internet addresses of visitors and customers, which enables it to advertise more effectively. Marketing is a very strong tool in this sector.

2.6.4 Kvety.sk: Hidden Champion

Whom do you turn to if you want to delight your VIP customer abroad with high-quality alcohol or luxury deserts? Or simply send a birthday gift of flowers to your mother who lives in another country? This is the domain of Kvety.sk, which operates in a very specific industry: a flower delivery service and Internet sales of supplementary products.

It is customers with some connection to Slovakia who create the market, but the latter extends to about 110 countries on all continents. This niche is very specific and can be defined as a premium market with exclusive products in the area of delivery of flowers and presents. Measuring global market share is hard, but in Slovakia this company holds 60 % of the market while the closest competitor has only 10 %. There are companies from Germany (Valentins.de and Florito.de) who are approximately five times larger and deliver low-cost bouquets (as opposed to kvety.sk's higher-end offering) but they compete only indirectly with a completely different business model; therefore any comparison somewhat loses its relevance. The company provides a guarantee for its customers that the recipient will be given the product exactly as it is seen on the webpage. Moreover, atypical requirements can be fulfilled through customization. In comparison with its competitors, the company provides exclusivity and a wide range of services.

Kvety.sk was founded in 1999 as a physical entity and in 2006 a limited liability company was established. It is small, currently employing only 25 people. Everything is conducted from one place, the village of Kriváň. Specific characteristics, in comparison with the competition, include co-operation with couriers, the use of the company's own product boxes, and imports of flowers from developing countries. ITo keep costs down and ensure maximum product standardization, Kvety.sk leases plantations and has the flowers delivered by air.

Kvety.sk has pioneered the market model where the customer who orders and pays for the product is not necessarily its recipient. In a market where 90 % of online purchases are paid with cash on delivery, this means that there is a huge level of trust in the company. It serves around 37,000 customers, paying an average of 42.35 euros per order. Currently, exports represent 10 % of sales. The company has expanded into foreign markets only recently, but sales are growing. The export numbers should be higher but the company currently faces a lack of resources for future expansion abroad. Total turnover is approximately 1.3 million euros and its growth is around 10–20 % per year.

Around 10–15 % of income is invested in research and development. Close relationships with customers are crucial to gain and maintain trust in the product and the company. CEO, Miroslav Očenáš, is very goal-oriented and admits that apart from innovation, endurance plays a very important role. He also believes in supporting students and sharing his experiences and knowledge at universities. The company is strong in marketing and advertising because of its their knowledge of the market and innovative advertising strategies. A proprietary system that monitors online access by visitors and purchasing statistics allows more effective tailoring of advertising campaigns.

While growth, especially abroad, is significantly restrained by lack of finances, the company still envisages further progress. Kvety.sk has the potential to become a regular HC.

Conclusion

For a small economy that has undergone massive transformation from a Soviet-style, centrally-planned and state-owned system, Slovakia possesses a surprisingly high number of HCs. Because of the characteristics of the market and the population, these are all very young companies, with the oldest of them in only their second decade of existence. This contrasts sharply with the HCs of Western Europe that are, on the whole, established companies with significant experience.

Another difference, of course, is that none of the Slovak HCs are family-owned and managed. In part, this is because their existence has been too short for generational change to occur. Also, the communist system only allowed state-owned companies; therefore this kind of continuity was impossible due to the non-existence of private ownership. It will take some time for the tradition of family-managed enterprises to emerge in post-communist countries.

Broadly speaking, we could divide the Slovak HCs into two groups—those in capital-heavy industries, and those that operate in niches that do not require significant upfront investment. Like their German counterparts, the members of the first group operate in manufacturing, machinery or construction. These companies take advantage of a well-educated and motivated workforce, which is nevertheless not as expensive to maintain as that in Western European countries. And because these companies strive to offer high-quality products, they can also successfully compete with their lower-cost competitors, located mostly in Asian. The latter may profit from even lower production costs, but are usually unable to match the quality or the customer service that Slovak HCs are able to offer.

The companies that operate in industries not requiring a heavy upfront investment underline even more the importance of a well-qualified workforce. These companies usually provide services or non-material products, such as software. It is therefore crucial for them to provide very good customer service and assure clients of the reliability of their products. Again, having access to a pool of educated workers helps these and all similar companies to flourish in Slovakia.

Three traits that Slovak companies share with HCs around the world are a relentless focus on innovation, a continuing pursuit of the high quality of their products, and the business-to-business service model. We know that the business-to-business market is particularly demanding in terms of product quality, value for money, and customer service. That these companies continue to develop and grow in this environment is a testimony to the competitiveness of their products in all three areas.

In these Slovak HCs we see dreams come true for a handful of ingenious and relentless individuals. In many cases, the leaders of these companies had no special preparation for their role as managers and CEOs. Often, they trained for something other than what ended up being the object of their business. This is additional evidence that while market capitalism is young in Slovakia, it is dynamic and rewards innovation. Slovak HCs are playing a role whose importance goes beyond commercial success—they are home-bred proof that imagination and resourcefulness will be rewarded.

References

Daborowski, T. (2011). *Slovakia's economic success and the global crisis*. Centre for Eastern Studies. http://www.osw.waw.pl/en/eksperci/tomasz-daborowski

Národná Banka Slovenska. (2010). *Annual report 2010*. http://www.nbs.sk

Uramová, M., & Kožiak, R. (2008). Regional disparities in Slovakia from the aspect of average nominal wage. *E+M Ekonomie a management, 11*(2), 6–17.

World Bank. (2013). *Data; countries and economies*. http://data.worldbank.org/country

Hidden Champions of Slovenia

Melita Balas Rant

Overview

Official name:	Republic of Slovenia
Type of government:	Parliamentary Democratic Republic
Population in 2011:	2,052,843
Land area:	20,140 km^2

History

1918	After the collapse of the Austro-Hungarian Empire, Slovenia joins the Kingdom of Serbs, Croats and Slovenes.
1929	The kingdom becomes known as Yugoslavia.
1941	Slovenia is occupied by Nazi Germany and Italy during World War II.
1945	At the end of the war, Slovenia becomes a constituent republic of socialist Yugoslavia.
1989	The Slovene parliament confirms the right of the country to secede from the Yugoslav Federation.
1991	Slovenia, along with Croatia, declares its independence. The Yugoslav federal army intervenes. Slovene forces defend the country. About 100 people killed. The EU brokers a ceasefire. The Yugoslav army withdraws.
1992	The EU recognizes Slovenia's independence, followed by the US. Slovenia joins the United Nations. First parliamentary and presidential elections in the newly independent country.
1993	Slovenia joins the International Monetary Fund.

M. Balas Rant (✉)
Department of Management and Organization, Faculty of Economics, University of Ljubljana, Ljubljana, Slovenia
e-mail: melita.balas.rant@ef.uni-lj.si

P. McKiernan and D. Purg (eds.), *Hidden Champions in CEE and Turkey*, 357
DOI 10.1007/978-3-642-40504-4_21, © Springer-Verlag Berlin Heidelberg 2013

2004 (March) Slovenia admitted to NATO.
2004 (May) Slovenia is 1 of 10 new states to join the EU.
2007 (January) Slovenia adopts the single European currency, the euro.
2008 (January) Slovenia takes over the EU presidency.

1 Introduction: Context

Slovenia has a small and open economy. In 2010 it was the 86th largest in the world with a GDP per person of 17,559 US dollars (Wikipedia 2010). Two million inhabitants live in an area of 20.140 km^2 squeezed between Italy, Austria, Hungary and Croatia. For a small country, exporting is an important way of reaching economies of scale. Despite of the country's openness, the majority of Slovenia's companies still remain small. Less than 1 % of them earn more than 4.5 million euros (Statistical Office of the Republic of Slovenia 2010).

To provide a backdrop for its economic history, I focus on those eighteenth and nineteenth century institutional arrangements that have had the strongest impact on Slovenia's economic development. In the nineteenth century, Slovenia was a part of the Austro-Hungarian Empire and primarily agrarian (Lazarević and Pančur 2010). The first savings bank was established in 1820. In the mid-nineteenth century, an agrarian reform was introduced allowing ordinary people to own land. This can be seen as the first mass privatization of Slovenia. At the same time, the Vienna-Trieste railroad opened up the country to broader competition. However, the lack of international competitiveness contributed to a deep and long-lasting depression, which resulted in slow, yet persistent transformation of the society towards industrialization and urbanization (Lazarevič 2009).

Slavic identification, as well as low standards of living, pushed Slovenia to unite with Serbia and Croatia. So, in 1918 a country of Serbs, Croats and Slovenes was formed, later renamed Yugoslavia. It was characterized by a socialist federalist arrangement in which Slovenia was the most technologically and industrially advanced republic in terms of GDP per person and exports. Slovenia has always exported to the West and hence served as a provider of foreign exchange currency for Yugoslavia. However, Slovenia was severely shaken by the 1929 banking system collapse in the USA, albeit with a time lag of 18 months, when Creditanstalt went bankrupt (Abramovič 2008). Exports and industrial production were reduced to a minimum. The crisis was most strongly felt in the agrarian sector, which was critically indebted.

During the Yugoslav era, Slovenian industry was celebrated and respected by many. Its well-educated and highly productive work force, systematic centrally-planned investments in heavy and light industry, as well as its strategic geographic position, contributed a great deal to the international competitiveness of many Slovenian companies. Already at that time, Slovenia produced some Hidden Champions (HCs), some of which are still around.

In particular, Slovenia was endowed with a set of high-profile companies in the industrial segment, especially in the engineering and automotive sectors, which were able to compete successfully on foreign markets and enjoy the benefits of economy of scale. Some of these companies like Fotona, Gorenje, successors of Iskra, are still major exporters today. In general, these companies were never particularly large compared to those of the USA or Western Europe (Purg 2010). They were mainly orientated towards Western Europe and still have a presence there. In the last decade, after the Western Balkans stabilized, Slovenian trade was successfully re-established in these markets. In general, the core exporting geography for Slovenian companies remains in Central and Eastern Europe.

However, in former Yugoslavia the development of trade, finance, tourism and transport was constrained as companies in those sectors were not used to dealing with foreign markets. After 1991, the immediate effect of separation from Yugoslavia was far from positive. The unemployment rate went up from 29,000 in 1989, to 130,000 in 1993. Workers organized more than 200 strikes in 1992 (Jamer 2010). However, after 1995 all underdeveloped economic segments, together with the construction industry, started blooming and hence contributed considerably to the economic growth of Slovenia. Apart from retail and transport, these sectors have remained domestically focused. Benefiting from macroeconomic stability and a favorable foreign debt position, Slovenia earned a high credit rating and was welcomed as a full EU member state in May 2004.

Nonetheless, the openness of its economy along with the under-developed industry, made Slovenia extremely sensitive to the economic cycles of its main trading partners, particularly Germany. Despite this, Slovenia successfully bypassed the economic slowdown in Europe in 2001–2003. However, the country was less fortunate during the 2008–2009 recession. Before 2008, Slovenia's GDP grew 2 % above the EU average, while after 2008 it dropped to 2 % below. In particular, GDP per capita shrunk by 8.7 % in 2009, which was the biggest fall in the European Union after the Baltic countries and Finland. The drop in Slovenian competitiveness was steep. In the IMD global competitiveness ranking for year 2010 Slovenia plummeted from number 32 to 52. In the World Economic Forum competitiveness ranking for the same year the drop was less severe but still significant, from 37 to 45.

The main reason for reduced competitiveness was the rise in labour costs. According to Eurostat, the labour costs index of Slovenia relative to the EU average was 84 in 2005. By 2010, this index had risen to 108, making Slovenia less able to compete internationally in labour-intensive industries. As a result, the labour intensive textiles and leather industries, once so significant in Yugoslavia, have experienced negative growth rates for a decade.

The recession in Slovenia was mainly due to a focus on domestic sectors such as construction, financial service, and trade (Wikipedia 2010). Yet, export-oriented companies, such as those in the automotive and industrial equipment sectors, also suffered because of reduced demand in 2008–2009. These sectors regained their sales strength in 2010 with many automotive companies posting near-record results. Still, this is hardly a cause for celebration since demand was largely created by

Exhibit 1 Core economic indicators

	1999	2000	2001	2002	2003	2004	2005	2006	2007	2008	2009	2010	2011
GDP per capita (current $US)	11,250.22	10,045.36	10,290.32	11,599.90	14,607.20	16,944.19	17,854.64	19,405.93	23,441.00	27,015.08	24,051.04	22,897.94	24,141.94
GDP per capita growth (annual %)	5.25	3.96	2.78	3.70	2.87	4.33	3.83	5.51	6.27	3.43	−8.84	0.94	−0.34
Long-term unemployment (% of total unemployment)	n/a	n/a	n/a	55.60	52.80	51.50	47.30	49.30	45.70	42.20	30.10	43.30	44.20
Foreign direct investment, net inflows (% of GDP)	0.48	0.68	2.46	7.17	1.03	2.46	2.72	1.77	3.98	3.34	−0.71	1.35	1.65
GDP (current $USm)	22,309.68	19,979.47	20,498.93	23,136.35	29,152.07	33,837.75	35,717.73	38,945.15	47,306.80	54,606.02	49,056.15	46,908.33	49,539.27
Exports of goods and services (current $USm)	10,536.64	10,728.77	11,311.74	12,743.05	15,683.06	19,561.23	22,208.56	25,914.29	32,905.34	36,663.79	28,643.63	30,689.63	35,815.26
Exports of goods and services (% of GDP)	47.23	53.70	55.18	55.08	53.80	57.81	62.18	66.54	69.56	67.14	58.39	65.42	72.30
Merchandise exports (current $USm)	8,560.08	8,769.77	9,266.57	10,365.68	12,765.55	16,361.37	19,247.72	23,229.87	30,101.74	34,127.71	26,177.19	29,200.27	34,730.82
Merchandise exports to high-income	86.40	85.00	83.92	82.07	82.41	81.71	80.40	79.94	78.46	76.69	78.06	79.35	n/a

economies (% of total merchandise exports)													
Merchandise exports to developing economies in Europe & Central Asia (% of total merchandise exports)	11.30	12.43	13.70	15.44	15.12	15.95	16.40	16.77	18.46	19.34	17.38	16.19	n/a
Ores and metals exports (% of merchandise exports)	3.78	4.21	4.26	3.75	3.73	4.16	4.44	5.49	5.14	4.12	3.29	4.42	4.76
Agricultural raw materials exports (% of merchandise exports)	1.57	1.55	1.37	1.25	1.19	1.07	1.14	1.10	1.51	1.57	1.81	1.73	1.65
Food exports (% of merchandise exports)	3.86	3.68	3.64	3.66	3.49	2.71	2.80	3.03	3.24	3.78	4.25	4.14	4.17
Fuel exports (% of merchandise exports)	0.62	0.67	0.97	1.11	1.37	1.61	2.10	2.70	1.97	3.04	3.29	4.31	6.31

(continued)

Exhibit 1 (continued)

	1999	2000	2001	2002	2003	2004	2005	2006	2007	2008	2009	2010	2011
Manufactures exports (% of merchandise exports)	90.16	89.67	89.56	90.06	90.02	90.24	89.36	87.51	87.97	87.26	87.16	85.22	82.92
High-technology exports (% of manufactured exports)	4.13	4.91	5.34	5.42	6.42	5.73	4.93	5.51	5.01	5.82	6.40	5.49	n/a

Source: World Bank (2013)

European schemes that offered financial incentives for buying new cars. In 2010, the automotive industry accounted for 12 % of the country's GDP Core foreign trade indicators of the Slovenian economy are presented in Exhibit 1.

Among the prospering companies, those that have specialized in mid to high-tech automotive and industrial equipment manufacturing are the strongest internationally. These organizations were able to grow and gain market share even in the darkest days of the global recession. The majority of them are now positioned as market leaders in narrow market segments in Europe and across the globe. In the following section we look in depth at examples of HCs primarily from these sectors.

A selection of Slovenian HCs is listed in alphabetic order in the table below. Roughly estimated, Slovenia has 15 HCs per one million inhabitants. There may be HCs that I have not been able to identify or interview. Among those listed, some hold a stronger international leadership position than others, and therefore I have given more attention to them. Those identified and interviewed are summarized in Exhibit 2. Some of the companies are strong champions with many of the characteristics of German HCs. Others are of a more regional nature, and some are start-up companies with an emerging competitive advantage, whose distinctive competitive positions are yet to be developed.

2 Six Case Studies

2.1 Akrapovič

Overview

Address:	Malo Hudo 8a, 1295 Ivančna Gorica, Slovenia
Tel:	+38617878404
Fax:	+38617878405
Email:	info@akrapovic.si
Web:	http://www.akrapovic.si

Company Information

Industry:	Manufacture of parts and accessories for motor vehicles
Year of establishment:	1990
Sales revenue in 2009:	€47.7 million
Sales revenue in 2000:	€1.7 million
Average number of employees in 2010:	415 (according to http://www.gvin.com)
Brain(s) behind the company:	Igor Akrapovič

Exhibit 2 Slovenian hidden champions

Name	Market leadership definition	Revenue 2010 (in €m)	Revenue 2000 (in €m)	Average employees 2010
Atech	First in Alpe Adria region in production and supply of electro-motors and navigation control systems for heaters on biomass	5.5	1.4	69
Akrapovič	First in the world in titanium exhaust systems for racing bikes	31.6	7.8	415
Bia Separations	First in the world (the only one) in CIM monolitic columns technology—the most cost efficiency technology used in purification stage of bio-drug production process	3.1	0.3	41
Bisol	First in the world (the only one) in top quality photovoltaic modules (highest electricity extraction ratio and lowest outwear of photovoltaic modules)	60.4	0	125
Euro Plus	Third in the world in the software service of design and printing of labels with bar codes and RFID labels	3.2	0.55	38
Hidria	Third in the world in diesel cold start systems for internal combustion engines. Proactive design manufacturer for OEM and tier 1 suppliers. First in the world in range extenders for hybrid electric vehicles. Proactive design manufacturer for OEM. Second in Europe in Alu die castings for automotive steering systems. Proactive design manufacturer for tier 1 and tier 2 suppliers	187[a]	77[b]	2,611
Genelitik	Number one in Slovenia in providing the product of "advice on optimal nutritional and lifestyle choices based on genetic analysis"; geographically in the process of refocusing on the EU market and Welness centres	0.13	n/a	2
GenePlanet	Number one in Slovenia in providing the product of "advice for prevention of potential (curable) diseases based on genetic analysis"; geographically in the process of expanding to CEE region and B2C market	0.42	n/a	3
Instrumentation Technologies	First in the world in production, supply and advice in instrumentation for beam particles, that is instrumentation for measuring the positions of elementary particles, in accelerators	5.4	0.18	51
Metrel	First in Europe in the production and supply of test and measurement	20[a]	12[b]	168

(continued)

Exhibit 2 (continued)

Name	Market leadership definition	Revenue 2010 (in €m)	Revenue 2000 (in €m)	Average employees 2010
	instruments for electrical safety of installations in low voltage electrical distribution industry			
Optotek	First in the world in OEM sales of ophthalmological laser for diagnostics and therapy. Used to be proactive designer. Transitioning from OEM to own branding strategy. In years 2011 60 % of revenue expected from own brand	4.38	2.1	51
Pipistrel	Number one in the world in the new and recently established categories of ultralight aircraft: first in the world in double seat motor gliders that can turn into pure gliders once in the air; first in the world in two-seat gliders with an auxiliary and in the category of electric two-seater airplanes; first in the world in newly established category of electric two seater gliders (not yet approved for flying in many countries).	7.2	0.67	53
Seaway Group	First in the world in sails and motor boat design for OEM. Proactive designer. Main revenue driver are royalties received throughout product life cycle from designed boats. Transitioning to own brands: Shipman—a line of carbon sailing yachts, Skagen—a range of world-girdling raised pilothouse motor yachts, and Greenline—a line of carbon boats with electric engine	34.3	4.58	185
Studio Moderna	First in Central and Eastern Europe in electronic retailing and direct marketing	250	25	4,500
Tajfun	First in Europe in the production and supply of three point logging winches	15.1	5.5	137

[a]Year 2009
[b]Year 1999
Source: Author of the chapter, http://www.gvin.com

2.1.1 Nature of Market Leadership

Akrapovič was the first company in the world to design and manufacture titanium exhaust systems for racing motorcycles. Since 2008 the company has also established itself as a global leader in custom-made exhaust systems for high-end cars. In its 23-year history, its products have been used by the winners of 63 world championships.

2.1.2 Nature of Competitive Advantage

In 2 decades of working with leading producers of racing motorcycles (Kawasaki, Yamaha, Honda, Ducati, Suzuki, etc.) Igor Akrapovič has accumulated a large stock of knowledge and experience in producing state-of-the-art exhaust systems and working with titanium composites, which is also the preferred material for fast transportation systems like airplanes and cars. This experience, along with the ability to learn fast, is the core of the company's business success.

2.1.3 Core Lessons Learned on the Path to Business Success

1. To deliver new ideas to the market faster than competitors, work directly with the most demanding customers who use your range of products.
2. If product excellence is what motivates you, pass management over to professionals and position yourself in the R&D department. As the core owner, you will still have enough discretionary power over the company's future.
3. Develop and invest in a distinctive knowledge base, strive for the toughest clients, win them, learn from them, and grow further from your superior knowledge base.

2.1.4 Akrapovič: Hidden Champion

The fastest racing motorcycles in the world have custom-made titanium exhaust systems, the best of which are produced by Slovenia's Akrapovič. Igor Akrapovič, who was one of the best super motorcycle racers in Yugoslavia, was dissatisfied with the state of exhaust systems for motorcycles. The power of an engine depends significantly on the quality of the exhaust system, and exhaust systems at that time were the most frequent reason for failure in the top races. Hence, Mr. Akrapovič started designing his own systems in his garage in the early 1990s. He came up with a titanium solution and offered it for testing to German racing teams. The superiority of titanium exhaust systems, particularly in terms of durability and power, won him a long-term cooperation with the Germans and other racing teams. Igor Akrapovič quickly discovered the importance of product quality. In one of his rare interviews he pointed out, "Racing bike teams do not care about politics; only about quality. If you have superior quality, doing business is pretty simple!". Quality breeds success. Akrapovič's company was open to learning and improving its exhaust systems by being actively engaged in top motorcycle racing, improving products on a race-by-race basis. The ability to learn and deliver new ideas to the market much faster than competitors was the key to Akrapovič's global market leadership.

His entrepreneurial behavior gave birth to one of the most successful Slovenian companies in the automotive sector. At present, the company counts more than 500 employees, producing more than 38 million euros in sales revenue. Recently, the company has grown at more than 20 % annually, which is a significant achievement taking into the account that the overall demand in this niche market fell almost 60 % after the 2008 recession, and many other companies failed.

In January 2009, Igor Akrapovič announced: “In the fall of 2008, when we were facing major challenges, I promised to say ‘thank you for your cooperation’ to anyone that I was not happy with. If that were me, I would replace myself as well. And today I am replacing myself. The new CEO of Akrapovič is Mr. Miloš Dežnak, ex-director of Johnson and Johnson for Central and Eastern Europe”. This act nicely illustrates the uncompromising leadership style that brought the company to its current level of success. Nonetheless, Mr. Akrapovič is still present and very active in the technological field.

Akrapovič’s resilience to recession was acquired through experience in the tough racing environment. In the 1999–2009 period, the company’s sales revenues grew from 3.5 million euros to 30 million whereas the number of employees rose from 30 to 415. To date, more than 60 super motorcycle world championships have been won using the Akrapovič exhaust system. No competitor can match Akrapovič here as he has the best exhaust system brand in the world of super motorcycle racing.

The next step is to leverage the company’s brand so as to strengthen its position in the wider consumer market. The Akrapovič brand is strong, and the price premium is significant. To move beyond the racing clientele, Akrapovič is building on its reputation, taking advantage of the fact that racing motorcycle owners identify with their champions and want the same motorcycles. Akrapovič is working to attach its brand to those of the racing motorcycles, such as Yamaha, Honda, or Ducati.

However, since 2008 the world of racing motorcycles has been in recession and growth in this segment has been limited. Nonetheless, Akrapovič has grown! While being a global brand is important, it is no longer sufficient for sustainable growth. In the Akrapovič’s case, growth is being achieved through related diversification built on two bases—product and capability—which are creating new market segments.

Akrapovič is now diversifying its expertise in titanium exhaust systems to penetrate two new global market segments: big scooters and high-performance cars. In both areas, Akrapovič is using its skills to shape its own distinctive market niche. In the area of high-performance cars, owners are replacing factory exhaust systems with custom-made ones. Akrapovič is the only company in the world offering after-market car exhaust systems made of titanium. The typical buyer in this market segment is well educated, knows what he wants, and is generally price-sensitive; so Akrapovič is becoming a preferred solution for BMW, Mercedes, Porsche, Maserati, Ferrari, and other companies.

However, underneath this growth pattern is a distinctive superior knowledge of moulding titanium and other composites. The organization invests a lot into the development of this capability. “We should never leave the ball here. We need to invest in new materials and technologies constantly, and aim for the top in the selected market niches. However, we will always be present in the world of motorcycles. This is our identity”. By bringing awareness to this distinctive capability, Akrapovič’s growth pattern has slightly changed in recent years.

Motorcycles are not the only source of growth. Instead, the company is striving to diversify, building on its expertise in exhaust systems.

Akrapovič is very satisfied with the company's performance over the last decade and sees bright future prospects. What specific lessons does Akrapovič teach us? Develop and invest in a distinctive knowledge base, strive for the toughest clients, win them, learn from them, and grow further from your superior knowledge base.

2.2 Hidria

Overview

Address:	Nazorjeva ulica 6, 1000 Ljubljana, Slovenia
Tel:	+38653756301
Fax:	+38653756470
Email:	info@hidria.com
Web:	http://www.hidria.si

Company Information

Industry:	Manufacture of electrical equipment
Year of establishment:	1971
Sales revenue in 2009:	€187 million
Sales revenue in 2009:	€77 million
Average number of employees in 2010:	2,611
Brain(s) behind the company:	The top management team

2.2.1 Nature of Market Leadership

Hidria is third in the world in the niche of diesel cold start systems for internal combustion engines in terms of sales volume. Additionally, one in every six vehicles in Europe contains a Hidria part in its steering system. The company is in the second place in Europe in the area of ALU Die Castings. Hidria holds 17 % of a 0.5 billion euro market.

2.2.2 Nature of Competitive Advantage

Hidria is a developmental supplier to Renault, PSA, Audi, and BMW, among others. Apart from its automotive branch, Hidria's construction branch offers complete climate system solutions covering ventilation and protection, heating and cooling, renewable energy sources and energy management systems. The core market for its climate systems is CEE, where it is positioned among the top-five companies. A strong leader in the CEE market in the HVAC business, Hidria is a real HC in the automotive sector in a period of uncertainty caused by a shift from internal combustion to electric power.

2.2.3 Core Lessons Learned on the Path to Business Success

1. When faced with fundamental change in the technology and the industry value chain is under transformation, refocus your innovation from products and processes to innovation of business models.
2. If you wonder which dimensions of your products, processes, and business models to change, and which to leave as they are, the best approach is to position yourself as a proactive developmental supplier for core OEMs (such as Renault, PSA, Audi and BMW) and pre-design a range of technical solutions for them so that they pick the most suitable ones.
3. If the company's stakeholders (employees, management, owners and local community) do not have at least some common interests it will be hard to take strategic action on an international scale. Very early on, Hidria's privatization involved employees and top management from the local region of Idrija. With this strategy the company aligned the interests of all employees, management, owners, and the local community, which led to harmonized strategic actions on international markets.

2.2.4 Hidria: Hidden Champion

According to the information on the company's website, every eighth vehicle in the world has a Hidria's start system, and the company holds the third position in the world in the niche of diesel cold-start systems for internal combustion engines. One in every six vehicles in Europe contains a Hidria part in its steering system.

Apart from its automotive branch, the company operates a construction branch that offers complete climate system solutions covering ventilation and protection, heating and cooling, renewable energy sources, and energy management systems. The core market for Klima is CEE, where it is positioned among the top five companies.

Hidria is an international corporation with production and sales representative facilities in 16 countries. Nowadays, close to 1,000 employees create 85 million euros in annual revenue. Contrary to typical HCs, Hidria was not started by an entrepreneurial manager. Instead, it is a successful offspring of the Iskra group, one of the most advanced equipment engineering groups from former Yugoslavia. In 1971, Iskra Rotomatika established a small motor assembly plant and quickly seized a piece of the international market under the management of its CEO, Edvard Svetlik. Svetlik may be one of the most successful Slovenian managers, effectively dealing with central planning and a market economy at the same time. In the mid-1990s, the company was efficiently privatized by its employees and top management. It ownership stabilized and all employees had a common interest—effective operation of the company for long-term penetration of foreign markets.

Today Hidria holds advanced technological knowledge in the area of vehicle powertrains and steering systems. It has a flexible, highly automated manufacturing system. However, one needs to bear in mind that the automotive industry is in a process of major technological transformation. The internal combustion engine (ICE) is at the end of its life cycle, and the emerging technology of electric vehicles is still highly ambiguous in terms of the platform that will become dominant. Hence, the industry value network in the automotive sector is under reconstruction. Being in an industry in which the value chain is under transformation presents great risks but also great opportunities. The sensitivity of top management to risky opportunities, while keeping the company on track, is critical to sustainable niche market leadership in the automotive sector.

And how is Hidria maintaining its leadership position? The company has become a proactive developmental supplier, able to offer a range of technical solutions for powertrains and steering systems for all technologies, including ICE, hybrid vehicles, and electrical vehicles. Hidria's president Iztok Seljak is a very thoughtful and sensitive manager. He sees "risk-management as well as on-time learning as critical to our success, hence we work from the core technological capabilities that we have in the area of steering systems and powertrains, and target selected opportunities in the area of green mobility".

This strategy of pursuing opportunities by using distinctive technological competences is creating significant results. Hidria is already the number-one company in the world in the niche of range extenders, a critical component in the area of electric vehicle technology. Range extenders are important parts of electric vehicle batteries, which assure that cars can run further even after the batteries have been depleted.

Last but not least, Hidria's top management is atypical of HCs. It is not characterized by single-mindedness, fearlessness, stamina, or perseverance. Instead, the top management consists of thoughtful decision-makers, highly sensitive to employees and other stakeholders; they are technically skilful and inspiring.

What particular lessons can Hidria teach us? One strategic way to success is through thoughtful organizational behaviour, with a strong focus on innovation in ambiguous business environments undergoing technological transformation.

2.3 Instrumentation Technologies

Overview

Address:	Velika pot 22, 5250 Solkan, Slovenia
Tel:	+38653352600
Fax:	+38653352601
Email:	info@i-tech.si
Web:	http://www.i-tech.si

Company Information

Industry:	Architectural and engineering activities; technical testing and analysis
Year of establishment:	1998
Sales revenue in 2010:	€5.4 million
Sales revenue in 2000:	€181,091
Average number of employees in 2010:	52
Brain(s) behind the company:	CEO and founder Rok Uršič

2.3.1 Nature of Market Leadership

Instrumentation Technologies is a world leader in the production and supply of, instrumentation for accelerator beam diagnostics, as well as consulting in that field. This market is now expanding from research institutes with accelerators and hadrons to applied industrial branches, such as medicine, manufacturing, and energy.

2.3.2 Nature of Competitive Advantage

The core of the company's competitive advantage is the constant stream of technology-led innovations in the area of instrumentations (measurement devices at the sub-atomic level). Recently, these innovations have been used in different industrial branches, with a view to creating new market niches. This company has a distinctive product and market position. It faces practically no direct competition.

2.3.3 Core Lessons Learned on the Path to Business Success

1. Brand your product, even if placed at the beginning of the industry value chain. However, Instrumentation Technology is a specific case because it is involved in fundamental research that can yield great potential benefits for society. It is publicly financed, unregulated, and not purely market driven.

2. If you are producing technology for highly specialized professionals, organize communities where these professionals can meet, share their problems and solutions, and come up with new products. Instrumentation Technologies has formed a community ("Libera") around a family of products. Its preferred expression is: "We create value by integrating technology and people".

3. Leadership is an artful activity. When you cannot easily think of a technical solution—which is normal—sensitivity to the beauty in the context, and comfort with uncertainty, can show you the way out.

2.3.4 Instrumentation Technologies: Hidden Champion

Instrumentation Technologies was established in 1998 by Rok Uršič in the house of his wife's mother in Solkan. As employees recollect, "Already back then, Rok believed we would create a company that employed the best scientists from the world of physics. First we offered consultancy to accelerators. Between the early beginnings and later success we lived through periods of failure and defeat, with occasional small successes. Our goals were far from clear. With the passage of time they have crystallized and become even more appealing. On the way here we needed to go through many in-depth conversations with our clients, from whom we learn the most. Now, we see ourselves as passionate designers of innovative solutions, aspired to be at the cutting edge of technology" (Krajnović et al. 2009).

In 2003, Instrumentation Technologies integrated digital and analogue technology with software in one product and named it Libera. It established a completely new product category and way of thinking and working in the world of particle accelerators. In less than a decade, the company created state-of-the-art technological knowledge of processors used for the stabilization of the beams of these accelerators. The umbrella brand of Libera also connects world-renowned scientists in the field of nano-instrumentation in a unique community of practice, where they share their experiences and knowledge at regular workshops and conferences. Libera is now "many instruments and many people working together". The company constantly learns from the best professionals and they help move its technical knowledge forward.

Before Libera, accelerator operators bought digital and electronic parts separately. They developed their software in-house, and spent significant amounts of time synchronizing these elements. The time required for such activities kept individuals from investing their time and contributions into research. Instrumentation Technologies established a completely new market niche. By now, more than 50 % of all research institutes with scientific accelerators no longer develop instrumentations for particle measurement.

The company's strongest competitors are researchers employed at institutions with accelerators. They challenge the company and push it forward with new ideas. In many areas, Instrumentation Technologies cooperates with them at Libera workshops. In the business world, the company faces one direct competitor from France that offers only a partly similar product (analogue instrumentation), although it has a wider array of products for scientific accelerators.

Deals are won through competitive tenders, where product customization and technical consultancy puts Instrumentation Technologies in a preferential position. However, winning tenders also depends, to a considerable extent, on the trust and closeness developed with core people and customers. Therefore, each bidding process is managed separately. Each deal is a unique collaborative project and a learning opportunity. "Our customers are the leading physicists in the world, who are very demanding, very knowledgeable, and have very strong personalities. In order to deal with them in the best contributing manner, we created a simple rule, handling each customer as our partner with whom we share a common mission to move the knowledge frontier further."

Nevertheless, the world of scientific accelerators is limited in size. Company growth would be constrained if the organization did not diversify its product offerings into related photons measuring technologies. With this approach, the number of employees at Instrumentation Technologies rose from 3 to 47 in the last decade. At the same time, revenue grew from 181,000 euros to 4.4 million in the same period.

In the process of growth the company sought the best experts in the world, those motivated to contribute to the creation of cutting-edge technical knowledge, and highly committed to the company's mission. Forty of the sixty employees hold PhDs. They see themselves as a "scientists in the world of business... not producing science but serving science". The composition of the management board is nationally and culturally diverse. It is also diverse in terms of its knowledge base; it attracts core global brains in the area of nano-instrumentations.

Company founder Rok Uršič is recognized as an exceptional entrepreneurial manager, who kicked off the business with his vision to "create something good for the local community of Solkan". In return, the local community is inspired by the will and power of Mr. Uršič . He is highly passionate, disciplined, and committed to technology. Business is a hobby that induces satisfaction and joy in Rok Uršič. Yet Mr. Uršič is perceived as highly compassionate leader, sensitive to the aesthetics of his work. In an interview for the Slovene Association of Managers in January 2009, Mr. Uršič reported: "There is no fine distinction between the energy for crazy ideas and entrepreneurial reality. Entrepreneurship is about creating artwork. Like artists, we entrepreneurs also struggle with moments of stuckness, restlesness and relentlessness before coming to moments of clarity, followed by action and ending with culmination, funnelled towards a period of serenity and rest. In business, as in arts, critical issues need to be sensed out of an ambiguous context with subjective certainty in what one is doing...I believe in men...into integrating technology with man. Technology is only the explication of man's ability to create outstanding products. If I said to my employees that we did not need to struggle for pure technological excellence, they would start leaving the company. If you walk around our company you can sense the passion employees have for the supremacy of technology. They are burning for Libera".

The company invests more than 40 % of its sales revenue in R&D. Innovations are not fuelled simply by technology, but also by the needs of customers. Although property rights at an international level protect Libera's products, the company remains selective over what to reveal by patenting, bearing in mind also the time-consuming bureaucratization involved. Nonetheless, the company is aware that in putting aside patent protection, "one should internalize the competitive dynamics and constant battle for remaining ahead in technological innovation...knowing that being first is always a transitory category. Competitors are just around the corner".

In 2010, Rok Uršič formed a strategic alliance with some of Slovenia's most advanced high-tech companies (Bia Separations, Cosylab, Systec) and established an applied research centre of excellence so as to design new products in the area of bio-sensorics. There is an expectation that completely new industry branches will be formed out of this project.

Finally, though growth opportunities are limited in the world of basic science, a company with state-of-the-art technical knowledge in the area of instrumentation has many possible leads for future growth. "We have a stock of technologies and knowledge that we can assemble into new products for different uses in different industries". Is this not powerful learning?

2.4 Atech Elektronika

Overview

Address:	Bač pri Materiji 30, 6242 Materija, Slovenia
Tel:	+386 (0)82008800
Fax:	+386 (0)82008801
Email:	info@atech.si
Web:	http://www.atech.si

Company Information

Industry:	Manufacture of other electrical equipment
Year of establishment:	1990
Sales revenue in 2010:	€5.5 million
Sales revenue in 2000:	€1.4 million
Average number of employees in 2010:	69 (data from http://www.gvin.com)
Brain(s) behind the company:	Davor Jakulin and Massimo Makovac

2.4.1 Nature of Market Leadership

ATech is a reliable partner to its customers, which helps it excel in its business. The company provides cost-effective solutions in the field of electronics design and manufacturing. It specializes in biomass combustion control, electronics manufacturing services (EMS), and in custom-designed motor controls for various markets, including home appliances, power tools, and industrial systems electronics.

2.4.2 Nature of Competitive Advantage

ATech's competitive advantage stems from the ability of customers to differentiate its products from others on the market. The company achieves this by providing innovative and cost-effective solutions that excel in terms of design, user friendliness, and energy efficiency.

2.4.3 Core Lessons Learned on the Path to Business Success

- Always try to understand your customer's business and needs.
- Consider how you can add value to your customer's business.
- Consider how you can help your customer bring benefits to his or her own customers.

2.4.4 Atech Elektronika: Hidden Champion

If you have a wooden cottage with a biomass combustion device that can be activated before your arrival home, you are likely to have a device produced by ATech. Especially in the Alpe-Adria region, Atech is the leading provider of such products.

In general, Atech is active in three distinctive markets. In the Slovenian market it is present predominantly as a leading electronics manufacturing service (EMS) provider, where its distinctive competence is in bundling additional services. In the EU market, ATech provides original design manufacturer (ODM) services, mostly in the motor controls segment for home appliances. ATech is known for effective solutions to the costs of energy consumption. The third market is a worldwide green segment of the heating business, where ATech offers premium-priced, superior quality electronic controllers for biomass combustion devices.

In 20 years, Atech evolved from a low-cost supplier to a developmental supplier. Most recently it started developing its own product brand. Atech was established in 1990 as a Swiss-Slovenian joint venture to produce low-cost electronics. In 1996, CEO Jakulin bought out the other shareholders and started to concentrate the company's activities around contracted electronics manufacturing. With this change in ownership and strategy, the company pressed for faster growth, especially after expanding its services to original design manufacturing. In 2007, ATech started to offer its own branded products. Atech is not a HC yet, though its development over the last decade is promising. In 2001 the share of export sales was almost 0; by 2010 it had reached 26 %.

ATech's growth is a result of the introduction of new value-added products and international expansion. Around 15 % of revenue goes back into product innovation. Being an ODM for motor controls for German companies provides access to high-end knowledge, technologies, and strategic foresight in the area of motor controls and efficient use of energy. The change to ODM provides new ideas for their own innovation processes.

Mr. Jakulin's leadership style involves a focus on three key objectives. As he personally described it: "I can feel successful only if I am acting responsibly towards people, the environment, and society. This is the core of my business success".

ATech provides examples of the typical challenges that a company faces while on its way to becoming a HC. A significant challenge for the company now is the problem of how to expand internationally with an effective approach to distribution and branding.

2.5 Bia Separations

Overview

Address: Mirce 21, 5270 Ajdovščina, Slovenia
Phone: +386 59 699 500

Fax: +386 59 699 599
Web: http://www.biaseparations.com

Company Information

Industry:	Manufacture of bio-chemical products
Year of establishment:	1994
Sales revenue in 2010:	€3.1 million
Sales revenue in 2000:	€300,000
Average number of employees in 2010:	41
Brain(s) behind the company:	Aleš Štrancar

2.5.1 Nature of Market Leadership

BIA Separations is an uncontested world leader in CIM monolithic columns technology—the most cost-efficient technology used in the purification stage of bio-drug production. The company holds around 30 % of market share in the world of intelligent filters. This is still an emergent niche with big prospects for the future.

2.5.2 Nature of Competitive Advantage

A critical phase in the bio-drug production process is the isolation of the right bio-molecules from organisms and then cleaning the product so that it has the right concentrations of the right substances. This purification process is the critical stage in bio-drug production and consumes a great deal of time, effort and money. BIA Separations has developed special intelligent filters that make this purification process 40 % more time- and cost-efficient. Though customers (large pharmaceuticals) are buying intelligent filters from BIA Separations in relatively small quantities, and big streams of revenues are yet to be created, once their drugs get FDA approvals, the expected revenue streams should be substantial.

2.5.3 Core Lessons Learned on the Path to Business Success

1. To sustain a small, high-tech company in a business where expected revenue streams are some way off in the future, leadership is a critical ingredient of growth and survival. Aleš Štrancar's persistence, passion, knowledge, and entrepreneurship, and his strong professional networks, are core drivers that have brought BIA Separations where it is today.
2. When more than 50 % of all revenues are reinvested in R&D, and product revenue streams are weak, financing may be an issue. If a company's assets are insufficient, banks will be unwilling to provide financing. In that case, venture capital funds or business angels can be crucial.
3. The professional networks of a company's CEO are sources of the best business opportunities. Make sure that you position yourself well and centrally in these networks.

2.5.4 Bia Separations: Hidden Champion

BIA Separations was established in 1994 as a spin-off from the Joseph Stephan Institute, the biggest institute for applied natural sciences in the Balkans. Soon after the formation of the company, it was joined by Dr Aleš Štrancar following his resignation from the university. Characterized by persistence, passion, knowledge, entrepreneurship, and good professional networks, Mr. Štrancar soon became the CEO.

Dr Štrancar succeeded in creating a distinctive competitive position in the narrow niche of intelligent bio-filters. Professionally speaking, the company has become a world leader in liquid separation bio chromatography by application of short monolithic column technology, which is currently the most cost-efficient process of biomolecular purification. BIA's products remove large molecules and nano-scale particles (viruses and virus-like particles) with 30–40 % lower costs.

Despite the product superiority, the growth of the company in the last decade has been modest. Revenue has risen from 0.3 million euros to 3.3 million. The growth curve is not steep as the company started from a very low base. Furthermore, one needs to acknowledge its growth in the context of the drug development process. BIA Separations is currently involved in drug development in over 500 global pharmaceutical companies, but it takes a decade or more for a new bio-drug (even one produced by cost-effective intelligent filters) to be launched on the market. Currently, large pharmaceuticals are buying intelligent filters in relatively small quantities, and larger streams of revenue are yet to be created. Nevertheless, it is estimated that BIA Separations holds 30 % of market share in the world of intelligent filters.

There are significant obstacles to growth and market proliferation in the bio-drug industry in general. These factors are particularly challenging for HCs. Firstly, for companies such as BIA Separations, the major threat comes from customers who outsource production to low-cost contract manufacturers, especially those who are also producing drugs using the competitive technology of bio-molecular purification. BIA's limited size is a second impediment. Large pharmaceuticals view small size as a risk factor: the smaller a company, the higher the likelihood that it will fail. The death of a supplier causes a major drop in revenue for the hiring firm because it has to stop sales and re-patent the drug, which is then subject to new approval processes at national NDAs. Therefore large pharmaceuticals prefer to select ingredient suppliers on the basis of size, cost, patents, and intellectual contribution in the drug development process.

Thirdly, selling products with a significant time lag in revenue is not appealing to external distributors. Hence, investment in their own distribution network consumes a lot of already scarce financial resources, not to mention the need to sustain a high level of innovative activity. On average, around 50 % of all revenue is reinvested in the development of new product variations. Finally, weak assets do not inspire banks to offer favourable loans, so the company is left to seek out venture capital and business angels.

In spite of a significantly superior product, the path to the stars is not simple. Nevertheless, being a real entrepreneur, Mr. Štrancar, can see it! As we have learned from real HCs, in most cases this leadership factor alone can be enough!

2.6 BISOL Group

Overview

Address:	Latkova vas 59a, 3312 Prebold, Slovenia
Tel:	+38637032250
Fax:	+38637032263
Email:	info@bisol.si
Web:	http://www.bisol.net

Company Information

Industry:	Manufacture of photovoltaic electrical equipment
Year of establishment:	2006
Sales revenue in 2010:	€60 million
Sales revenue in 2000:	n/a
Average number of employees in 2010:	125 (data from http://www.gvin.com)
Brain(s) behind the company:	Uroš Merc

2.6.1 Nature of Market Leadership

BISOL is one of the top three producers of high-quality photovoltaic modules (i.e., modules with the highest yield electricity extraction and lowest degradation over time) in the world.

2.6.2 Nature of Competitive Advantage

BISOL's engineering team designs PV systems that have the highest possible yield. After successfully targeting Western Europe with its photovoltaic modules, the company has expanded into the construction of turnkey photovoltaic installations. BISOL is a leader in the emerging Slovene market, and has had its power plants built in the Czech Republic, Italy, and other CEE countries. In this way, BISOL has become the most efficient solar electricity producer.

2.6.3 Core Lessons Learned on the Path to Business Success

1. Understand the customer's needs in detail, and use your scientific knowledge and business competences to satisfy those needs better than anyone else.

2. Always question the existing technological solutions by tapping deeper into your knowledge domain and elsewhere to produce cost-effective and top-quality products.
3. To extract more value from the emerging industry, move forward and appropriate those areas where value-adding can be generated. BISOL has evolved from being a producer of a single component—photovoltaic modules—into an engineer of photovoltaic installations, an installer of turnkey photovoltaic installations, and now a solar energy provider.
4. A company is its people. You cannot grow if you do not have high-quality employees. BISOL does a good deal of work in attracting the greatest potential from the region.

2.6.4 BISOL Group: Hidden Champion

"Photovoltaic" has lately become a buzzword in the media, business, and politics, yet few of us really understand what it is all about and how it may impact on our future.

BISOL, a fast growing Slovene company, understands these dynamics very well. BISOL was established in 2008 by Dr Uroš Merc, a doctor of physics who earned his experience, knowledge, and ideas at the most advanced institutes in Europe. The company started out as a manufacturer of high-quality photovoltaic modules for solar power plants. It offered premium-priced PV modules that were characterized by an excellent energy efficiency ratio, product durability, and longevity. On average 15 % of sales revenue has been re-invested in innovation efforts. Patenting is an important barrier to the entry of competitors in the field of premium-priced photovoltaic modules.

From its early days, BISOL successfully targeted Western Europe with its photovoltaic modules, and soon after started to expand into the construction of large-scale turnkey photovoltaic installations. Many of their competitors did the same. However, in this emerging niche market BISOL is one of the leaders in CEE. BISOL solar power plants have been built in the Czech Republic, Slovenia, Italy and some other CEE countries; however this niche is still in its infancy; therefore it is difficult to define reliable market share estimates.

Nonetheless, one can quickly grasp that BISOL possesses an important skill—the ability to navigate quickly though an emerging market landscape and seize close and distant business opportunities. Being able to make quick adjustments to the growth strategy in the early stages of a company's life is an advantage on the way to becoming a HC. The truth of this proposition transpires through BISOL's own fast growth. In 4 years, its revenue grew to 55 million euros and a total of 250 staff, mainly highly educated engineers and experts in photovoltaic technology—were taken onboard. BISOL's distinctive growth and international competitiveness stem partly from its superior product quality, and partly from management's sensitivity and fast sense-making of emergent business opportunities.

Conclusion

Taking into account the size of its economy, we can conclude that Slovenia does have some globally competitive companies able to hold international market leadership, though mostly in quite narrow market segments. With this in mind, how are their business practices similar to those of German HCs and in what do they differ?

Like German HCs (Simon 2009), Slovenian HCs are positioned mainly in the business-to-business segment in manufacturing, where economies of scale breed significant benefits. Close proximity to their customer base is an important element in their business models, and an essential ingredient of innovation. Products are of a very high quality, and priced at a premium level. Going for the most demanding customers and winning their trust is important for shaping product excellence and navigating the innovation efforts. HCs have the capacity to handle customer uniqueness with care and flexibility. Yet their level of professional marketing can at times be weak. The role of an entrepreneurial manager is also crucial in the majority of these companies, though not all. Typically, company leaders are highly visionary, tough, passionate, and totally committed to their businesses. They also possess great product knowledge.

Unlike the German HCs, Slovenian companies focus mainly on the European market or even narrower, on CEE. Their goals are not defined in terms of growth, although technological leadership and excellence are core components of their mission. Hence, they grow not only through focus and internationalization, but in many cases also through related diversification and selected internationalization. In general, they are much smaller than their competitors. Smallness and limited resources can partly explain why wider internationalization is not economically feasible; bigger investments are required for building up the global distribution and sales system. Yet, they do grow in terms of value adding, by transitioning from low to higher value adding. Many Slovenian companies positioned themselves as ordinary suppliers in their earlier stages, then restructured to become developmental suppliers, and in the last stage created their own brands. Nevertheless, there are still many that remain in the developmental supplier position, trying to create their own distinctive consultancy niche. Cases such as Seaway, Pipistrel or Akrapovič are good examples.

Some Slovenian HCs are innovative also in their business models and organizational processes, in addition to their products. Smallness and flexibility are put forward as justifications for selective patenting policy. Many are actively involved in communities of practice through which they promote their innovation efforts. A lack of financing does constrain growth in many cases—especially in small companies that do not possess enough fixed assets, have postponed revenue streams, or make high R&D investments.

Unlike the German leaders, those of Slovenia in many cases justify their actions through their identity ("This is who we are") than through rationality ("This is what we do because we expect benefits"). Many simply dare to challenge the future of their business. They succeed through interplay of luck, professionalism, and fast learning through failure. None of the Slovenian leaders stand still. They act even when they do not know where the path leads. Though some admitted that on occasion they lose sight of their goal, they never lose their enthusiasm for technological knowledge, passion for learning, and commitment to business. Perhaps this is the behavior that brings the future to the present and makes HCs successful!

References

Abramovič, K. (2008). *Kaj se lahko naučimo iz preteklih finančnih kriz?* Bilten NLB Skladi, 7. Accessed May 19, 2011, from http://www.nlbskladi.si/bilten07-2008-kaj-se-lahko-naucimo-iz-preteklih-financnih-kriz

Jamer, N. (2010). *Štiri velike gospodarske krize na Slovenskem.* Ljubljana: Faculty of Economics.

Krajnović, E., Faganelj, A., & Svetina, P. (2009). *Moč črpam iz slepe točke*, MQ. Accessed 21 April, 2011, from http://www.zdruzenje-manager.si/storage/4843/

Lazarevič, Ž. (2009). *Plasti prostora in časa.* Ljubljana: Inštitut za novejšo zgodovino.

Lazarević, Ž., & Pančur, A. (2010). *Economic history of Slovenia from the 19th to the 20th century*, Videolectures. Accessed April 16, 2011, from http://videolectures.net/sadovi_pancur_lazarevic_gzslo

Purg, D. (2010). *Skriti zmagovalci v Sloveniji.* Ljubljana: Planet GV0.

Simon, H. (2009). *Hidden champions of the twenty-first century* (p. 2009). Berlin: Springer.

Statistical Office of the Republic of Slovenia. (2010). Accessed June 10, 2011, from http://www.stat.si

Wikipedia. (2010). *Economy of Slovenia.* Accessed April 10, 2011, from http://en.wikipedia.org/wiki/Economy_of_Slovenia#cite_note-13

World Bank. (2013). *Data; countries and economies.* http://data.worldbank.org/country

Hidden Champions of Turkey

Türkan Yosun and Dilek Çetindamar

Overview

Official name:	Republic of Turkey
Type of government:	Parliamentary Democratic Republic
Population in 2011:	73,639,596
Land area:	769,630 km^2

History

1920	After its defeat in WWI, the Ottoman Empire is gradually partitioned by the Allies, a period finalized by the Treaty of Sévres in 1920, leaving a minor Turkish territory.
1923	Turkey wins its War of Independence and the Republic of Turkey is established. The Treaty of Lausanne determines new borders, preserved to the present day. The state initiates industrialization efforts to create a domestic market.
1952	Turkey becomes a member of NATO.
1960	Fear in the army that the government is threatening Turkey's secular state leads to a military intervention. In the same period, import substitution industrialization becomes the official economic development policy, aimed at minimizing imports and creating domestic production by means of quotas, tariffs, and exchange regulations.

T. Yosun (✉) • D. Çetindamar
School of Management, Sabanci University, Istanbul, Turkey
e-mail: turkanyosun@sabanciuniv.edu

P. McKiernan and D. Purg (eds.), *Hidden Champions in CEE and Turkey*,
DOI 10.1007/978-3-642-40504-4_22, © Springer-Verlag Berlin Heidelberg 2013

1980	Internal tensions due to a severe economic crisis and left and right political movements lead to another military coup. An export-led growth policy set up with IMF and WB support, continues after the coup, aiming to liberalize the Turkish economy by means of export subsidies, privatization, free currency exchange, and open financial markets.
1996	Turkey is fully integrated into the Customs Union. Import taxes, which had been gradually decreased since 1990, are cancelled altogether for imports from the European Union and EFTA countries.
1999	Turkey becomes a candidate for full membership of the EU negotiations begin on 3 October, 2005.
Membership of international economic organizations:	IMF (1947), OECD (1961), ECO (1985), BSEC (1992), WTO (1997), D-8 (1997)

1 Introduction: Context

After centuries of increasing preeminence on three continents, the Ottoman Empire started losing its power by the end of the seventeenth century. Prevailing religious conservatism had resulted in its lagging behind Western countries in terms of intellectual and technological development. The decreased power of the military led to defeat in several wars. Consequently, nationalistic ideas, which had spread to the Empire by the nineteenth century, caused many of the nations under its control to declare war for their own independence. The reorganization and modernization efforts in the military, finance, industry, and civil rights—starting in the mid-nineteenth century—were not able to prevent the empire from dissolving or becoming economically dependent on foreign countries. Lastly, after its defeat in World War I, the Ottoman Empire's territory was gradually partitioned by the Allies, a period finalized by the Treaty of Sevres in 1920, leaving only a minor Turkish territory. In 1923, Turkey won its War of Independence, and the Treaty of Lausanne determined new borders that have not changed since then. The establishment of the Republic of Turkey followed on 29 October, 1923.

The newly established Republic of Turkey was a wounded country, as its physical and social capital had eroded in the preceding periods. Industrialization efforts were initiated by the state to create a domestic market for consumer goods. Following the shift to a multi-party electoral regime in 1945, The Demokrat Party came to power in 1950, bringing with it a strong emphasis on agriculture-led growth in line with the Marshall Plan of the US (Pamuk 2010). During these years, Turkey became a member of several international political and economic institutions, including the IMF (1947), NATO (1952) and OECD (1961). In 1960, fear that Turkey's government was a threat to the secular state led to a military intervention. In the same period, import substitution industrialization became the official economic development policy. It aimed at minimizing imports and creating domestic production by means of implementation of quotas, tariffs, and exchange regulations. In 1980, a severe economic crisis, caused by lack of foreign exchange and left and right political movements, led to internal tensions and another military coup followed. Nonetheless, the export-led growth policy, arranged with the IMF and the WB just before the coup, was continued with a view to liberalize the Turkish economy by means of export subsidies, privatization, free currency exchange, and open financial markets. In 1996, Turkey was fully integrated into the Customs Union, and import taxes were cancelled for imports from the European Union and EFTA countries. In 1997, Turkey became a member of the WTO. While having an average annual economic growth of 3.04 % for the last 20 years, the country has also suffered several economic crises. The biggest of these, the crisis of 2001, was followed by macroeconomic stabilization and structural reforms, especially in the banking sector, which shielded the economy to some extent from the 2009 world economic crisis.

Turkey was recognized as a candidate for full membership of the EU in 1999, and negotiations started in 2005. Since then, to comply with the requirements of the EU, several legislations have been changed and new institutions have been established to administer the economy, health, the environment, and civil rights. Despite the accomplishment of the requirements, Turkey's accession to the EU has caused a major political controversy among member states.

Turkey has the world's 15th largest GDP at PPP and the 17th largest nominal GDP. It is in a period of rapid growth and industrialization with the help of newly established market-oriented institutions. The major international economic institutions considered Turkey an emerging economy. It has a number of attractive features: a large domestic market (a population of 73 million in 2011) and a geographical and cultural proximity to both Eastern and Western markets. Some more economic data are shown in Exhibit 1.

Turkey has a dynamic economy, characterized by a mix of modern industry, commerce, and a traditional agriculture sector. The share of agriculture in total employment fell from 80 % in 1950 to 51 % in 1980 (Pamuk 2010), and 25 % in 2010 (OECD 2010). The largest industrial sector is textiles and clothing, accounting for one-third of industrial employment. The automotive and electronic industries are growing in importance and have recently surpassed textiles in export composition. In 2009, 46.0 % of Turkey's exports were bound for EU countries, followed by the Middle-Eastern region with a share of 18.8 %. In the same period, Turkey's main export partners were Germany (9.6 %), France (6.1 %), the UK (5.8 %), Italy (5.8 %), and Iraq (5.0 %) (Turkish Statistics Institute, 2009).

While Turkey has some natural resources, such as coal, iron, copper, uranium and chromium, it imports nearly all of its oil and natural gas, which fosters the country's foreign trade deficit. Historically, this deficit has been financed by foreign borrowing. However, increased domestic long-term borrowing and foreign direct

Exhibit 1 Core economic indicators of Turkey

	1999	2000	2001	2002	2003	2004	2005	2006	2007	2008	2009	2010	2011
GDP per capita (current $US)	3,983.75	4,189.48	3,036.73	3,553.07	4,567.50	5,832.69	7,087.72	7,687.13	9,246.03	10,297.51	8,553.74	10,049.77	10,524.00
GDP per capita growth (annual %)	−4.83	5.21	−7.04	4.70	3.85	7.90	6.96	5.47	3.28	−0.66	−6.05	7.80	7.20
Long-term unemployment (% of total unemployment)	27.30	20.40	20.90	28.30	23.40	38.50	39.40	35.70	30.30	26.90	25.30	28.60	26.50
Foreign direct investment, net inflows (% of GDP)	0.31	0.37	1.71	0.47	0.56	0.71	2.08	3.80	3.41	2.67	1.37	1.24	2.07
GDP (current $USm)	249,751.47	266,567.53	196,005.29	232,534.56	303,005.30	392,166.27	482,979.84	530,900.09	647,155.13	730,337.50	614,553.92	731,144.39	774,983.42
Exports of goods and services (current $USm)	48,551.40	53,574.40	53,785.58	58,638.96	69,674.96	92,361.27	105,557.06	120,354.56	144,466.00	174,608.49	143,292.03	155,069.45	183,987.57
Exports of goods and services (% of GDP)	19.44	20.10	27.44	25.22	22.99	23.55	21.86	22.67	22.32	23.91	23.32	21.21	23.74
Merchandise exports (current $USm)	26,588.00	27,775.00	31,334.00	36,059.00	47,253.00	63,167.00	73,476.00	85,535.00	107,271.75	132,027.20	102,142.61	113,883.22	134,971.55
Merchandise exports to high-income economies (% of total merchandise exports)	74.83	75.41	73.23	73.12	71.80	71.14	67.83	67.25	64.69	61.92	58.83	57.91	n/a
Merchandise exports to developing economies in	8.76	9.22	9.54	10.11	10.69	10.88	12.22	13.67	15.97	16.70	13.40	14.47	n/a

Europe & Central Asia (% of total merchandise exports)													
Ores and metals exports (% of merchandise exports)	2.78	2.57	2.20	2.00	1.99	2.17	2.46	3.31	3.49	3.40	3.21	4.40	4.21
Agricultural raw materials exports (% of merchandise exports)	1.34	1.12	0.86	0.81	0.80	0.66	0.52	0.51	0.45	0.39	0.39	0.44	0.55
Food exports (% of merchandise exports)	15.36	12.80	12.75	10.09	10.01	9.31	10.49	9.32	8.44	8.30	10.83	10.58	10.61
Fuel exports (% of merchandise exports)	1.27	1.06	1.42	1.92	2.08	2.27	3.61	4.17	4.82	5.85	4.00	3.93	4.70
Manufactures exports (% of merchandise exports)	79.12	81.24	81.75	83.93	83.71	84.55	81.57	81.40	81.69	80.97	80.23	79.18	78.31
High-technology exports (% of manufactured exports)	4.14	4.83	3.87	1.79	1.93	1.90	1.47	1.85	1.89	1.62	1.74	1.93	n/a

Source: World Bank (2013)

investment (FDI) inflows have also been effective, especially in the last decade. In 2010, Turkey became the 15th most attractive destination for FDI in the world (UNCTAD World Investment Prospects Survey, 2008–2010). The privatization of major state-owned enterprises, planned in the liberalization efforts in 1980s but initiated in the last decade, also contributed to the increase in FDI inflows. Turkey's outward FDI has also been rising in recent years, due to both push and pull factors. The liberalization of the economy has made the domestic market much more competitive, forcing Turkish firms to look abroad for profitable opportunities. Meanwhile, the emergence of independent republics in Central Asia and the political and economic developments in the Middle East have created new opportunities for them.

When it comes to competitiveness and a balanced sustainable economic development, Turkey cannot always show a bright performance. In 2010, Turkey was ranked 63rd of 135 countries in the Global Competitiveness Index measured by the World Economic Forum, and 83rd in the Human Development Index. Although value-adding has increased in some conventional industries in recent years, mainly by localization of parts supply, the economy lacks high value-added activity and innovation in general. Holding companies have a huge slice of the economic pie in Turkey. They have typically based their growth on unrelated diversification strategies, taking advantage of institutional voids, motivated by their risk-averse nature, or in the pursuit of new opportunities (Buğra 1995). More recently, a surge of competition in the domestic market, along with the liberalization of the economy and the increased global competition, has forced them to focus on particular industries and emphasize innovation. While the financial system has been developing with new regulations and agencies, the country lacks institutions for providing small firms with access to capital. The adequacy and efficiency of incentive systems regarding R&D are questionable, and firms typically lack the capital for a scale-up period after their innovations. Still, in this period of modernizing its economic structure, Turkey ranks 83rd in property rights and 117th in intellectual property rights, out of 136 countries.

Hidden Champions (HCs) are not widely known to the general public; therefore, finding them requires some exploration. We first analysed business journals and newspapers, and found a small sample based on the statements of company managers regarding their global or regional leadership. Next, we analyzed the Top-500 Companies list provided by the Istanbul Chamber of Industry, focusing on firms with export activities. We identified candidate companies, and we crosschecked their market data claims with the trade and industry associations' web pages. We also contacted the Federation of Industrial Associations (SEDEFED) of Turkey, and requested their help in finding more HCs. By 2009, there were 11 Turkish firms with annual revenues higher than 4 billion US dollars, which we directly excluded because they exceeded the revenue criteria. One interesting point was that there were plenty of Turkish firms claiming leadership in Europe and the Middle East in terms of production; however, very few of them claimed regional leadership in terms of sales. This is an indicator that Turkish firms

Exhibit 2 Hidden champions from Turkey

Name	Market leadership description	Revenue 2009 (€m)	Employees 2009
Aksa	#1 in USA in acrylic fiber for outdoor products	503	900
Alvimedica	Technological innovation leader in interventional cardiology products	7	200
Arbel	#1 in the world in red lentil	200	750
Ege Cooling Systems (Safkar)	#1 in Eastern Europe and Middle East	n/a	296
Eko Textile (Suwen, Gossard)	3 in Europe in lingerie and underwear (biggest producer in CEE, Europe, and Middle East)	22	1,590
Kanca Hand Tools	#1 in Europe in vise production	52	420
Kordsa	#1 in the world in cord fabric for tire reinforcement and mechanical rubber	650	6,000
Mutlu Batteries	#1 in Russia and CIS in transportation and industrial batteries (biggest manufacturer in Middle East and Eastern Europe)	112	695
Şişecam Group (Paşabahçe)	#1 in CEE, Middle East and Middle Central Asia, #2 in Europe, #3in the world in glassware	1.700	17,983
Yünsa	#1 in Europe in worsted yarn fabric	64	1.516

Source: Authors of the chapter

do not only focus on particular markets to become regional leaders, but expand towards dispersed regions. A final list of ten HCs that responded to our survey can be found in Exhibit 2.

2 Ten Case Studies

2.1 AKSA (Akrilik Kimya Sanayi A.Ş.)

Overview

Address: Miralay Şefik Bey Sk. Ak-Han No:15 34437 Gümüşsuyu Istanbul, Turkey
Tel: +902122514500
Email: aksa@aksa.com
Web: http://www.aksa.com/

Company Information

Industry:	Manufacture of chemicals and chemical products
Year of establishment:	1968
Sales revenue in 2009:	€503 million
Sales revenue in 1999:	€347 million
Average number of employees in 2009:	900
Brain(s) behind the company:	CEO Mustafa Yilmaz

2.1.1 Nature of Market Leadership

AKSA is the biggest producer of acrylic fibre under one roof; it owns 12.5 % of the global production. This company is number one in the USA, in both revenue and output volume, in acrylic fibre for outdoor products.

2.1.2 Nature of Competitive Advantage

The company sees its uniqueness in its customer-focused model. Customer feedback is much valued; customers are often visited and their satisfaction level measured once a year by an independent public relations company. Production is tailored according to the production system and the needs of the customer, so that the latter can achieve high performance and efficiency. In addition, the product range is increased and continuously improved with new and innovative products. The company's long history is also a big asset, as it provides a source of accumulated market knowledge and management skills.

2.1.3 Core Lessons Learned on the Path to Business Success

1. When faced with price competition in basic goods, instead of cutting prices, invest in R&D to come up with more sophisticated products that can justify higher profit margins.
2. Creating new and efficient uses and tailoring the production mode and product design to customer demands, and intensive pre-sales and after-sales services, promotes customer loyalty and thus maximizes value-added for both the company and its customers.
3. When faced with increasing competition, and decreasing market demand and prices, your superior market knowledge and intuition as a leader can help the firm sustain, and even increase, its market share. A highly qualified and motivated work force, together with a strong company culture, can be complementary resources.

2.1.4 AKSA: Hidden Champion

The Akkök Group of companies established AKSA in 1968. It reached a capacity of 308,000 tons by 2009, making it the "world's largest acrylic fiber producer under a single roof". It also has a plant in Egypt. AKSA provides 12.5 % of the global production using the world's most developed manufacturing technology. It has been exporting through the trading company of the group since 1977, and today it exports 40 % of its production to a customer portfolio of approximately 300 firms in more than 50 countries, in five continents. The firm has recently started production of carbon fibre, which requires state-of-the-art technology and is mainly used in aircraft, wind turbine blades, pressure vessels, and the marine industry.

2.2 Alvimedica Medical Technologies

Overview

Address:	Istanbul Trakya Free Zone 34540 Çatalca Istanbul, Turkey
Tel:	+902127866080
Email:	contact@alvimedica.com
Web:	http://www.alvimedica.com/

Company Information

Industry:	Manufacture of basic pharmaceutical products and pharmaceutical preparations
Year of establishment:	2007
Sales revenue in 2009:	€7 million
Sales Revenue in 1999:	n/a
Average number of employees in 2009:	200
Brain(s) behind the company:	CEO Cem Bozkurt

2.2.1 Nature of Market Leadership

A world leader in technological innovation in the interventional cardiology sector, with products, such as the 100 % soluble polymer coated stent, invented and produced for the first time by Alvimedika. The market is growing both in size and volume, along with a rise in the price of the products.

2.2.2 Nature of Competitive Advantage

The company's competitive advantage arises from making worldwide innovations both in design and production. Its innovations are aimed at making consumers' lives easier. In addition, a special branch monitors all the processes that concern customers, and customer satisfaction is maintained by providing superior service quality.

2.2.3 Core Lessons Learned on the Path to Business Success

1. Collaborate with universities and companies all around the world for R&D. Do not focus only on improvement and innovation of products that deliver immediate solutions, but also on long-term research to make radical innovations.
2. Your main goal must be satisfying customer needs, rather than competition. Create the necessary conditions for the employees' self-improvement to tap all their potential. Together these elements will create a competitive advantage.
3. Set ambitious goals. Act as a big company with an established, well developed, and globally available product line, but still carry the heart and soul of a small innovative company. This versatility will provide rapid development of new products and technologies.

2.2.4 Alvimedica Medical Technologies: Hidden Champion

Turkish scientists and businessmen living in Denmark and Sweden established Alvimedica in 2007. The company invests and transforms SMEs operating in health care and the medical technology industry into prestigious world-class companies. It manufactures diagnostic catheters, guiding catheters, PTCA balloon catheters, and SDSs, with a world-class production technology. The company operates a 5,500 m^2 manufacturing facility (with the biggest Class 10 clean-rooms in Europe) located in Catalca-Istanbul, opened in February 2009. Despite its short history, Alvimedica sells its products to more than 30 countries around the world through a rapidly expanding distributor network in Europe, Latin America, Africa, the Middle- and Far East, Russia, and CIS.

2.3 ARBEL A.Ş.

Overview

Address:	Yeni Mahalle, Cumhuriyet Bulvarı No: 73/4, Kazanlı Mersin, Turkey
Tel:	+903242411111
Email:	arbel@arbel.com.tr
Web:	http://www.arbel.com.tr

Company Information

Industry:	Crop and animal production, and related services
Year of establishment:	1980
Sales revenue in 2009:	€200 million
Sales revenue in 1999:	n/a
Average number of employees in 2010:	750
Brain(s) behind the company:	CEO and owner Hüseyin Arslan

2.3.1 Nature of Market Leadership

ARBEL A.Ş. produces lentils, chickpeas, bulgur, wheat, beans, peas, rice, and pasta. For the past 3 years, it has been number one in the world in red lentils production in terms of revenue and volume. It has 25 % of the global market compared to the 5 % of its closest competitor.

2.3.2 Nature of Competitive Advantage

Using its market experience and management skills, ARBEL has collaborated with grain producing companies and institutions to create new hybrid grains to satisfy the needs of the world lentil market. Product quality creates a gap between ARBEL and its closest competitors. Although its price and product range are similar, ARBEL provides higher quality products. As the sole producer and supplier of a unique variety of lentils, ARBEL has a prominent position in the customer's mind. ARBEL has registered licences for the production of various kinds of lentils and guarantees delivery deadlines and production locations in line with customer expectations.

2.3.3 Core Lessons Learned on the Path to Business Success

1. The leadership style of the company's CEO includes fairness in every decision and an emphasis on teamwork. For him, employee satisfaction is equally important to company growth as it helps the company sustain product improvement and keep its market position.
2. Providing high-quality products at comparable market prices, being customer-focused during product development, and registering its unique products creates a high market share for the firm.
3. Collaborate with suppliers to help you deliver superior product quality at comparable costs and prices.

2.3.4 ARBEL A.Ş: Hidden Champion

ARBEL was established in 1980. With its 10 brands, it is a leading processor and exporter of grains, pulses, and other food products for domestic and international markets. Its facilities in Turkey, located on a 100,000 m^2 compound in the Mersin Free Zone, provide logistical advantages in sea and land connections for the shipment of products to global markets. In 2009, all food-related operations of ARBEL A.Ş. where acquired by Alliance Grain Traders, which had 21 facilities in Canada, the US, Australia, and Turkey.

2.4 Eko Tekstil Sanayi ve Ticaret Ltd. ŞTİ.

Overview

Address: N. Kemal Mah. Cengiz Opel Cad. Billur Sok. No:30 Ümraniye Istanbul, Turkey

Tel: +902164431958
Email: info@ekotex.com
Web: http://www.ekotex.com/ or http://www.suwen.com.tr/

Company Information

Industry:	Manufacture of wearing apparel
Year of establishment:	1994
Sales revenue in 2009:	€22 million
Sales revenue in 1999:	€3 m
Average number of employees in 2009:	1,590
Brain(s) behind the company:	CEO and founder Özcan Sumer

2.4.1 Nature of Market Leadership

The company operates as both contract manufacturer and manufacturer of its own brands in the lingerie and underwear market. It is number three in Europe in terms of revenue and output volume, and is the biggest producer of lingerie in CEE, Europe, and the Middle East. It is also a leader in evaluating trends, developing new products, and concern for research and development.

2.4.2 Nature of Competitive Advantage

Eko Tekstil differentiates itself from competitors with its speed, high quality, wide and flexible product lines, and trendy designs created through continuous investments in R&D and design. Even prestigious contractor companies prefer Eko Tekstil designs to their own. The company works collaboratively with its suppliers and customers, so that they can use new and fashionable materials in their designs and offer superior products. A unique coordination capability enables Eko Tekstil to have its products manufactured in the most convenient regions and sell to markets where there is most potential. The entrepreneurship of the owner, his planning skills, deep intuition, and dedication to developing the capabilities of the firm, have together helped the company to maintain its competitive advantage.

2.4.3 Core Lessons Learned on the Path to Business Success

1. Even if production shifts towards lower-cost countries in the industry, you can reverse this situation by responding quickly to trends and developing fashionable and differentiated products.
2. Knowing the markets intimately is necessary for providing flexibility and speed in delivery, while cultural proximity helps Eko Tekstil to design product lines superior to those of competitors from more distant countries.
3. "The key to our rapid success is our mentality of working for success, not for money. If you work for success, money comes later as well", says Özcan Sumer.

2.4.4 Eko Tekstil: Hidden Champion

Eko Tekstil was founded in 1994, merchandizing in Germany the lingerie that it produced in Turkey. In 1999, the company started its own production facilities, operating as a contractual manufacturer of lingerie and underwear for foreign brands. In 2003, it extended its product line to include outwear made of combed cotton. It continued to grow by establishing new plants in Turkey, Egypt, Morocco, and Ukraine, and by building its own brands and acquiring existing ones. Exports constitute 95 % of total sales, and product destinations include Europe, the US, the Middle East and Asia.

2.5 KANCA EL ALETLERi DÖVME ÇELIK A.Ş.

Overview

Address:	Taysad Organize Sanayi Bölgesi 41480, Şekerpınar-Çayirova Kocaeli, Turkey
Tel:	+902626788600
Email:	info@kanca.com.tr
Web:	http://www.kanca.com.tr

Company Information

Industry:	Manufacture of fabricated metal products, except machinery and equipment
Year of establishment:	1974
Sales revenue in 2009:	€52 million
Sales revenue in 1999:	n/a
Average number of employees in 2009:	420
Brain(s) behind the company:	CEO and owner Alper Kanca

2.5.1 Nature of Market Leadership

KANCA produces hand tools and forged parts. With its major product line—bench vices—it is a market leader in Europe in terms of sales volume and revenue. The company has a 36 % market share in Europe, compared to the 25 % share of its closest competitor.

2.5.2 Nature of Competitive Advantage

A competitive advantage has been achieved by creating high customer satisfaction, applying an appropriate quality/price ratio, opening a local branch so as to be close to customers and satisfy their need for spare parts and retail, making frequent regular customer visits, and by quickly introducing new products according to the needs of the customers.

2.5.3 Core Lessons Learned on the Path to Business Success

1. Form well-established customer relations; be close to the customers, not only by opening branches nearby, but also by visiting them frequently.
2. Even if operating in a very low-tech industry, invest considerable amounts in R&D to design and develop new products.
3. Design the products according to customer needs and introduce them to the market rapidly. Be quick and flexible in delivering the products.

2.5.4 KANCA: Hidden Champion

KANCA started to produce hand tools as a family-owned business in 1966. In the following years, the company widened its product range in both hand tools and forged parts, the latter deriving from demand from the auto industry. Capacity was gradually increased, finally reaching 20,000 tons per year. The company uses a 25,000 m^2 factory facility with an adjoining 30,000 m^2 open area. It exports 50 % of its production mainly to Europe through five agencies in Europe, one in North America, and a branch and advanced distribution center in Germany.

2.6 KORDSA Global

Overview

Address:	Sabancı Centre Kulesi 2, Kat 17, 4. Levent, Beşiktaş Istanbul, Turkey
Tel:	+902123858657
Email:	info@kordsaglobal.com
Web:	http://www.kordsaglobal.com

Company Information

Industry:	Manufacture of textiles
Year of establishment:	1973
Sales revenue in 2010:	€650 million
Sales revenue in 2000:	€120 million
Average number of employees in 2010:	6,000
Brain(s) behind the company:	CEO Hakan Tiftik

2.6.1 Nature of Market Leadership

In terms of market share, revenue, and profitability, KORDSA Global is a worldwide market leader in high denier nylon-polyester industrial yarn, cord fabrics, industrial fabrics, and single-end cord products. Its main customers are leading manufacturers of vehicle tyres in the mechanical rubber goods industry.

2.6.2 Nature of Competitive Advantage

Major competencies that distinguish KORDSA from its competitors are product quality and a higher price-performance ratio. These are followed by the ability to build and maintain relationships with customers, both before and after sales. The provision of service facilities close to customers, flexibility of orders, superiority in distribution channels, and cooperation with suppliers, are further advantages. The scope of the company's R&D activities, and innovation and excellence, are the core elements of corporate culture.

2.6.3 Core Lessons Learned on the Path to Business Success

1. Operating excellence comes with the combination of achieving competitive local costs at all sites, having production capacity aligned with the market demand, and establishing a global supply chain with flexible products.
2. One can be a successful partner to customers by improving connections with their technical and operational departments, using advanced materials and know-how, providing customized services, and having an open innovation culture to achieve new solutions.
3. Using a balanced global approach is necessary for global success, which consists of product management with global customers, global functions driving global synergies, and developing the technical ability to satisfy various customer wants.

2.6.4 KORDSA Global: Hidden Champion

KORDSA Global was established in 1973 by one of the biggest Turkish conglomerates, the Sabanci Holding. It is the world's leading producer of nylon and polyester cord fabric for at the tyre-reinforcement and mechanical rubber markets. It operates with 11 facilities located in nine countries in five continents, and a 4,500-strong workforce. It exports 97 % of its production to more than 80 countries.

2.7 MUTLU AKÜ VE MALZEMELERI SAN. A.Ş.

Overview

Address:	Tepeören Mahallesi, Eski Ankara Yolu Cad No: 60 Tuzla Istanbul, Turkey
Tel:	+902163041590
Email:	ygulmez@mutlu.com
Web:	http://www.mutlu.com.tr/

Company Information

Industry:	Manufacture of electrical equipment
Year of establishment:	1945
Sales revenue in 2009:	€112 million
Sales revenue in 1999:	€108 million
Average number of employees in 2010:	695
Brain(s) behind the company:	CEO Atilla Turker

2.7.1 Nature of Market Leadership

MUTLU Batteries is the biggest battery manufacturer in Turkey, the Middle East, and Eastern Europe. The company sells transportation and industrial batteries to more than 25 countries throughout Europe, Russia, South Africa, the Middle East, the Far East, and North and Central Asia. It holds a strong market position in Russia, Turkey and the CIS countries. The company is a leader in Russia in terms of sales volume and revenue.

2.7.2 Nature of Competitive Advantage

Although global giants, especially from the US, dominate the battery industry in other regions, they have yet to fully enter the geographical scope of MUTLU.

MUTLU's products are of higher quality compared to those of its main competitors. The company also has superior design capabilities and the ability to develop specialized products according to customer demands. Employees are provided with international training at the most hi-tech battery plants, by producers of battery production machines in Europe and in the US, with whom MUTLU cooperates.

2.7.3 Core Lessons Learned on the Path to Business Success

1. Producing for branches of multinational firms in the home market creates network advantages that bring high success during internationalization.
2. Taking advantage of the opportunities arising from political developments in particular markets, and being the first-mover, enables rapid and deep penetration into the market.
3. Dedication to recycling your used products, particularly in the battery business, creates tremendous savings for the company.

2.7.4 MUTLU Akü: Hidden Champion

MUTLU Batteries, the original and leading company of MUTLU Incorporated, was established in 1945 as a trading company. In 1955, it started producing batteries for the auto industry. Since then, the company's capacity has grown steadily; it has adapted new technologies and widened its product range to include various types of batteries for different end uses. MUTLU Akü establishes sales contracts with original equipment manufacturers by the use of its own sales teams. With its modern 230,000 m^2 facility, it has become the biggest battery manufacturer in Turkey, the Middle East, and Eastern Europe.

2.8 SAFKAR (EGE SOĞUTMACILIK KLİMA ve SOĞUK HAVA TESİSLERİ İHR. İTH. SAN. ve TİC. A.Ş.)

Overview

Address:	Ulukent Sanayi Bölgesi 10001 Sokak, No. 15 Ulukent Izmir, Turkey
Tel:	+902328333764
Email:	info@safkar.com
Web:	http://www.safkar.com.tr/

Company Information

Industry:	Manufacture of machinery and equipment
Year of establishment:	1988
Sales revenue in 2009:	n/a
Revenues in 1999:	n/a
Average number of employees in 2010:	296
Brain(s) behind the company:	CEO Doruk Aydın

2.8.1 Nature of Market Leadership

SAFKAR operates in every segment of mobile climate control. It is a leader in Eastern Europe and the Middle-Eastern markets, where it competes with other global firms. In Europe, it is among the top five companies in its sector. It also claims to be a leader in R&D and project development with customers.

2.8.2 Nature of Competitive Advantage

SAFKAR provides high-quality products at low prices, while offering a 100 % guarantee on parts and service to its customers, thus fulfilling their most important needs. The company operates as project partner for its customers and designs products according to their specific needs. It has established its market in Central Asia and the Middle East by early introduction of its products and the provision of comprehensive after-sales service.

2.8.3 Core Lessons Learned on the Path to Business Success

1. If you can offer a favourable price/performance ratio, and flexible designs according to customer wants, market capture soon follows.

2. Establishing manufacturing facilities close to the customer enables flexibility in delivery and lowers transportation costs, which can be reflected in sales prices.
3. While strengthening customer relations, the extensive after-sales services provided by the company enables the customers to use the products correctly and get maximum efficiency from them, thus reducing warranty costs to the company.

2.8.4 SAFKAR: Hidden Champion

Ege Cooling Systems started its operations in 1988 in Izmir, manufacturing under the brand of SAFKAR, later introducing the Penguin brand. The initial product range included bus and mini-bus air conditioners. It was quickly expanded by means of intensive research and development investments, which resulted in the addition of frigorific systems, commercial vehicle air-conditioning systems, railroad vehicle air-conditioning systems, and special applications: ambulances, military vehicles, construction machinery, and so forth. The company now operates with a capacity of 15,000 units per year. In 2000, the company started production in Algeria. SAFKAR now exports to 33 countries worldwide through its established dealer network, consisting of 336 dealers.

2.9 ŞİŞECAM: TÜRKİYE ŞİŞE VE CAM FABRİKALARI A.Ş.

Overview

Address:	Iş Kuleleri Kule 3 Kat: 23, 4. Levent Istanbul, Turkey
Tel:	+902123505050
Email:	info@sisecam.com
Web:	http://www.sisecam.com.tr/

Company Information

Industry:	Manufacture of non-metallic mineral products
Year of establishment:	1935
Sales revenue in 2009:	€1.7 billion
Sales revenue in 1999:	€1.2 billion
Average number of employees in 2010:	17,673
Brain(s) behind the company:	CEO Ahmet Kirman

2.9.1 Nature of Market Leadership

In the glassware sector, ŞIŞECAM is a leader in terms of sales volume and revenue in the region that it calls "Our Vital Geography", i.e., Eastern Europe, the Balkans, and the Middle East,. The group is ranked second in Europe with a market share of 25 %, and third in the world with a market share of 9 %.

2.9.2 Nature of Competitive Advantage

The group's tangible and intangible resources, particularly its market knowledge and customer relations acquired over its long history, have helped it achieve a leadership position. The highly qualified and loyal workforce, together with a strong company culture, also provides a key intangible resource. The financial strength of the company enables it to be more innovative while fostering its success.

2.9.3 Core Lessons Learned on the Path to Business Success

1. Use collective intellect; listen, discuss, and make strategic decisions collectively when possible and diffuse them to the shareholders. Make right decisions at the right times.
2. Set off with a proper industrial enterprise, which includes corporate governance, and insist on long-term strategic planning and specialization. Restructure the firm when necessary and focus on a market geography that you can define as your "vital region".
3. Use joint ventures for accessing knowledge of the markets and for benefiting the network of the local manufacturer.

2.9.4 ŞİŞECAM: Hidden Champion

The ŞİŞECAM Group was established in 1935 as a subsidiary of İŞBANK. After serving only domestic demand during the early period of industrialization in Turkey, it had begun to enter foreign markets by the 1960s. Today, ŞİŞECAM is a global group with diversified operations in eight countries, selling its products in 140 countries. Its production activities cover all basic needs for glass; including float glass, glass household articles, glass packaging, and glass fiber, as well as soda and chromium compounds. Glassware is exported mainly from the branches in Bulgaria, Russia, the US, Germany, China, Spain and Japan.

2.10 YÜNSA YÜNLÜ SANAYİ VE TİCARET A.Ş.

Overview

Address:	Sabanci Centre Kat 19–20 4. Levent Istanbul, Turkey
Tel:	+902123858700
Email:	yunsa@yunsa.com
Web:	http://www.yunsa.com

Company Information

Industry:	Manufacture of textiles
Year of establishment:	1973
Sales revenue in 2009:	€63 million
Sales revenue in 1999:	€42 million
Average number of employees in 2010:	1,516
Brain(s) behind the company:	CEO Cem Çelikoğlu

2.10.1 Nature of Market Leadership

In terms of revenue, YÜNSA has been the largest worsted wool fabric producer and seller in Europe for the last 2 years, ranking fifth in the world. Its principle markets are the EU, North America, and Eastern countries. Its market share is 7 % in Europe and 4 % in the world. Over the last decade, there has been some conservative growth in the size of the market and in sales volume, with a corresponding increase in prices.

2.10.2 Nature of Competitive Advantage

Strong customer relationships, superior market knowledge, and professional marketing skills establish the core of the company's competitive intangible resources, complemented by a very strong corporate culture among the highly qualified and dynamic workforce. Highly capable in flexible production, the company can fill small-scale special orders in addition to large-scale ones, with a guarantee of delivery on time. A core advantage of YÜNSA's products over those of its rivals is the ability to satisfy specific design needs for the customer, at a lower price and higher efficiency ratio.

2.10.3 Core Lessons Learned on the Path to Business Success

1. In times of crisis, do not simply focus on cutting costs, but also embrace an assertive strategy by introducing new products to the market, at lower prices.
2. Global success comes from a combined strategy: a customer-centered approach, exceptional design skills, an ability to adapt to market dynamics and trends, high product quality, flexibility in production, and delivery on time.
3. Anticipating the market and one's competitors is vital for business success. Strong connections and collaborations with customers worldwide are also necessary.

2.10.4 YÜNSA: Hidden Champion

YÜNSA was established in 1973 as part of the Sabanci Group, producing worsted yarn and fabric, a product differentiated from woolen fabrics by its cooler and lighter nature and satin-like appearance. Since then, the company has grown sustainably to become a champion. In its strong international network, YÜNSA has more than 900 customers in more than 60 countries. The company has sales offices in United Kingdom, Germany, United States, and China, and has agents in many other countries. Exports constitute approximately 70 % of its fabric production. The company has a yearly production capacity of around 12,000 km of fabric, and 3,600 tons of worsted yarn.

Conclusion

The leaders of the Turkish HCs define themselves with words such as "dynamic", "analytic", and as having "a wide vision". In addition, they emphasize the importance of participative teamwork and self-development of their employees. Hüseyin Arslan, founder and CEO of Arbel, sees himself as a leader "who gives importance to fair work and teamwork", while Cem Bozkurt, CEO of Alvimedika, suggests that he "gives birth to new leaders" by encouraging employees to take the initiative and become leaders of their own businesses.

All HCs in Turkey have strong manufacturing competencies developed through licenses or contract manufacturing. They have realized their ambitions of building sustainable corporations by investing in innovation, quality, and customer relations. The nature of competition in their environment is different to the situation described in Simon's (2009) study, because Turkey's HCs face on average 20 competitors while Simon's subjects faced only 6 or 7. Price is a more important factor in the markets of the former group, so most of them cannot charge prices that are much higher than those of their rivals in the way that Simon's global firms do. In general, Turkish HCs seem to sell higher quality goods for cheaper prices. Since firms operate with the highest quality and lowest prices, they have high market share but relatively low profits. The negative return on assets for some companies suggests that they are not profitable. Making profit can be a major challenge for them. They need to seek ways to charge higher prices while preserving their market share.

The innovation management practices and emphasis on innovation in the Turkish sample are similar to those described in Simon's findings. However, the innovativeness of our companies does not necessarily show up in the number of patents that the firms have. It is important to note that these companies are process-based. Their innovativeness comes from their processes and is not easily transferred into patents. Some firms intentionally keep their processes as trade secrets. Those that interact directly with end customers can react to demands and try to build intellectual assets around patents, utility models, and brands. Even heavy manufacturers try to be close to their customers—who are themselves producers—so that they can benefit from the innovative ideas from the customer end. This closeness is also kept alive through distributorships and newly established after-sales service structures. In addition, Turkish HCs open offices, branches and service centres to have flexibility in supply. These companies emphasize their ability in tailored design and work closely with customers for product development.

Turkish HCs grow by exporting their own brands to different regions or by acquiring existing brands. They also extend their markets by innovative products within the niche. They perform related diversifications in which they can improve the common core technologies. Yet, these are not necessarily the soft diversifications of Simon's champions, because the Turkish HCs are entering new businesses with new products that have different customer bases.

With one exception, Alvimedika, Turkish HCs operate in the country's leading export industries: auto, textiles, and food. Auto parts producers initially benefited from high domestic demand. Then—having increased their capabilities over time—they have expanded abroad with the help of existing ties with multinational corporations operating in Turkey.

While developments in China and India have constituted big threats to Turkish HCs in recent years, they have been able to maintain their position relative to Eastern businesses mainly by guaranteeing higher quality, tailored design, flexible production, and after-sales service. In addition, Turkey is closer to the European market and the newly emerging Middle East market where demand is increasing. Furthermore, geographic proximity enables delivery on time with lower transportation costs, while cultural intimacy with both Eastern and Western markets helps Turkish firms to understand their customers better and therefore design products that they prefer.

Turkish HCs have used the first-mover advantage in former Soviet Union countries, as well as in the Middle East where wealth is increasing. Penetration into these markets has offered them a competitive advantage for the future. However, in Western Europe and the US, Turkish HCs face the liability of newness; competitors already have quite strong brands and market penetration. In these competitive markets, flexibility in production and price efficiency are the saviours of Turkish HCs. Meanwhile, Turkey is still a low-cost country in comparison to Europe and North America, which creates advantages—some businesses in advanced countries cannot move their factories to a low-cost environment, nor can they achieve the desired quality at the same price.

But nothing is guaranteed in the long term. East Asian firms are gradually increasing the level of quality, and Western multinational corporations are starting to enter those emerging markets where Turkish businesses have been first-movers. Therefore, Turkish HCs are not able to avoid fully global competition anymore, whether they operate regionally or globally. Some of them are opening factories in lower-cost countries such as Egypt and China, aiming at producing basic products in these regions. Meanwhile, being aware of the unsustainable nature of price-based competition, Turkish HCs are very keen on innovation. They are not exactly major technology initiators, yet they are quick implementers. In addition, they mostly rely on incremental or architectural innovations for differentiating their products. While this strategy is less risky and less costly, it also carries the risk of lagging behind the competition if radical innovators quickly capture the market.

In addition to the goals of extending their customer base, high-quality production, and differentiation, Turkish HCs also invest in R&D with the aim of cost reduction through process innovations. This approach usually enables them to provide a superior efficiency/price ratio compared to that of their competitors. Other created efficiencies that decrease production costs include high capacity usage rates, production of their own energy within the plants, and the recycling and reuse of scrap.

An emphasis on process innovation has enabled the Turkish HCs to cope with the impacts of the financial crisis. During the crisis, they have implemented extensive cost-cutting programs by means of good managerial practices, without having to lay off employees or reduce R&D expenditure. They have also expanded into markets that are less affected by the crisis.

As most of the Turkish HCs are new global or regional players with brands that do not command a strong reputation, they aim at doing many things better than their competitors to create customer loyalty. Still, they are usually unable to charge higher prices. To fully exploit their leadership advantage, Turkish HCs can establish stronger brand images, or target smaller niches where they will face less competition. Some champions are attempting to build brands by acquiring established firms.

Turkish HCs operate with a customer-focused model, which includes designing products according to customer demands and being flexible in terms of production quotas and mode of production. This approach builds customer loyalty and helps extend the market share, while increasing the skill base of firms. Yet, this customer orientation might not allow for high profit margins in the long run. Becoming a trend-setter, instead of adapting to market dynamics and trends, may be a useful approach for Turkish firms to increase their profit margins.

References

Buğra, A. (1995). *Devlet ve işadamları*. İstanbul: İletişim Yayınevi.

OECD. (2010). *OECD science, technology and industry outlook*. OECD. Retrieved January 31, 2011, from 10.1787/sti_outlook-2010-en

Pamuk, Ş. (2010). Economic growth and institutional change in Turkey before 1980. In T. Çetin & F. Yılmaz (Eds.), *Understanding the process of economic change in Turkey*. New York, NY: Nova Science.

Simon, H. (2009). *Hidden champions of the 21st century: Success strategies of unknown world market leaders*. New York, NY: Springer.

Turkish Statistics Institute. *Foreign Trade Statistics*. Database http://www.turkstat.gov.tr/PreTablo.do?alt_id=1046

World Bank. (2013). *Data; countries and economies*. http://data.worldbank.org/country

Hidden Champions of Ukraine

Nataliia Palii and Viktor Oksenyuk

Overview

Official name:	Ukraine
Type of government:	Unitary semi-presidential republic
Population in 2011:	45,706,100
Land area:	579,320 km^2

History

1917/1919	The collapse of the Russian and Austro-Hungarian Empires is followed by several attempts to establish an independent Ukrainian state (Ukrainian National Republic, West Ukrainian National Republic, Ukrainian State, and so forth).
1919	The Ukrainian Soviet Socialist Republic is formally established.
1922	The Ukrainian Soviet Socialist Republic becomes one of the founding republics of the Soviet Union.
1939	After the partitioning of Poland, the western parts of modern Ukraine are annexed to the Ukrainian Soviet Socialist Republic. The last region to be transferred to modern Ukraine is Crimea in 1954.
1941	The Ukrainian Soviet Socialist Republic is occupied by Nazi Germany.
1945	The Ukrainian Soviet Socialist Republic becomes one of the founding members of the United Nations.

N. Palii (✉)
PR consultant, Kyiv, Ukraine
e-mail: Natalka.Paliy@gmail.com

V. Oksenyuk
Kyiv-Mohyla Business School (KMBS), Kyiv, Ukraine

P. McKiernan and D. Purg (eds.), *Hidden Champions in CEE and Turkey*,
DOI 10.1007/978-3-642-40504-4_23, © Springer-Verlag Berlin Heidelberg 2013

1990	Declaration of Independence.
1991	After the dissolution of the Soviet Union, Ukraine becomes an independent country. The first presidential elections take place. Ukraine, Belarus, and Russia form the Commonwealth of Independent States (CIS).
1992	Ukraine joins the Organization for Security and Cooperation in Europe (OSCE).
1996	A new currency, the hryvnia, is introduced and a new Ukrainian constitution is adopted.
1999/2001	Ukraine serves as a non-permanent member of the UN Security Council.
1998	The European Union's Partnership and Cooperation Agreement (PCA) with Ukraine comes into force.
2004	The Democratic Orange Revolution takes place.
2008	Ukraine joins the World Trade Organization.

1 Introduction: Context

In 2010, Ukraine's service sector accounted for 65.8 % of the country's GDP, followed by the industrial sector (27 %), and agriculture (7.2 %). For the last 20 years, Ukraine's exports have mostly consisted of metals (iron ore, metal-roll, pipes), chemicals (nitrogen fertilizers), machinery (railroad engines), and agricultural goods (oil, grain, oil seeds, including rapeseed).

This structure of Ukraine's exports was inherited from the USSR period when mining, metals, and agriculture were actively developed in the country. However, after the collapse of the Soviet Union, many industries in Ukraine faced the problem of broken cycles. For example, machinery producers were unable to access all the necessary raw materials, and metal producers could not sell their entire product range as they lacked customers. As a result, some of the machinery segments declined, while exports were concentrated more around raw materials and semi-finished products.

One of the key reasons that these products (metals and agricultural goods) are attractive exports is the low cost of production in comparison to competing products from Europe and Asia. In particular, this low cost is a result of Ukraine's cheap labour force. On the other hand, the export share of the metal industry is gradually declining, and it is expected to continue doing so because of the use of outdated technologies and the extremely high levels of energy involved. However, top metal producers have commenced infrastructure renewals through initiation of long-term, billion-dollar projects. Exports of machinery have decreased, and raw materials have become the main export product.

According to forecasts, agriculture is to become one of the most dynamic industries in Ukraine in the coming years. The country is among the main exporters of grain, although this is mostly forage grain. In 2010 and 2011, Ukraine exported

12.1 million tons of grain. Analysts forecast that this figure will expand by a factor of 2.5 by 2015. In the same period, exports of seed oil exceeded 2.6 million tons, representing half of the world's total exports of this product. More core foreign trade indicators are provided in Exhibit 1.

Forecasts are optimistic for the export of fats and oils, as a large number of stakeholders are international corporations. Big international companies from the US and Switzerland took part in the formation of agricultural holdings in Ukraine by investing in agro-industrial firms and processing enterprises. Thus companies have the opportunity to raise additional funding, including investments and innovations funds. The fats and oils industry is one of the most technologically advanced agricultural industries in Ukraine. Agricultural holdings owned by Ukrainians also show positive dynamics, recently making a series of acquisitions.

Raw materials and commodity goods account for the greater part of Ukraine's exports. As noted above, the metal and chemical industries involve mostly raw materials and semi-finished products, together making up almost 37 % of Ukrainian exports. Moreover, due to product specifics on the one hand (materials and goods are processed using large-scale facilities with complex technological cycles), and general operating conditions of the small and medium-sized enterprises on the other, the main exporters in these sectors are mainly large holdings. According to official data, small and medium-sized companies account for 30 % of national GDP.

The current fiscal, regulatory, and legal framework is not advantageous for the development of small and medium-sized companies; rather, it is oriented towards large financial and industrial groups. In numerous ratings of international research and financial structures (IMD-Lausanne, WEF, World Bank, Transparency International, etc.), Ukraine is constantly ranked low in competitiveness, in simplicity of doing business, and in sensitivity to corruption. The reasons for this include the inconsistency of public policy which impedes the competitiveness of companies by regulations and legal provisions, the low level of competitive legislation, the low adaptation capacity of public policy to economic changes, bureaucracy, corruption, inaccessibility of stock markets, insufficient simplicity of doing business, and more. For instance, the WB's *Doing Business* ranks Ukraine 181st of 183 countries on effectiveness of the tax system.

The procedure for creating new firms is rather complicated in Ukraine. Moreover, the new Tax Code cuts the existing tax benefits for small and medium-sized businesses. The aforementioned legal framework and regulations have a negative impact on opportunities for small and medium-sized companies.

Ukrainians operating small companies are not willing to make their activities public. This is a consequence of several factors: the threat of undesirable mergers or acquisitions, a reluctance to inform public authorities of their business successes, and the fact that it is not customary to accept investments and delegate business management functions. For the vast majority of small and medium-sized enterprises, the owner and the senior manager tend to be the same person. Still, a growing number of owners are progressing from intuitive to systematic management; they are obtaining business degrees and implementing best-practice global management. They reserve shareholder positions for themselves while hiring

Exhibit 1 Selected indicators of competitiveness of Ukraine

	1999	2000	2001	2002	2003	2004	2005	2006	2007	2008	2009	2010	2011
GDP per capita (current $US)	635.77	635.71	780.74	879.48	1,048.52	1,367.35	1,828.72	2,303.02	3,068.61	3,891.04	2,545.48	2,973.98	3,615.38
GDP per capita growth (annual %)	0.75	6.97	10.30	6.25	10.29	12.95	3.46	8.03	8.55	2.86	-14.42	4.61	5.58
Long-term unemployment (% of total unemployment)	n/a	n/a	n/a	n/a	n/a	n/a	n/a	n/a	n/a	n/a	n/a	n/a	n/a
Foreign direct investment, net inflows (% of GDP)	1.57	1.90	2.08	1.63	2.84	2.64	9.06	5.20	7.14	5.94	4.07	4.73	4.36
GDP (current $US m)	31,580.64	31,261.53	38,009.34	42,392.90	50,132.95	64,883.06	86,142.02	107,753.07	142,719.01	179,992.41	117,227.77	136,418.62	165,245.01
Exports of goods and services (current $US m)	16,960.00	19,521.22	21,080.21	23,352.98	28,952.31	39,715.74	44,344.45	50,239.01	64,000.99	84,458.35	54,364.41	69,227.57	88,854.40
Exports of goods and services (% of GDP)	53.70	62.44	55.46	55.09	57.75	61.21	51.48	46.62	44.84	46.92	46.38	50.75	53.77
Merchandise exports (current $US m)	11,582.00	14,573.00	16,265.00	17,957.10	23,066.80	32,666.10	34,228.40	38,368.00	49,296.10	66,954.40	39,782.00	51,478.00	68,460.00
Merchandise exports to high-income economies (% of total merchandise exports)	39.16	37.80	37.92	40.55	40.62	40.40	36.19	36.17	32.60	34.06	29.26	29.70	n/a
Merchandise exports to developing economies in Europe & Central Asia (% of total merchandise exports)	38.73	42.61	41.23	37.40	34.43	38.64	42.44	44.82	49.44	46.80	43.69	47.17	n/a
Ores and metals exports (% of merchandise exports)	11.31	11.96	9.17	7.67	5.79	5.59	6.36	6.05	5.64	6.16	6.11	7.42	8.05

Agricultural raw materials exports (% of merchandise exports)	1.61	1.69	1.49	1.81	1.85	1.55	1.47	1.36	1.29	0.86	1.15	1.13	1.07
Food exports (% of merchandise exports)	12.00	9.19	10.93	13.06	11.55	10.41	12.37	12.02	12.56	16.05	23.79	19.20	18.64
Fuel exports (% of merchandise exports)	5.91	5.34	7.02	8.98	11.72	10.30	9.60	6.41	5.12	5.97	5.23	6.93	8.11
Manufactures exports (% of merchandise exports)	65.53	69.44	69.44	67.33	67.80	71.04	69.43	73.11	74.51	70.49	62.89	64.64	63.55
High-technology exports (% of manufactured exports)	4.38	5.23	4.66	4.86	6.92	6.30	3.72	3.40	3.65	3.29	5.55	4.34	n/a

Source: World Bank (2013)

professional managers to run their ventures. Companies are becoming more productive and predictable.

The unwholesome Ukrainian business environment demands optimization of a company's activities, and causes companies to remain private and reluctant to address their issues. Accordingly, companies are skeptical about participating in research, improving or sharing management practices, or practicing social responsibility. Because of this, Ukrainian Hidden Champions (HCs) prefer to remain hidden, literally, to avoid threats; they see no advantage in public announcements of their successes.

However, an increasing number of Ukrainian companies are approaching international markets. Primarily, these are enterprises in the agricultural field, the food industry, and a booming IT sphere. In view of this, the phenomenon of niche leaders in Ukraine's economy is yet to grow and expand.

The task of finding HCs in Ukraine was not easy. Firstly, many leaders choose to stay in the dark so as not to demonstrate their accomplishments to state bodies. Secondly, because the cultural and business practice of revealing financial data is undeveloped, most company-related information is kept private. Also, the domestic market is relatively large; therefore many successful companies are still operating within its range. The metal industries and agriculture constitute the bulk of Ukraine's exports, and one would assume that HCs are to be found here. However, these companies are private and reluctant to communicate with researchers or journalists. The research team was not able to identify HCs in these industries.

The IT field is currently booming in Ukraine because of its highly skilled yet comparatively low-cost IT specialists. One of the HCs analysed below is operating in the IT market. Possibly, a few more Ukrainian software companies will become HCs in the very near future. The Ukrainian HCs in our study were identified as a result of interviews with market experts and media monitoring. Twelve companies were selected in this way. Seven of them, including companies specializing in holograms, CRM Systems, yeast, gliders and model aircraft, charcoal, and meter seals, refused to participate in the research because of a reluctance to become public or popularize their experience. Interviews were held with five companies, whose nature of market leadership is summarized in Exhibit 2.

2 Five Case Studies

2.1 Eleks Software

Overview

Address: ELEKS Ltd, 7g Naukova St., Lviv 79060, Ukraine
Tel: +38 032297–125
Fax: +38 032244–7002
Email: eleksinfo@eleks.com
Web: http://www.eleks.com

Exhibit 2 A selection of the Ukrainian hidden champions

Name	Short market leadership description	Turnover 2010	Turnover 2000	Employees 2010
Eleks Software	One of world top companies on programming real-time automated complex systems in entertainment industry	6 mio EUR	0.05 mio EUR	450
Kakhovka plant of electric welding equipment (KZESO)	World's leading enterprise on manufacturing of rail welding equipment			1,200
Malyn Paper Mill	Company #1 in the CIS in production of pulp-insulating materials (for example, electrical insulating board obtained by hot pressing) for the electrical industry	Appr. 20 mio EUR	Appr. 10 mio EUR	585
PocketBook International	Company #1 in the CIS in production of e-book readers	120 mio EUR (2007)	30 mio EUR (2010)	150
Ukrainian Beer Company (UBC Group)	Company #1 in the world in production of beer coolers; company #1 in the CIS in producing beer promo products (caps, cafeteria carts, tent products, ceramic beer faucets, etc.)	250 mio EUR	35 mio EUR	4,500

Source: Authors of the chapter

Company Information

Industry:	Software
Year of establishment:	1995
Turnover in 2010:	€6 million
Turnover in 2000:	€50,000
Average number of employees in 2010:	450
Brain(s) behind the company:	CEO Oleksiy Skrypnyk

2.1.1 Nature of Market Leadership

In 2000, the company started operating in the entertainment industry and later with Hollywood filmmakers. Blockbuster directors are always striving for the ultimate sense of reality, and special effects are not created by drawing, but are filmed and processed by computer software. Eleks Software is a developer of these programmes, which the company is creating together with American IT company FTSI. Eleks Software, in collaboration with FTSI, is one of the top-five world companies in creating complex automated systems for the entertainment industry.

2.1.2 Nature of Competitive Advantage

The company has great technical capabilities, and its employees are among the top experts in Ukraine. These two factors, along with an informal work environment, provide for the production of a great number of break-through innovations. Eighty percent of the company's revenue is reinvested in these innovative solutions. Moreover, the company is capable of maintaining competitive prices.

2.1.3 Core Lessons Learned on the Path to Business Success

1. Employees are the only assets of a service company.
2. The main role of the leader is to develop talents and deliver a vision to the team.
3. The entertainment industry is becoming one of the biggest customers of innovative software products in the world.

2.1.4 Eleks Software: Hidden Champion

If you are a fan of action and science fiction movies, such as *Agent 007, The Hulk, Indiana Jones, Spiderman, The Phantom of the Opera,* or *Harry Potter*, then your experience has been enhanced by special software produced by Eleks Software. Oleksiy Skrypnyk, the visionary father of the company, established Eleks Software in 1995 in the city of Lviv, the centre of IT in Ukraine.

Initially the company specialized in developing computer programs for the domestic market. However, the demand for IT programmes in Ukraine was minor in comparison to the global market. This brought the company to IT outsourcing, mainly for American companies. Ekeks Software currently provided services include IT outsourcing, original software development, software localization, as well as web-studio services.

In 2000, the company started operating in the entertainment industry and later with Hollywood film-makers. ELEKS Software is a developer of these programmes, which the company creates together with American IT company, FTSI.

The company's programmers have contributed to the creation of stunts in many action movies, but the movie industry is not their only field of operations. Ekeks also develops synchronization software and stage scenery for leading shows in Tokyo, Las Vegas, and California.

Eleks Software has four engineering centres in Ukraine, and three representative offices in the US; the company has 450 employees. The compound annual growth rate is 30 %. The company's revenue in 2010 was 6 million euros. The brain behind this success is company founder Oleksiy Skrypnyk, a man of great charisma and an influential public leader with the ability to attract, inspire, and develop IT talents. He is the company's visionary whose mind is far into the future in many ways, so that he can wrestle well with the uncertainty of current realities.

Because the entertainment industry is complex and diverse, with a huge number of highly specialized IT-companies, it is difficult to define their market share precisely. However, Eleks collaborates closely with FTSI, and jointly they rank among the top-five companies in the world in the business of developing complex automated systems for entertainment.

The company has great technical capabilities. Its employees are the pick of Ukraine's IT experts, each with a high passion for the technology. Eleks excels in its pre- and post-market services, innovative solutions, quality of product, safety practices, and its correspondence with international standards. And it is still capable of maintaining a competitive price. However, in spite of being highly competitive in all these dimensions, Elek's rivals appear to receive more recognition in the global market. The company's great potential for future growth depends on improving this shortfall.

Elek's business is basically continuous innovation of IT programs for entertainment companies; hence, 80 % of its revenue is focused on development of novel software solutions. Though innovations are driven by consumer demands, they are also coupled with the innovative ideas from company employees. However, the only source of funding are the internal assets of the company, which suggests that funding limits Elek's growth.

Oleksiy Skrypnyk believes that the company will remain attractive to its core market in the future; but he also thinks it will become more challenging to achieve the growth rates of the past. His aspiration is to reach the position of European and American software companies over the next 5 years, and strengthen Elek's presence in Europe by continuing to nourish an inspirational culture that attracts Ukraine's best IT minds to the company.

2.2 Kakhovka Plant of Electric Welding Equipment (KZESO)

Overview

Address:	109, Pushkin Str., 74800 Kakhovka, Kherson region, Ukraine
Tel:	+380 553620003
Fax:	+380 553641041, 2590
Email:	info@kzeso.com
Web:	http://kzeso.com/en/

Company Information

Industry:	Manufacturing electric welding equipment
Year of establishment:	1959
Turnover in 2010:	n/a
Turnover in 2000:	n/a
Average number of employees in 2010:	1,200
Brain(s) behind the company:	CEO Yaroslav Ivanovych Mykytyn

2.2.1 Nature of Market Leadership

KZESO produces 97 % of the world's mobile rail welding machines and close to 63 % of all stationary machines.

2.2.2 Nature of Competitive Advantage

The company's key competitive advantages are innovations and product quality. KZESO constantly searches for the best available components. Close cooperation with the Scientific Institute of Electric Welding plays an important role in the product manufacturing process. All advanced solutions have been developed at the Institute and transformed into a manufactured product by KZESO. The company's strengths include a charismatic leader who has been leading the enterprise for more than 20 years and has complete knowledge of all technical aspects.

2.2.3 Core Lessons Learned on the Path to Business Success

1. While others assemble machines of yesterday, a leader must work on the machines of the day after tomorrow.
2. Partnerships with scientific institutions allow one to be on the cutting edge in the industry.
3. Technology is not enough to be successful. A leading company is also the best in sales.

2.2.4 KZESO: Hidden Champion

The KZESO Kakhovka company is in the business of manufacturing modern electric welding equipment. The company's history dates back to 1929, when it was established to manufacture small farm machinery. In 1959, the E. O. Paton Scientific Institute of Electric Welding—a globally recognized institution, holding thousands of patents—decided to find a partner for the commercial implementation of its innovative solutions. From five candidates in the USSR, it selected the Kakhovka plant. This marked a new stage for the factory, an era of electric welding.

Since 1970, OJSC KZESO has developed a range of innovative, high-quality machinery for the welding of rail track. The export of these machines to global markets had already been initiated in earlier Soviet times. Hence, rails in the New York Metro were welded with machines produced by KZESO.

The collapse of the Soviet Union brought tough times for the enterprise, mostly because of lost connections with the international offices responsible for sales and promotion of company products. At that time, Yaroslav Ivanovych Mykytyn, an engineer and designer of more than 30 patents, saw the problem as a call for him to do something. He took over the management of the company and, with a prodigious reputation at home and abroad, he committed himself to re-establishing the lost connections with foreign organizations.

Soon, the enterprise signed a cooperation agreement with an Austrian company, Plasser & Theurer, for the worldwide distribution of its products. The company also opened its own foreign sales offices, and established close ties with the Kakhovka company in Russia and Paton International Holdings in Canada. The latter was responsible for equipment sales in North and South America, India, and Australia.

In less than a decade, the company became a leading global manufacturer of electric rail-welding machines. Its revenue has quadrupled in the last 10 years. Nowadays, KZESO has around 1,200 employees and operates in 76 countries; 65 % of its products are exported.

In general, these machines can be divided into two types—mobile and stationary. KZESO has 97 % of the market for the former and 63 % for the latter. The company develops and manufactures not only machines for rail-welding, but also universal welding equipment with over 100 items available. Their main competitor is Swiss company Shlatter. It held a strong position in the 1990s but its market share has decreased since then.

A key decision factor for purchasing these machines includes product quality and a reasonable price. As CEO Mr. Mykytyn said: "While others are assembling machines of yesterday, we are already working on the machines of the day after tomorrow". The company is always searching for the best components. Bosch supplies parts for the hydraulic systems, and Siemens supplies computer equipment. Some components are manufactured using KZESO's own high-tech equipment.

Close cooperation with Ukraine's E.O. Paton Institute of Electric Welding plays an important role in the manufacturing process. All advanced solutions have been developed at the Institute, and transformed into a product by KZESO. To maintain its leading position, KZESO directs significant investments into its R&D activities, the output of which is a range of patents. Suggestions for innovative solutions come from the market and from clients' needs; personnel and the director of the Paton Institute also generate ideas.

The main driver of the company's success is its charismatic leader Yaroslav Mykytyn, who has state-of-the art technical expertise in welding and has been in charge for more than 20 years. The business of electric welding equipment is a specific field, as machines are customized and the demand is limited. The average life cycle of these products is 20 years. The market for rail welding machines is expanding at the moment. Among the contributing factors for this expansion is the development of infrastructure in India and China, and an increased volume of passenger and cargo traffic worldwide. Railroad cargo and passenger transport are the most profitable.

Mr. Mykytyn is satisfied with the way that the enterprise has been operating for the last 10 years, even though KZESO was affected by the recession. Shortly before the recession, the company invested its own assets and raised bank loans for the construction of a new plant to manufacture welding machines and components previously imported into Ukraine from abroad. However, the financial obstacles have now been resolved and, with capacity expansion, the company is planning to increase the pace of its growth again.

2.3 Ukrainian Beer Company Group (UBC Group)

Overview

Address:	7, Lermontovska St., Kharkiv, 61024, Ukraine
Tel:	+380 577009031
Fax:	+380 577009055
Email:	e@beer-co.com
Web:	http://www.beer-co.com

Company Information

Industry:	Manufacture of cooling equipment products of wood and cork, of paper and paperboard, of containers, and more.
Year of establishment:	1993
Turnover in 2010:	€250 million
Turnover in 2000:	€35 million
Average number of employees in 2010:	4,500
Brain(s) behind the company:	President Igor Gumennyy

2.3.1 Nature of Market Leadership

UBC Group is a world leader in the production of beer coolers and a CIS leader in producing beer promotion products: caps, cafeteria carts, tent products, ceramic beer faucets, and so forth. Almost all world-famous beer producers use cooling equipment manufactured by this Ukrainian company. It is the certified supplier of beer coolers for InBev, Molson Coors, Anheuser Bush, Heineken, and other companies.

2.3.2 Nature of Competitive Advantage

The company's modern technology and strict control over distribution channels are among the main reasons that it is a market leader. Reinforcement of market position is associated with a constant increase of operational efficiency and thorough planning of all business processes. While designing new equipment, UBC Group takes into account all the quality standards and equipment requirements of their clients.

2.3.3 Core Lessons Learned on the Path to Business Success

1. Soft skills and emotional intelligence are important factors of market leadership. Powerful leadership and a consistent strategy play important roles in the establishment of a company able to live through the challenges of a crisis.

2. It is quite easy for the Group to compete in the global market because its ownership structure, level of technology, and production efficiency, are similar to those of its nearest competitors.
3. One of the best approaches to winning and retaining market leadership is to become highly client-oriented, and be flexible so as to achieve customer satisfaction. Strict control over distribution channels is also considered a competitive advantage.

2.3.4 Ukranian Beer Company Group: Hidden Champion

UBC Group is a trade and industrial holding founded in 1993. The company operates in several industries: food manufacturing, HoReCa, and beer distribution. It also has two divisions involved in the manufacture of beverage cooling equipment and promotional beer products. These subsidiaries are the typical HCs of Central and Eastern Europe and in the world.

UBC Cool is the number-one world producer of beer coolers whereas UBC Promo is the number- one producer of beer promotional products (caps, cafeteria carts, tent products, ceramic beer faucets, etc.) in the CIS.

UCB Promo's share of the CIS market is 35 %, while its biggest competitor has only 20 %. Its share of the BRIC market is 15 %, whereas its biggest competitor has around 10 %. UBC Cool's share of the BRIC market is 50 %, while the share of its biggest competitor is only 5–10 %. The UBC Group's total turnover in 2010 was 250 million euros.

In 2000, UBC Promo began as a small enterprise specializing in the manufacture of caps. By 2004, it had developed several new lines. In the same year it purchased its own production facilities. In 2008, in order to form a flexible operating structure, the group reorganized and merged its six separate manufacturing enterprises. UBC Cool's facility began production in 1998. And in 2006, it was manufacturing not only beer coolers but also refrigerator boxes and cooling cabinets.

The group's products are rather complex, technologically advanced, and capital-intensive. The life cycle of cooling equipment is 5–7 years, whereas promotional products last between 1 and 7 years, depending on their type.

Products do not require special after-sales technical support, but consumers should have the most comprehensive information before buying them. The quality of the product, flexibility of supply, and on-time delivery, are very important factors to clients. Maintaining strict control over distribution channels helps to fulfill these criteria.

The company's management emphasizes the importance of rapid technological innovations to maintain competitive advantages in the market. This is especially important for the UBC Cool division. The company pays much attention to improving the quality of its cooling equipment. A special research team of competent experts, with numerous patents for cooling equipment, works at achieving this goal. Modernization is based on a profound analysis of consumer needs. About 10 % of the company's income is assigned to this process. According to UBC Group data, the average ROI has been 30 % over the past 10 years.

CEO, Igor Gumennyy and two vice presidents head the UBC GROUP. They have held their posts for 18 years—since the company's incorporation. Several large shareholders own UBC and represent its governing body. Igor Gumennyy suggests that his main qualities as a leader are his desire to achieve new goals, creativity, enthusiasm, and his temperament. The company's personnel are crucial business assets; therefore a lot of attention is given to forming a strong and unique corporate culture, and gathering together a solid team of loyal and highly professional employees. This leadership strategy has been consistently applied throughout the history of the company.

A key lesson in the training of company personnel involves customer satisfaction. The company wins global market leadership by winning local markets. For example, the goal of UBC Cool is to be the world's number one manufacturer of refrigeration equipment for the food industry, with a 30 % share of the world market in coolers. The goal of UBC Promo is to be world leader in promotional beer products. However, a major challenge for these businesses today is their operational efficiency.

The group demonstrates a powerful growth dynamic. For example, over the past 10 years, its total turnover has increased from 35 million euros to 250 million. This growth has been fuelled by the company's internationalization. The share of exports has increased from 15 to 45 % of total sales revenue; the value of authorized capital has increased as well.

From the point of view of management, modern technology and the company's strict control over distribution channels are among the main reasons for its leading position in the market. Its market position (UBC Group has been market leader in its divisions for at least 5 years) is ensured by its constant improvement of perational efficiency and thorough planning of all business processes.

UBC Group is a strong competitor in regional markets. One reason for that is the quality of its products, achieved through advanced applied technologies. But he managers think that high quality is only one of the success factors. Proximity to clients, on-time delivery, effective co-operation with suppliers, and favourable location of production facilities and divisions (offices and production facilities are located in several big industrial cities in Ukraine and Russia), are additional competitive advantages of equal importance.

The core strategy of the company is client-oriented, so a great deal of attention is paid to flexibility of delivery, detailed information about the products, after-sales service, and establishing long-lasting partnerships. The company controls product quality at all stages of production and after assembly. While designing new equipment, UBC takes into account all the quality standards and equipment requirements of its clients. Because of this approach, UBC Cool has obtained certificates of conformity from leading beer producers, such as InBev, Molson Coors, and Anheuser Bush. UBC Cool became an official supplier of refrigeration equipment for Heineken only after producing innovative coolers that fully satisfied their design requirements. UBC also pays special attention to logistics. A network of branches is established according to the geographic location of clients, ensuring immediate supply. Hence, the company has representative offices throughout the CIS, Europe, and North and South America.

Soft skills and emotional intelligence are equally important factors. Powerful and decisive leadership has played an important role in growing market share in different geographies, as well as wrestling through the challenges of financial crises. UBC has dealt with the problems better than many in the industry.

The company reinforces employee motivation through a special incentive system: The highest awards go to those who better conform to the company's culture, driven by the principle that the business should not only be a source of work and money, but a major part of life as well. It should be a fascinating game, of value to the people involved. People who share these values create a collaborative team with ambitious goals. Hence, the informal structure of the company, which unites the holders of various company awards, does not conform to a commonly encountered organizational structure. Next to that, the company combines professional marketing, deep understanding of the trade, and strong entrepreneurial instincts. The senior managers consider these important competitive advantages.

However, UBC's management is concerned that conditions for further business development will become more severe. Such a situation may be caused by several factors, including changes in market conditions, new companies approaching the market, the macroeconomic situation, and deterioration of the business environment in Ukraine. Thus, the UBC Group actively works on further improving capacity utilization and cost control through more efficient organization design. Indeed, it was the optimization of its organizational structure before the crisis that helped the company reduce its risks.

The goal of the UBC Group is to achieve global leadership among manufacturers of cooling equipment for the food industry and manufacturers of beer promotional products. Currently, the company has three or four major competitors in different regions and in different segments of the business. In each segment, competitors are quite similar to UBC. Although the nature of competition is tough and intensifying, the company is betting on economies of scope; they operate in complementary business segments—beer coolers and beer promotional materials.

Such synergies create greater benefits for the company's global clients. UBC offers them not only refrigeration equipment but also promotional products that add value to their beverages. Recently, soft-drink manufacturers, such as Pepsi-Cola, and Coca-Cola, have also become core company clients. The treatment of each client is highly personalized, leading to mutual trust.

UBC's winning formula appears to be client-oriented; it involves a customized approach to each client, an emphasis on satisfying clients' needs, and maintaining control of distribution channels. This formula is considered a competitive advantage.

2.4 Weidmann Malyn Paper Mill, JSC

Overview

Address:	Prykhodko Str. 66, 11602 Malyn, Zhytomyr region, Ukraine
Tel:	+380 413367222
Email:	wicor@wicor.kiev.ua
Web:	http://www.weidmann-electrical.com

Company Information

Industry:	Manufacture of paper and paperboard
Year of establishment:	1871
Turnover in 2010:	€20 million
Turnover in 2000:	€10 million
Average number of employees in 2010:	585
Brain(s) behind the company:	Head of the Board Andrii Panchenko

2.4.1 Nature of Market Leadership

This company produces pulp-insulating materials for the electrical industry. For almost 20 years, Malyn Paper has been leading the pulp and paper industry in the CIS market. One of its unique products is electrical insulating cardboard obtained by hot pressing. Malyn is the only company in the CIS region that produces such material. Currently, market demand for this insulating board is rather strong. Production is characterized by a standardized level of applied technologies and high capital intensity.

2.4.2 Nature of Competitive Advantage

This particular insulating board is an essential element for fabricating transformers and other electrical equipment. Consumers generally have a vested interested in establishing lasting relations with their supplier, therefore Malyn Paper's long production history and traditional market leadership, combined with adequate demand and technological innovations, provide the company with competitive advantages. Besides owning a unique technical solution (Malyn Paper Mill is the only producer of this type of electrical insulating board obtained by hot pressing), the company's strongest competitive advantages are in its pre- and after-sales service, and reliable delivery.

2.4.3 Core Lessons Learned on the Path to Business Success

1. It is essential to keep a leading position in the CIS market with the company's long and successful client history. Strategic location of production facilities and proximity to the client are key competitive advantages.

2. Innovation and distribution continue to be important factors for Malyn Paper's success. High quality, a good price/performance ratio, trust, and experience, are all very important.
3. Studying clients' needs and expansion of international relations will provide sustainable development for the company.

2.4.4 Weidmann Malyn Paper Mill: Hidden Champion

Founded in the nineteenth century as a paper mill, Malyn[1] has undergone many changes in both ownership and product range. Fifty years ago, the company established market leadership in pulp-insulating materials in the USSR, and re-established it again in the CIS region 19 years ago.

During the Soviet era, Malyn Paper was a monopoly in the production of some types of industrial paper, which it supplied to the Soviet republics and Warsaw Pact countries. After affiliating with WICOR Holding AG (Weidmann International Corporation), the company had the resources to expand its product range and improve distribution channels.

Weidmann Malyn Paper Mill was incorporated as an open joint-stock company in 1994. Malyn Paper has its headquarters in Switzerland, operating as a separate entity competing in the CIS market, while Weidmann Corporation sells its products in other regional markets and tries to expand the company globally.

Malyn has been the only company in the CIS region that produces this unique material. Over the last decade, the industry has undergone some changes; prices have increased and the market has grown. This has resulted in sales growth for the mill—market share in the CIS region is now around 60–70 %. In the same period, the company's annual turnover has increased from 10 million euros to 20 million, and the share of export sales has gone from 50 to 70 % of the total sales income.

The company's hot press technology is distinct from the technology of its competition. As a consequence, productivity, volumes, and ownership structures also differ considerably. Furthermore, Malyn Paper is far more experienced, being the oldest firm in the business. Compared to its rivals, the company excels in several areas: price, delivery time, technical capability, and quality; together resulting in a very favourable price/performance ratio. Most important, the company builds its winning position on loyalty.

Despite a favourable market trend in the last decade, the mill's management is concerned about intensifying competition and market segmentation. Thus, the company directs investments towards technological innovations aimed at improving the quality of the product, and broadening the potential for its use. In general, investment in innovations is around 0.7–1 % of income, and the average ROI in the past 10 years is about 25 to 30 %. The company tries to maintain close proximity and cooperation with core clients—an easy task since it has worked with them for more than a century. On the other hand, these experiences can result in tacit

[1] The mill itself was set up in 1871, and was registered as an OJSC. It manufactured pulp-insulating materials for the electrical industry.

knowledge and routines that impede the company's flexibility; a potential problem considering it already has a high level of capital intensity and narrowly specialized expertise. To counter this, the company constantly encourages improvements to its internal structure and culture. A great deal of attention is paid to the development of a favourable working atmosphere for committed employees.

2.5 PocketBook International

Overview

Address:	5, Tampere St., Kiev, 02105, Ukraine
Tel:	+380-44-5010647, ext. 172
Fax:	+380-44-5010645
Email:	info@pocketbook.com,ua
Web:	http://www.pocketbook-int.com.ua

Company Information

Industry:	Manufacture of computer, electronic and optical products
Year of establishment:	2007
Turnover in 2010:	€120 million
Turnover in 2008:	€30 million
Average number of employees in 2010:	150
Brain(s) behind the company:	The CEO

2.5.1 Nature of Market Leadership

Since its establishment in 2007, PocketBook International has become one of the leading producers in various regional segments of the world market for electronic reading devices. The market of e-book reading devices is rather new, fast growing, and innovative. During the early period of its development, it belonged to big international companies. However, Ukraine's PocketBook International is not only the leading producer in the CIS market, but is now seizing market share in Europe and other regions.

2.5.2 Nature of Competitive Advantage

Some very important factors for PocketBook International, which ensure the company's leading position and business growth, include: an understanding of the industry, marketing, productive relations with clients, risk management, innovation, and employees' qualifications and motivation. The company owns patents, and invests about 50 % of its income in product development. Most manufacturers of electronic reading devices use electronic ink (E Ink) technology. PocketBook multifunctional electronic devices are unique in their design and tailor-made software (constantly upgraded); they support all e-book formats, and feature a simple multilingual interface and pre-installed content.

2.5.3 Core Lessons Learned on the Path to Business Success

1. The technology described above is typical and widespread in the market. Therefore, producers must introduce alternative competitive advantages to convince the users. The main purchasing criteria for consumers are product quality, information system, after-sales service, and product popularity.
2. Taking into consideration global market conditions, competition with world-recognized brands, and end-customer orientation of the product, one needs to make marketing efforts to expand market share.
3. New high-tech companies with innovative multi-functional products will enter this market, but PocketBook International can maintain its position through ongoing development of its own innovations.

2.5.4 PocketBook International: Hidden Champion

The market for e-book reading devices is rather new, fast growing, and innovative. During the early period of its development it belonged to big international companies like Sony, Amazon's Kindle and Nook. But now a Ukrainian company is also gaining market share.

PocketBook International, set up in 2007, is now a market leader in the CIS region with a 40 % share of sales, while the share of its biggest competitor is only 1 %. In the period between 2008 and 2010, turnover increased from 30 million euros to 120 million, mostly because of the company's strengthened position in Western Europe and the Middle East. Export operations nowadays accounts for more than 90 % and are carried out through the company's own sales subsidiaries. From the outset, market demand for e-book reading devices has been growing exponentially, corresponding with rising consumer awareness of this product category. Experts believe that this trend will continue for several years.

With the growing demand, it is expected that there will be competitive battles between increasing numbers of high-tech companies entering this market with innovative multifunctional devices. The outcome for the industry's structure will be determined by the interplay of these market forces. PocketBook International tries to increase its market share by investing in novel product solutions (about 50 % of its income goes into product development), and utilizing its strategic foresight acquired through close, productive relations with clients. In particular, the company develops all core product dimensions that win over consumers: simple interface, support for all formats, customer service, software upgrades, and pre-installed content. The management believes that improved capacity utilization and cost reductions can also make important contributions to the company's future performance.

Taking into consideration global market conditions, competition with world recognized brands, and key purchasing factors for the end-consumer, PocketBook is still to navigate through risky business waters.

Conclusion

Overall, Ukrainian HCs have much in common with the HCs described by Hermann Simon. Ambitious goals appear to be the main success driver of the companies that were analysed. A priority function of senior managers is to determine those long-term goals and communicate them to the team.

Compared to the businesses studied by Simon (2009), the Ukrainian HCs are relatively small in terms of scale and turnover. Two important factors that can explain this contrast are the different levels of development and economic transparency in the two countries. In the case of the Ukrainian champions, the postulate regarding the family business predominance does not apply. The majority of Ukraine's HCs belong to one owner or several unrelated owners. Moreover, owners might include foreign companies.

From the point of view of globalization, there are two types of HCs in Ukraine: those that operate across the world and those that operate only in some regions. The explanation of this fact is, primarily, in the product: if the niche is too narrow, it is wise to look for additional clients worldwide. If the transportation of goods to distant countries is justified, then the company can establish direct contacts with specific clients all over the world, rather than just local regions.

Four of these five companies are operating in the business-to-business market. Their fields vary from paper manufacturing to solar batteries. They also vary in age, property structure, innovations, and size, but a common key advantage lies in their specialization; growth can be fostered only though internationalization. These companies had no other choice but to compete successfully on a global scale.

Two of the five Ukrainian HCs consider their competition to be not just regional, but global. For them, "the sky is the limit, not the national border!" They possess cutting-edge global technologies. None of them are public—financial information is kept private.

HCs in Ukraine have existed in incorporated format for less than 20 years, although the origins of some go back to USSR times. Sources of innovation for these HCs include the market, internal ideas, and technologies; although the more innovative a company is, the more likely it is that ideas are generated by the team itself rather than the market.

Interestingly, while the range of products of a particular Ukrainian HC may be rather broad, it is associated with a narrow key competence. For example, KZESO produces more than 100 varied products for different markets and customers, but they are united by one common feature—electric welding. Eleks Software also has a diverse offering for the market, but it involves a single competence—developing computer software for custom projects; for example, software for filming special effects.

Both authors of this research were impressed that all Ukrainian HCs produce and export high added-value, hi-tech products. This fact refutes the perception of Ukrainian HCs being mere suppliers of raw material for international corporations. When interviewing company CEOs, the authors had the impression that they were focused more on the quality and innovative character of a product than on the financial performance of the company. They are not just making money, but fulfilling themselves. They have long-term plans, and financial issues can bring only minor adjustments to their objectives.

The uniqueness of the companies comes from within, as well as from the situation on the external market; many of them internationalized in the face of favourable market demand. Recently, many owners of Ukrainian companies have realized that they needed to move away from operational management and have hired professionally trained managers. This raises a question that worries the owners today: how to keep a company unique.

In general, Ukrainian HCs do not resort to scaled credit financing or attract investment from external loan markets. In this way they are similar to the HCs described in Simon's study. Because of the country's unfavourable business environment and lack of tradition for business transparency, Ukrainian HCs usually refuse to disclose potentially risky information about themselves.

One of the main features of these companies is their relatively young age. Even though some of them were established several decades ago, they have functioned no more than 15 years in their present form. PocketBook began operating as recently as 2007. The position of some HCs is not proven yet; they are still in a stage of rapid development. There is a chance that in a few years their structure will change dramatically.

The Ukrainian economy and the state itself are only 22 years old. This time is marked by gradual satiety of the domestic market, capital distribution, and increased competition. Today, the economy is entering a stage of foreign expansion; therefore in the next years we can expect new Ukrainian HCs to emerge and evolve.

References

Simon, H. (2009). *Hidden champions of the twenty-first century: The success strategies of unknown world market leaders*. London: Springer.

World Bank. (2013). *Data; countries and economies*. http://data.worldbank.org/country

Author Biographies

Peter Baloh. is Assistant Professor of Technology and Innovation Management at IEDC—Bled School of Management and a member of the executive board at BISOL.

Dr. Baloh holds a Ph.D. and M.Sc. in Information Systems and Management at University of Ljubljana, Faculty of Economics; and a M.Phil. degree in Knowledge Management from a 6* RAE IRIS-Informatics Research Institute at University of Salford Business School, Manchester, UK.

His research interests lie in the areas of (1) management of technology and innovation, (2) strategic project management, (3) learning and knowledge management.

He has held visiting positions at RMIT and Victoria universities in Australia, at National University of Singapore, several universities in South Korea, the University of Salford in the UK and at the University of Washington, Seattle, US.

Denis Berberović, M.Sc. started his academic career as a research assistant in 2004. Since 2007 he works as senior Research and teaching assistant at the School of Economics and Business, Department of Marketing, University in Sarajevo. In 2010 he was a Chevening scholar at the Bradford School of Management (UK). Since then he holds a master of science degree (with distinction). Today he is a Ph.D. candidate. Denis' main professional interests are in strategic marketing, marketing research, marketing communications, consumer behaviour, tourism and building reputation. Denis is member of the AIPES Alumni, IAA Young Professionals and CEEMAN IMTA 2008 Alumni. He has co-authored book chapters and papers on these issues.

Tamara Bobáková. works as a consultant for Simon-Kucher & Partners. She advises clients on pricing, strategy, and marketing challenges. Her interests include fostering democracy, entrepreneurship and innovation in post-communist countries, especially her native Slovakia. She became interested in Hidden Champions after her first meeting with the founder of her company, Professor Simon, and has written and spoken on this subject in the Central European region.

Dr. Nenad Brkić, Ph.D. is a professor in the School of Economics and Business, Department of Marketing at Faculty of Economics in Sarajevo, University of

P. McKiernan and D. Purg (eds.), *Hidden Champions in CEE and Turkey*,
DOI 10.1007/978-3-642-40504-4, © Springer-Verlag Berlin Heidelberg 2013

Sarajevo. He teaches "Marketing", "Marketing Communication", "Sales and Sales Management" and "Public Relations and Corporate Communication", at the undergraduate and graduate level. Also teaches at the graduate school of Faculty of Economics in Zagreb, where he teaches "Strategic planning integrated marketing communications."

Before joining the Faculty of Economics in Sarajevo he worked at UPI Institute for Research and Development in Sarajevo (1989–1993) and at the Ministry of Foreign Trade of the Government of Republic of BiH (1994–1996) in Sarajevo.

His professional interests are in marketing communications, strategic marketing, tourism, and sales management. He has published several books, book chapters, and papers on these issues.

Dilek Cetindamar. is a professor at Sabanci University. She received her B.S. degree from Industrial Engineering Department at Boğaziçi University, her M.A. degree from Economics Department at BU, and her Ph.D. degree from Management Department at Istanbul Technical University in 1995. Before her appointment to the Faculty of Management at Sabanci University in 1999, she worked at: Boğaziçi University, Case Western Reserve University (USA), Portland State University (USA), and Chalmers University of Technology (Sweden). She was at Cambridge University, UK as a visiting professor in 2008. She participated in many international projects, including UN and EU projects. She has more than 50 publications, including 9 books. She received an "encouragement award" from Turkish Academy of Sciences in 2003. Her main interest and research topics are Entrepreneurship and Technology and Innovation Management. She has memberships in the following associations: Technology Management Association, International Association for Management of Technology, Schumpeterian Society, European Institute for Technology and Innovation Management, and Academy of Management.

Jaroslav Ďad'o. works as university professor at the Faculty of Economics of Matej Bel University in Banska Bystrica, Slovakia. His teaching activities are focused on strategic marketing, international marketing, service marketing and marketing communication. His research activities are in the fields of relationship marketing, positioning, marketing audit and marketing management. He is a supervisor of the master degree program Marketing and Management of Enterprises, including the English version.

Pavel Daneyko. is Chairman of the Supervisory Board of the Institute for Privatization and Management, and member of the supervisory boards of Silvano Fashion Group (Estonia), JSC Milavitsa (Belarus), CJSC UNITER (Belarus), and CASE (Ukraine). He has 20 years of managerial and consulting experience. He has authored more than 50 articles covering multiple aspects of the transition from a planned to-a market economy, and co-authored books, articles, policy papers, and analytical reports on economics and business-related issues in Belarus, with a focus on small- and medium-sized business development. His areas of expertise include strategic management, enterprise restructuring, and transformational economy.

Vesna Rašković Depalov, Ph.D. is an assistant on projects (Best Technology Innovation Competition, Enterprise Europe Network Serbia, and UNESCO Chair for Entrepreneurial Studies) at the Faculty of Engineering, University of Novi Sad, Serbia. This work was partly supported by Project No 47005 financed by the Ministry of Education and Science Republic of Serbia. Her research interest lies in the area of innovation, strategic management and strategic marketing.

Dr. Nenad Filipović. graduated in Electrical Engineering from the University of Zagreb, Croatia, where he also received his Masters degree in Computer Science. He obtained his Ph.D. in Management from Free University of Amsterdam. He also completed the Stanford Executive Program at Graduate School of Business, Stanford University, as well as Harvard University's "Central and East European Teachers Program".

Since 1991 Dr. Filipović is Assistant Professor, MBA Project Director and Academic Director of the IEDC—Bled School of Management. He teaches courses in General Management and Business Ethics. He is the author or co-author of six books and more than thirty case studies. Dr. Filipović has been a visiting faculty of a number of business schools in Europe and North America.

Pavel Golenchenko. is Dean of IPM (Institute for Privatization and Management) Business, and general manager of Adizes Management Consulting (Belarus). He has more than 10 years of managerial and consulting experience. He has completed more than ten consulting projects covering multiple aspects of organizational transformation, focusing on expanding the capabilities of small and medium enterprises and rejuvenation aging post-Soviet companies in Belarus, Russia, Ukraine and other countries. His areas of expertise include: organizational transformation, strategic management, and marketing.

Ljubomir Kekenovski. is a full time professor at Ss Cyril and Methodius University, Faculty of Economics – Skopje. Prof. Kekenovski is teaching the subjects such as Economics of the public sector and Economics of the public utilities and public administrations. He has published over 300 papers and research work reports. Among other positions he was a President of the Anti-monopoly Commission from 2000 to 2003 and President of the Council of Governors of the National Bank of Macedonia from 2000 to 2007. In 2008 he attended MIT Sloan, and in 2010 he attended Humboldt University as a guest lecturer.

Anisa Kume. is part-time lecturer at the Faculty of Economics, Tirana University, and some other private universities in Tirana. She works full time for the Albanian Ministry of Finance. She has finished a Master in Economic European Studies in Rome, Italy, and is now in a doctoral program. Her work concentrates on human resource management, business communication, and macro-environment in Albania.

Vasilika Kume. is professor at the Faculty of Economics, Tirana University. She is a member of the Department of Management and deals with Strategic Management and Managerial Decision Making subjects. Since 1998 she has been Executive Director of the Master's Program in this Faculty. She has published articles and research works in strategic management, public administration analysis and policies, SME management and development, long-term planning for public and private organizations, and managerial decision making.

Pavel Lebedev. is a consultant and educator in the field of financial and strategic management. He holds an MBA degree along with professional certification of the Association of Chartered Certified Accountants (ACCA). He is a Ph.D. student at IEDC-Bled School of Management. Among the clients of his projects there are Russian companies from TOP-50 as well as multinationals operating in CIS and CEE. Pavel is currently holding a position of Deputy Director of the Banking Management Center, Department of Finance and Banking of the Russian Presidential Academy of National Economy and Public Administration. He is also a visiting faculty at MIRBIS and HSE. His experience includes establishing and running his own consulting company in Moscow, being in charge of management accounting in a big international company, taking a position of corporate finance director at investment banking boutique and financial director of media-holding.

Dr. Anu Leppiman. is a marketing professor at Tallinn University of Technology in School of Economics and Business Administration. She is the Head of the Chair of Marketing. Dr. Leppiman is a Certified Experience Expert and Communication and Interaction Skills trainer. Her research interests lies in the area of experience marketing, business communication and service design.

Sanja Marinković, Ph.D. is an assistant professor at the Faculty of Organizational Sciences, University of Belgrade. She is the author of the book *Innovation Management in Services* and coauthor of the books *Management of Innovation and Technology Development* and *Management of Sustainable Development* (all published in Serbian). This work was partly supported by Project No 47003 funded by the Ministry of Education and Science Republic of Serbia. Her research and teaching interests are in the fields of technology and innovation management, sustainable development and strategic management.

Prof. Peter McKiernan. Professor of Management at University of Strathclyde, Glasgow, United Kingdom.

Previously he was Dean of the School of Management and Governance at Murdoch University in Australia and Head of School of Management at the University of St Andrews in Scotland.

He was President of the European Academy of Management and President of the British Academy of Management. He is a Fellow of EURAM and of BAM, a Companion of the Association of Business Schools, an Academician of the Academy of Social Sciences and a Fellow of the Royal Society of the Arts.

He has published widely in the area of strategic management and foresight, including the international best seller “Sharpbenders”.

Zhanna B. Musatova, Ph.D. is associate professor at the Marketing Department of Plekhanov Graduate School at Plekhanov Russian University of Economics (Moscow, Russia http://www.rea.ru) and Deputy Dean of the School. Her research areas are marketing planning, Internet marketing, and marketing for young active consumers.

Mr. Viktor Oksenyuk. is a research coordinator at Kyiv-Mohyla Business School (KMBS), Ukraine. His key research interests are in the area of managerial innovation.

Dr. Mislav Ante Omazić. is an assistant professor at the Faculty of Economics and Business, University of Zagreb, Department for Organization and Management. His research interests are in the area of change management, event management, project management and corporate social responsibility.

Nataliia Palii. During the “Hidden Champions in CEE” project, Ms. Nataliia Palii was a project coordinator at the International Management Institute (MIM-Kyiv), Ukraine. At the time, her research interests were in competitiveness of economies and enterprises, business environment, and the national conditions of business development.

Prof. Danica Purg. is President of the IEDC-Bled School of Management, Slovenia and President of CEEMAN, the International Association for Management Development in Dynamic Societies.

In 2010 Prof. Purg received the 2010 Educator of the Year Award by the Academy of International Business (AIB) for her outstanding achievements in international business education. In 2013 Prof. Purg became the Chair of the UN Global Compact PRME (Principles of Responsible Management Education) Steering Committee.

Prof. Purg is professor of leadership and effective management. Her special field of interest is looking for inspirations for managers from art and other professions. She authored and co-authored several books and numerous articles. She is a frequent guest speaker at European and American universities and international conferences.

Prof. Purg is also member of several international advisory boards. President of the Republic of Slovenia awarded her with the “Honorary Order of Freedom” for her contribution to management development in Slovenia and CEE. She has been awarded doctor honoris causa by three universities.

Melita Balas Rant. is an assistant professor at the Management and Organization Department at the Faculty of Economics, University of Ljubljana, Slovenia and former assistant professor at IEDC-Bled School of Management. Her research interest covers organization design, focusing on three major domains: the role of strategic cognition in strategy formation and execution, business model architecture seen through the lenses of integration and coordination processes, and barriers to change of business models along the triple-bottom-line as the core measure of business sustainability. She has presented her work at several academic and business conferences, and published articles in academic and professional journals.

Rein Riisalu. is a marketing lecturer at Tallinn University of Technology focusing on business simulations, cases and team work training. Apart from his academic job, he serves as a management consultant.

Bogdan Rusu. is an associate professor in the Engineering and Management Department of "Gh. Asachi" Technical University of Iasi (TUIASI), Romania. He received a Bachelor in Mechanical Engineering from TUIASI, an MBA from Derby University UK and his Ph.D. in Management from "Alexandru Ioan Cuza" University of Iasi. He was an associate professor for Romanian-Canadian MBA in Bucharest teaching Consumer Behavior, and Director of CETEX Iaşi. He is teaching Quality Management and Management of SMEs subjects to undergraduate and master students. His research interest includes Opportunity Identification and exploitation by SMEs, Growth and Customer Satisfaction.

Prof. Olga V. Saginova, Ph.D. is Head of the Comparative Economics and Entrepreneurship Department at Plekhanov Russian University of Economics (Moscow, Russia http://www.rea.ru). Her most important research areas are brand management, marketing of higher education, and cross-cultural marketing. She was initiator and leader of several innovative educational projects: International Business School Plekhanov (and Plekhanov Graduate School. She has a variety of publications in leading international journals with a high impact factor (including *European Business Review, Marketing Theory*, etc.). Olga Saginova is member of the European Marketing Academy and the Russian Marketing Guild. E-mail address: saguinova@rea.ru, saginova@yandex.ru.

Mijalce Santa. is a teaching assistant at Ss Cyril and Methodius University, Faculty of Economics – Skopje and PhD student at University Paris 1 – Pantheon – Sorbonne in France. He is involved in the courses of e-business, systems analysis and innovation. He has published in international conferences and acts as a reviewer to international journals. He is also board member of the YES incubator.

Dr. Arnis Sauka. is Academic Vice-Rector of Ventspils University College, director of the Centre for Entrepreneurship, Innovation and Regional Development at Ventspils University College and Research Fellow at the Stockholm School of Economics in Riga. At the beginning of 2008, Arnis earned a Ph.D. in business administration (magna cum laude) from the University of Siegen (Germany). Prior to that, he was a visiting Ph.D. candidate at Jönköping International Business School (Sweden) and a teaching fellow at SSEES/University College London (U.K.).

Arnis has more than 15 years of practical experience in entrepreneurship, business management and consultancy. His main research interests include competitiveness and social contribution of entrepreneurship, value creation and tax evasion, business start-ups and exits, and entrepreneurship policies in transition economies.

Prof. Irina I. Skorobogatykh, Ph.D. is Head of the Marketing Department at Plekhanov Russian University of Economics (Moscow, Russia http://www.rea.ru), the oldest marketing department in Russia (established in 1990). Her most important research areas are relationship marketing, consumer behaviour, history of marketing thought, and luxury brand management. She has more than 60 publications in these areas in leading Russian and international journals with a high impact factor and books. Irina Skorobogatykh is also editor-in-chief of the leading professional journal in Russia, titled *Marketing and Marketing Research* (Grebennikov Publishing House, hyyp://www.grebennikov.ru), established 15 years ago and still one of the leading professional marketing journals in Russia and the CIS. Irina is a member of the European Marketing Academy, the Academy of Marketing Science, and the Russian Marketing Guild, and a member of the board of directors of the Russian Marketing Association. E-mail address: skorobogatykh@rea.ru, iskorobogatykh@yahoo.com.

Miklós Stocker. is assistant professor at the Department of Business Studies at Corvinus University of Budapest, teaching and researching strategic management and knowledge-intensive organizations.

Ian Sutherland. Born and raised in Newfoundland and Labrador, Canada, Dr. Ian Sutherland is Deputy Dean for Research and Director of Ph.D. Studies at IEDC–Bled School of Management in Slovenia. An internationally recognized expert in the intersection of the arts and business, Dr. Sutherland was originally trained as a professional musician. Today he has an active international career as a researcher, educator and consultant combining expertise in sociology, philosophy, creativity and leadership studies. In particular his work is focused on leadership practice, creative and strategic processes, leveraging diversity and experiential arts-based methods of management and leadership development. He is a co-founding editor of the journal *Music and Arts in Action* and the author/co-author of articles appearing in *Management Learning; Business Leadership Review; Journal of Arts Management, Law and Society*; *Organizational Aesthetics; Journal of Visual Art Practice; Music and Arts in Action*; *Emotion Review*. He is also co-author of the book *Key Concepts in Leadership* (Sage 2012) with Prof. Jonathan Gosling and Dr. Stephanie Jones. A sought after speaker and facilitator he has delivered courses, workshops, seminars and lectures in over 20 countries around the world and worked with companies from the pharmaceuticals, consumer electronics, telecommunications, financial services and defense industries.

Péter Szlávik. is managing partner at Boda & Partners, and honorary associate professor at Budapest Business School.

Janka Táborecká-Petrovičová. works as a senior lecturer and deputy head of department at the Faculty of Economics at Matej Bel University in Banská Bystrica, Slovakia. Her research and teaching interests cover areas such as strategic marketing, consumer behaviour, relationship marketing and market research. She was involved as a lecturer and module leader in an MBA programme in co-operation with Nottingham Trent University. She is a supervisor of five courses, a member of two editorial boards and author of various books and scientific papers.

Marija Todorović. is a teaching assistant at the Faculty of Organizational Sciences, University of Belgrade. This work was partly supported by Project No 179081 funded by the Ministry of Education and Science Republic of Serbia. Her research interest lies in the area of project management and strategic management.

Rebeka Danijela Vlahov. MBA is a teaching and research assistant at the Faculty of Economics and Business, University of Zagreb, Department for Organization and Management. Her research interests are in the area of change management, event management, project management and management of sports organizations.

Dr. Arnold Walravens. is Professor Emeritus of Economic Sociology at the University of Technology, Delft, The Netherlands where he served as the dean of the Faculty of Philosophy and Social Sciences. He received his Ph.D. from the University of Technology, Twente, the Netherlands and served as faculty member at the Free University of Amsterdam. Since 1993 Dr. Walravens is Academic Director of the Presidents' MBA Program at the IEDC—Bled School of Management and since 2001 a member of the Senate of Faculty of Postgraduate Studies at the same institution. He teaches the courses of Corporate Governance in EMBA and General Management Programs at IEDC—Bled School of Management.

He is author of five books and more than 90 articles. He has recently co-authored a new book titled, Leaders And Teams—The Winning Partnership, jointly written by well-known professors of leadership: Danica Purg, Pierre Casse, Lynn Isabella, and Paul Claudel.

Prof. Walravens is a former President of the Supervisory Board of Eureko BV, Sneep Industries, and member of the supervisory board of Rabobank and Atag. He was on the boards of multinationals as CSM and Wolters-Kluwer and served as President of the Board of Connexxion, the largest personal transport company in the Netherlands.

Türkan Yosun. is a Ph.D. student at Sabanci University. She received her B.A. Degree from Management Department at Bilkent University in 2002. Before starting her Ph.D. at Sabancı University, she worked at Yapı ve Kredi Bank, Garanti Bank, Toyota Tsusho Europe and Fiat Turkey for a total of 6 years in corporate sales, treasury management, and financial controlling departments. Her main academic interests are internationalization of emerging market enterprises and social enterprise strategies.

Dr. Nadya Zhexembayeva. is the Coca-Cola Chair of Sustainable Development at IEDC-Bled School of Management, the European executive education business school based in Slovenia, where she teaches leadership and sustainability strategy. In 2011, together with Chris Laszlo, Nadya co-authored *Embedded Sustainability: The Next Big Competitive Advantage*, published by Stanford University Press in the US and Greenleaf Publishing in the UK. Nadya earned her Doctorate Degree in Organizational Behavior at the Weatherhead School of Management, Case Western Reserve University, USA, where she also served as an Associate Director at the Center for Business as an Agent of World Benefit, now Fowler Center for Sustainable Value, until 2008. She received Bachelor of Arts in Management and Bachelor of Arts in Psychology from Hartwick College, USA.

MIX
Papier aus verantwortungsvollen Quellen
Paper from responsible sources
FSC® C105338

If you have any concerns about our products,
you can contact us on
ProductSafety@springernature.com

In case Publisher is established outside the EU,
the EU authorized representative is:
Springer Nature Customer Service Center GmbH
Europaplatz 3, 69115 Heidelberg, Germany

Printed by Libri Plureos GmbH
in Hamburg, Germany